THE TRUTH OF THE CHRISTIAN RELIGION

NATURAL LAW AND
ENLIGHTENMENT CLASSICS

Knud Haakonssen
General Editor

Hugo Grotius

NATURAL LAW AND
ENLIGHTENMENT CLASSICS

Hugo Grotius

The Truth of the Christian Religion

With Jean Le Clerc's Notes
and Additions

Translated by John Clarke (1743)

Edited and with an Introduction by
Maria Rosa Antognazza

Major Legal and Political Works of Hugo Grotius

LIBERTY FUND

Indianapolis

This book is published by Liberty Fund, Inc., a foundation established to encourage study of the ideal of a society of free and responsible individuals.

The cuneiform inscription that serves as our logo and as the design motif for our endpapers is the earliest-known written appearance of the word "freedom" (*amagi*), or "liberty." It is taken from a clay document written about 2300 B.C. in the Sumerian city-state of Lagash.

Frontispiece: Portrait of Hugo de Groot by Michiel van Mierevelt, 1608; oil on panel; collection of Historical Museum Rotterdam, on loan from the Van der Mandele Stichting. Reproduced by permission.

C   10   9   8   7   6   5   4   3   2   1
P   10   9   8   7   6   5   4   3   2   1

Library of Congress Cataloging-in-Publication Data
Grotius, Hugo, 1583–1645.
[De veritate religionis Christianae. English]
The truth of the Christian religion: / Hugo Grotius; with Jean Le Clerc's notes and additions; translated by John Clarke; edited and with an introduction by Maria Rosa Antognazza.
p. cm. — (Natural law and enlightenment classics)
"Major legal and political works of Hugo Grotius."
Includes bibliographical references and index.
ISBN 978-0-86597-514-9 (hbk.: alk. paper) — ISBN 978-0-86597-515-6 (pbk.: alk. paper)
1. Apologetics—Early works to 1800. 2. Indifferentism (Religion)
I. Clarke, John, 1682–1757. II. Antognazza, Maria Rosa, 1964– III. Title.
BT1103.G76313 2012
239—dc23   2012011439

LIBERTY FUND, INC.
8335 Allison Pointe Trail, Suite 300
Indianapolis, Indiana 46250-1684

CONTENTS

INTRODUCTION

Religion and Politics in the United Provinces

In June 1619 Hugo Grotius was imprisoned at Loevestein Castle, in the south of the United Provinces, sentenced to life imprisonment for treason. For any thirty-six-year-old, this would have been a grim prospect; even more so for one who had been born a member of the governing elite of the United Provinces and had already enjoyed prestige and success. The De Groots (Latinized as *Grotius*) were a prominent family in the Dutch city of Delft, where Hugo was born on 10 April 1583.

As regents of the city—that is, members of the oligarchy which ruled many Dutch towns, including Delft—the De Groots belonged to the social class at the core of the political, economic, and religious life of the seven northern provinces of the Netherlands that in 1579 had declared their independence from one of the superpowers of the time, the Catholic Spanish monarchy. Protestant, wealthy, and well educated, they had high stakes in the economic and military activities which were at the root of the Dutch golden age of prosperity—the overseas trade carried out by one of the most powerful economic organizations of the early modern period: the private corporation which went under the name of Dutch East India Company.

As a young and virtually unique political entity, the United Provinces in the first decades of Grotius's life were still settling their form of government. While pondering the expediency of choosing a new monarch, the seven United Provinces assumed the status of a republic and governed themselves through a complex and not altogether clear system in which power was shared between the provincial Statholders (that is, the old royal governors now appointed by the provinces themselves) and the Estates (that is, the representative assemblies of the provinces), which in turn sent delegates to an Estates General of the Union at The Hague.

Inevitably, perhaps, a power struggle simmered under the brittle surface of the recently created union between forces favoring a more centralized form of government and the monarchical element of the United Provinces constitution on the one side, and forces favoring the autonomy of the provinces and the republican element on the other. This tension was compounded by economic and religious differences in the provinces, and by the fact that most of them had chosen the same Statholder, namely the Prince of Orange, effectively making of him almost a king *in pectore*.

These diverse forces had been bound together in their struggle to overthrow their Catholic ruler not least by their common desire to win the freedom necessary to practice their Protestant religion undisturbed. But the protestantism in question was by no means a seamless fabric, and these varying strands of religious allegiance soon became inextricably interwoven with economic and political interests. Indeed, the most important proximate cause of the appeals by Grotius (and other Dutch thinkers) to religious toleration was not primarily the clashes between Christians and non-Christians, or between Catholics and Protestants, or even between Lutherans and Calvinists, but the war which broke out between two different camps in the Reformed community, which were rooted, in turn, in different social and economic sections of the Dutch population.

In religion, the rural and less wealthy provinces tended to embrace a strict Calvinism characterized by a hard-line doctrine of predestination; in politics, they looked to the Prince of Orange as their protector and as the enforcer of the purer Calvinist confession. On the other hand, the urbanized, commercial, and richer provinces (including first and foremost Grotius's own province of Holland) emphasized their autonomy against central government and tended to side with the followers of the Dutch Reformed theologian, Jacobus Arminius (1560–1609).

Arminius had rejected the rigid doctrine of predestination, arguing (in line with the humanistic tradition of Erasmus) that election did take into account the individual's response to divine grace. In 1610, shortly after Arminius's death, his position was systematized by Simon Episcopius and Jan Uytenbogaert into five "articles of remonstrance," for which the followers of Arminius were called "Remonstrants."

The opposition of hard-line Dutch Calvinists against the Remonstrants was fierce and uncompromising. They called for a general synod of international Calvinism to cleanse the Dutch Reformed church of these defections from strict Calvinism and to proclaim their own views as official orthodoxy. The principle of church authority—thrown out through the door by the Protestant Reformation in favor of *sola Scriptura*—was coming back through the window in order to settle this intra-Calvinist dispute arising from the vexed question of what in fact Scripture taught on issues such as election and predestination.

Grotius grew up in the midst of this political and religious unrest. He was educated in the humanist tradition which the new University of Leiden had deeply institutionalized and come to exemplify, gained a doctorate in law in 1598 from the University of Orléans, and soon distinguished himself for his exceptional rhetorical gifts and extraordinary erudition. A brilliant political and diplomatic career seemed certain when the young prodigy was enlisted as adviser to Johann van Oldenbarnevelt (1547–1619), the de facto prime minister of the United Provinces. Instead, this close association with the political and religious program of Oldenbarnevelt led Grotius to his prison cell in Loevestein Castle.

Supporting Oldenbarnevelt's efforts to protect the Remonstrants, Grotius called for toleration of religious views diverging from strict Calvinism and opposed the convocation of the synod demanded by hard-line Calvinists. The call for toleration and religious freedom on the part of a religious group which stands in danger of being outlawed is not in itself surprising. In Grotius, however, this appeal was part of a broader, coherent religious vision which sought to overcome divisions among Christians on the basis of that very principle of *sola Scriptura* which had been one of the original leitmotifs of the Protestant Reformation. Following in particular the teaching of Franciscus Junius senior (1545–1602), Grotius embraced the doctrine of fundamental and nonfundamental articles of faith. All fundamental articles of faith necessary to salvation were clearly contained in Scripture.[1] All issues not explicitly determined by Scripture, instead of being established as necessary dogmas by church

---

1. See Franciscus Junius (François Du Jon), *Eirenicum de pace Ecclesiae Catholicae inter Christianos,* Leiden, 1593.

authority, should be considered as *adiafora:* that is, as "indifferent" matters, or matters of opinion and free interpretation.

In this power struggle, Oldenbarnevelt's party was routed. In July 1617, Prince Maurice of Orange declared himself firmly on the side of the counter-Remonstrants. In August 1618, he arrested Oldenbarnevelt and his associates on charges of high treason. Strict Calvinists likewise succeeded in their efforts to call a general synod of Reformed churches, which met in Dort (Dordrecht) from 13 November 1618 to 9 May 1619 and resulted in a comprehensive condemnation of Remonstrant doctrines. Oldenbarnevelt was beheaded on 13 May 1619; Grotius received a sentence of life imprisonment. After several months under arrest at The Hague, he settled into his prospective lifetime's incarceration at Loevestein Castle, devoting himself to study and writing.

De Veritate Religionis Christianae

His time as a prisoner was extremely productive: he returned to the study of jurisprudence, meditated on moral philosophy (translating into Latin ethical excerpts from Greek poets and dramatists), and resumed his earlier writing on theology. It was at Loevestein that the first version of his work on the truth of the Christian religion was written in the form of a Dutch poem, *Bewijs van den waren godsdienst* ("Proof of the True Religion").[2] In March 1621, however, with the help of his wife, he escaped from prison. Eventually he reached Paris, where he began life in exile under the protection of friends and, in due course, of the French king.

The *Bewijs van den waren godsdienst* was published in 1622. In 1627 it was followed by the appearance in Leiden and Paris of a Latin book which, under the title *Sensus librorum sex, quos pro veritate religionis Christianae Batavice scripsit Hugo Grotius,* reworked and recast in prose the themes covered in the Dutch poem. This little book with the cumbersome title was the first edition of *De Veritate Religionis Christianae,* a work destined to become a world-famous treatise advocating the truth

---

2. A detailed account of the genesis of this poem is offered by J. P. Heering, *Hugo Grotius as Apologist for the Christian Religion: A Study of His Work "De veritate religionis christianae" (1640),* trans. J. C. Grayson (Leiden and Boston: Brill, 2004), pp. 1–25.

of the Christian religion.[3] The second edition, bearing the simplified title *De Veritate Religionis Christianae,* was published in Leiden in 1629. Written in a plain and direct language for his countrymen and "especially Seamen, that they might have an Opportunity to employ that Time which in long Voyages lies upon their Hands, and is usually thrown away,"[4] this short work aimed to confirm to those who came into contact with pagans, Muslims, and Jews that the Christian religion was the true revealed religion. In addition to "fortifying" the beliefs of Grotius's countrymen, the treatise was also intended for missionary purposes, namely for convincing non-Christians that "the Christian Religion recommends itself above all others" and "it self is most true and certain."[5]

Grotius's intention to target a readership of seamen was not as implausible as it might appear at first glance, if one recalls that the first version of Grotius's apology was not only in the vernacular but also in verse, to add pleasure to the reading and to aid retention in the memory. Seamen were, of course, central to the Dutch Republic's standing as the greatest commercial country of the age: it dominated the Baltic trade, which furnished western Europe with many of its basic staples, and through the Dutch East India Company, the Dutch had displaced the Portuguese in the more exotic and prestigious (if less profitable) trade with India and the Far East.

A work aimed both at fortifying the Christian faith of those who were increasingly confronted with alternative and often competing systems of beliefs, and at gaining converts to Christianity through peaceful means of persuasion, was highly topical not only for genuine religious reasons but also for the political, social, and economic stability of the United Provinces. That Grotius was encouraged to prepare a Latin version indicates that an international readership more educated than the average sailor also appreciated his agile compendium of arguments in support of the Christian religion.

3. The editions of *De Veritate Religionis Christianae* are listed in Jacob Ter Meulen and P. J. J. Diermanse, *Bibliographie des écrits imprimés de Hugo Grotius* (The Hague: Nijhoff, 1950), pp. 467–535 (Nos. 944–1090).

4. Hugo Grotius, *The Truth of the Christian Religion,* ed. Jean Le Clerc, trans. John Clarke (London: Printed for John and Paul Knapton, 1743), pp. 2–3. All quotations are from this edition, which is the basis of the present volume.

5. Ibid., pp. 86–87.

Originality and philosophical sophistication were not in fact Grotius's main concern. It has rightly been observed that the arguments presented by Grotius can be traced quite closely to existing literature[6] and tend to fall short of the argumentative rigor found in other classical theological and philosophical works. Grotius's genius lay not in new or more philosophically sophisticated proofs (which would have been unintelligible to most readers, let alone the average sailor) but in selecting, organizing, and presenting in clear and compelling language arguments which could be easily followed and understood.

Like the original Dutch poem, *De Veritate* was divided into six books. The first three contained positive arguments for the truth of the Christian religion; the remaining three offered comparisons with paganism, Judaism, and Islam designed to display their inferiority. The key argumentative strategy was "to show the Reasonableness of believing and embracing the Christian Religion"[7] based on three considerations: its agreement with the conclusions of natural reason concerning the existence of God and his attributes; the authenticity and reliability of Scripture; and the morally excellent teaching contained especially in the New Testament. Accordingly, the first book offered some of the traditional proofs of the existence of God; a discussion of his attributes; and a response to some classical objections to the existence of an omnipotent, completely good, and provident God in the face of so much evil in the world.

The second book turned from natural theology to the Christian revelation, defending the truth of the historical facts on which Christianity rested, that is, the life and scandalous death of Jesus of Nazareth. Such an ignominious death and the ensuing persecutions would normally have meant the end of a sect. Amazingly, Grotius argued, Christianity instead spread and was embraced by "very many" men "of good Judgment, and of no small Learning," who acknowledged that reports of Jesus's miracles were "true, and founded upon sufficient Testimony" and that "some of the Works of Christ were such as seem to declare God himself to be the Author of them."[8] After this class of arguments "drawn from Matters

---

6. See especially Heering, *Hugo Grotius,* pp. 93–162.
7. John Clarke in the preface to his translation of *De Veritate* (p. 13 in this volume).
8. Grotius, *The Truth of the Christian Religion,* pp. 90–91, 93.

of Fact," Grotius turned to "those which are drawn from the Nature of the Doctrine,"[9] that is, to the moral superiority of its commandments.

The third book focused on philological and historical considerations aiming to establish the authenticity, reliability, and lack of significant corruption of biblical texts, with special regard to the New Testament.

In 1640 a new Latin edition of *De Veritate* appeared, in which Grotius had added a formidable apparatus of learned notes designed to support the main text's arguments by referring to a vast array of ancient, patristic, medieval, and contemporary sources. Here the author's exceptional humanistic erudition flooded the entire text of *De Veritate*. Although the arguments in the body of the work remained unchanged, Grotius's convenient little book was thereby transformed into a treatise which even the most determined sailor who did not happen to be an accomplished humanist would have found difficult to digest.

Success and Polemics

With or without notes, *De Veritate* received a remarkably warm welcome throughout the international Christian community of almost all parties. As one of the early translators of Grotius's work, John Clarke, wrote, "this Piece of *Grotius*" has met in the world with "general Acceptation."[10] Its success can only be described as overwhelming. Already before Grotius's death, in 1645, ten Latin, one German, one English, and two French editions had appeared. This was, however, only the tip of an iceberg. By the middle of the nineteenth century there had appeared sixty-four editions in Latin, seven in German, forty-five in English, eight in French, seven in Dutch, four in Scandinavian languages, three in Welsh, one in Hungarian, one in Polish, and one in Italian, plus six in Oriental languages, clearly meant as missionary tools.

The one dissonant voice in this choir of praise was that of Grotius's old enemies, the hard-line Calvinists who had condemned the Remonstrants and zealously continued to attack them as, among other things, crypto-Socinians. Among this group in particular, Socinianism was at the time

9. Ibid., p. 100.
10. Page 13 of the present volume.

almost synonymous with heresy. More specifically, the movement (which derived its name from its Italian founder, Faustus Socinus) denied the dogma of the Trinity—and therefore the divinity of Jesus Christ—on two main grounds: first, in its view, the Trinitarian doctrine was against reason; and second, being irrational, the dogma of the Trinity could not be (and indeed was not) contained in Scripture.

The charge of Socinianism was routinely thrown at the Remonstrants for their minimalist attitude toward dogmas and their emphasis on Scripture as the sole source of the articles of faith that Christians should be required to embrace. It was not long before this accusation fell upon Grotius as well, and *De Veritate* was branded as leaning toward Islam and Socinianism.[11] To the modern, untutored eye, the charge of favoring Islam might appear quite extravagant directed at a work which devotes an entire book to showing in sometimes even disturbingly firm terms the superiority of Christianity to Islam. But in the eyes of the anti-Remonstrant Calvinists who attacked Grotius, this charge was united with that of Socinianism and was grounded in the fact that both Socinians and Muslims denied the distinctive dogma of the Christian revelation, the Trinity, a dogma conspicuous for its absence from *De Veritate.*

Grotius tried his best not to be dragged into the ensuing polemic but felt compelled to explain himself to his friends. His line of defense was clear. *De Veritate,* as befitted a work addressed not only to Christians but also to non-Christians, was not the place to discuss the doctrine of the Trinity. This was a central truth unique to Christian revelation which could not be reached by natural reason. Attempts to prove the Trinity by means of rational arguments or through reference to pre-Christian authors, such as Plato and the neo-Platonists, were misguided, in Grotius's view, since Scripture and only Scripture was the source of revealed truths.[12]

11. See H. Grotius to W. de Groot, 17 March 1640 (*Briefwisseling van Hugo Grotius.* 17 vols. 's-Gravenhage: Nijhoff, 1928–2001, vol. 11, No. 4561, p. 146; hereafter *BW*). For a rich and detailed account of *De Veritate*'s reception see Heering, *Hugo Grotius,* pp. 199–241.

12. See H. Grotius to W. de Groot, 25 September 1638 (*BW* vol. 9, No. 3775, p. 589); H. Grotius to G. J. Vossius, 1 January 1639 (*BW* vol. 10, No. 3917, pp. 12–14); H. Grotius to W. de Groot, 12 April 1620 (*BW* vol. 2, No. 600, pp. 30–31).

In *De Veritate* he had taken people as far in the knowledge of God as was possible on the basis of natural reason, then focused on proving the authenticity and reliability of the Scriptures, in which doctrines surpassing the natural light of reason were revealed.[13] As Grotius pointed out, the (Catholic) doctors of the Sorbonne who had examined *De Veritate* before its publication, and who certainly were not known for their dogmatic leniency, had failed to detect any shadow of Socinianism. Instead, the Sorbonne doctors had probably found Grotius quite in line with the teaching of Thomas Aquinas, who argued that natural reason provided the *praeambula fidei* but was incapable of reaching supernatural truths, for which revelation was needed.

Interestingly, *De Veritate* sailed through the Spanish and Venetian Inquisitions almost without a scratch, and the prominent Cardinal Francesco Barberini (1597–1679) was reported to have kept it constantly to hand, in case an opportunity for evangelizing should present itself. The Lutherans also greeted the work with approval, as testified by Christoph Köler's German translation of 1631.[14] In short, in this particular instance those who vociferously denounced the absence of dogmas were the representatives, not of the Roman church so often stigmatized for its zeal for rigid doctrinal definitions, but of a branch of Reformed Protestantism which regarded itself as an unyielding defender of Calvinist orthodoxy.

As for Grotius, the approach to the Christian religion chosen in *De Veritate* was perfectly in line with his long-standing view that division among Christians could and should be overcome on the basis of the distinction between fundamental and nonfundamental articles of faith coupled with the crucial claim that all fundamental articles are explicitly contained in Scripture. For him as for others, this claim also provided a solid criterion for religious toleration. In *De Veritate*, instead of embarking on an inappropriate dogmatic treatment of what Christians should

13. See H. Grotius to N. van Reigersberch, 26 December 1637 (*BW* vol. 8, No. 3397, p. 814).

14. See H. Grotius to W. de Groot, 22 October 1637 (*BW* vol. 8, No. 3310, p. 667). On the verdict of the Spanish and Venetian Inquisitions, see Ter Meulen–Diermanse, *Bibliographie*, No. 944, note 6 and No. 988, note 2; the 1640 edition appeared with the approval of the (Catholic) king of France.

believe, he had limited himself to proving the reliability and authenticity of Scripture—the only voice to which one was required to listen. Once its divine inspiration had been established, one had only to let it speak to discover all fundamental Christian truths.

It is remarkable that a man who wrote the first version of this work in a state of life imprisonment as a consequence (at least in a significant measure) of religious divisions should spend no ink to condemn in it the views of his opponents. Despite the high personal price he paid for the intestine fights within the Reformed camp, in *De Veritate* he rose above them to focus on what he regarded as the agreement among Christians "in the principal things." The opportunity for reestablishing unity among Christians, in other words, was provided by precisely "those Commands" by which the Christian religion recommended itself above other faiths as well. The certainty of Christianity was confirmed by the very fact that "those who[,] being highly enraged against one another, have fought for Matter of Disagreement, never ventured to go so far as to deny, that these were the Precepts of Christ."[15]

Christianity was thus presented in *De Veritate* as an eminently reasonable religion, though in a manner quite different from Grotius's deistic successors: Christianity was reasonable, in Grotius's view, not because there was not room within it for supernatural truths such as the Trinity, the divinity of Christ, and miracles (in fact, miracles did heavy duty within his argumentation), but because it agreed with what natural reason could discover about God, it contained nothing irrational or contradictory, it was based on texts the authenticity and reliability of which could be proved, and (finally and most importantly) it displayed and advocated superior moral standards.

Le Clerc's Additions

Among the posthumous Latin editions of *De Veritate,* the most important and influential were those of Jean Le Clerc (1657–1736). Born and raised in Geneva and transplanted successively to Grenoble and Saumur in France and for six months also to London, Le Clerc settled in

---

15. See Grotius, *The Truth of the Christian Religion,* pp. 124–25.

Amsterdam where (from 1684) he taught philosophy, literature, and Hebrew in the Remonstrant seminary. At the death of his close friend, the
leading Dutch Remonstrant theologian Philip V. Limborch (1633–1712),
Le Clerc was also appointed to the chair of church history. Befriended
by John Locke (whom he met during the English thinker's exile in the
United Provinces between 1683 and 1688), he established himself as a key
figure of the European republic of letters through his work as a biblical
scholar, theologian, and especially as editor of one of the learned jour-
nals central to contemporary intellectual life, the *Bibliothèque Universelle
et Historique* (26 volumes, 1686–1694, 1718), continued as *Bibliothèque
Choisie* (28 volumes, 1703–1713, 1718), and then *Bibliothèque Ancienne et
Moderne* (29 volumes, 1714–1727, 1730).

Le Clerc's first edition of Grotius's *De Veritate Religionis Christianae*,
published in 1709, supplemented the original work in three respects: it
corrected numerous mistakes, especially in quotations from ancient
sources; it provided a series of notes in addition to those of Grotius; and
it subjoined an additional book to the six of Grotius's original work. The
new book was devoted to the question of which Christian church should
be chosen, and in it Le Clerc advanced two main conclusions which were
in line with Grotius's views but were not as explicit in *De Veritate* as
Le Clerc thought necessary. First, nothing else ought to be imposed on
Christians aside from what they can gather from the New Testament; and
second, the purest Christian doctrine is professed by those who propose
as necessary to be believed only those things on which Christians agree.

Le Clerc's edition, including his "seventh book," was translated into
English in 1711 by John Clarke senior (1682–1757). Brother of Samuel
Clarke (1675–1729) and an accomplished mathematician, John Clarke was
a clergyman who served as chaplain to the king and (from 1728) as dean
of Salisbury.

In 1718 Le Clerc published a second, revised edition, on the basis
of which Clarke published his second English edition in 1719, followed
by a third in 1729.

The third and definitive Latin edition by Le Clerc appeared in The
Hague in 1724. It included an "eighth book" in which Le Clerc argued
against those who "imagine it to be quite indifferent, what Party of Christians we really join ourselves with, or indeed only profess to join ourselves

with."[16] While "we ought not hastily to condemn" those who have different religious beliefs, the hypocrisy of those who join a certain religious denomination against their "own Conscience" is never permissible.[17] The 1724 edition served as a basis for Clarke's fourth English edition, which appeared in London in 1743 and included Le Clerc's "eighth book."

Especially in the English-speaking world, the two books added by Le Clerc became classic documents in their own right, alongside the original work by Grotius. Testimony to this are the seventeen reprints of Clarke's definitive English edition of 1743. In its preface, Clarke endorsed the view, shared by Grotius and Le Clerc, that the way to end fighting among Christians was to return to *sola Scriptura,* in which all the articles of faith necessary for salvation are clearly contained: "the only Remedy that can heal these Divisions amongst Christians . . . is, in one Word, making the Scripture the only Rule of Faith. Whatever is necessary for a Christian to believe, in order to everlasting Salvation, is there declared."[18]

16. Jean Le Clerc, "Against Indifference in the Choice of our Religion," in Grotius, *The Truth of the Christian Religion,* p. 325.

17. Ibid., pp. 332, 334.

18. Page 16 of the present volume.

A NOTE ON THE TEXT

The impetuous flood of editions of Grotius's *De Veritate* shrinks to a trickle from 1950 onward. A facsimile reprint of the first English translation (London, 1632; probably based on the Leiden Latin edition of 1629) was published in Amsterdam and New York in 1971. An Italian translation by Fiorella Pintacuda De Michelis—based on the text of *De Veritate* in Grotius's *Opera omnia theologica* (Amsterdam, 1679) but excluding the extensive notes added by Grotius in 1640—appeared in 1973. Finally, a photographic reproduction of the 1818 edition of John Clarke's translation was published in 2004.

The current edition presents John Clarke's English translation of 1743 of Jean Le Clerc's definitive Latin edition of 1724. It does not attempt to provide a critical edition of a text with so many and such complex layers of revisions, additions, and corrections by Grotius, Le Clerc, and Clarke. Its aim is much more modest: namely, to help the modern reader appreciate a classic work that had a massive impact on western culture. This aim is pursued in the "Authors and Works Cited by Grotius and Le Clerc" (pp. 299–332), via the identification of the authors and works mentioned by Grotius and Le Clerc in their countless allusions and more or less implicit references, and in explanatory annotations to the text itself. Given the already formidable apparatus of notes by Grotius, Le Clerc, and occasionally Clarke, I have kept my own annotations to a minimum. John Clarke's translation, although far from blameless, has been treated as a period piece in its own right. I have therefore limited my interventions to silently correcting only clear typographical errors.

ACKNOWLEDGMENTS

The bulk of the work on this edition was done during a period of research leave for which I am grateful to King's College London. It is a pleasure to record my thanks also to Hamilton Bryson, Noel Malcolm, Maria Grazia and Mario Sina, M. A. Stewart, Stefania Tutino, and Joanna Weinberg for helping me with the identification of some of the most obscure authors and works cited by Grotius and Le Clerc. In this challenging task Richard Hewitt's "Catalogus Librorum a Grotio et Clerico Laudatorum," appended to the edition of Grotius's *De Veritate Religionis Christianae* published in Oxford in 1807, has provided a valuable starting point. Thank you to Paul Dimmock for checking Hebrew and Ancient Greek words. I am greatly indebted to Knud Haakonssen for his support over the years and for his advice as the general editor of the series of which this volume is part. Thanks are also due to Laura Goetz and Diana Francoeur of Liberty Fund, for being gracious and competent editors, and to the library of Harris Manchester College (Oxford) for allowing me to consult the 1743 edition. As always, the deepest debt of all is to my family. My husband, Howard Hotson, has been my constant intellectual companion, sharing the pleasure of this work and helping me to endure its frustrations when Grotius and Le Clerc's elusive citations proved difficult to track down. They prompted our son John, however, to try his hand at scholarly work. Our daughters, Sophia and Francesca, might or might not try some other time.

To John

THE TRUTH OF THE CHRISTIAN RELIGION

THE

TRUTH

OF THE

Christian Religion.

IN

SIX BOOKS

BY

HUGO GROTIUS.

Corrected and Illustrated with NOTES,
By Mr. LE CLERC.
To which is added, a SEVENTH BOOK,
Concerning this QUESTION,
What Christian Church we ought to join ourselves to.
By the said Mr. LE CLERC.

The FOURTH EDITION, with ADDITIONS:

*Particularly one whole BOOK of Mr. LE CLERC's,
Against Indifference of what Religion a Man is of.*

Done into *English* by JOHN CLARKE, D.D.
Dean of SARUM.

LONDON:

Printed for JOHN and PAUL KNAPTON, at the *Crown* in *Ludgate-Street.*

MDCCXLIII.

Most Reverend Prelate
THOMAS,[1]
Lord Archbishop of *Canterbury,*
Primate of all *England,* and Metropolitan, and Privy-Counsellor
to her most Serene Majesty the Queen of *Great-Britain.*[2]

Upon the Reprinting this excellent Piece of that great Man *Hugo Grotius,* concerning the Truth of the Christian Religion; whereunto I thought fit to add something of my own, and also some Testimonies, from which the good Opinion he had of the Church of *England,* is evident; there was no other Person, most Reverend Prelate, to whom I thought it so proper for me to Dedicate this Edition, with the Additions, as the Primate and Metropolitan of the whole Church of *England.* I therefore present it to you, as worthy your Protection upon its own Account, and as an Instance of my Respect and Duty towards you. I will not attempt here, either to praise or defend *Grotius;* his own Virtue and distinguishing Merits in the Commonwealth of Christians, do sufficiently commend and justify him amongst all good and learned Men. Neither will I say any thing of the Appendix which I have added; it is so short, that it may be read over almost in an Hour's time. If it be beneath *Grotius,* nothing that I can say about it will vindicate me to the Censorious; but if it be thought not beneath him, I need not give any Reasons for joining it with a Piece of his. Perhaps it might be expected, most illustrious Prelate, that I should, as usual, commend you and your Church; but I have more than once

1. Thomas Tenison (1636–1715), archbishop of Canterbury from 1694 to 1715.
2. Anne, queen of Great Britain and Ireland (1665–1714; reigned 1702–14).

performed this Part, and declared a thing known to all: Wherefore for-bearing that, I conclude with wishing that both you and the Reverend Prelates, and the rest of the Clergy of the Church of *England*, who are such brave Defenders of the true Christian Religion, and whose Con-versations are answerable to it, may long prosper and flourish; which I earnestly desire of Almighty God.

Amsterdam, *the Calends*
of March, MDCCIX.[3]

JOHN LE CLERC.

3. 1 March 1709.

READER

The Bookseller having a Design to reprint this Piece of *Grotius*'s, I gave him to understand that there were many great Faults in the former Editions, especially in the Testimonies of the Ancients, which it was his Business should be mended, and that something useful might be added to the Notes: Neither would it be unacceptable or unprofitable to the Reader, if a Book were added, to show where the Christian Religion, the Truth of which this great Man has demonstrated, is to be found in its greatest Purity. He immediately desired me to do this upon his Account, which I willingly undertook, out of the Reverence I had for the Memory of *Grotius,* and because of the Usefulness of the thing. How I have succeeded in it, I must leave to the *candid Reader*'s Judgment. I have corrected many Errors of the Press, and perhaps should have done more, could I have found all the Places. I have added some, but very short Notes, there being very many before, and the thing not seeming to require more. My Name adjoined, distinguishes them from *Grotius*'s. I have also added to *Grotius*'s a small Book, concerning chusing our Opinion and Church amongst so many different Sects of Christians; in which I hope I have offered nothing contrary to the Sense of that great Man, or at least to Truth. I have used such Arguments, as will recommend themselves to any prudent Person, easy, and not far-fetched; and I have determined that Christians ought to manage themselves so in this Matter, as the most prudent Men usually do, in the most weighty Affairs of Life. I have abstained from all sharp Controversy, and from all severe Words, which ought never to enter into our Determinations of Religion, if our Adversaries will suffer it. I have declared the Sense of my Mind in a familiar Stile, without any Flourish of Words, in a Matter where Strength of Argument and not the Enticement of Words is required. And herein I have imitated *Grotius,* whom I think All ought to imitate who attempt to write seriously, and with a Mind deeply affected with the Gravity of the Argument, upon such Subjects.

As I was thinking upon these things, the Letters which you will see at the End, were sent me by that honourable and learned Person, to whose singular good Nature I am much indebted, the most Serene Queen of *Great Britain*'s Embassador Extraordinary to his Royal Highness the most Serene Great Duke of *Tuscany.*[4] I thought with his Leave they might conveniently be published at the End of this Volume, that it might appear what Opinion *Grotius* had of the Church of *England;* which is obliged to him, notwithstanding the Snarling of some Men, who object those inconsistent Opinions, Socinianism, Popery, nay, even Atheism itself, against this most learned and religious Man; for fear, I suppose, his immortal Writings should be read, in which their foolish Opinions are intirely confuted. In which Matter, as in many other things of the like Nature, they have in vain attempted to blind the Eyes of others: But God forgive them, (for I wish them nothing worse,) and put better Thoughts into their Minds, that we may at last be all joined by the Love of Truth and Peace, and be united into one Flock, under one Shepherd Jesus Christ. This, *Kind Reader,* is what you ought to desire and wish with me; and may God so be with you, and all that belong to you, as you promote this Matter as far as can be, and assist to the utmost of your Power.

Farewel.

Amsterdam, *the Calends*
of March, MDCCIX.[5]

---

4. See p. 289 in this volume.
5. 1 March 1709.

TO THE
READER.

I have nothing to add to what I said Eight Years since, but only, that in this my second Edition of *Grotius,* I have put some short Notes, and corrected a great many Faults in the Ancient Testimonies.

Amsterdam, *the Calends*
of June, MDCCXVII.[6]

J. C.[7]

6. 1 June 1717.
7. Jean Le Clerc.

Most Noble and Most Excellent

HIERONYMUS BIGNONIUS,[8]

The King's Sollicitor in the Supreme Court of Audience at PARIS.

Most Noble and Excellent Sir,
I should offend against Justice, if I should divert another way that time which you employ in the Exercise of Justice in your high Station: But I am encouraged in this Work, because it is for the Advancement of the Christian Religion, which is a great Part of Justice, and of your Office; neither would Justice permit me to approach any one else so soon as you, whose Name my Book glories in the Title of. I do not say I desire to employ part of your Leisure; for the Discharge of so extensive an Office allows you no Leisure. But since Change of Business is instead of Leisure to them that are fully employed, I desire you would in the midst of your forensick Affairs, bestow some Hours upon these Papers. Even then, you will not be out of the way of your Business. Hear the Witnesses, weigh the Force of their Testimony, make a Judgment, and I will stand by the Determination.

Paris, August 27,
ↀ ↄↄ XXXIX.[9]

HUGO GROTIUS.

---

8. Jérôme Bignon (1589–1656), French lawyer and tutor to the dauphin (afterward Louis XIII, king of France from 1610 to 1643). Under Louis XIII Bignon held the positions of advocate-general to the grand council, councillor of state, and advocate-general to the *parlement* of Paris.
   9. 27 August 1639.

Translator's Preface

Christian READER.

The general Acceptation this Piece of *Grotius* has met with in the World, encouraged this Translation of it, together with the Notes; which, being a Collection of Antient Testimonies, upon whose Authority and Truth the Genuineness of the Books of Holy Scripture depends, are very useful in order to the convincing any one of the Truth of the Christian Religion. These Notes are for the most Part *Grotius*'s own, except some few of Mr. *Le Clerc*'s, which I have therefore translated also, because I have followed his Edition, as the most Correct.

The Design of the Book, is to show the Reasonableness of believing and embracing the Christian Religion above any other; which our Author does, by laying before us all the Evidence, that can be brought, both Internal and External, and declaring the Sufficiency of it; by enumerating all the Marks of Genuineness in any Books, and applying them to the Sacred Writings; and by making appear the Deficiency of all other Institutions of Religion, whether *Pagan, Jewish,* or *Mahometan.* So that the Substance of the whole is briefly this; that as certain as is the Truth of Natural Principles, and that the Mind can judge of what is agreeable to them; as certain as is the Evidence of Mens Bodily Senses in the most plain and obvious Matters of Fact; and as certainly as Mens Integrity and Sincerity may be discovered, and their Accounts delivered down to Posterity faithfully; so certain are we of the Truth of the Christian Religion; and that if it be not true, there is no such Thing as true Religion in the

World, neither was there ever or can there ever be any Revelation proved to be from Heaven.

This is the Author's Design to prove the Truth of the Christian Religion in general, against Atheists, Deists, *Jews,* or *Mahometans;* and he does not enter into any of the Disputes which Christians have among themselves, but confines himself wholly to the other. Now as the State of Christianity at present is, were a Heathen or *Mahometan* convinc'd of the Truth of the Christian Religion in general, he would yet be exceedingly at a Loss to know what Society of Christians to join himself with; so miserably divided are they amongst themselves, and separated into so many Sects and Parties, which differ almost as widely from each other as Heathens from Christians, and who are so zealous and contentious for their own particular Opinions, and bear so much Hatred and ill Will towards those that differ from them, that there is very little of the true Spirit of Charity, which is the Bond of Peace, to be found amongst any of them: This is a very great Scandal to the Professors of Christianity, and has been exceedingly disserviceable to the Christian Religion; insomuch that great Numbers have been hindered from embracing the Gospel, and many tempted to cast it off, because they saw the Professors of it in general agree so little amongst themselves: This Consideration induced Mr. *Le Clerc* to add a Seventh Book to those of *Grotius;* wherein he treats of this Matter, and shows what it becomes every honest Man to do in such a Case; And I have translated it for the same Reason. All that I shall here add, shall be only briefly to enquire into the Cause of so much Division in the Church of Christ, and to show what seems to me the only Remedy to heal it. First, to examine into the Cause, why the Church of Christ is so much divided: A Man needs but a little Knowledge of the State of the Christian Church, to see that there is just Reason for the same Complaint St. *Paul* made in the primitive Times of the Church of *Corinth;* that some were for *Paul,* some for *Apollos,* and some for *Cephas;* so very early did the Spirit of Faction creep into the Church of God, and disturb the Peace of it, by setting its Members at Variance with each other, who ought to have been all of the same common Faith, into which they were baptized; and I wish it could not be said that the same Spirit has too much remained amongst Christians ever since. It is evident that the Foundation of the Divisions in the

Church of *Corinth*, was their forsaking their common Lord and Master, *Jesus Christ*, into whose Name alone they were baptized; and uniting themselves, some under one eminent Apostle or Teacher, and some under another, by whom they had been instructed in the Doctrine of Christ; whereby they were distinguished into different Sects, under their several Denominations: This St. *Paul* complains of as a Thing in itself very Bad, and of pernicious Consequence; for hereby the Body of Christ, that is, the Christian Church, the Doctrine of which is one and the same at all Times and in all Places, is rent and divided into several Parts, that clash and interfere with each other; Which is the only Method, if permitted to have its natural Effect, that can overthrow and destroy it. And from the same Cause have arisen all the Divisions that are or have been in the Church ever since. Had Christians been contented to own but one Lord, even *Jesus Christ*, and made the Doctrine delivered by him the sole Rule of Faith, without any Fictions or Inventions of Men; it had been impossible but that the Church of Christ must have been one universal, regular, uniform Thing, and not such a Mixture and Confusion as we now behold it. But when Christians once began to establish Doctrines of their own, and to impose them upon others by humane Authority as Rules of Faith, (which is the Foundation of Antichrist,) then there began to be as many Schemes of Religion as there were Parties of Men who had different Judgment, and got the Power into their Hands. A very little Acquaintance with Ecclesiastical History does but too sadly confirm the Truth of this, by giving us an Account of the several Doctrines in Fashion, in the several Ages of the Christian Church, according to the then present Humour. And if it be not so now, how comes it to pass that the Generality of Christians are so zealous for that Scheme of Religion, which is received by that particular Church of which they profess themselves Members? How is it that the Generality of Christians in one Country are zealous for *Calvinism*, and in another Country as zealous for *Arminianism?* It is not because Men have any natural Disposition more to the one than the other, or perhaps that one has much more Foundation to support it from Scripture than the other; But the Reason is plain, *viz.* because they are the established Doctrines of the Places they live in; they are by Authority made the Rule and Standard of Religion, and Men are taught them from the Beginning; by this Means, they are so deeply fixed and rooted in their Minds, that they become prejudiced in Favour of them, and have so strong a Relish of them, that they cannot read a Chapter in the Bible but it appears exactly agreeable to the received Notions of them both, tho' perhaps those Notions are directly contradictory to each other: Thus instead of making the Scripture the only Rule of Faith, Men make Rules of Faith of their own, and interpret Scripture according to them; which being an easy Way of coming to the Knowledge of what they esteem the Truth, the Generality of Christians sit down very well satisfy'd with it. But whoever is indeed convinced of the Truth of the Gospel, and has any Regard for the Honour of it, cannot but be deeply concerned to see its sacred Truths thus prostituted to the Power and Interests of Men; and think it his Duty to do the utmost he is able to take it out of their Hands, and fix it on its own immoveable Bottom. In order to contribute to which, I shall in the Second Place show what seems to be the only Remedy that can heal these Divisions amongst Christians; and that is, in one Word, making the Scripture the only Rule of Faith. Whatever is necessary for a Christian to believe, in order to everlasting Salvation, is there declared, in such a Way and Manner as the Wisdom of God, who best knows the Circumstances and Conditions of Mankind, has thought fit. This God himself has made the Standard for all Ranks and Orders, for all Capacities and Abilities; And to set up any other above, or upon the Level with it, is dishonouring God and abusing of Men. All the Authority in the World cannot make any Thing an Article of Faith, but what God has made so; neither can any Power establish or impose upon Men, more or less, or otherwise than what the Scripture commands. God has given every Man proportionable Faculties and Abilities of Mind, some stronger and some weaker; and he has by his own Authority made the Scripture the Rule of Religion to them all; It is therefore their indispensible Duty to examine diligently, and study attentively this Rule, to instruct themselves in the Knowledge of Religious Truths from hence, and to form the best Judgment they can of the Nature of them. The Scripture will extend or contract itself according to the Capacities of Men; The strongest and largest Understanding will there find enough to fill and improve it, and the narrowest and meanest Capacity will fully acquiesce in what is there required of it. Thus all Men are obliged to form a Judgment of Religion for themselves, and to be continually rectifying and improving it; They may be very helpful and assisting to each other in the Means of coming to this Divine Knowledge, but no one can finally determine for another; every Man must judge for himself; and for the Sincerity of his Judgment he is accountable to God only, who knows the Secrets of all Hearts, which are beyond the Reach of humane Power: This must be left till the final Day of Account, when every Man shall be acquitted or condemned according as he has acted by the Dictates of his Conscience or no. Were all Christians to go upon this Principle, we should soon see an End of all the fierce Controversies and unhappy Divisions which now rend and confound the Church of Christ: Were every Man allowed to take the Scripture for his only Guide in Matters of Faith, and, after all the Means of Knowledge and Instruction used, all the Ways of Assurance and Conviction try'd, permitted quietly to enjoy his own Opinion, the Foundation of all Divisions would be taken away at once: And till Christians do arrive at this Temper of Mind, let them not boast that they are endued with that excellent Virtue of Charity which is the distinguishing Mark of their Profession; for if what St. *Paul* says be true, that Charity is greater than Faith, it is evident no Christian ought to be guilty of the Breach of a greater Duty upon Account of a lesser; They ought not to disturb that Peace and Unity which ought to be amongst all Christians, for the Sake of any Matters of Faith, any Differences of Opinion; because it is contrary to the known Law of Charity: And how the far greatest Part of Christians will clear themselves of transgressing this plain Law, I know not. Wherefore if ever we expect to have our Petitions answered, when we pray that God would make us one Flock under one Shepherd and Bishop of our Souls, *Jesus Christ;* we must cease to make needless Fences of our own, and to divide ourselves into small separate Flocks, and distinguish them by that whereby Christ has not distinguished them. When this Spirit of Love and Unity, of forbearing one another in Meekness, once becomes the prevailing Principle amongst Christians; then, and not till then, will the Kingdom of Christ in its highest Perfection and Purity flourish upon the Earth, and all the Powers of Darkness fall before it.

JOHN CLARKE.

THE CONTENTS[1]

1. The page numbers given in the Contents are those from the present Liberty Fund edition. The original page numbers appear in the angle brackets.

BOOK II.

BOOK III.

BOOK IV.

II. And first of Paganism. That there is but One God. That created Beings are either good or bad. That the Good are not

BOOK V.

The Contents of Mr. Le Clerc's two Books.

BOOK I.

BOOK II.

To the Honourable
Hieronymus Bignonius,[1]
His Majesty's Sollicitor
in the chief court of *PARIS*.

〽 BOOK I 〽

Sect. I. *The Occasion of this Work.*

You have frequently enquired of me, worthy Sir, (whom I know to be
a Gentleman that highly deserves the Esteem of your Country, of the
learned World, and, if you will allow me to say it, of myself also;) what
the Substance of those Books is, which I wrote in defence of the Christian Religion, in my own Language.[2] Nor do I wonder at your Enquiry;
For you, who have with so great Judgment read every thing that is worth
reading, cannot but be sensible with how much Philosophick Nicety (*a*)
Raemundus Sebundus, with what entertain-<2>ing Dialogues *Ludovicus
Vives,* and with how great Eloquence your *Mornaeus,* have illustrated this
Matter. For which Reason it might seem more useful, to translate some

---

1. Jérôme Bignon (see note 6 above).
2. The first version of Grotius's work on the truth of the Christian religion was written in the form of a Dutch poem, *Bewijs van den waren godsdienst* ("Proof of the True
Religion"). See p. xii and note 2 of the introduction.
a. *Raemundus Sebundus,* &c.] These were the chief Writers upon this Subject in
Grotius's Time; but since then a great Number have wrote concerning the Truth of the
Christian Religion, especially in *French* and *English;* moved thereto by the Example
of *Grotius,* whom they imitated, and sometimes borrowed from him: So that the Glory
of so pious and necessary a Method of Writing chiefly redounds to him. *Le Clerc.*

of them into our own Language, than to undertake any thing new upon this Subject. But though I know not what Judgment others will pass upon me, yet have I very good Reason to hope that you, who are so fair and candid a Judge, will easily acquit me, if I should say, that after having read not only the fore-mentioned Writings, but also those that have been written by the *Jews* in behalf of the antient *Jewish* Dispensation, and those of Christians for Christianity, I chuse to make use of my own Judgment, such as it is; and to give my Mind that Liberty which at present is denied my Body; For I am persuaded that Truth is no other way to be defended but by Truth, and *That* such as the Mind is fully satisfied with; it being in vain to attempt to persuade others to that which you yourself are not convinced of: Wherefore I selected, both from the Antients and Moderns, what appeared to me most conclusive; leaving such Arguments as seemed of small Weight, and rejecting such Books as I knew to be spurious, or had Reason to suspect to be so. Those which I approved of, I explained and put in a regular Method, and in as popular a manner as I could, and likewise turned them into Verse, that they might the easier be remembred. For my Design was to undertake something which might be useful to my Countrymen, especially Seamen, that they might have an Opportunity to employ that Time which in long Voyages lies upon their <3> Hands, and is usually thrown away: Wherefore I began with an Encomium upon our Nation, which so far excells others in the Skill of Navigation; that by this means I might excite them to make use of this Art, as a peculiar Favour of Heaven; not only to their own Profit, but also to the propagating the Christian Religion: For they can never want Matter, but in their long Voyages they will every where meet either with *Pagans* as in *China* or *Guinea;* or *Mahometans,* as in the *Turkish* and *Persian* Empires, and in the Kingdoms of *Fez* and *Morocco;* and also with *Jews* who are the professed Enemies of Christianity, and are dispersed over the greatest part of the World; And there are never wanting prophane Persons, who, upon occasion, are ready to scatter their Poison amongst the Weak and Simple, which Fear had forced them to conceal: Against all which Evils, my Desire was, to have my Countrymen well fortified; that they who have the best parts, might employ them in confuting Errors; and that the other would take heed of being seduced by them.

Sect. II. *That there is a God.*

And that we may show that Religion is not a vain and empty thing; it shall be the Business of this first Book to lay the Foundation thereof in the Existence of the Deity: Which I prove in the following manner. That there are some Things which had a Beginning, is confessed on all Sides, and obvious to Sense: But these Things could not be the Cause of their own Existence; because that which has no Being, cannot act; for then it would have *been* before it *was,* which is impossible; whence it follows, that it derived its Being from something else: This is true not only of those Things which are now before our Eyes, or which we have formerly seen; but also of *those things* <4> out of which *these* have arisen, and so on, (*a*) till we arrive at some Cause, which never had any Beginning, but exists (as we say) necessarily, and not by Accident: Now this Being whatsoever it be (of whom we shall speak more fully by and by) is what we mean by the Deity, or God. Another Argument for the Proof of a Deity may be drawn from the plain Consent of all Nations, who have any Remains of Reason, any Sense of Good Manners, and are not wholly degenerated into Brutishness. For, Humane Inventions, which depend upon the arbitrary Will of Men, are not always the same every where, but are often changed; whereas there is no *Place* where this Notion is not to be found; nor has the Course of Time been able to alter it, (which is observed by (*b*) *Aristotle* himself, a Man not very credulous in these Matters;) wherefore we must assign it a Cause as extensive as all Mankind; and That can be no other than a Declaration from God himself, or a Tradition derived down from the first Parents of Mankind: If the former be granted, there needs

a. *Till we arrive at some Cause,* &c.] Because as their manner of speaking is, there can be no such thing as going on for ever; for of those Things which had a Beginning, either there is some first Cause, or there is none. If it be denied that there is any first Cause; then those Things which had a Beginning, were without a Cause; and consequently existed or came out of nothing of themselves, which is absurd. *Le Clerc.*

b. *Aristotle himself,* &c.] *Metaphys.* Book XI. Ch. 5. where, after relating the Fables of the Gods, he has these Words, "Which if any one rightly distinguishes, he will keep wholly to this as the principal Thing; that to believe the Gods to be the first Beings, is a divine Truth: and that tho' Arts and Sciences have probably been often lost, and revived; yet this Opinion hath been preserved as a Relict to this very Time." *Le Clerc.*

no further Proof; if the latter, it is hard to give a good Reason why our first Parents should deliver to Posterity a Falsity in a Matter of so great <5> Moment. Moreover, if we look into those Parts of the World, which have been a long time known, or into those lately discovered; if they have not lost the common Principles of Human Nature, (as was said before) this Truth immediately appears; as well amongst the more dull Nations as amongst those who are quicker, and have better Understandings; and, surely, these *latter* cannot all be deceived, nor the *former* be supposed to have found out something to impose upon each other with: Nor would it be of any force against *this,* if it should be urged, that there have been a few Persons in many Ages, who did not believe a God, or at least made such a Profession; For considering how few they were, and that as soon as their Arguments were known, their Opinion was immediately exploded; it is evident, it did not proceed from the right use of that Reason which is common to all Men; but either from an Affectation of Novelty, like the Heathen Philosopher who contended that Snow was black; or from a corrupted Mind, which like a vitiated Palate, does not relish Things as they are: Especially since History and other Writings inform us, that the more vertuous any one is, the more carefully is this Notion of the Deity preserved by him: And it is further evident, that they who dissent from this antiently established Opinion, do it out of an ill Principle, and are such Persons whose Interest it is that there should be no God, that is, no Judge of human Actions; because whatever Hypotheses they have advanced of their own, whether an infinite Succession of Causes, without any Beginning; or a fortuitous Concourse of Atoms, or any other (a) it is attend-<6>ed with as great, if not greater Difficulties, and not at all more credible than what is already received; as is evident to any one that considers it ever so little. For that which some object, that they don't believe

a. *It is attended with as great,* &c.] *Grotius* might have said, and that not rashly, that there are much greater Difficulties in the Opinions of those, who would have the World to be eternal, or always to have *been:* such as, that it must have come out of nothing of *it self,* or that it arose from the fortuitous Concourse of *Atoms;* Opinions full of manifest Contradictions, as many since *Grotius's* Time have exactly demonstrated; amongst whom is the eminent and learned Dr. *Ralph Cudworth,* who wrote the *English* Treatise *Of the intellectual System of the Universe:* There are also other very excellent *English* Divines and natural Philosophers. *Le Clerc.*

a God, because they don't see him; if they can see any thing, they may see how much it is beneath a Man, who has a *Soul* which he cannot see, to argue in this manner. Nor if we cannot fully comprehend the *Nature* of God, ought we therefore to deny that there is any *such* Being; for the *Beasts* don't know of what sort Creatures *Men* are, and much less do they understand how Men, by their Reason, institute and govern Kingdoms, measure the Course of the Stars, and sail cross the Seas: These Things exceed their Reach: And hence *Man,* because he is placed by the Dignity of his *Nature* above the *Beasts,* and *that* not by himself, ought to infer; that *He* who gave him this Superiority above the Beasts, is as far advanced beyond *Him,* as *He* is beyond the *Beasts;* and that therefore there is a *Nature,* which, as it is more Excellent, so it exceeds his Comprehension.

Sect. III. *That there is but one God.*

Having proved the Existence of the Deity: we come next to his Attributes; the first whereof is, That there can be no more Gods than One. Which may be gathered from hence; because (as was before said) God exists necessarily, or is self-<7>existent. Now that which is *necessary* or *self-existent,* cannot be considered as of any Kind or Species of Beings, but as actually existing, (*a*) and is therefore a single Being: For if you imagine many Gods, you will see that *necessary Existence* belongs to none of them; nor can there be any Reason why two should rather be believed than three, or ten than five: Beside the Abundance of particular Things of the same kind, proceeds from the Fruitfulness of the Cause, in proportion to which more or less is produced; but God has no Cause, or Original. Further, particular different Things, are endued with peculiar Properties, by which they are distinguished from each other; which do not belong to God, who is a necessary Being. Neither do we find any Signs of many

a. *And is therefore a single Being,* &c.] But a great many single Beings, are a great many individual Beings; this Argument therefore might have been omitted, without any detriment to so good a Cause. *Le Clerc.*

Whoever would see the Argument for the Unity of God, drawn from his *necessary* or *Self-existence,* urged in its full force, may find it at the beginning of Dr *Sam. Clarke's* *Boyle's Lectures.*[3]

3. Added by John Clarke.

Gods; for this whole Universe makes but one World, in which there is but (a) *One* Thing that far exceeds the rest in Beauty; *viz.* the Sun; and in every Man there is but *One Thing* that governs, that is, the Mind: Moreover, if there could be two or more Gods, free Agents, acting according to their own Wills, they might *will* contrary to each other; and so *One* be hindered by the *Other* from effecting his Design; now a Possibility of being hindred is inconsistent with the Notion of God. <8>

Sect. IV. *All Perfection is in God.*

That we may come to the Knowledge of the other Attributes of God; we conceive all that is meant by *Perfection,* to be in Him, (I use the Latin Word *Perfectio,* as being the best that Tongue affords, and the same as the Greek τελειότης). Because whatever Perfection is in any Thing, either had a Beginning, or not; if it had no Beginning, it is the Perfection of God; if it had a Beginning, it must of necessity be from something else: And since none of those things that exist, are produced from nothing, it follows, that whatever *Perfections* are in the Effects, were first in the Cause, so that it could produce any thing endued with *them;* and consequently they are *all* in the first Cause. Neither can the first Cause ever be deprived of any of its Perfections: Not from any thing else; because that which is Eternal, does not depend upon any other thing, nor can it at all suffer from any thing that they can do: Nor from itself, because every Nature desires its own Perfection.

Sect. V. *And in an infinite Degree.*

To this must be added, that these Perfections are in God, in an infinite Degree: Because those Attributes that are finite, are therefore limited, because the Cause whence they proceed has communicated so much of them and no more; or else, because the Subject was capable of no more. But no other Nature communicated any of its Perfections to God; nor

---

a. *One Thing that far exceeds,* &c.] At least to the Inhabitants of this our *Solar System* (as, we now term it;) as those fiery Centers the *Stars,* are to other *Systems. Le Clerc.*

does he derive any thing from any One else, he being (as was said) necessary or self-existent. <9>

Sect. VI. *That God is Eternal, Omnipotent, Omniscient and compleatly Good.*

Now seeing it is very evident, that those Things which have *Life* are more perfect, than those which have not; and those which have a *Power of Acting,* than those which have none; those which have *Understanding,* than those which want it; those which are *good,* than those which are not so; it follows from what has been already said, that these Attributes belong to God, and *that* infinitely: Wherefore he is a *living infinite* God; that is *eternal,* of *immense Power,* and every way *good* without the least Defect.

Sect. VII. *That God is the Cause of all Things.*

Every Thing that is, derives its Existence from God; this follows from what has been already said. For we conclude that there is but One necessary self-existent Being; whence we collect, that all other Things sprung from a Being different from themselves: For those Things which are derived from something else, were all of them, either immediately in themselves, or mediately in their Causes, derived from Him who had no Beginning, that is, from God, as was before evinced. And this is not only evident to Reason, but in a manner to Sense too: For if we take a Survey of the admirable Structure of a Humane Body, both within and without; and see how every, even the most minute Part, hath its proper use, without any Design or Intention of the Parents, and with so great Exactness as the most excellent Philosophers and Physicians could never enough admire; it is a sufficient Demonstration that the Author of Nature is the most *compleat Understanding.* Of this a great deal may <10> be seen in (*a*) *Galen,* especially where he examines the Use of the Hands and Eyes; And

---

a. *In Galen,* &c.] Book III. ch. 10. Which Place is highly worth reading, but too long to be inserted. But many later Divines and natural Philosophers in *England* have explained these Things more accurately. *Le Clerc.*

the same may be observed in the Bodies of dumb Creatures; for the Figure and Situation of their Parts to a certain End, cannot be the Effect of any Power in Matter. As also in Plants and Herbs, which is accurately observed by the Philosophers. *Strabo* (*a*) excellently well takes notice hereof in the Position of Water, which, as to its Quality, is of a middle Nature betwixt Air and Earth, and ought to have been placed betwixt them, but is therefore interspersed and mixed with the Earth, lest its Fruitfulness, by which the Life of Man is preserved, should be hindred. Now it is the Property of intelligent Beings only to act with some View. Neither are particular Things appointed for their own peculiar Ends only, but for the Good of the Whole; as is plain in Water, which (*b*) contrary to its own Nature is raised upwards, <11> lest by a *Vacuum* there should be a Gap in the Structure of the Universe, which is upheld by the continued Union of its Parts. Now the Good of the Whole could not possibly be designed, nor a Power put into Things to tend towards it, but by an intelligent Being to whom the Universe is subject. There are moreover some Actions, even of the Beasts, so ordered and directed, as plainly discover them to be the Effects of some small degree of Reason: As is most manifest in Ants and Bees, and also in some others, which, before they have experienced them, will avoid Things hurtful, and seek those that are profitable to them.

a. *Strabo,* &c.] Book XVII. Where after he had distinguished betwixt the Works of *Nature,* and those of *Providence,* he adds; "After the Earth was surrounded with Water, because Man was not made to dwell in the Water, but belongs partly to the Earth, and partly to the Air, and stands in great need of light; (Providence) has caused many Eminences and Cavities in the Earth, that in these, the Water, or the greatest Part of it, might be received; whereby that part of the Earth under it might be covered; and that by the other, the Earth might be advanced to cover the Water, except what is of Use for Men, Animals, and Plants." The same hath been observed by *Rabbi, Jehuda Levita,* and *Abenesdra,* amongst the *Jews,* and St. *Chrysostom* in his 9th Homily of Statues, among Christians.

b. *Contrary to its own Nature,* &c.] This was borrowed from the *Peripatetick* Philosophy, by this great Man; which supposed the Water in a Pump to ascend for fear of a *Vacuum;* whereas it is now granted by all, to be done by the Pressure of the Air. But by the Laws of Gravitation, as the Moderns explain them, the Order of the Universe, and the Wisdom of its Creator, is no less conspicuous. *Le Clerc.*

That this Power of searching out and distinguishing, is not properly in themselves, is apparent from hence, because they act always alike, and are unable to do other Things which don't require more Pains; (*a*) wherefore they are acted upon by some foreign *Reason;* and what they do, must of necessity proceed from the *Efficiency* of that *Reason* impressed upon them: Which *Reason* is no other than what we call *God.* <12> Next, the Heavenly Constellations, but more especially those eminent ones, the Sun and Moon, have their Courses so exactly accommodated to the Fruitfulness of the Earth, and to the Health of Animals, that nothing can be imagined more convenient: For though otherwise, the most simple Motion had been along the Equator, yet are they directed in an oblique Circle, that the Benefit of them might extend to more Places of the Earth. And as other Animals are allowed the Use of the Earth; so Mankind are permitted to use those Animals, and can by the Power of his Reason tame the fiercest of them. Whence it was that the (*b*) *Stoicks* concluded that the World was made for the Sake of Man. But since the Power of Man does not extend so far as to compel the Heavenly Luminaries to serve Him, nor is it likely they should of their own accord submit themselves to him; hence it follows, that there is a superior *Understanding,* at whose Command those beautiful Bodies afford their perpetual Assistance to Man, who is placed so far beneath them: Which *Understanding* is none other

a. *Wherefore they are acted upon,* &c.] No, they are done by the Soul of those Beasts, which is so far reasonable as to be able to do such Things, and not others. Otherwise God himself, would act in them instead of a *Soul,* which a good Philosopher will hardly be persuaded of. Nothing hinders but that there may be a great many Ranks of sensible and intelligent Natures, the lowest of which may be in the Bodies of Brute Creatures; for no Body I think, really believes with *Ren. Cartes* that Brutes are mere corporeal Machines. But you will say, when Brute Creatures die, what becomes of their Souls? That indeed I know not, but it is nevertheless true that Souls reside in them. There is no necessity that we should know all Things, nor are we therefore presently to deny any thing, because we cannot give account of it. We are to receive those Things that are evident, and be content to be ignorant of those Things which we cannot know. *Le Clerc.*

b. *The Stoicks concluded,* &c.] See *Tully* in his first Book of Offices, and his second of the Nature of the Gods.

than the Maker of the Stars and of the Universe. (*a*) The Eccentrick Motions of the Stars, and the Epicycles, as they term them, manifestly show, that they are not the Effects of Matter, but the Appointment of a free Agent; <13> and the same Assurance we have from the Position of the Stars, some in one Part of the Heavens, and some in another; and from the unequal Form of the Earth and Seas: Nor can we attribute the Motion of the Stars, in such a Direction, rather than another, to any thing else. The very Figure of the World, which is the most perfect, *viz.* round, inclosed in the Bosom of the Heavens, and placed in wonderful Order, sufficiently declares that these Things were not the Result of Chance, but the Appointment of the most excellent Understanding: For can any one be so foolish, as to expect any thing so accurate from Chance? He may as soon believe that pieces of Timber, and Stones, should frame themselves into a House; (*b*) or from Letters thrown at a venture, there should arise a Poem; when the Philosopher, who saw only some Geometrical Figures on the Sea-shore, thought them plain Indications of a Man's having been there, such Things not looking as if they proceeded from Chance. Besides, that Mankind were not from Eternity, but date their Original from a certain Period of Time, is clear, as from other Arguments, so from the *Improvement of Arts, <14> and those desart Places, which came afterwards to be inhabited; and is further evidenced by the Lan-<15>guage

    a. *The Eccentrick Motions,* &c.] This Argument is learnedly handled by *Maimonides,* in his *Ductor Dubitantium,* Part II. c. 4. And if you suppose the Earth to be moved, it amounts to the same thing in other Words.

    Ibid. These and some of the following Things are according to the vulgar Opinion, which is now exploded; but the Efficacy of the Divine Power, is equally seen in the constant Motion of the Planets in Ellipses, about the Sun, through the most fluid Vortex; in such a manner as not to recede from, or approach to their Centre, more than their wonted Limits, but always cut the Sun's Equator at like Obliquity. *Le Clerc.*

    b. *Into a House,* &c.] or Ship or Engine.

    * *The Improvement of Arts,* &c.] *Tertullian* treats of this Matter, from History in his Book concerning the Soul, Sect. 30. *We find* (says he) *in all Commentaries, especially of Humane Antiquities, that Mankind increase by Degrees,* &c. And a little after, *The World manifestly improves every Day, and grows wiser than it was.* These two Arguments caused *Aristotle's* Opinion, (who would not allow Mankind any Beginning) to be rejected by the learned Historians, Especially the *Epicureans.*

    If Heaven and Earth had no Original,
    How is it, that before the *Trojan* War,

No Poets sung of Memorable Things;
But Deeds of Hero's dy'd so oft with them;
And no where, Monuments rais'd to their Praise?
This shews the World is young and newly Born,
Whence 'tis that Arts are every Day encreas'd,
And published anew; Ships are improved,
And Musick, to delight the Ear.

                    Lucretius, Book V.

With a great deal more to the same purpose.

—— From these first Principles
All Things arose, hence sprung the tender World.

                    Virgil, Eclogue VI.

And in his *Georgicks.*

Use first produced those various Arts we see,
By small degrees; this taught the Husbandman
To plow and sow his Fields; from the hard Flint
To fetch the hidden Sparks; then Men began
With hollow Boats to cross the Stream; Pilots
To name the Stars, the Pleiades, Hyades,
And *Charles's* Wain: Then Sportsmen spread their Nets
To catch wild Beasts, and Dogs pursu'd their Game.
Some drain the Rivers, and some seek the Main,
Stretching their Nets to inclose the finny Prey:
Others with Iron forge sharp Instruments
To cleave the yielding Wood, Then Arts arose.

When first Mankind began to spread the Earth.
Like Animals devoid of Speech, they strove
With utmost Strength of Hands, for Dens and Acorns
From thence to Clubs, and then to Arms advanc'd,
Taught by Experience; 'Till Words express'd
Their Meaning, and gave proper Names to Things:
Then Wars were ended; Cities built, and Laws
To punish Thieves, Adulterers, and Villains.

                    Horace, Book I, Satyr III.

Pliny in his third Book of Natural History, about the Beginning; *Wherefore I would be so understood, as the Words themselves signify, without the flourish of Men; and as they were understood at the Beginning, before any great Exploits were performed.* The same Author affirms that the *Hercinian* Wood (in *Germany*) was coaeval with the World, Book XVI. *Seneca,* in *Lactantius, 'Tis not a Thousand Years since Wisdom had a Beginning. Tacitus's* Annals III. *The first Men, before Appetite and Passion swayed them, lived without Bribes, and without Iniquity; and needed not to be restrained from Evil by Punishment:*

of Islands, plainly derived from the neighbouring Continents. There are moreover certain Ordinances so universal amongst Men, that they don't seem so much to owe their Institution to the Instinct of Nature, or the Deductions of plain Reason; as to a constant Tradition, scarce interrupted in any Place, either by Wickedness or Misfortune: <16> Of which sort were formerly Sacrifices, amongst holy Rites; and now Shame in Venereal Things, the Solemnity of Marriage, and the Abhorrence of Incest.

Neither did they stand in need of Reward, every one naturally pursuing Virtue; for so long as nothing was desired contrary to Morality, they wanted not to be restrained by Fear: But after they laid aside Equity; and Violence and Ambition succeeded in the Room of Honesty and Humility; then began that Power which has always continued amongst some People. And *Aristotle* could not fully persuade himself, any more than others of the truth of his own *Hypothesis,* that Mankind never had any Beginning. For he speaks very doubtfully of the Matter in many places, as *Moses Maimonides* observes in his *Ductor Dubitantium,* Part II. In the Prologue to his Second Book concerning the Heavens, he calls his Position, only a Persuasion, and not a Demonstration; and there is a Saying of the same Philosopher in the third Book of the Soul; Chap III. *That Persuasion is a Consequence of Opinion.* But his principal Argument is drawn from the Absurdity of the contrary Opinion, which supposes the Heavens and the Universe not to be created, but generated; which is inconsistent. Book XI. of his *Metaphysicks,* Chap. 8. he says, *'Tis very likely that Arts have often been lost, and invented again.* And in the last Chapter of the Third Book of the *Generation of Animals,* he has these Words, *It would not be a foolish Conjecture concerning the first Rise of Men, and Beasts, if any one should imagine, that of old they sprung out of the Earth one of these two ways, either to have been like Maggots, or to have come from Eggs.* After his Explication of each of these, He adds, *If therefore Animals had any Beginning, it is manifest it must be one of these two ways.* The same *Aristotle,* in the First of his *Topicks,* Chap. XI. *There are some Questions against which very good Arguments may be brought; (it being very doubtful which side is in the right, there being great Probability on either hand,) we have no Certainty of them: and tho' they be of great weight, we find it very difficult to determine the Cause and Manner of their Existence; as for Instance, whether the World were from Eternity, or no: For such Things as these are disputable.* And again, disputing about the same thing in his First Book of the Heavens, Chap. 10. *What shall be said, will be the more credible, if we allow the Disputants Arguments their due weight.* *Tatian* therefore did well not to pass by this, where he brings his Reasons for the Belief of the Scriptures, *That what they deliver concerning the Creation of the Universe, is level to every one's Capacity.* If you take *Plato,* for the World's having a Beginning, and *Aristotle* for its having had none; you will have seen both the Jewish and Christian Opinions.

Sect. VIII. *The Objection concerning the Cause of Evil, answered.*

Nor ought we to be in the least shaken in what has been said, because we see many Evils happen, the Original of which cannot be ascribed to God, who, as was affirmed of Him, is perfectly good. For when we say, that God is the Cause of all Things, we mean of all such Things as have a real Existence; which is no Reason why those Things themselves should not be the Cause of some Accidents, such as Actions are. God created Man, and some other Intelligences superior to Man, with a Liberty of Acting; which Liberty of Acting is not in itself Evil, but may be (*a*) the Cause of something that is Evil. And to make God the Author of Evils of this kind, which are called Moral Evils, is the highest Wickedness. But there are other Sorts of Evils, such as Loss or Pain inflicted upon a Person, which may be allowed to come from God, suppose for the Reformation <17> of the Man, or as a Punishment which his Sins deserve: For here is no Inconsistency with Goodness; but on the contrary, these proceed from Goodness itself, in the same manner as Physick, unpleasant to the Taste, does from a good Physician.

Sect. IX. *Against Two Principles.*

And here, by the way, we ought to reject their Opinion, who imagine that there are (*b*) two Active Principles, the one Good, and the other Evil.

a. *The Cause of something that is Evil,* &c.] God indeed foresaw, that free Agents would abuse their Liberty, and that many natural and moral Evils would arise from hence; yet did not this hinder him from permitting such Abuse, and the Consequences thereof; any more than it hindred his creating Beings endued with such Liberty. The Reason is plain. Because a free Agent being the most Excellent Creature, which discovers the highest Power of the Creator, God was unwilling to prevent those Inconveniencies which proceed from the Mutability of their Nature; because He can amend them as He pleases, to all Eternity; in such a manner as is agreeable to his own Goodness, tho' he has not yet revealed it to us. Concerning which we have largely treated in *French,* in a Book wrote against *Pet. Bayle,* the seeming Advocate of the *Manichees. Le Clerc.*

b. *Two active Principles,* &c.] This has respect to the ancient Disciples of *Zoroastres,* and to the *Manichees. Le Clerc.*

For from Two *Principles,* that are contradictory to each other, can arise no regular Order, but only Ruin and Destruction: Neither can there be a self-existent Being perfectly Evil, as there is One Self-existent perfectly Good: Because Evil is a Defect, which cannot reside but in something which has a Being; (*a*) and the very having a Being is to be reckoned amongst the Things which are Good.

Sect. X. *That God governs the Universe.*

That the World is governed by the Providence of God, is evident from hence: That not only Men, who are endued with Understanding; but Birds, and both Wild and Tame Beasts, (who are lead by Instinct, which serve them instead of Understanding) take care *of,* and provide *for* their Young. Which Perfection, as it is a Branch of Goodness, ought not to be excluded from God: And so much the rather, because He is All-wise, and All-powerful, and cannot but know every thing that is done, or is to be done, and with the greatest Fa-<18>cility direct and govern them; To which we may add, what was before hinted, concerning the Motion of particular Things, contrary to their own Nature, to promote the Good of the Whole.

Sect. XI. *And the Affairs of this lower World.*

And they are under a very great Mistake, who confine this Providence (*b*) to the Heavenly Bodies; As appears from the foregoing Reason, which holds as strong for all created Beings; and moreover from this Consideration, that there is an especial Regard had to (*c*) the Good of Man, in the

a. *And the very having a Being,* &c.] But here, (the Author) was speaking of moral and not of natural Good. It had therefore been better to have forborn such kind of Reasoning. *Le Clerc.*

b. *To the Heavenly Bodies,* &c.] This was the Opinion of *Aristotle.* See *Plutarch* concerning the Opinions of the Philosophers, Book II. ch. 3. and *Atticus* in *Eusebius's* Gospel Preparation, Book V. ch. 5. *Le Clerc.*

c. *The Good of Man,* &c.] Though not for Man only, (for it doth not appear, that there are no other Intelligent Beings, in other Planets,) yet partly for Him, and so far as He makes use of them without any Detriment to other Creatures. Because we cannot

Regulation of the Course of the Stars, as is confessed by the best Philosophers, and evident from Experience. And it is reasonable to conceive, that greater Care should be taken of *that,* for whose Sake the *other* was made, than of *that* which is only subservient to it.

And the Particulars in it.

Neither is Their Error less, (*a*) who allow the Universe to be governed by Him, but not the <19> particular Things in it. For if He were ignorant of any particular Thing (as some of them say,) He would not be thoroughly acquainted with himself. Neither will his Knowledge be Infinite (as we have before proved it to be) if it does not extend to Individuals. Now if God knows all Things, what should hinder his taking care of them; Especially since Individuals, as such, are appointed for some certain End, either Particular or General: And Things in General (which they themselves acknowledge to be preserved by God) cannot subsist but in their Individuals: So that if the Particulars be destroyed by Providence's forsaking them, the Whole must be destroyed too.

Sect. XII. *This is further proved by the Preservation of Empires.*

The Preservation of Commonwealths hath been acknowledged, both by Philosophers and Historians, to be no mean Argument for the Divine Providence over Humane Affairs. *First,* in General; (*b*) because where

---

live without the Sun; we may well conclude it was made upon our account; unless we can imagine that Chance provided every Thing that is necessary for us; which is very absurd: Just like a Man, who happening upon a House well furnished, should deny that it was built for the Convenience of Men, who are alone capable of enjoying it. *Le Clerc.*

a. *Who allow the Universe,* &c.] This was the Opinion of the Stoicks; See *Arrius's* Dissertations upon *Epictetus,* Book I. ch. 12. and *Justin Lipsius* in his *Stoical Physiology. Le Clerc.*

b. *Because where ever good Order,* &c.] Because without it, there is no such thing as humane Society; and without Society Mankind cannot be preserved; Whence we may collect, that Men were created by divine Providence, that they might live in Society, and make use of Laws, without which there neither is, nor can be any Society. *Le Clerc.*

ever good Order in Government and Obedience hath been once admitted, it has been always retained; and in particular, certain Forms of Government have continued for many Ages; as that of Kings among the *Assyrians, Aegyptians* and *Franks;* and that of *Aristocracy* among the *Venetians.* Now though Humane Wisdom may go a good way towards this; yet if it be duly considered, what a Multitude of wicked Men there are, how many external Evils, how liable Things are in their own Nature to change; we can hard-<20>ly imagine any Government should subsist so long without the peculiar Care of the Deity. And this is more visible where it has pleased God (*a*) to change the Government; For all Things (even those which do not depend upon Humane Prudence) succeed beyond their Wish (which they do not ordinarily in the variety of Humane Events) to those whom God has appointed Instruments for this Purpose, as it were destined by him; (suppose *Cyrus, Alexander, Caesar* the Dictator, (*b*) the *Cingi* amongst the *Tartars,* (*c*) *Namcaa* amongst the *Chinese:*) Which wonderful Agreeableness of Events, and all conspiring to a certain End, is a manifest Indication of a Provident Direction. For though a Man may now and then throw a particular Cast on a Die by Chance; yet if he should do it a hundred times together, every Body would conclude there was some Art in it.

Sect. XIII. *And by Miracles.*

But the most certain Proof of Divine Providence is from Miracles, and the Predictions we find in Histories: It is true indeed, that a great many of

a. *To change the Government,* &c.] Thus *Lucretius.*
Some secret hidden Cause confounds the Exploits of Men.

b. *The Cingi amongst the Tartars,* &c.] He seems to mean *Genghiz-Can,* who came out of Eastern *Tartary,* and out of the City *Caracarom,* and subdued not only *Tartary,* but also the Northern *Sina,* and *India.* From him sprung the *Mogul* Kings, and the Princes of the lesser *Tartary.* His Life is written in *French,* and published at *Paris,* in 1710. *Le Clerc.*

c. *Namcaa amongst the Chinese,* &c.] Here in Justice *Manca Capacus* ought to be named, who was the Founder of the Empire of *Peru.* (See *Garsilazzi de la Vega, in Incarum Historia.*)[4]

4. Reference to Garcilaso de la Vega added by Le Clerc.

those Relations are fabulous; but there is no Reason to dis-believe those which are attested by credible Witnesses, to have been in their Time, Men whose Judgment and Integrity have never been called in question. For since God is All-<21>knowing and All-powerful, why should we think him not able to signify his Knowledge or his Resolution to Act, out of the ordinary Course of Nature, which is his Appointment, and subject to his Direction and Government? If any one should object against this, that inferior intelligent Agents may be the Cause of them, it is readily granted; and this tends to make us believe it the more easily of God: Beside, whatever of this Nature is done by such Beings, we conceive God does by them, or wisely permits them to do them; in the same manner as in well regulated Kingdoms, nothing is done otherwise than the Law directs, but by the Will of the Supreme Governor.

Sect. XIV. *But more especially amongst the* Jews, *who ought to be credited upon the account of the long Continuance of their Religion.*

Now that some Miracles have really been seen, (though it should seem doubtful from the Credit of all other Histories) the *Jewish* Religion alone may easily convince us: which though it has been a long time destitute of Humane Assistance, nay exposed to Contempt and Mockery, yet it remains (*a*) to this very Day, in almost all parts of the World; <22> when

---

a. *To this very Day,* &c.] *Hecataeus* concerning the *Jews,* which lived before the Time of *Alexander,* has these Words: "Though they be severely Reproached by their Neighbours and by Strangers, and many times harshly treated by the *Persian* Kings and Nobility; yet cannot they be brought off from their Opinion, but will undergo the most cruel Torments and sharpest Death, rather than forsake the Religion of their Country." *Josephus* preserved this place, in his first Book against *Appion,* and he adds another Example out of the same *Hecataeus,* relating to *Alexander's* Time, wherein the *Jewish* Soldiers peremptorily refused to assist at the Repairing the Temple of the God *Belus.* And the same *Josephus* has very well shown, in his other Book against *Appion,* that the firm Persuasion of the *Jews* of old, concerning God's being the Author of their Law, is from hence evident, because they have not dared, like other People to alter any thing in their Laws; not even then, when in long Banishments, under foreign Princes, they have been tried by all sorts of Threatnings and Flatteries. To this we may add something of *Tacitus,* about the Proselites: "All that are converted to them do the like; for the first (*a*) all other Religions (except the Christian, which is as it were the Perfection of the *Jewish*) have either disappeared as soon as they were forsaken by the Civil Power and Authority, (as all the *Pagan* Religions did;) or else they are yet maintained by the same Power as *Mahometanism* is: For if any one should ask, whence it is that the *Jewish* Religion hath taken so deep Root in the Minds of all the *Hebrews,* as never to be plucked out; there can be no other possible Cause assigned or imagined than this; That the present *Jews* received it from their Parents, and they from theirs, and so on, till you come to the Age in which *Moses* and *Joshua* lived; they received, I say, (*b*) by a certain and uninterrupted Tradition, the Miracles which were worked as in other Places, so more especially at their coming out of *Aegypt,* in their Journey, and at their Entrance into *Canaan;* of all which, their Ancestors themselves were Witnesses. Nor is it in the least credible, that a People of so obstinate a Disposition, could ever be persuaded any otherwise, to submit to a Law loaded with so many Rites and <23> Ceremonies; or that wise Men, amongst the many Distinctions of Religion which Humane Reason might invent, should chuse Circumcision; which could not be performed (*c*) without great Pain, and (*d*) was laughed at by all Strangers, and had nothing to recommend it but the Authority of God.

Principle they are instructed in, is to have a Contempt of the Gods; to lay aside their Love to their Country, and to have no Regard for their Parents or Brethren." That is, when the Law of God comes in competition with them; which this profane Author unjustly blames. See further what *Porphyry* has delivered about the Constancy of the *Jews,* in his Second and Fourth Books against Eating of living Creatures; where He mentions *Antiochus,* and particularly the Constancy of the *Essenes* amongst the *Jews.*

a. *All other Religions,* &c.] Even those so highly commended Laws of *Lycurgus,* as is observed by *Josephus* and *Theodoret.*

b. *By a certain and uninterrupted Tradition,* &c.] To which we give credit, because it was worthy of God to institute a Religion in which it was taught, that there was one God the Creator of all Things, who is a spiritual Being, and is alone to be worshipped. *Le Clerc.*

c. *Without great Pain,* &c.] *Philo* says, It was done *with very great Pain.*

d. *Was laughed at,* &c.] The same *Philo* says, It was a Thing laughed at by every Body: Whence the *Jews* by the Poets, are called Cropt, Circumcised, Fore-skinned.

Sect. XV. *From the Truth and Antiquity of* Moses.

This also gives the greatest Credit imaginable to the Writings of *Moses,* in which these Miracles are recorded to Posterity; not only because there was a settled Opinion and constant Tradition amongst the *Jews,* that this *Moses* was appointed by the express Command of God himself to be the Leader and Captain of this People; but also because (as is very evident) he did not make his own Glory and Advantage his principal Aim, because He himself relates those Errors of his own, which He could have concealed; and delivered the Regal and Sacerdotal Dignity to others, (permitting his own Posterity to be reduced only to common *Levites.*) All which plainly show, that he had no occasion to falsify in his History; as the Style of it further evinces, it being free from that Varnish and Colour, which uses to give Credit to Romances; and is very natural and easy, and agreeable to the Matter of which it treats. Moreover, another Argument for the undoubted Antiquity of *Moses*'s Writings, which no other Writings can pretend to, is this; That the *Greeks* (from whom all other Nations derived their Learning) own, that they (*a*) had their Letters from others; which

---

a. *Had their Letters,* &c.] *Herodotus* in his *Terpsichors,* says, "That the *Ionians* learned their *Letters* of the *Phoenicians,* and used them, with very little variation; which afterwards appearing, those *Letters,* were called *Phoenician,* (as they ought to be) from the *Phoenicians* bringing them into *Greece.*" He calls them

The Phoenician Counsellors of *Cadmus.*

And *Calimachus.*

—— Cadmus, from whom the *Greeks,* derive their written Books.

And *Plutarch* calls them *Phoenician* or *Punick* Letters, in his Ninth Book, and Third Prob. of his *Symposiacks,* where he says, that *Alpha* in the *Phoenician* Language, signifies an *Ox,* which is very true. *Eupolemus,* in his Book of the Kings of *Judaea,* says, "That *Moses* was the first wise Man, and that Letters were first given by him to the *Jews,* and from them the *Phoenicians* received them," That is, the ancient Language of the *Jews* and *Phoenicians* was the same, or very little different. Thus *Lucian. He spake some indistinct Words, like the* Hebrew *or* Phoenician. And *Choerilus* in his Verses concerning the *Solimi,* who, he says, dwelt near the Lake, I suppose he means *Asphaltites.*

These with their Tongue pronounced *Phoenician* Words.

See also the *Punick* Scene of *Plautus,* where you have the Words that are put in the *Punick* Language, twice, by reason of the double writing; and also the *Latin* Translation,

Letters <24> of theirs, have the same Order, Name (*a*) and Shape, as the *Syriack* or *Hebrew:* And further still, the most antient (*b*) *Attick* Laws, from whence the <25> *Roman* were afterwards taken, owe their Original to the Law of *Moses.*

---

whence you may easily correct what is corrupted. And as the *Phoenican* and *Hebrew* Language were the same, so are the ancient *Hebrew* Letters the same with those of the *Phoenicians.* See the great Men about this Matter. *Joseph Scaliger's Diatriba* of the *Eusebian* Year cIↃ Iↄcxvii,[5] and the First Book, Chap X. of *Gerrard Vossius's Grammar* (and particularly *Sam. Bochart,* in his *Chanaan*).[6] You may add also, if you please, *Clement* of *Alexandria,* Strom. Book I. and *Eusebius's Gospel Preparation,* Book X. Chap. 5.

5. The year 1617.

6. Reference to Samuel Bochart added by Le Clerc.

a. *And Shape,* &c.] He means the *Samaritan* Letters, which are the same as the *Phoenician,* as *Lud. Capel. Sam Bochart,* and others have shown. I also have treated of the same in *French* in the Biblioth. Select. Vol. XI. *Le Clerc.*

b. *Attick Laws,* &c.] You have a famous Instance of this, in Thieves that rob by Night, which we have treated of in the Second Book of *War* and *Peace,* Ch. I. Sect. 12, and another in that Law, which *Sopater* recites, *Let him that is next akin possess the Heiress;* which is thus explained by *Terence.*

There is a Law, by which Widows ought to be married to the next Kinsmen, and the same Law obliges these Kinsmen to marry them.

Donatus remarks upon this place thus: *That the Widow should be married to the next Kinsman, and he marry her, in the Attick Law; viz.* taken from the Law of *Moses* in the last Chapter of *Numbers,* which we shall have opportunity of speaking more of afterwards. A great many other Things may be found to this purpose, if any one search diligently for them: As the Feast in which they carried Clusters of Grapes, taken from the Feast of Tabernacles: the Law that the High Priest should marry none but a Virgin, and his Countrywoman; that next after Sisters, Kinsmen by the Father's side should inherit:[7] Wherefore the *Attick* Laws agree with many of the *Hebrew,* because the *Atticks* owe many of their Customs to *Cecrops* King of *Egypt;* and because God established many Laws amongst the *Hebrews,* very much like those of the *Egyptians,* to which they had been accustomed, only reforming such Things, as were bad in them; as we have often observed in our Notes upon the *Pentateuch,* and before us, *John Spencer* in his Book about the Ritual Laws of the Jews. *Le Clerc.*

7. The following portion of the note was added by Le Clerc.

Sect. XVI. *From Foreign Testimonies.*

To these we may add the Testimony of a great Number, who were Strangers to the *Jewish* Religion, which shows that the most ancient Tradition among all Nations, is exactly agreeable to the Relation of *Moses*. For his Description of the Original of the World, is almost the very same as in the (*a*) ancient *Phoenician* Histories which are tran-<26>slated by *Philo Bib-*

---

a. *Ancient Phoenician Histories,* &c.] *Eusebius* has preserved them for us, in his First Book, Chap. 10. of his *Preparation.* "The Theology of the *Phoenicians* supposes the Foundation of the Universe to have been a Dark and Windy Air, or the Breath of a dark Air, and a dismal Chaos, covered with thick Darkness; that these were Infinite, and had no Bounds for many Ages. But when This Spirit or Breath placed its Desire or Love on these first Principles, and a Mixture was produced thereby, this Conjunction was called *Love;* This was the Beginning of the Creation of all Things; But the Breath, or Spirit, was not created, and from its Embraces proceeded *Μώτ Mot,* which some call *Mud,* others the Corruption of a watry Mixture; This was the Seminary and from hence were all things produced." In *Moses's* History we find the Spirit or Breath, and the Darkness; and the *Hebrew* Word מרחפת *Merachepheth* signifies *Love. Plutarch, Symposiac.* VIII. *Prob.* I. explaining of *Plato,* says, That God is the Father of the World, not by the Emission of Seed, but by a certain Generative Power infused into Matter; which he illustrates by this Similitude.

The Female Bird is oft impregnated by the Wind's quick Motion ——

And *Μώτ, Mot,* מוט whence the *Greeks derive their Μόθος, Mothos,* signifies in Hebrew תהום *Tehom,* in Greek Ἄβυσσος, an *Abyss* already in Motion: For Ἄβυσσος *Abyssos,* is in *Ennius* nothing else but Mud, if I understand him right.

Black slimy Mud from the *Tartarean* Body proceeded.

This Mud separated into Earth and Sea. *Apollonius* in the IVth of his *Argonauticks.*

The Earth's produced from Mud.

Upon which place the Scholiast says: *"Zeno* affirms, That the Chaos in *Hesiod* is Water, of which all Things were made; the Water subsiding made Mud, and the Mud congealing made solid Earth." Now this *Zeno* was a *Phoenician,* a Colony of whom were planted in *Cittium* whence the *Hebrews* call all beyond the Seas, כתים *Chittim.* Not much different from which is that of *Virgil, Eclogue* VI.

Then Earth began to harden, and include
The Seas within its Bounds, and Things to take
Their proper Forms.

Numenius, cited by *Porphyry* about the Nymph's Den, affirms, *It was said by the Prophet* (meaning *Moses*) *That the Spirit of God was moved upon the Waters;* The same Expression which *Tertullian* uses concerning Baptism. Now because the Hebrew Word מרחפת *Merachepheth* signifies properly the Brooding of a Dove upon her Eggs; therefore it follows in *Sanchuniathon,* that the Living Creatures, that is, the Constellations, were in that Mud, as in an Egg; and hence That Spirit is called by the Name of the *Dove:* Under the Similitude of which Dove. *Rabbi Solomon* explains the Word מרחפת *Merachepheth, Nigidius* in the Scholiast of *Germanicus:* says, "That there was found an Egg of a huge Bigness, which being rolled about, was cast upon the Earth, and after a few Days *Venus* the Goddess of *Syria* was hatched thereby." *Lucius Ampelius* in his Book to *Matrinus;* says, "It is reported that in the River *Euphrates,* a Dove sat many Days upon a Fish's Egg, and hatched a Goddess very kind and merciful to the Life of Man." *Macrobius* resembles the World to an Egg, in the VIIth Book and 16th Chapter of his *Saturnalia.* It is said to be *the Beginning of Generation,* in the *Orphick* Verses mentioned by *Plutarch, Symposiack. XI. Ch. 3.* and *Athenagoras.* And hence, *the Syrian Gods* are called by *Arnobius, the Offspring of Eggs;* by which Gods he means the Stars. For it follows in the *Phoenician* Theology, that *The Mud was illuminated with Light, whence came the Sun and Moon, and great and little Stars.* You see here as in *Moses,* that Light was before the Sun. The Word that *Moses,* uses immediately after, I mean ארץ *Erets,* where evidently that which was dryed from the Water is called יבשה *Jabashah;* the same *Pherecydes,* from the Authority of the *Syrians* expresses thus, (as we are informed by others, but particularly by *Josephus,* in his first Book against *Appion;*) Chthonia *was the Name given to the Earth after that* Jupiter *had honoured it.* This Place we find in *Diogenes Laertius* and Others; and *Anaximander* calls the Sea, *that which remained of the first Moisture of Things.* That Things were confused before their Separation, (concerning which you have the very Words of *Moses* in *Chalcidius's* Explication of *Timaeus*) *Linus* informs us, as he was himself taught.

In the Beginning all Things were confused.

So *Anaxagoras, All Things were blended together, till the* (Divine) *Mind separated them, and adorned and regulated that which was confused.* And for this Reason, was the Name *Mind* given by *Anaxagoras,* as *Philiasius* assures us in his *Timon:*

> For *Anaxagoras* that noble Hero,
> Was term'd a *Mind,* 'cause that was thought by him
> A *Mind,* which from Confusion Order brought.

All this came from the *Phoenicians,* who held a very ancient Correspondence with the *Greeks.* The Ancients say that *Linus* descended from *Phoenix:* So *Orpheus* had his Opinions from the *Phoenicians,* one of which was this in *Athenagoras, That Mud proceeded from Water.* After which he mentions a great Egg split into two Parts, Heaven and Earth. From the same *Orpheus,* *Timotheus* the Chronographer cites this Passage. "The Chaos was dark as Night, in which Darkness all Things under this Sky were involved; the Earth could not be seen by reason of the Darkness, till Light breaking from the Sky illuminated every Creature." See the Place in *Scaliger* in the Beginning of the first Book

lius from *Sanchuniathon*'s Col-<27><28>lection; and a good Part of it
is to be found (*a*) among the *Indians* (*b*) and *Egyptians;* whence it is,

---

of the *Greek* Chronicle of *Eusebius.* In that which follows of *Sanchuniathon,* it is called
βάκη, which is certainly the בהו *bohu* of *Moses;* And the Winds, which is there called
κολπία *Kolpía,* is the same with קל־פי־יה *Kalphijah,* the Voice of the Mouth of God.

a. *Among the Indians,* &c.] *Megasthenes,* in the Fifteenth Book of *Strabo,* expresses
their Opinion thus: "That in many Things they agree with the *Greeks;* as that the
World had a Beginning, and will have an End; that it is of a Spherical Figure; that
God the Creator and Governor of it, penetrates all Things; that Things had different
Beginnings; and that the World was made of Water." *Clement* has preserved the Words
of *Megasthenes* himself out of his Third Book of the *Indian* History, Strom. I. "All that
was of old said concerning the Nature of Things, we find also said by the Philosophers
who lived out of *Greece,* the *Brachmans* among the *Indians,* and they that are called
Jews in *Syria.*"

b. *And Egyptians,* &c.] Concerning whom see *Laertius* in his *Proaemium;* "The
Foundation was a confused Chaos, from whence the Four Elements were separated,
and Living Creatures, made." And a little after, "That as the World had a Beginning, so
it will have an End." *Diodorus Siculus* explains their Opinion thus: "In the Beginning
of the Creation of all Things, the Heavens and the Earth had the same Form and Appearance, their Natures being mixed together; but afterwards the Parts separating from
one another, the World received that Form in which we now behold it, and the Air a
continual Motion. The Fiery Part ascended highest, because the Lightness of its Nature
caused it to tend upwards; for which Reason, the Sun and Multitude of Stars go in a
continued Round; the Muddy and grosser Part, together with the Fluid sunk down, by
reason of its Heaviness. And this rolling and turning itself continually round, from its
Moisture produced the Sea and from the more Solid Parts proceeded the Earth, as yet
very soft and miry; but when the Sun began to shine upon it, it grew firm and hard;
and the Warmth causing the Superficies of it to ferment, the Moisture, in many places
swelling, put forth certain putrid Substances covered with Skins, such as we now see in
Fenny Moorish Grounds, when the Earth being cool, the Air happens to grow warm,
not by a gradual Change, but on a sudden: Afterwards the forementioned Substances,
in the moist Places, having received Life from the Heat in that manner, were nourished
in the Night by what fell from the Cloud surrounding them, and in the Day they were
strengthened by the Heat. Lastly, When these *Foetus*'s were come to their full growth,
and the Membranes by which they were inclosed broke by the Heat, all sorts of Creatures immediately appeared; those that were of a hotter Nature, became Birds, and
mounted up high; those that were of a Grosser and Earthy Nature, became Creeping
Things, and such like Creatures which are confined to the Earth; and those which
were of a Watry Nature, immediately betook themselves to a Place of the like Quality, and were called Fish. Now the Earth being very much dried and hardned, by the
Heat of the Sun, and by the Wind, was no longer able to bring forth Living Creatures,
but they were afterwards begotten by mixing with each other. *Euripides* seems not to

<29><30> that, (*a*) in *Linus,* (*b*) *Hesiod,* and many other <31> *Greek* Writers, mention is made of a *Chaos,* (sig-<32>nified by some under the Name

---

contradict this Account, who was the Scholar of *Anaxagoras* the Philosopher: For he says thus in his *Menalippe;*

> Heaven and Earth at first were of one Form,
> But when their different Parts were separated,
> Thence sprung Beasts, Fowls, and all the Shoals of Fish,
> Nay, even Men themselves.

This therefore is the Account we have received of the Original of Things. And if it should seem strange to any one, that the Earth should in the Beginning have a Power to bring forth Living Creatures, it may be further confirmed by what we see comes to pass even now. For as *Thebais* in *Egypt,* upon the River *Nile*'s very much overflowing its Banks, and thereby moistning the Ground, immediately by the Heat of the Sun is caused a Putrefaction, out of which arises an incredible Number of Mice. Now if after the Earth has been thus hardned, and the Air does not preserve it's original Temperature, yet some Animals are notwithstanding produced. From hence, they say, it is manifest, that in the Beginning all sorts of Living Creatures were produced out of the earth in this manner." If we add to this, that God is the Creator, who is called by *Anaxagoras* a *Mind,* you will find many Things agreeing with *Moses,* and the Tradition of the *Phoenicians;* The Heavens and Earth being mixed together, the Motion of the Air, the Mud or Abyss, the Light, the Stars, the Separation of Heaven and Earth, and Sea, the Birds, the Creeping Things, Fishes and other Animals; and last of all, Mankind. *Macrobius* in his Seventh of his *Saturnalia,* Chap. 16. transcribed these Words from the *Egyptians;* "If we allow, what our Adversaries affirm, that the Things which now are, had a Beginning; Nature first formed all sorts of Animals perfect; and then ordained, by a perpetual Law, that their Succession should be continued by Procreation. Now that they might be made perfect in the Beginning, we have the Evidence of very many Creatures produced perfect, from the Earth and the Water; as in *Egypt* Mice, and in other Places Frogs, Serpents, and the like." And it is with just Reason that *Aristotle* prefers *Anaxagoras* before any of the ancient *Greek* Philosophers, *Metaphys.* Book I. ch. 3. as a sober Man, when the rest were drunken; because they referred every thing to Matter, whereas this Man added also a Cause, which acts with Design; which Cause *Aristotle* calls Nature, and *Anaxagoras* Mind, which is better; and *Moses,* God; and so does *Plato.* See *Laertius,* where he treats concerning the first Principles of Things according to the Opinion of *Plato;* and *Appuleius* concerning the Opinions of *Plato. Thales,* who was before *Anaxagoras,* taught the same; as *Vellieus* in *Cicero* tells us, in his first Book of the Nature of the Gods: "For *Thales Milesius,* who was the first that enquired into such Things as these, says, that Water was the Beginning of all Things; and that God was that Mind which formed all Things out of Water." Where, by *Water,* he means the *Chaos,* which *Xenophon* and others call *Earth;* all of them well enough, if we rightly apprehend them.

a. *In Linus,* &c.] In the Verse quoted above.
b. *Hesiod,* &c.] In his *Theogonia:*

The Rise of all Things was a Chaos rude.
Whence sprang the spacious Earth, a Seat for Gods;
Who dwell on high *Olympus* Snowy Top,
Nor are excluded from the dark Abyss
Beneath the Earth; from hence the God of Love.
Most amiable of all, who frees the Breasts
Of Men and Gods from anxious Cares and Thoughts;
And comforts all of them with soft Delight;
From hence rose *Erebus,* and gloomy Night.
These produced *Aether,* and the gladsome Day,
As Pledges of their Love.

If we compare this, with those of the *Phoenicians* now quoted, it will seem to be taken from them. For *Hesiod* lived hard by the *Theban Boeotia,* which was built by *Cadmus the Phoenician.* Ἔρεβος, *Erebus,* is the same as *Moses's* ערב *Ereb,* which Night and Day follow in the Hymns that are ascribed to *Orpheus.*

The Original of all Things was a vast Chaos.

In the *Argonauticks,* which go under the same Name:

In Verse he sang the Origin of Things,
Nature's great Change; how Heaven's high Roof was fram'd,
The Earth establish'd, and the Sea was bounded.
How Love, the Cause of all Things, by his Power
Creating every Thing, gave each his Place.

So also *Epicharmus,* the most ancient Comic Poet, relating an old Tradition.

'Tis said that Chaos was before the Gods themselves.

And *Aristophanes,* in his Play called the *Birds,* in a Passage preserved by *Lucian,* in his *Philopatris,* and by *Suidas.*

First of all was *Chaos* and Night, dark *Erebus* and gloomy Tartarus;
There was neither Earth, nor Air, nor Heaven, till dusky Night,
By the Wind's Power on the wide Bosom of *Erebus,* brought forth an Egg,
Of which was hatch'd the God of Love (when Time began;) who with his
    Golden Wings,
Fixed to his Shoulders, flew like a mighty Whirlwind; and mixing with black
    Chaos;
In *Tartarus* dark Shades, produc'd Mankind, and brought them into Light.
For, before Love joined all Things, the very Gods themselves had no Existence;
But upon this Conjunction, all Things being mixed and blended, *Aether* arose;
And Sea and Earth, and the blessed Abodes of the Immortal Gods.

These appear, upon a very slight View, to be taken from the Tradition of the *Phoenicians,* who held an ancient Correspondence with the Inhabitants of *Attica,* the most ancient of the *Ionians.* We have already spoken of *Erebus. Tartarus* is תהום *Tehom.*

of an Egg,) and of the framing of Animals, and also of Man's Formation after the Divine Image, and the Dominion given him over all living Creatures; which are to be seen in many Writers, particularly (*a*) in <33> *Ovid,*

Ἄβυσσος *Abyssos,* and מרחפת *Merachepheth,* signifies Love, as was shewn before: To which agrees that of *Parmenides,*

Love was the first of all the Gods.

a. *In Ovid,* &c.] The Place is no further than the First Book of his *Metamorphosis,* and is very well worth reading; the principal Things in it being so very like those of *Moses,* and almost the same Words, that they afford much Light to what has been already said, and are likewise much illustrated by it:

Before the Sea and Earth, and Heaven's high Roof
Were framed, Nature had but one Form, one Face;
The World was then a Chaos, one huge Mass,
Gross, undigested; where the Seeds of Things
Lay in Confusion, and Disorder hur'ld,
Without a Sun to cherish with his Warmth
The rising World; or paler horned Moon.
No Earth, suspended in the Liquid Air,
Born up by his own Weight; no Ocean vast
Through unknown Tracts of Land to cut his Way;
But Sea and Earth and Air are mix'd in one;
The Earth unsettled, Sea innavigable,
The Air devoid of Light; no Form remain'd:
For each resisted each, being all confin'd;
Hot jarr'd with Cold, and Moist with Dry contended;
Hard, Soft, Light, Heavy strove with mighty Force.
'Till God and Nature did the Strife compose,
By severing Heav'n from Earth, and Sea from Land,
And from gross Air the liquid Sky dividing;
All which from lumpish Matter separated,
Had each his proper Place, by Law decreed:
The Light and fiery Parts upwards ascend,
And fill the Region of the Arched Heavens;
The Air, as next to them in Weight, and then
The Earth (drawing the Elements) possessed
And last, the solid Orb by the Ocean girt.
Thus the well order'd Mass divided was
Into chief Parts, by the Divine Command;
And first, the Earth not stretched into a Plain,
But like an Artificial Globe condensed;
Upon whose Surface winding Rivers glide,
And stormy Seas, whose Waves each Shore rebound.

Here Fountains send forth Streams, there one broad Lake
Fills a large Plain: Thus mixed with Pools and Springs,
The gentle Streams, which roll along the Ground,
Are some by the thirsty hollow Earth absorb'd:
Some in huge Channels to the Ocean bend,
And leave their Banks to beat the Sandy Shoar.
By the same Power were Plains and Vales produc'd.
And shady Woods and rocky Mountains rais'd.
The Heaven begirt with Zones: two on the Right,
Two on the Left, the torrid One between.
The same Distinction does the Earth maintain,
By Care Divine into five Climates mark'd:
Of which the middle, through its Heat immense
Has no Inhabitants; two with deep Snow
Are covered; what remain are temperate.
Next, between Heav'n and Earth the Air was fix'd,
Lighter than Earth, but heavier than Fire.
In this low Region Storms and Clouds were hung,
And hence loud Thunder timerous Mortal frights,
And forked Lightning, mix'd with Blasts of Wind.
But the wise Framer of the World did not
Permit them every where; because their Force
Is scarce to be resisted (when each Wind
Prevaileth in its Turn;) but Nature shakes,
Their Discord is so great. And first the East
Possesses the Morn, *Arabia's* desart Land;
And *Persia's* bounded by the rising Sun.
Next *Zephyr's* gentle Breeze, where *Phoebus* dips
Himself into the Sea; then the cold North,
At whose sharp Blasts the hardy *Scythians* shake.
And last the South, big with much Rain and Clouds.
Above this stormy Region of the Air,
Was the pure *Aether* plac'd, refin'd and clear.
When each had thus his proper Bounds decreed,
The Stars, which in their grosser Mass lay hid,
Appear'd, and Heaven's whole Orb illuminated.
The lower Regions, pressed by its own Weight;
Now living Creatures did each place possess:
The Gods and Stars coelestial Regions fill,
The Waters with large Shoals of Fishes throng'd,
The Earth with Beasts, the Air, with Birds replete.
Nothing seem'd wanting, but a Mind endu'd
With Soul and Reason to rule o'er the rest;
Which was supply'd by Man, the Seed Divine
Of Him who did the Frame of all Things make;

who transcribed them from the *Greek*. That <34> all Things were made by the Word of God, is <35> asserted by (*a*) *Epicharmus*, and (*b*) the

---

> Or else when Earth from Sky was separated,
> Some of the Heavenly Seed remain'd, which sown
> By *Japhet*, and with watry Substance mix'd,
> Was form'd into the Image of the Gods.
> And when all Creatures to the Earth were prone,
> Man had an upright Form to view the Heavens,
> And was commanded to behold the Stars.

Here you see Man has the Dominion over all inferior Creatures given him; and also that he was made after the Image of God, or Divine Beings. To the same purpose are the Words of *Eurysus* the *Pythagorean* in his Book of Fortune; "His *(that is, Man's)* Tabernacle, or Body, is like that of other Creatures, because it is composed of the same Materials; but wrought by the best Workman, who framed it according to the Pattern of himself." Where the Word σκῆνος is put for *Body,* as in *Wisdom,* Chap. IX. Ver. 15. and 2 *Cor.* V. 1. and 4. To which may be added, that of *Horace,* who calls the Soul,

> —— A Particle of Breath Divine.

And *Virgil,*

> An Aethereal Sense.

And that of *Juvenal,* Satyr XV.

> —— Who alone
> Have Ingenuity to be esteem'd,
> As capable of Things Divine, and fit
> For Arts; which Sense we Men from Heav'n derive,
> And which no other Creature is allow'd;
> For He that fram'd us both, did only give
> To them the Breath of Life, but us a Soul.

And those remarkable Things, hereto relating, in *Plato's Phaedon* and *Alcibiades. Cicero,* in the Second Book of the Nature of the Gods, says thus: "For when He *(that is, God)* left all other Creatures to feed on the Ground; he made Man upright, to excite him to view the Heavens, to which he is related, as being his former Habitation." And *Salust,* in the Beginning of the *Cataline* War. "All Men, that desire to exceed other Animals, ought earnestly to endeavour not to pass away their Days in Silence, like the Beasts which Nature has made prone, and Slaves to their Bellies." And *Pliny,* Book II. Ch. 26. "The never enough to be admired *Hipparchus;* than whom none more approved of the Relation betwixt Man and the Stars, and our Souls being a Part of the Heavens."

a. *Epicharmus,* &c.] "Man's Reason is derived from that of God."

b. The *Platonists,* &c.] *Amelius* the *Platonick,* "And this is that Reason, or Word, by which all Things that ever were, were made; according to the Opinion of *Heraclitus:* That very Word, or Reason, the *Barbarian* means, which set all Things in Order in the

Platonists; <36> and before them, by the most antient Writer, (I do not mean of those Hymns which go under his Name,) but of those Verses which were (*a*) of Old called *Orpheus*'s; not because *Orpheus* composed

---

Beginning, and which was with God before that Order, and by which every Thing was made, and in which was every Creature; the Fountain of Life and Being." The *Barbarian* he here speaks of, is St. *John* the Evangelist, a little later than whose Time *Amelius* lived. *Eusebius* has preserv'd his Words in the Eleventh Book and 19th Chapter of his *Preparation;* and *Cyril* in his Eighth Book against *Julian,* St. *Austin* mentions the same Place of *Amelius* in his Tenth Book and 29th Chapter of the *City of God,* and in the Eighth Book of his *Confessions.* And *Tertullian* against the *Gentiles.* "It is evident, says he, that with your Wise Men, the Λόγος, *Logos,* Word or Reason, was the Maker of the Universe; for *Zeno* would have the *Word* to be the Creator, by whom all Things were disposed in their Formation." This Place of *Zeno* was in his Book περί οὐσίας, *concerning Being,* where he calls τό ποιοῦς the *Efficient Cause,* Λόγος the *Word* or *Reason;* and in this he was followed by *Cleanthes, Chrysippus, Archedemus,* and *Possidonius,* as we are told by *Laertius* in his Life of *Zeno. Seneca,* in his LXVth Epistle, calls it the *Reason which maketh.* And *Chalcidius* to *Timaeus* says, "That the Reason of God, is that God who has a Regard to Humane Affairs, and who is the Cause of Mens living well and happily, if they do not neglect the Gift of God bestowed on them by the most High God." And in another Place, speaking of *Moses,* he has these Words: Who is clearly of Opinion, "that the Heaven and Earth were made by the Divine Wisdom: and at length, that the Divine Wisdom was the Foundation of the Universe."

a. *Of Old called Orpheus's,* &c.] The Verses are these:

I swear by that first Word the Father spake,
When the Foundation of the Earth was laid.

They are extant in the Admonition to the *Greeks* among the Works of *Julian:* As also these;

I speak to those I ought, be gone, Prophane,
Away: But do thou hearken, O *Musaeus,*
Begotten by the Moon; I speak the Truth;
Let not vain Thoughts, the Comfort of thy Life
Destroy; the Divine Reason strictly view,
And fix it in thy Mind to imitate;
Behold the great Creator of the World,
Who's only Perfect; and did all Things make,
And is in all; though we with mortal Eyes
Cannot discern him; but he looks on us.

These we find in the Admonition to the *Greeks;* as also in a Book concerning the Monarchy of the World, in the Works of *Justin Martyr;* in *Clemens Alexandrinus,* Strom. 5. and in the XIIIth Book of *Eusebius's Gospel Preparation* from *Aristobulus.*

them, but because they contained his Doctrines. (*a*) And <37> *Empedocles* acknowledged, that the Sun was not the Original Light, but the Receptacle of Light, (the Storehouse and Vehicle of Fire, as the antient Christians express it.) (*b*) *Aratus,* and (*c*) *Catullus* thought the Divine Residence was above the starry Orb; in which, *Homer* says, there is a continual Light. (*d*) *Thales* taught from the antient Schools, That God was the oldest of Beings, because not Begotten; that the World was most beautiful, because the Workmanship of God; that Darkness was before Light, which latter we find (*e*) in *Orpheus's* Verses, (*f*) and *Hesiod;* whence it was, that (*g*) the <38> Nations who were most tenacious of antient

a. *And Empedocles acknowledged,* &c.] Of whom *Laertius* says, "That he affirmed the Sun to be a great Heap of Fire." And he that wrote the *Opinions of the Philosophers,* has these Words; "*Empedocles* said that the *Aether* was first separated, then the Fire, and after That the Earth, the Superficies of which being streightned by the violent Motion, the Water burst out; whence the Air was exhaled: That the Heavens were composed of *Aether,* and the Sun of Fire." And Chap. 20. *Empedocles* affirms, "There are two Suns, one the Original, and the other the Apparent." And *Philolaus,* as we there also read, says, "That the Sun is of the same Nature as Glass, receiving its Splendor from the Fire that is in the World, and transmitting its Light to us." *Anaxagoras, Democritus, Metrodorus,* affirmed the Sun to be a certain Mass of Fire; as you find it in the same Place. And *Democritus* shows, that these were the most antient Opinions, as *Laertius* relates.

b. *Aratus,* &c.] Aratus;

As far as the dire Gulph *Eridanus,*
Under the Footsteps of the Gods extends.

c. *Catullus,* &c.] *Catullus* the Interpreter of *Callimcabus* introduces *Berenices Hair,* speaking after this Manner,

Tho' in the Night the Gods upon me tread.

d. *Thales taught,* &c.] As we see *Diogenes Laertius;* and *Herodotus* and *Leander* assert him to have been originally a *Phoenician.*

e. *In Orpheus's Verses,* &c.] In his Hymn to Night:

I sing the Night, Parent of Men and Gods.

f. *And Hesiod,* &c.] Whose Verses upon this Subject are cited above.

g. *The Nations who were the most tenacious,* &c.] *The* Numidians *in* Lybia *reckon their Time not by Days, but by Nights,* says *Nicolaus Damascenus.* And *Tacitus* affirms of the Germans, *that they do not, like us, compute the Number of the Days, but of the Nights; so they appoint and decree; Night seems to usher in the Day.* See the *Speculum Saxonicum,* Book I. Art. 3.67. and in other Places. And also the learned *Lindebrogius,* upon the

Customs, reckoned the Time by Nights. (*a*) *Anaxagoras* affirmed, that all Things were regulated by the Supreme Mind; (*b*) *Aratus*, that the <39> Stars were made by God; (*c*) *Virgil*, from the *Greeks*, that Life was infused

---

Word *Night*, in his *Vocabulary* of the *German Laws*. The Neighbouring People of *Bohemia* and *Poland* preserve this Custom to this very Day, and the *Gauls* used it of old. *Caesar*, in his Sixth Book of the *Gallick War* says, *That all their Distances of Time were counted, not by the Number of Days, but of Nights.* And *Pliny* concerning the *Druids*, in the Sixteenth Book of his *Natural History*, says, *The Moon with them began their Months and Years.* It is a known Custom amongst the *Hebrews. Gellius* in his Third Book, Chap. II. adds the *Athenians*, who in this Matter were the Scholars of the *Phoenicians.*

    a. *Anaxagoras affirmed*, &c.] His Words are quoted above, which are to be found in *Laertius*, the Writer of the Opinions of the Philosophers, and others: As are also the Verses of *Timon* concerning his Opinion.

    b. *Aratus*, &c.] In the Beginning of his *Phoenomena;*

> Begin with *Jupiter*, whose Essence is
> Ineffable by mortal Man, whose Presence
> Does all Things fill; Assemblies, Courts, and Markets.
> The deep Abyss, and Ports are fill'd with Him.
> We all enjoy him, all his Offspring are,
> Whose Nature is benign to Man; who stirs
> Them up to work, the Good of Life consulting.
> 'Tis He appoints the Time to Plow and Sow,
> And Reap the fruitful Harvest ——
> 'Twas He that in the Heavens fix'd the Stars,
> Allotting each his Place to teach the Year,
> And to declare the Fate us Men attends;
> That all Things are by certain Laws decreed.
> Him therefore let us first and last appease.
> O Father, the great Help we Mortals have.

That by *Jupiter* we are here to understand God, the true Maker of the World, and all Things in it, St. *Paul* shews us in the Seventeenth Chapter of the *Acts*, Ver. 28. And we learn from *Lactantius*, that *Ovid* ended his *Phoenomena* with these Verses:

> Such both in Number and in Form, did God
> Upon the Heavens place, and give in Charge
> To 'nlighten the thick Darkness of the Night.

And *Calcidius* to *Timaeus:* "To which thing the *Hebrews* agree, who affirm that God was the Adorner of the World, and appointed the Sun to rule the Day, and the Moon to govern the Night; and so disposed the rest of the Stars, as to limit the Times and Seasons of the Year, and to be Signs of the Productions of Things."

    c. *Virgil, from the Greeks*, &c.] In the Sixth Book of his *Aeneads*, which *Servius* says was composed from many of the antient *Greek* Writings.

into Things by the Spirit of God; (*a*) *Hesiod,* (*b*) *Homer,* <40> and (*c*)

> At first the Heaven and Earth and watry Seas,
> The Moon's bright Globe, and all the glittering Stars,
> Were by the Divine Spirit each sustain'd:
> For the whole World is acted by a Sun,
> Which throughly penetrates it; whence Mankind,
> And Beasts and Birds have their Original;
> And Monsters in the Deep produc'd: The Seed
> Of each is a Divine and Heavenly Flame.

Which may be explain'd by those in his *Georgicks* IV.

> By such Examples taught, and by such Marks.
> Some have affirm'd that Bees themselves partake
> Of the Coelestial Mind, and Breath Aetherial,
> For God pervades the Sea, and Earth, and Heavens;
> Whence Cattle, Herds, Men, and all Kinds of Beasts
> Derive the slender Breath of fleeting Life.

a. *Hesiod,* &c.] In his Poem upon *Labour* and *Days:*

> Then ordered *Mulciber,* without Delay,
> To mix the Earth and Water, and infuse
> A Human Voice.

b. *Homer,* &c.] *Ilias* VIII.

> You all to Earth and Water must return.

For all Things return from whence they came. *Euripides* in his *Hipsipyle* (as *Stobaeus* tells us in the Title) uses this Argument, for bearing patiently the Events of Things, which is transcribed by *Tully* in his Third Book of *Tusculan* Questions:

> —— All which in vain, us Mortals vex,
> Earth must return to Earth, for Fate ordains
> That Life, like Corn, must be cut off, in all.

To the same Purpose *Euripides* in his *Supplicants*

> Permit the Dead to be entomb'd in Earth,
> From whence we all into this Body came;
> And when we die, the Spirit goes to Air,
> To Earth the Body; for we can possess
> Life only for a Time; the Earth demands
> It back again.

All which, you see, exactly agree with *Moses,* Gen. III. 19. and *Solomon,* Eccl. XII. 7.

c. *Callimachus,* &c.] Who in his *Scazon* calls Man, *Prometheus's Clay.* Of this Clay we find mention made in *Juvenal* and *Martial.* To which we may add this Place of *Cen-*

Callimachus, that Man was formed of Clay; lastly, (*a*) *Maximus Tyrius* asserts, that it <41> was a constant Tradition received by all Nations, that there was One Supreme God, the Cause of all Things. And we learn (*b*) from *Josephus*, (*c*) *Philo*, (*d*) *Tibullus*, (*e*) *Clemens Alexandrinus*, and (*f*)

---

sorinus; Democritus *the* Abderite *was of Opinion, that Men were first formed of Clay and Water; and* Epicurus *was much of the same Mind.*

    a. *Maximus Tyrius,* &c.] In his First Dissertation: "Notwithstanding the great Discord, Confusion, and Debates that are amongst Men; the whole World agree in this one constant Law and Opinion, that God is the sole King and Father of all; but that there are many other Gods; the Offspring of Him, who assists in his Government. This is affirmed by the *Greek* and the *Barbarian;* by him who dwells in the Continent, and by him who lives on the Sea-shore; by the Wise and by the Foolish." To which may be added those Places cited in the Second Book of *War and Peace,* Ch. XX. 9, 45. And that of *Antisthenes,* related by *Tully* in his First Book of the *Nature of the Gods, That there are many Vulgar Gods, but there is but one Natural God.* And *Lactantius,* Book I. Chap 5. adds, from the same *Antisthenes.*

    The Maker of the whole World,

So likewise *Sophocles:*

> There is really but One God,
> The Maker of Heaven and Earth,
> And Sea, and Winds.

To which may be added that Place of *Varro,* cited by St. *Austin,* in the Fourth Book, and Chap. 31. of his *City of God.*

    b. *From Josephus,* &c.] Against *Appion,* about the End of the Second Book, where he says, There is no City, *Greek* or *Barbarian,* in which the Custom of Resting on the Seventh Day is not preserved, as it is amongst the *Jews.*

    c. *Philo,* &c.] Concerning the Seventh Day; *It is a Festival celebrated, not only in one City or Country, but throughout the whole World.*

    d. *Tibullus,* &c.] *The Seventh Day is sacred to the* Jews.

    e. *Clemens Alexandrinus,* &c.] Who in his *Strom.* V. quotes, out of *Hesiod, that the Seventh Day was sacred.* And the like out of *Homer* and *Callimachus.* To which may be subjoined, what *Eusebius* has taken out of *Aristobulus,* Book XIII. Ch. 12. *Theophilus Antiochenus,* Book XI. to *Antolychus; Concerning the Seventh Day, which is distinguished by all Men.* And *Suetonius,* in his *Tiberius* XXXII; Diogenes *the Grammarian uses to dispute at* Rhodes *upon the Sabbath Day.* (The seventh Day of the Month ought not to be confounded with the last Day of the Week. See what *John Selden* has remarked upon this Subject, in his Book of the *Laws of Nature and Nations,* Book III. Chap. 17. *Le Clerc.*)

    f. *Lucian,* &c.] Who tells us in his *Paralogist, That Boys were used to play on the seventh Day.*

Lucian (for I need not mention the *Hebrews*) that the Memory of the Seven Days Work was preserved not only among the *Greeks* and *Italians,* by honouring the Seventh Day; but also (*a*) amongst the *Celtae* and *Indians,* who all measured the Time by Weeks; as we learn from (*b*) *Philostratus,* (*c*) *Dion* <42> *Cassius,* and *Justin Martyr;* and also (*d*) the most ancient Names of the Days. The *Egyptians* tell us, that at first Men led their Lives (*e*) in great Simplicity, (*f*) their Bodies being naked; whence arose the Poet's Fiction of the Golden Age, famous among the *Indians,* (*g*)

a. *Amongst the Celtae,* &c.] As is evident by the Names of the Days among the different Nations of the *Celtae,* viz. *Germans, Gauls,* and *Britons. Helmoldus* tells us the same of the *Sclavonians,* Book I. Chap. 48.

b. *Philostratus,* &c.] Book III. Chap. 13. speaking of the *Indians.*

c. *Dion Cassius,* &c.] Book XXXIII. *The Day called Saturn's.* Where he adds, that the Custom of computing the Time by Weeks was derived from the *Egyptians* to all Mankind. And that this was not a new, but a very ancient Custom, *Herodotus* tells us in his Second Book: To which may be added *Isidore* concerning the *Romans,* Book V. Chap. 30. and 32.

d. *The most ancient Names,* &c.] See the *Oracle,* and *Orpheus's* Verses in *Scaliger's Prolegomena* to his Emendation of Times. (I suspect that the Foundation of Weeks was rather from the Seven Planets, than from the Creation of the World in Seven Days. *Le Clerc.*)

e. *In great Simplicity,* &c.] See what we have said of this Matter, Book II. Chap. 1. Sect. XI. concerning *the Right of War,* and the Notes belonging to it.

f. *Their Bodies being naked,* &c.] Whose Opinion *Diodorus Siculus* thus relates, "The first Men lived very hardy, before the Conveniencies of Life were found out; being accustomed to go naked and wanting Dwellings and Fires; and being wholly ignorant of the Food of civilized Nations." And *Plato,* in his *Politicks:* "God their Governor fed them, being their Keeper; as Man, who is a more divine Creature, feeds the inferior Creatures." And a little after: "They fed naked and without Garments in the open Air." And *Dicearchus* the *Peripatetick,* cited both by *Porphry,* in his Fourth Book against eating Living Creatures; and to the same Sense by *Varro,* concerning Country Affairs: "The Ancients, who were nearest to the Gods, were of an excellent Disposition, and led so good Lives, that they were called a Golden Race."

g. *As Strabo remarks,* &c.] Book XV. where he brings in *Calanus* the *Indian* speaking thus: "Of old we met every where with Barley, Wheat and Meal, as we do now adays with Dust. The Fountains flowed, some with Water, some with Milk; and likewise some with Honey, some with Wine, and some with Oil: But Men, through Fulness and Plenty, fell into Wickedness; which Condition *Jupiter* abhorring, altered the State of Things; and ordered them a Life of Labour."

as *Strabo* remarks. (*a*) *Mai-<43>monides* takes notice, that (*b*) the History of *Adam*, of *Eve*, of the Tree, and of the Serpent, was extant amongst the idolatrous *Indians* in his Time: And there are many (*c*) Witnesses in our Age, who testify, that the same is still to be found amongst the *Heathen* dwelling in *Peru*, and the *Phillippine* Islands, People belonging to the same *India;* the Name of *Adam* amongst the *Brachmans;* and that it was reckoned (*d*) Six Thousand Years since the Creation of the World, by those of *Siam*. (*e*) *Berosus* in his History of *Chaldea*, *Manethos* in <44> his of *Egypt*, *Hierom* in his of *Phoenicia*, *Hestiaeus*, *Hecataeus*, *Hillanicus* in theirs of *Greece;* and *Hesiod* among the Poets; all assert, that the Lives of those who descended from the first Men, were almost a thousand Years in length; which is the less incredible, because the Historians of many

a. *Maimonides*, &c.] In his *Guide to the Doubting*, Part III. Chap. 29.

b. *The History of Adam*, &c.] In those Places which *Philo Biblius* has translated out of *Sanchuniathon:* The *Greek* Word πρωτόγενος, *First-born*, is the same with the *Hebrew* אדם *Adam;* and the *Greek* Word αἰών, *Age*, is the same with the *Hebrew* Word חוה *Chavah, Eve*. The first Men found out the Fruit of Trees. And in the most ancient *Greek Mysteries*, they cried out *Εὖα, Eva,* and at the same time shewed a *Serpent*. Which is mentioned by *Hesychius*, *Clemens* in his Exhortations, and *Plutarch* in the Life of *Alexander. Chalcidius* to *Timaeus*, has these Words: "That, as *Moses says*, God forbad the first Man to eat the Fruit of those Trees, by which the Knowledge of Good and Evil should steal into their Minds." And in another Place: "To this the *Hebrews* agree, when they say, that God gave to Man a Soul by a divine Breath, which they call Reason, or a Rational Soul; but to dumb Creatures, and wild Beasts of the Forest, one void of Reason: The living Creatures and Beasts being, by the Command of God, scattered over the Face of the Earth; amongst which was that Serpent, who by his evil Persuasions deceived the first of Mankind."

c. *Witnesses in our Age*, &c.] See amongst others *Ferdinand Mendesius de Pinto*.

d. *Six Thousand Years*, &c.] What *Simplicius* relates out of *Porphyry*, Comment XVI. upon Book II. concerning Heaven, agrees exactly with this Number; that the Observations collected at *Babylon*, which *Calisthenes* sent to *Aristotle*, were to that Time cI‫כ‬ Ic ccccii I.[8] which is not far from the Time of the Deluge.

8. The year 1903.

e. *Berosus in his History*, &c.] *Josephus* in the First Book, Chap. 4. of his Ancient History, quotes the Testimony of all these Writers whose Books were extant in his Time; and besides these, *Acusilaus*, *Ephonus*, and *Nicholaus Damascaenus*. *Servius* in his Notes upon the Eighth Book of *Virgil's Aeneids*, remarks that the People of *Arcadia* lived to three hundred Years.

Nations, (particularly (*a*) *Pausanias* and (*b*) *Philostratus* amongst the *Greeks,* and (*c*) *Pliny* amongst the <45> *Romans*) relate, that (*d*) Mens

a. *Pausanius,* &c.] In his *Laconicks,* he mentions the Bones of Men, of a more than ordinary Bigness, which were shewn in the Temple of *Aesculapius* at the City of *Asepus:* And in the First of his *Eliacks,* of a Bone taken out of the Sea, which aforetime was kept at *Piso,* and thought to have been one of *Pelops*'s.

b. *Philostratus,* &c.] In the Beginning of his *Heroicks,* he says, that many Bodies of Gyants were discovered in *Pallene,* by Showers of Rain and Earthquakes.

c. *Pliny,* &c.] Book VII. Chap. 16. "Upon the bursting of a Mountain in *Crete* by an Earthquake, there was found a Body standing upright, which was reported by some to have been the Body of *Orion,* by others the Body of *Ection. Orestes*'s Body, when it was commanded by the Oracle to be digged up, is reported to have been seven Cubits long. And almost a Thousand Years ago, the Poet *Homer* continually complained, that Mens Bodies were less than of old." And *Solinus,* Ch. 1. "Were not all who were born in that Age less than their Parents? And the Story of *Orestes*'s Funeral, testifies the Bigness of the Ancients, whose Bones, when they were digged up, in the Fifty Eighth Olympiad at *Tegea,* by the Advice of the Oracle, are related to have been seven Cubits in length. And other Writings, which give a credible Relation of ancient Matters, affirm this, That in the War of *Crete,* when the Rivers had been so high as to overflow and break down their Banks; after the Flood was abated; upon the cleaving of the Earth, there was found a Humane Body of three and thirty Foot long; which *L. Flaccus* the Legate, and *Metellus* himself, being very desirous of seeing, were much surprised, to have the satisfaction of seeing, what they did not believe when they heard." See *Austin*'s Fifteenth Book, Chap. 11. of the *City of God,* concerning the Cheek Tooth of a Man, which he himself saw.

d. *Mens Bodies,* &c.] *Josephus,* Book V. Chap. 2. of his Ancient History: "There remains to this Day some of the Race of the Giants, who by reason of the Bulk and Figure of their Bodies, so different from other Men, are wonderful to see, or hear of: Their Bones are now shewn, far exceeding the Belief of the Vulgar." *Gabinius,* in his History of the *Mauritania,* said, that *Antaeus*'s Bones were found by *Sertorius,* which joined together were sixty Cubits long. *Phlegon Trallianus,* in his Ninth Chapter of *Wonders,* mentions the digging up of the Head of *Ida,* which was three times as big as that of an ordinary Woman. And he adds also, that there were many Bodies found in *Dalmatia,* whose Arms exceeded Sixteen Cubits. And the same Man relates out of *Theopompus,* that there was found in the *Cimmerian Bosphorus,* a Heap of Humane Bones twenty four Cubits in length. And there is extant a Book of the same *Phlegon,* concerning *Long Life,* which is worth reading. (That in many Places of old time, as at the present, there were Men of a very large Stature, or such as exceeded others, some few Feet, is not very hard to believe; but that they should all of them have been bigger, I can no more believe, than that the Trees were taller, or the Channels of the Rivers deeper. There is the same Proportion between all these, and Things of the like kind now, as there was formerly, they answering to one another, so that there is no Reason to think they have undergone any Change. See *Theodore Rickius*'s Oration about Giants. *Le Clerc.*)

Bodies, upon opening their Sepulchres, were found to be much larger in old time. And (*a*) *Catullus*, after many of the <46> *Greeks*, relates, that divine Visions were made to Men before their great and manifold Crimes did as it were, hinder God and (*b*) those Spirits that attend him, from holding any Correspondence with Men. We almost every where (*c*) in the *Greek* and (*d*) *Latin* Historians, meet with the Savage Life of the Giants, mentioned by *Moses*. And it is very remarkable concerning the Deluge, that the Memory of almost all Nations ends in the History of it, even those Nations which were unknown till our Forefathers discovered them: (*e*) So that *Varro* calls all *that* the unknown Time. <47> And all those

a. *Catullus*, &c.] In his *Epithalamium on Peleus and Thetis:*

But when the Earth was stain'd with Wickedness
And Lust, and Justice fled from every Breast:
Then Brethren vilely shed each other's Blood,
And Parents ceas'd to mourn their Childrens Death.
The Father wish'd the Funeral of his Son;
The Son to enjoy the Father's Relique wish'd:
The impious Mother yielding to the Child,
Fear'd not to stain the Temple of the Gods:
Thus Right and Wrong by furious Passion mix'd,
Drove from us the divine propitious Mind.

b. *Those Spirits that attend him*, &c.] Of this, see those excellent Things said by *Plutarch* in his *Isis; Maximus Tyrius* in his First and Sixteenth Dissertation, and *Julian's* Hymn to the Sun. The Name of *Angels* is used, when they treat of this Matter, not only by the *Greek* Interpreters of the Old Testament, but also by *Labeus, Aristides, Porphyry, Jamblicus, Chalcidius,* and by *Hostanes,* who was older than any of them, quoted by *Minutius:* The forementioned *Chalcidius* relates an Assertion of *Heraclitus,* That such as deserved it, were forewarned by the Instruction of the Divine Powers.

c. *In the Greek,* &c.] *Homer, Iliad* 9. and *Hesiod* in his *Labours.* To this may be referred the *Wars of the Gods,* mentioned by *Plato* in his Second *Republick;* and those distinct and separate Governments, taken notice of by the same *Plato* in his Third Book of *Laws.*

d. *Latin Historians,* &c.] See the First Book of *Ovid's Metamorphosis,* and the Fourth Book of *Lucan,* and *Seneca's* Third Book of *Natural Questions,* Quest. 30. where he says concerning the Deluge: *That the Beasts also perished, into whose Nature Men were degenerated.*

e. *So that* Varro *calls,* &c.] Thus *Censorinus:* "Now I come to treat of that Space of Time which *Varro* calls Historical. For he makes three Distinctions of Time; The first from the Creation of Man to the first Flood, which, because we are ignorant of it, is called unknown: The second, from the first Flood to the first Olympiad; which is

Things which we read in the Poets wrapped up in Fables, (a Liberty they allow themselves,) are delivered by the ancient Writers according to Truth and Reality, that is, agreeable to *Moses;* as you may see in *Berosus's* (*a*) History of *Chaldea,* (*b*) *Abydenus's* of <48><49> *Assyria,* (*c*) who men-

---

called Fabulous, because of the many fabulous Stories related in it: The third, from the first Olympiad to our Time, which is called Historical, because the Things done in it are related in a true History." The Time which *Varro* calls unknown, the *Hebrew Rabbins* call *void. Philo* in his Book of the *Eternity of the World* remarks, that the Shells found on the Mountains are a Sign of the universal Deluge.

a. *Berosus's History,* &c.] Concerning whom *Josephus* says thus, in his first Book against *Appion:* "This *Berosus,* following the most antient Writings, relates, in the same Manner as *Moses,* the History of the Flood, the Destruction of Mankind, the Ark or Chest in which *Noah* the Father of Mankind was preserv'd, by its resting on the Top of the Mountains of *Armenia.*" After having related the History of the Deluge, *Berosus* adds these Words, which we find in the same *Josephus,* Book I. and Chap. IV. of his antient History: "It is reported that Part of the Ship now remains in *Armenia,* on the *Gordyaean* Mountains, and that some bring Pitch from thence, which they use for a Charm."

b. *Abydenus's of Assyria,* &c.] *Eusebius* has preserved the Place in the Ninth Book of his *Preparation,* Chap. 12. and *Cyril* in his First Book against *Julian.* "After whom reigned many others, and then *Sisithrus,* to whom *Saturn* signified there should be an abundance of Rain on the fifteenth Day of the Month *Desius,* and commanded him to lay up all his Writings in *Heliopolis,* a City of the *Sipparians;* which when *Sisithrus* had done, he sailed immediately into *Armenia,* and found it true as the God had declared to him. On the third Day after the Waters abated, he sent out Birds to try if the Water was gone off any Part of the Earth; but they finding a vast Sea, and having no where to rest, returned back to *Sisithrus:* In the same manner did others: And again the third Time, (when their Wings were daubed with Mud.) Then the Gods took him from Men; and the Ship came into *Armenia,* the Wood of which the People there use for a Charm." *Sysithrus* and *Ogyges,* and *Deucalion,* are all Names signifying the same Thing in other Languages, as *Noah* does in the *Hebrew,* in which *Moses* wrote; who so expressed proper Names, that the *Hebrews* might understand the Meaning of them: For Instance, *Alexander* the Historian writing *Isaac* in *Greek,* calls him Γαλωΐα, *Laughter,* as we learn from *Eusebius;* and many such like we meet with among the Historians; as in *Philo* concerning Rewards and Punishments; "The *Greeks* call him *Deucalion,* the *Chaldeans Noach,* in whose Time the great Flood happen'd." It is the Tradition of the *Egyptians,* as *Diodorus* testifies in his First Book, that the universal Deluge was that of *Deucalion. Pliny* says it reached as far as *Italy,* Book III. Chap. 14. But to return to the Translation of Names into other Languages, there is a remarkable Place in *Plato's Critias* concerning it: "Upon the Entrance of this Discourse, it may be necessary (says he) to premise the Reason, lest you be surprized when you hear the Names of *Barbarians* in *Greek.* When *Solon* put this Relation into Verse, he enquired into the Signification of the Names, and found that the first *Egyptians,* who wrote of these Matters,

tions the Dove that was sent out of the Ark; and in *Plutarch* from the *Greeks;* (*a*) and in *Lucian,* who says, that in *Hierapolis* of <50> *Syria,* there

---

translated them into their own Language; and he likewise searching out their true Meaning, turned them into our Language." The Words of *Abydenus* agree with those of *Alexander* the Historian, which *Cyril* has preserved in his forementioned First Book against *Julian;* "After the Death of *Otiartes,* his Son *Xisuthrus* reigned eighteen Years; in whose Time, they say, the great Deluge was. It is reported that *Xisuthrus* was preserved by *Saturn's* foretelling him what was to come; and that it was convenient for him to build an Ark, that Birds and creeping Things, and Beasts might sail with him in it." The most High God is named by the *Assyrians,* and other Nations, from that particular Star of the Seven (to use *Tacitus's* Words) by which Mankind are governed, which is moved in the highest Orb, and with the greatest Force: Or certainly the *Syriack* Word, איל *Il,* which signifies *God,* was therefore translated Κρόνος, Kronos, by the *Greek* Interpreters, because he was called איל *Il* by the *Syrians, Philo Biblius,* the Interpreter of *Sanchuniathon,* hath these Words; Ilus, *who is called* Saturn. He is quoted by *Eusebius:* In whom it immediately follows from the same *Philo, That* Kronos *was the same the* Phoenicians *call* Israel; but the mistake was in the Transcriber, who put Ἰσραὲλ *Israel,* for ἰλ, which many times amongst the *Greek* Christians is the Contraction of Ἰσραὲλ, when ἰλ is, as we have observed, what the *Syrians* call איל *Il,* and the *Hebrews* אל *El.* [It ought not to be overlooked, that in this History, *Deucalion,* who was the same Person as *Noah,* is called ἀνήοπύρρᾶς, that is, איש אדמה *a Man of the Earth,* that is, *a Husband-man.* See my Notes upon *Gen.* ix. 20. *Le Clerc.*]

c. *Who mentions the Dove,* &c.] In his Book where he enquires which have most Cunning, Water or Land Animals: "They say *Deucalion's* Dove, which he sent out of the Ark, discovered at its Return, that the Storms were abated, and the Heavens clear." It is to be observed, both in this place of *Plutarch's,* and in that of *Alexander* the Historian, as well as in the Books of *Nicolaus Damascenus,* and the Writers made use of by *Theophilus Antiochenus* in his Third Book, that the *Greek* Word λάρναξ *Larnax,* answers to the *Hebrew* Word תבה *Tebah,* and so *Josephus* translates it.

a. *And in Lucian,* &c.] In his Book concerning the Goddess of *Syria,* where having begun to treat of the very antient Temple of *Hierapolis,* he adds: "They say this Temple was founded by *Deucalion* the Scythian, that *Deucalion,* in whose Days the Flood of Water happened. I have heard in *Greece* the Story of this *Deucalion* from the *Greeks* themselves, which is thus: The present Generation of Men is not the Original one, for all that Generation perished; and the Men which now are, came from a second Stock, the whole Multitude of them descending from *Deucalion.* Now concerning the first Race of Men, they relate thus: They were very obstinate, and did very wicked Things; and had no Regard to Oaths, had no Hospitality or Charity in them; upon which Account many Calamities befel them. For on a sudden the Earth sent forth abundance of Water, great Showers of Rain fell, the Rivers overflowed exceedingly, and the Sea overspread the Earth, so that all was turned into Water, and every Man perished: *Deucalion* was only saved alive, to raise up another Generation, because of his Prudence

was remaining a most antient History of the Ark, and of the preserving a few not only of Mankind, but also of other living Creatures. The same History was extant also in (*a*) *Molo* and in (*b*) *Nicolaus Damascenus;* which latter names the <51> Ark, which we also find in the History of *Deucalion* in *Apollodorus:* And many *Spaniards* affirm, that in several (*c*)

---

and Piety. And he was preserved in this Manner; He and his Wives and his Children entered into a large Ark, which he had prepared; and after them went in Bears, and Horses, and Lions, and Serpents, and all other Kinds of living Creatures that feed upon the Earth, two and two; he received them all in, neither did they hurt him, but were very familiar with him, by a divine Influence. Thus they sailed in the same Ark, as long as the Water remained on the Earth: This is the Account the *Greeks* give of *Deucalion.* Now concerning what happened afterwards; There was a strange Story related by the Inhabitants of *Hierapolis,* of a great Hole in the Earth in that Country which received all the Water; after which *Deucalion* built an Altar, and reared a Temple to *Juno,* over the Hole. I saw the Hole myself; it is but a small one, under the Temple; whether it was larger formerly, I know not; I now am sure this which I saw, was but small. To preserve this Story, they perform this Ceremony; Twice every Year Water is brought from the Sea into the Temple; and not only the Priests, but all the People of *Syria* and *Arabia* fetch it; many go even from the River *Euphrates* as far as the Sea to fetch Water, which they pour out in the Temple, and it goes into the Hole, which, though it be but small, holds a vast Quantity of Water: When they do this, they say it was a Rite instituted by *Deucalion,* in Memory of that Calamity, and his Preservation. This is the antient Story of this Temple."

a. *In Molo,* &c.] *Eusebius* relates his Words in his Ninth Book of the *Gospel Preparation,* Chap. 19. "At the Deluge, the Man and his Children that escaped, came out of *Armenia,* being driven from his own Country by the Inhabitants, and having passed through the Country between, went into the mountainous Part of *Syria,* which was then uninhabited."

b. *Nicolaus Damascenus,* &c.] *Josephus* gives us his Words out of the Ninety Sixth Book of his *Universal History,* in the fore-cited Place: "There is above the City *Minyas,* (which *Strabo* and *Pliny* calls *Milyas*) a huge Mountain in *Armenia,* called *Batis,* on which they say a great many were saved from the Flood, particularly One who was carried to the Top of it by an Ark, the Reliques of the Wood of which was preserved a great while: I believe it was the same Man that *Moses* the Lawgiver of the *Jews* mentions in his History." To these Writers we may add *Hieronymus* the *Egyptian,* who wrote the Affairs of *Phoenicia,* and *Mnaseas,* mentioned by *Josephus.* And perhaps *Eupolemus,* which *Eusebius* quotes out of *Alexander* the Historian, in his *Gospel Preparation,* Book IX. Chap. 17.

c. *Parts of America,* &c.] See *Josephus Acosta,* and *Antonius Herera.*

Parts of *America*, as *Cuba, Mechoacana, Nicaraga,* is preserved the Memory of the Deluge, the saving alive of Animals, especially the Raven and Dove; and the Deluge it self in that Part called *Golden Castile.* (*a*) That Remark of *Pliny's*, that *Joppa* was built before the Flood, discovers what Part of the Earth Men inhabited before the Flood. The Place where the Ark rested after the Deluge (*b*) on the *Gordyaean* Mountains, is evident from the constant Tradition of the *Armenians* from all past Ages down (*c*) to this <52> very Day. (*d*) *Japhet,* the Father of the *Europeans,* and from him, *Jon,* or, as they formerly pronounced it, (*e*) *Javon* of the *Greeks,* and

a. *That Remark of Pliny's,* &c.] Book V. Chap. 13. *Mela* and *Solinus* agree with *Pliny.* Compare it with that which we have quoted out of *Abydenus.*

b. *On the Gordyaean Mountains,* &c.] Which *Moses* calls *Ararath,* the *Chaldean* Interpreters translate it *Kardu; Josephus, Gordiaean, Cortius, Cordaean; Strabo* writes it *Gordiaean,* Book XVI. and *Pliny,* Book VI. and *Ptolemaeus,* (These, and what follows in relation to the sacred Geography and the Founders of Nations, since these of *Grotius* were published, are with great Pains and much more Accuracy searched into by *Sam. Bochart* in his Sacred Geography, which add Weight to *Grotius's* Arguments. *Le Clerc.*)

c. *To this very Day,* &c.] *Theophilus Antiochenus* says, in his Third Book, that the Reliques of the Ark were shewn in his Time And *Epiphanius* against the *Nazarites; The Reliques of* Noah's *Ark are shewn at this Time in the Region of the* Cordiaeans: And *Chrysostom* in his Oration of Perfect Love. And *Isidore,* Book XIV. Chap. 8. of his Antiquities; "*Ararath,* a Mountain in *Armenia,* on which Histories testify the Ark rested after the Deluge; where at this Day are to be seen some Marks of the Wood." We may add the Words out of *Haiton* the *Armenian,* Chap. 9. "There is a Mountain in *Armenia* higher than any other in the whole World, which is commonly called *Ararath,* on the Top of which Mountain the Ark first rested after the Deluge." See the *Nubian Geographer,* and *Benjamin's Itinerary.*

d. *Japhet,* &c.] It is the very same Word יפת *Japheth;* for the same Letter פ is by some pronounced like π *p,* by others φ *ph;* and the same Difference is now preserved among the *Germans* and *Dutch. Hieronymus* upon *Daniel* has observed this of the *Hebrew* Letter.

e. *Javon,* &c.] For ἰαονες *iaones* is often found amongst the antient Writers. The *Persian* in *Aristophanes's* Play, called *Acharnenses,* pronounces it ἰαοναν *iaonan.* Now it was a very antient Custom to put a *Digamma* between two Vowels, which afterwards began to be wrote by a *V,* formerly thus *F.* In like Manner that which was ἀυὼς *auos,* is now ἀὼς *aos,* and ἠὼς *eos,* ταιως *tanos,* ταώς *taos,* a Peacock; τὼς Ἔλλφας καλυσω ἰαῦτας *iaunas,* Suidas.

(a) *Hammon* of the *Africans,* are Names to be seen in *Moses,* (b) and *Josephus* and others observe the like <53> Footsteps in the Names of other Places and Na-<54>tions. And which of the Poets is it, in which we

a. *Hammon,* &c.] For the *Greeks* sometimes render the *Hebrew* Letter ח *Cheth* by an Aspirate, and sometimes omit it; as חצר־מות *Chatzarmuth,* Ἀδράμυστος *Adramyttos,* or Ἀδράμυστος *Hadramyttos:* חכמות *Chachmoth,* ἀχμοῖθ *Achmuth* in *Irenaeus* and others: חביה *Chabrah,* a *Companion,* by the antient *Greeks,* ἄβρα *abra;* חיה *Chajah,* αἰών *aion,* an Age. חנה *Hanno* or *Anno;* חני־בעל *Hannibal* or *Annibal,* חצר־בעל *Hasdrubal* or *Asdrubal;* חשים *Cashim,* ἄξυμῖται *axoumitai;* for ων *on* is a *Greek* ending. This Father, not only of the *Libyans,* but also of many other Nations, is consecrated by them into the Star *Jupiter.*

> *Jupiter Ammon* is the only God
> Amongst the happy *Arabs,* and amongst
> The *Indians* and Aethopians. *Lucan,* Book IX.

And the sacred Scripture puts *Egypt* amongst them, *Psalm* lxxviii. 51. cv. 23, 27, cvi. 22. *Hieronymus* in his *Hebrew* Traditions on *Genesis* has these Words, *From whom,* Egypt *at this very Day, is called the Country of* Ham *in the* Egyptian *Language.*

b. *And Josephus and others,* &c.] He says, Γομαρεῖς *Gomareis,* the *Galatians,* is derived from גמר *Gomer,* where *Pliny's* Town *Comara* is. The People of *Comara* we find in the First Book of *Mela.* The *Scythians* are derived from מגוג *Magog,* by whom the City *Scythopolis* in *Syria* was built, and the other City *Magog; Pliny,* Book V. Chap. 23. which is called by others *Hierapolis* and *Bambyce.* It is evident that the *Medes* are derived from מדי *Medi;* and as we have already observed, *Javones, Jaones, Jones,* from יון *Javen, Josephus* says, the *Iberians* in *Asia* come from תבל *Thebal,* near to whom *Ptolemy* places the City of *Thabal,* as preserving the Marks of its ancient Original. The City *Mazaca,* mentioned by him, comes from משך *Masach,* which we find in *Strabo,* Book XII. and in *Pliny,* Book VI. 3. and in *Ammianus Marcellinus,* Book XX. Add to this the *Moschi* mentioned by *Strabo,* Book XI. and in the First and Third Book of *Mela,* whom *Pliny* calls *Moscheni,* Book VI. Chap. 9. and we find in them and *Pliny* the *Moschican* Mountains. *Josephus* and others agree, that the *Thracians* were derived from תירס *Tiras,* and the Word itself shews it, especially if we observe that the *Greek* Letter ξ *x* at first answered to the *Syriack* Letter ס *s,* as the Place of it shews. Concerning those that are derived from אשכנז *Aschanaz,* the Place is corrupt in *Josephus;* but without doubt *Ascania,* a Part of *Phrygia* and *Mysia,* mentioned in *Homer,* comes from thence; concerning which see *Strabo,* Book XII. and *Pliny,* Book V. Chap 32. The *Ascanian* Lake, and the River flowing from it, we find in *Strabo,* Book XIV. and in *Pliny's* forecited Fifth Book, Chap. 32. The *Ascanian* Harbour is in *Pliny,* Book V. Chap. 30. and the *Ascanian* Islands also, Book IV. Ch. 12. and Book V. Chap. 31. *Josephus* says the *Paphlagonians* are derived from ריפת *Riphath,* by some called *Riphataeans,* where *Mela* in his First Book puts the *Riphacians.* The same *Josephus* tells us, that the ἀιολεῖς *aioleis* come from אלישה *Alishah;* and the *Jerusalem* Paraphrast agrees with him in naming the *Greeks, Aeolians;* putting the Part for the Whole; nor is it much unlike *Hella,* the Name of the

Country. The same *Josephus* also says, that the *Cicilians* are derived from תרשיש *Tarsh-ish*, and proves it from the City *Tarsus;* for it happens in many Places that the Names of the People are made the Names of Cities. We have before hinted, that κίττιον *Kit-tion* is derived from כתים *Chitim*. The *Aethiopians* are called *Chusaeans* by themselves and their Neighbours, from כיש *Cush*, now; as *Josephus* observed they were in his Time; from whence there is a River so called by *Ptolemy*, and in the *Arabian* Geographer, there are two Cities, which retain the same Name. So likewise Μισώρ in *Philo Biblius* is derived from מִצְרִים *Mitzraim;* those which the *Greeks* call *Egyptians*, being called by themselves and their Neighbours *Mesori;* and the Name of one of their Months is Μεσιρι *Mesiri*. *Cedrenus* calls the Country itself Μέσρα, and *Josephus* rightly conjec-tures that the River in *Mauritania* is derived from פוט *Phut*. *Pliny* mentions the same River, Book V. Chap. 1. Phut, *and the Neighbouring* Phutensian *Country, is so called to this Day*. *Hieronymus*, in his *Hebrew* Traditions on *Genesis*, says, it is not far from *Fesa*, the Name remaining even now. The כנען *Chenaan* in *Moses* is contracted by *Sanchu-niathon*, and from him by *Philo Biblius*, into Χνᾶ *Chna*, you will find it in *Eusebius*'s Preparation, Book I. Chap. 10. and the Country is called so. *Stephanus*, of Cities, says, Chna *was so called by the* Phoenicians. And St. *Austin* in his Book of Expositions on the Epistle to the *Romans*, says, in his Time, if the Country People that lived at *Hippo* were asked who they were, they answered *Canaanites*. And in that place of *Eupolemus*, cited by *Eusebius, Praepar. IX. 17.* the *Canaanites* are called *Mestraimites*. *Ptolemy*'s *Regema* in *Arabia Felix* is derived from רעמה *Raamah*, by changing ע into γ g, as in *Gomorrah*, and other Words. *Josephus* deduces the *Sabins* from סבא *Saba*, a known Nation, whose chief City *Strabo* says, Book XVI. was *Saba;* where *Josephus* places the *Sabateni*, from סבתה *Sabatah;* where *Pliny* places the City *Sobotale*, Book VI. Chap. 28. The Word להבים *Lehabim* is not much different from the Name of the *Lybians;* nor the Word נפתהים *Nephathim* from *Nepata*, a City of *Ethiopia*, mentioned by *Pliny*, Book VI. Chap. 29. Nor *Ptolemy*'s *Nepata;* or the *Pharusi* in *Pliny*, Book V. Ch. 8. from פתרסים *Phatstrasim*, the same as *Ptolemy*'s *Phaurusians* in *Ethiopia*. The City *Sidon*, famous in all Poets and Historians, comes from צידן *Tzidon*. And *Ptolemy*'s Town *Gorasa*, from גרגשי *Gorgashi;* And *Arca*, a City of the *Phoenicians*, mentioned by *Ptolemy* and *Pliny*, Book V. Chap. 18. from ערקי *Arki*. And *Aradus*, an Island mentioned in *Strabo*, Book XVI. and *Pliny*, Book V. Chap. 20. and *Ptolemy* in *Syria*, from ארדי *Arodi;* and *Amathus* of *Arabia*, mentioned by *Herodotus* in his *Euterpe* and *Thalia*, from המתי *Hamathi;* and the *Elymites*, Neighbours to the *Medes*, from עילם *Eelim*, mentioned by *Strabo*, Book XVI. *Pliny*, Book V. Ch. 26. and *Livy*, Book XXXVII. Their Descendents in *Phrygia* are called *Elymites* by *Athanaeus*, Book IV. Every one knows, that the *Assyrians* are derived from אשור *Ashur*, as the *Lydians* are from לוד *Lud;* from whence comes the *Latin* Word *Ludi*. Those which by the *Greeks* are called *Syrians*, from the City ציר *Tzur*, are called *Aramites* to this Day from ארם *Aram:* For צ tz, is sometimes translated τ t, and some-times σ s; whence the City צור *Tzur*, which the *Greeks* call *Tyre*, is by *Ennius* called *Sarra*, and by others *Sina* and *Tina*. *Strabo*, Book XVI. towards the end: *The Poet mentions the* Arimites, *whom* Possidonius *would have us to understand, not to be any Part of* Syria, *or* Cilicia, *or any other Country, but* Syria *itself*. And again, Book XIII. *Some mean* Syr-ians *by* Arimites, *whom they now call* Aramites. And in the First Book, *For those we call*

<55><56> do not find mention made of the (*a*) Attempt to <57> climb

Syrians, *are by themselves called* Aramites. The Country *Ausanitis,* mentioned by the Seventy in *Job,* is derived from הוץ *Hutz. Aristaeus* calls it *Austias.* And the City *Cholla,* placed by *Ptolemy* in *Syria* from חול *Chol;* and the City *Gindarus* in *Ptolemy,* from גחר *Geher;* and the *Gindaren* People in *Pliny,* Book V. Chap. 23. in *Coelo-Syriae.* And the Mountain *Masius,* not far from *Nisibus,* mentioned by *Strabo,* Book XI. and *Ptolemy* in *Mesopotamia* is derived from מש *Mash.* The Names יקטן *Joktan,* and חצרמות *Hatzoramuth,* and חולן *Holan,* are represented by the *Arabian* Geographers under the Names of *Balsatjaktan, Hadramuth,* and *Chaulan,* as the learned *Capell* observes. The River *Ophar,* and the People called *Opharites,* near *Maeotis, Pliny,* Book VI. 7. if I mistake not, retain the Name איפר *Ophar;* and those Cities which *Moses* mentions in this Place, appear to be the most ancient by comparing of Authors. Every one knows from whence *Babylon* is derived. ארך *Arach* is *Aracca,* placed by *Ptolemy* in *Susiana;* from whence come the *Aracaean* Fields in *Tibullus,* as the famous *Salmasius,* a Man of vast Reading observes. *Acabene,* a Corruption of *Acadene,* is derived from אכד *Achad,* as is probably conjectured by *Franciscus Junius,* a diligent Interpreter of Scripture, who has observed many of those Things we have been speaking of. כלנה *Chalnah* is the Town *Gaunisus* on the River *Euphrates;* whose Name *Ammianus* tells us in his Twenty third Book continued to his time. The Land שנער *Senaar,* is the *Babylonian Sennaas* in *Haestiaeus Milesus,* which Place *Josephus* has preserved in his ancient History, Book I. Chap. 7. and in his *Chronicon;* as has *Eusebius* in his *Preparation.* He wrote the Affairs of *Phoenicia;* whom also *Stephens* had read. Again ע being changed into *γ, g, Ptolemy* from hence calls the Mountain *Singarus* in *Mesopotamia.* And *Pliny* mentions the Town *Singara,* Book V. Chap. 24. and hence the *Singaranaen* Country in *Sextus Rufus* נינוה *Nineveh* is undoubtedly the *Ninos* of the *Greeks* contracted; thus in *Sardanapalus's* Epitaph.

> I who great *Ninus* rul'd, am now but Dust.

The same Name we find in *Theognis* and *Strabo,* Book XVI. and *Pliny,* Book XI. Ch. 13. whose Words are these. Ninus *was built upon the River* Tygris, *towards the West, a beautiful City to behold. Lucan,* Book III. *Happy* Ninus, *as Fame goes.* The Country *Calachena* has its Name from the principal City כלה *Chala: Strabo,* Book XI. and afterwards, in the Beginning of Book XVI. רסן *Resin* is *Resaina* in *Ammianus,* Book XXIII, *Sidon* every one knows. עזה *Azzah* is without doubt rendered *Gaza* in *Palestine,* by changing, as before, the Letter ע into *γ, g:* It is mentioned by *Strabo,* Book XVI. and *Mela,* Book I. who calls it a large and well fortified Town; and *Pliny,* Book XV. Ch. 13. and Book VI. Chap. 28. and elsewhere. ספרה *Sephirah,* is *Heliopolis,* a City of the *Sipparians,* in that place of *Abydenus* now quoted. *Sippara* is by *Ptolemy* placed in *Mesopotamia,* איר *Ur* is the Castle *Ur,* mentioned by *Ammianus,* Book XXV. חרן *Caran* is *Carra,* famous for the Slaughter of the *Crassi.*

    a. *The Attempt to climb the Heavens,* &c.] See *Homer,* Odys. 30. and *Ovid's Metamorphosis,* Book I.

> The Giants, by Report, would Heaven have storm'd.

the Heavens? (*a*) *Diodorus Siculus,* (*b*) *Strabo,* (*c*) <58> *Tacitus,* (*d*) *Pliny,*

———

See also *Virgil's* First *Georgick,* and *Lucan,* Book VII. It is a frequent way of speaking amongst all Nations, to call those Things which are raised above the common Height, *Things reaching to Heaven,* as we often find in *Homer,* and *Deut.* I. 29. and IX. 1. *Josephus* quotes one of the *Sybils,* I know not which, concerning the unaccountable Building of that Tower; the Words are these: "When all Men spoke the same Language, some of them built a vast high Tower, as if they would ascend up into Heaven; but the Gods sent a Wind, and overthrew the Tower, and assigned to each a particular Language, and from hence the City *Babylon* was so called." And *Eusebius,* in his Preparation, Book IX. Ch. 14. *Cyril,* Book I. against *Julian,* quotes these Words out of *Abydenus:* "Some say that the first Men, who sprang out of the Earth, grew proud upon their great Strength and Bulk, and boasted they could do more than the Gods, and attempted to build a Tower, where *Babylon* now stands; but when it came nigh the Heavens, it was overthrown upon them by the Gods, with the Help of the Winds; and the Ruins are called *Babylon.* Men 'till then had but one Language, but the Gods divided it, and then began the War betwixt *Saturn* and *Titan.*" It is a false Tradition of the *Greeks,* that *Babylon* was built by *Semiramis,* as *Berosus* tells us in his *Chaldaicks,* and *Josephus* in his First Book against *Appion;* and the same Error is refuted by *Julius Firmicus* out of *Philo Biblius,* and *Dorotheus Sidonius.* See also what *Eusebius* produces out of *Eupolemus* concerning the Giants and the Tower, in his *Gospel Preparat.* Book XX. Chap. 17.

    a. *Diodorus Siculus,* &c.] Book XIX. where he describes the Lake *Asphaltitis:* "The neighbouring Country burns with Fire, the ill Smell of which makes the Bodies of the Inhabitants sickly, and not very long-lived." (See more of this in our *Dissertation* added to the *Pentateuch,* concerning the Burning of *Sodom. Le Clerc.*)

    b. *Strabo,* &c.] Book XVI. after the Description of the Lake *Asphaltitis:* "There are many Signs of this Country's being on Fire; for about *Masada* they show many cragged and burnt Rocks, and in many Places Caverns eaten in, and Ground turned into Ashes, drops of Pitch falling from the Rocks, and running Waters stinking to a great Distance, and their Habitations overthrown; which give Credit to a Report amongst the Inhabitants, that formerly there was thirteen Cities inhabited there, the chief of which was *Sodom,* so large as to be sixty Furlongs round; but by Earthquakes and Fire breaking out, and by hot Waters mixed with Bitumen and Brimstone, it became a Lake as we now see it; the Rocks took Fire, some of the Cities were swallowed up, and others forsaken by those Inhabitants that could flee."

    c. *Tacitus,* &c.] In the Fifth Book of his History: "Not far from thence are those Fields which are reported to have been formerly very fruitful, and had large Cities built in them, but they were burnt by Lightning; the Marks of which remain, in that the Land is of a burning Nature, and has lost its Fruitfulness. For every thing that is planted, or grows of itself, as soon as it is come to an Herb or Flower, or grown to its proper Bigness, vanishes like Dust into nothing."

    d. *Pliny,* &c.] He describes the Lake *Asphaltitis,* Book V. Chap. 16. and Book XXXV. Chap. 15.

(*a*) *Solinus* speak of the Burning of *Sodom*. (*b*) *Herodotus, Diodo-*<59>*rus* (*c*),

a. *Solinus*, &c.] In the 36th Chap. of *Salmanus*'s Edition: "At a good Distance from *Jerusalem* a dismal Lake extends itself, which was struck by Lightning, as appears from the black Earth burnt to Ashes. There were two Towns there, one called *Sodom,* the other *Gomorrah;* the Apples that grow there cannot be eaten, though they look as if they were ripe; for the outward Skin incloses a kind of sooty Ashes, which pressed by the least Touch, flies out in Smoke, and vanishes into fine Dust."

b. *Herodotus*, &c.] With some little Mistake. The Words are in his *Euterpe:* "Originally only the *Colchians,* and *Egyptians,* and *Ethiopians* were circumcised. For the *Phoenicians* and *Syrians* in *Palaestine* confess they learned it from the *Egyptians*. And the *Syrians* who dwell at *Thermodoon,* and on the *Parthenian* River, and the *Macrons* their Neighbours say, they learnt it of the *Colchians*. For these are the only Men that are circumcised, and in this Thing agree with the *Egyptians*. But concerning the *Ethiopians* and *Egyptians,* I cannot affirm positively which learned it of the other." *Josephus* rightly observes, that none were circumcised in *Palaestine Syria* but the *Jews;* in the Eighth Book, Chap. 14. of his ancient History, and First Book against *Appion.* Concerning which *Jews, Juvenal* says, *They take off their Foreskin;* and *Tacitus, That they instituted circumcising themselves, that they might be known by such distinction:* See *Strabo,* Book XVII. But the *Jews* are so far from confessing that they derived this Custom from the *Egyptians,* that on the contrary, they openly declare that the *Egyptians* learnt to be circumcised of *Joseph.* Neither were all the *Egyptians* circumcised, as all the *Jews* were, as we may see from the Example of *Appion,* who was an *Egyptian,* in *Josephus. Herodotus* undoubtedly put the *Phoenicians* for the *Idumaeans;* as *Aristophanes* does in his Play, called the *Birds,* where he calls the *Egyptians* and *Phoenicians, The Circumcised. Ammonius,* of the Difference of Words, says, *The* Idumaeans *were not originally* Jews, *but* Phoenicians *and* Syrians. Those *Ethiopians* which were circumcised, were of the Posterity of *Keturah,* as shall be observed afterwards. The *Colchians* and their Neighbours were of the Ten Tribes that *Salmanasar* carried away, and from thence some came into *Thrace.* Thus the *Scholiast* on *Aristophanes*'s *Acharnenses,* says, *That the Nation of the* Odomants *is that of the* Thracians; *they are said to be* Jews. Where, by *Jews,* are to be understood, improperly, *Hebrews,* as is usual. From the *Aethiopians,* Circumcision went over Sea into the new World, if it be true what is said of that Rite's being found in many Places of that World. (The Learned dispute whether Circumcision was instituted first amongst the *Egyptians* or amongst the *Jews,* concerning which see my Notes upon *Genes.* XVII. 30. *Le Clerc.*)

c. *Diodorus*, &c.] Book I. of the *Colchians:* "That this Nation sprang from the *Egyptians,* appears from hence, that they are circumcised after the manner of the *Egyptians,* which Custom remains amongst this Colony, as it does amongst the *Jews.*" Now since the *Hebrews* were of old circumcised, it no more follows from the *Colchians* being circumcised, that they sprang from the *Egyptians,* than that they sprang from the *Hebrews,* as we affirm they did. He tells us, Book III. that the *Troglodites* were circumcised, who were a Part of the *Aethiopians.*

Strabo (*a*), *Philo Byblius* (*b*), testify the ancient Custom of Circumcision, which is confirmed by those Nations (*c*) descended from *Abraham,* not only *Hebrews,* but also (*d*) *Idumaeans,* <60> (*e*) *Ismaelites,* (*f*) and others.

a. *Strabo,* &c.] Book XVI. concerning the *Troglodytes: Some of these are circumcised, like the* Egyptians. In the same Book he ascribes Circumcision to the *Jews.*

b. *Philo Byblius,* &c.] In the Fable of *Saturn* in *Eusebius,* Book I. Chap. 10.

c. *Descended from Abraham,* &c.] To which *Abraham* that the Precept of Circumcision was first of all given, *Theodorus* tells us in his Poem upon the *Jews;* out of which *Eusebius* has preserved these Verses in his *Gospel Preparation,* Book IX. Chap. 22.

> He who from Home the righteous *Abraham* brought,
> Commanded him and all his House, with Knife
> To circumcise their Foreskin. He obeyed.

d. *Idumaeans,* &c.] So called from *Esau,* who is called Οὑσωὸς *Ousoos,* by *Philo Byblius.* His other Name was *Edom,* which the *Greeks* translated Ἐρυθρᾶν *Eruthran,* from whence comes the *Erythraean* Sea, because the ancient Dominions of *Esau* and his Posterity extended so far. They who are ignorant of their Original, confound them, as we observed, with the *Phoenicians. Ammonius* says, the *Idumaeans* were circumcised; and so does *Justin* in his *Dialogue* with *Trypho,* and *Epiphanius* against the *Ebionites.* Part of these were *Homerites,* who, *Epiphanius* against the *Ebionites* tells us, were circumcised in his Time.

e. *Ismaelites,* &c.] These were circumcised of old, but on the same Year of their Age as *Ismael. Josephus,* Book I. Ch. 12 and 13. *A Child was born to them.* (viz. *Abraham* and *Sarah) when they were both very old, which they circumcised on the Eighth Day; and hence the Custom of the* Jews *is to circumcise after so many Days. But the* Arabians *defer it Thirteen Years; for* Ismael, *the Father of that Nation, who was the Child of* Abraham *by his Concubine, was circumcised at that Age.* Thus *Origen* in his excellent Discourse against Fate, which is extant in *Eusebius,* Book VI. Chap. 11. And in the *Greek* Collection, whose Title is Φιλοκαλία; "I don't know how this can be defended, that there should be just such a Position of the Stars upon every one's Birth in *Judaea,* that upon the Eighth Day they must be circumcised, made sore, wounded, lamed, and so inflamed, that they want the Help of a Physician as soon as they come into the World. And that there should be such a Position of the Stars to the *Ismaelites* in *Arabia,* that they must be all circumcised when they are Thirteen Years old; for so it is reported of them." *Epiphanius,* in his Dispute against the *Ebionites,* rightly explains these *Ismaelites* to be the *Saracens;* for the *Saracens* always observed this Custom, and the *Turks* had it from them.

f. *And others,* &c.] Namely those that descended from *Keturah,* concerning whom there is a famous Place of *Alexander* the Historian in *Josephus,* Book I. Ch. 16. which *Eusebius* quotes in his *Gospel Preparation,* Book IX. Ch. 20. Cleodemus *the Prophet, who is called* Malchus, *in his Relation of the* Jews, *gives us the same History as* Moses *their Lawgiver,* viz. "That *Abraham* had many Children by *Keturah,* to three of which he gave the Names, *Afer, Asser,* and *Afra. Assyria* is so called from *Asser;* and from the other two, *Afer* and *Afra,* the City *Afra* and the Country *Africa* is denominated These fought

The History of <61> *Abraham, Isaac, Jacob* and *Joseph,* agreeable with *Moses,* (*a*) was extant of old in (*b*) *Philo Byblius* out of *Sanchuniathon,* in (*c*) *Berosus,* (*d*) *Hecataeus,* (*e*) <62> *Damascenus,* (*f*) *Artapanus, Eupolemus,*

---

with *Hercules* against *Lybiae* and *Antaeus.* Then *Hercules* married his Daughter to *Afra:* He had a Son of her, whose Name was *Deodorus,* of whom was born *Sophon,* whence the *Barbarians* are called *Sophaces.*" Here the other Names, through the Fault of the Transcribers, neither agree with *Moses,* nor with the Books of *Josephus* and *Eusebius,* as we have them now. But *Αφιρ,* is undoubtedly the same as אפר *Apher* in *Moses.* We are to understand by *Hercules,* not the *Thebean Hercules,* but the *Phoenician Hercules,* much older, whom *Philo Byblius* mentions, quoted by *Eusebius* often, in the forementioned 10th Chapter of the First Book of his *Gospel Preparation.* This is that *Hercules,* who *Salust* says in his *Jugurthine* War, brought his Army into *Africa.* So that we see whence the *Aethiopians* who were a great Part of the *Africans,* had their Circumcision, which they had in *Herodotus's* Time; and even now those that are Christians retain it, not out of a Religious Necessity, but out of Respect to so antient a Custom.

a. *Was extant of old,* &c.] *Scaliger* thinks that several things which *Eusebius* has preserved out of *Philo Byblius,* certainly relate to *Abraham;* see himself in his *Appendix* to the *Emendation of Time.* There is some reason to doubt of it.

b. *Philo Byblius,* &c.] How far we are to give Credit to *Philo's Sanchuniathon,* does not yet appear; for the very learned *Henry Dodwell* has rendred his Integrity very suspicious, in his *English* Dissertation on *Sanchuniathon's Phoenician* History, published at *London,* in the Year M DCLXXXI, to whose Arguments we may add this, that in his *Fragments* there is an absurd Mixture of the Gods unknown to the *Eastern Graecians* in the first Time, with the Deities of the *Phoenicians,* which the Streightness of Paper will not allow me to enlarge upon. *Le Clerc.*

c. *Berosus,* &c.] *Josephus* has preserved his Words in his antient History, Book. I. C. 8. *In the Tenth Generation after the Flood, there was a Man amongst the* Chaldaeans, *who was very Just and Great, and sought after Heavenly Things.* Now it is evident from Reason, that this ought to be referred to the Time of *Abraham.*

d. *Hecataeus,* &c.] He wrote a Book concerning *Abraham,* which is now lost, but was extant in *Josephus's* Time.

e. *Damascenus,* &c.] *Nicolaus,* that famous Man, who was the Friend of *Augustus* and *Herod,* some of whose Reliques were lately procured by that excellent Person, *Nicholas Peiresius,* by whose Death, Learning and Learned Men had a very great Loss. The Words of this *Nicolaus Damascenus, Josephus* relates in the forecited Place: "*Abraham* reigned in *Damascus,* being a Stranger who came out of the Land of the *Chaldaeans,* beyond *Babylon;* and not long after, he and those that belonged to him, went from hence into the Land called *Canaan,* but now *Judaea,* where he and those that descended from him dwelt, of whose Affairs I shall treat in another Place. The Name of *Abraham* is at this Day famous in the Country about *Damascus,* and they show us the Town, which from him is called *Abraham's* Dwelling."

f. *Artapanus, Eupolemus,* &c.] *Eusebius* in his Preparation, Book IX. Chap. 16, 17, 18, 21, 23. has quoted several Things under these Mens Names out of *Alexander* the

Demetrius, and partly (*a*) in the antient Writers of the Orphick Verses; and something of it is still extant in (*b*) *Justin,* out of *Trogus Pompeius.* (*c*) By almost <63> all which, is related also the History of *Moses,* and his principal Acts. The Orphick Verses expressly mention (*d*) his being taken

---

Historian, but the Places are too long to be transcribed; no body has quoted them before *Eusebius.* But the Fable of the *Bethulians,* which *Eusebius* took out of *Philo Byblius,* Prepar. Book I. Chap. 10. came from the Altar of *Bethel,* built by *Jacob,* mentioned *Gen.* 36.

a. *In the antient Writers,* &c.] For certainly those that we find in *Clemens Alexandrinus,* Strom. V. and *Eusebius,* Book XIII. Chap. 12. can be understood of no other.

> The Maker of all Things is known to none,
> But One of the *Chaldean* Race, his Son
> Only begotten, who well understood,
> The starry Orb, and by what Laws each Star
> Moves round the Earth, embracing all Things in it.

Where *Abraham* is called *only Begotten,* as in *Isaiah* LI. 2. אחד *Achad.* We have before seen in *Berosus,* that *Abraham* was famous for the Knowledge of Astronomy; and *Eupolemus,* in *Eusebius,* says of him, *that he was the Inventor of Astronomy amongst the* Chaldeans.

b. *In Justin,* &c.] Book XXXVI. Ch. 2. "The Original of the *Jews* was from *Damascus,* an eminent City in *Syria,* of which afterwards *Abraham* and *Israel* were Kings." *Trogus Pompeius* calls them Kings, as *Nicolaus* did; because they exercised a Kingly Power in their Families; and therefore they are called *Anointed,* Ps. CV. 15.

c. *By almost all which,* &c.] See *Eusebius* in the forementioned Book IX. Ch. 26, 27, 28. Those things are true which are there quoted out of *Tragicus Judaeus Ezechiel,* part of which we find in *Clemens Alexandrinus,* Strom. I. who reports out of the Books of the Priests, that an *Egyptian* was slain by the Words of *Moses;* and Strom. V. he relates some things belonging to *Moses,* out of *Artapanus,* tho' not very exactly. *Justin,* out of *Trogus Pompeius,* says of *Moses,* "He was Leader of those that were banished, and took away the sacred Things of the *Egyptians;* which they endeavouring to recover by Arms, were forced by a Tempest to return home; and *Moses* having entered into his own Country of *Damascus,* he took Possession of Mount *Sinah;*" and what follows, which is a Mixture of Truth and Falsehood. Where we find *Arvas* written by him, it should be read *Arnas,* who is *Aaron,* not the Son, as he imagines, but the Brother of *Moses,* and a Priest.

d. *His being taken out of the Water,* &c.] As the great *Scaliger* has mended the Place; who with a very little Variation of the Shape of a Letter, instead of ὑλογενὴς *hulogenes,* as it is quoted out of *Aristobulus,* by *Eusebius,* in his Gospel Preparation, Book XIII. Ch. 12. bids us read ὑδογενὴς *hudogenes, Born of the Water.* So that the Verses are thus:

> So was it said of Old, so he commands
> Who's born of Water, who received from God
> The two great Tables of the Law.

out of the Water, and the two Tables that were given him by God. To these we may add (*a*) *Polemon.* (*b*) And <64> several Things about his coming out of *Egypt,* from the *Egyptian* Writers, *Manetho, Lysimachus, Chaeremon.* Neither can any prudent Man think it at all credible, that *Moses,* (*c*) who had so many Enemies, not only of the *Egyptians,* but also of many other Nations, as the (*d*) *Idumaeans,* (*e*) *Arabians,* and (*f*) *Phoenicians,* would venture to relate any thing concerning the Creation of the World, or the Original of Things, which could be confuted by more antient Writings, or was contradictory to the antient and received Opinions:

The antient Writer of the Orphick Verses, whoever he was, added the Words after he had said there was but one God to be worshipped, who was the Creator and Governor of the World.

a. *Polemon,* &c.] He seems to have lived in the Time of *Ptolemy Epiphanes;* concerning which, see that very useful Book of the famous *Gerard Vossius,* of the *Greek* Historians. *Africanus,* says the *Greek* Histories, were wrote by him; which is the same Book *Athenaeus* calls Ἑλλαδικον. His Words are these: "In the Reign of *Apis* the Son of *Phoroneus,* part of the *Egyptian* Army went out of *Egypt,* and dwelt in *Syria,* called *Palestine,* not far from *Arabia.*" As *Africanus* preserved the Place of *Polemon,* so *Eusebius* in his Chronology, preserved that of *Africanus.*

b. *And several Things,* &c.] The Places are in *Josephus* against *Appion* with abundance of Falsities, as coming from People who hated the *Jews;* and from hence *Tacitus* took his Account of them. But it appears from all these compared together, that the *Hebrews* descended from the *Assyrians,* and possessing a great Part of *Egypt,* led the Life of Shepherds; but afterwards being burthen'd with hard Labour, they came out of *Egypt* under the Command of *Moses,* some of the *Egyptians* accompanying them, and went through the Country of the *Arabians* unto *Palaestine Syria,* and there set up Rites contrary to those of the *Egyptians:* But *Josephus* in that learned Book has wonderfully shown, how the *Egyptian* Writers, in the Falsities which they have here and there mix'd with this History, differ with one another, and some with themselves, and how many Ages the Books of *Moses* exceed theirs in Antiquity.

c. *Who had so many Enemies,* &c.] From whom they went away by Force, whose Laws the *Jews* abolish'd. Concerning the implacable Hatred of the *Egyptians* against the *Jews,* see *Philo* against *Flaccus,* and in his *Embassy;* and *Josephus* in each Book against *Appion.*

d. *The Idumaeans,* &c.] Who inherited the antient Hatred between *Jacob* and *Esau;* which was encreased from a new Cause, when the *Idumaeans* denied the *Hebrews* Passage, *Numb.* XX. 14.

e. *Arabians,* &c.] Those, I mean, that descended from *Ismael.*

f. *Phoenicians,* &c.] Namely the *Canaanites,* and the Neighbouring Nations, who had continual Wars with the *Hebrews.*

or that he would relate any thing of Matters in his own Time, that could be confuted by the Testimony of many <65> Persons then alive. (*a*) *Diodorus Siculus,* and (*b*) <66> *Strabo,* and (*c*) *Pliny,* (*d*) *Tacitus,* and after them (*e*) *Dionysius Longinus,* (concerning Loftiness of Speech) make

a. *Diodorus Siculus,* &c.] In his first Book, where he treats of those who made the Gods to be the Authors of their Laws, he adds; *Amongst the* Jews *was* Moses, *who called God by the Name of* Ἰάω *Iao,* where by Ἰάω, *Iao,* he means, יהוה *Jehovah,* which was so pronounced by the Oracles, and in the Orphick Verses mentioned by the Ancients, and by the *Basilidian* Hereticks, and other Gnosticks. The same Name the *Tyrians,* as we learn from *Philo Byblius,* pronounced Ἰευὼ *Ieno,* others Ἰαὺ *Iaou,* as we see in *Clemens Alexandrinus.* The *Samaritans* pronounced it, Ἰαβαὶ *Iabai,* as we read in *Theodoret;* for the *Eastern* People added to the same Words, some one Vowel and some another; from whence it is that there is such difference in the proper Names in the Old Testament. *Philo* rightly observes, that this Word signifies *Existence.* Besides *Diodorus,* of those who make mention of *Moses,* the Exhortation to the *Greeks,* which is ascribed to *Justin,* names *Appion, Ptolemy Mendesius, Hellanicus, Philochorus, Castor, Thallus, Alexander* the Historian: And *Cyril* mentions some of them in his first Book against *Julian.*

b. *Strabo,* &c.] The Place is in his sixteenth Book, where he thinks that *Moses* was an *Egyptian* Priest; which he had from the *Egyptian* writers, as appears in *Josephus:* Afterwards he adds his own Opinion, which has some Mistakes in it. "Many who worshipped the Deity, agreed with him *(Moses;)* for he both said and taught, that the *Egyptians* did not rightly conceive of God, when they likened him to wild Beasts and Cattle; nor the *Lybians,* nor the *Greeks,* in resembling him by a humane Shape; for God is no other than that Universe which surrounds us; the Earth, and the Sea, and the Heaven, and the World, and the Nature of all Things, as they are called by us. Who (says he) that has any Understanding would presume to form any Image like to these Things that are about us? Wherefore we ought to lay aside all carved Images, and worship him in the innermost Part of a Temple worthy of him, without any Figure." He adds, that this was the Opinion of good Men: He adds also, that sacred Rites were instituted by him, which were not burdensome for their Costliness, nor hateful, as proceeding from Madness. He mentions Circumcision, the Meats that were forbidden, and the like: and after he had shown that Man was naturally desirous of civil Society, he tells us, that it is promoted by Divine and Human Precepts, but more effectually by Divine.

c. *Pliny,* &c.] Book XXX. Chap. 1. *There is another Sect of Magicians which sprang from* Moses. And *Juvenal;*

They learn, and keep, and fear the *Jewish* Law,
Which *Moses* in his secret Volume gave.

d. *Tacitus,* &c.] History V. Where, according to the *Egyptian* Fables, *Moses* is called *one of those that were banished.*

e. *Dionysius Longinus,* &c.] He lived in the Time of *Aurelian* the Emperor, a Favourite of *Zenobia,* Queen of the *Palmyrians.* In his Book of the *Sublime,* after he had

mention of *Moses*. (*a*) Besides the <67> *Talmudists*, (*b*) *Pliny*, and (*c*) *Apuleius*, speak of *Jamnes* and *Mambres*, who resisted *Moses* in *Egypt*. (*d*) Some things there are in other Writers, and many things amongst the (*e*)

---

said, that they who speak of God, ought to take care to represent him, as Great, and Pure, and without Mixture: He adds, "Thus does he who gave Laws to the *Jews*, who was an extraordinary Man, who conceived and spoke worthily of the Power of God, when he writes in the Beginning of his Laws, God spake: What? Let there be Light, and there was Light: Let there be Earth, and it was so." *Chalcidius* took many Things out of *Moses*, of whom he speaks thus. "*Moses* was the wisest of Men, who, as they say, was enlivened, not by human Eloquence, but by Divine Inspiration."

a. *Besides the Talmudists*, &c.] In the *Gemara*, in the Title, *Concerning Oblations*, and the Chapter, *All the Oblations of the Synagogue*. To which add the *Tanchuma* or *Ilmedenu*. Mention is there made of the chief of *Pharaoh's* Magicians, and their Discourse with *Moses* is related. Add also *Numenius*, Book III. concerning the *Jews: Eusebius* quotes his Words, Book VIII. Chap. 8. "Afterwards *Jamnes* and *Mambres*, *Egyptian* Scribes, were thought to be famous for Magical Arts, about the time that the *Jews* were driven out of *Egypt;* for these were they who were chosen out of the Multitude of the *Egyptians* to contend with *Musaeus* the Leader of the *Jews*, a Man very powerful with God by Prayers; and they seemed to be able to repel those sore Calamities which were brought upon *Egypt* by *Musaeus*." Where *Moses* is called *Musaeus*, a Word very near it, as is customary with the *Greeks;* as others call *Jesus, Jason;* and *Saul, Paul. Origen* against *Celsus* refers us to the same Place of *Numenius. Artapanus* in the same *Eusebius*, Book IX. Chap. 27. calls them the *Priests* of *Memphis*, who were commanded by the King to be put to Death, if they did not do things equal to *Moses*.

b. *Pliny*, &c.] In the forecited Place.

c. *Apuleius*, &c.] In his second Apologetick.

d. *Some things there are*, &c.] As in *Strabo, Tacitus,* and *Theophrastus,* quoted by *Porphyry* in his second Book against eating living Creatures, where he treats of Priests and Burnt-offerings; and in the fourth Book of the same Work, where he speaks of Fishes and other living Creatures that were forbidden to be eaten. See the place of *Hecataeus* in *Josephus's* first Book against *Appion*, and in *Eusebius's Preparat.* Book IX. Chap. 4. You have the Law of avoiding the Customs of strange Nations in *Justin's* and *Tacitus's* Histories; of not eating Swines Flesh, in *Tacitus, Juvenal, Plutarch's Sympos.* iv. and *Macrobius* from the Ancients. In the same place of *Plutarch* you will find mention of the *Levites,* and the pitching of the Tabernacle.

e. *Pythagoreans*, &c.] *Hermippus* in the Life of *Pythagoras,* quoted by *Josephus* against *Appion,* Book II. "These Things he said and did, imitating the Opinion of the *Jews* and *Thracians,* and transferring them to himself; for truly this Man took many Things into his own Philosophy from the *Jewish* Laws." To abstain from Creatures that die of themselves, is put amongst the Precepts of *Pythagoras*, by *Hierocles,* and *Porphyry* in his Epistle to *Anebo,* and *Aelian,* Book IV. that is, out of *Levit.* iv. 15. *Deut.* xiv. 21. *Thou shalt not engrave the Figure of God on a Ring,* is taken out of *Pythagoras*, in *Malchus's* or *Porphyry's* Exhortation to Philosophy, and in *Diogenes Laertius;* and this from the Second Commandment. *Take not away that which thou didst not place,*

Pythagoreans, <68> about the Law and Rites given by *Moses,* (*a*) *Strabo* and *Justin,* out of *Trogus,* remarkably testify concerning the Religion and Righteousness of the ancient *Jews:* So that there seems to be no need of mentioning what is found, or has formerly been found, of *Joshua* and others, agreeable to the *Hebrew* Books; seeing that whoever gives Credit to *Moses* (which it is a Shame for any one to refuse) cannot but believe those famous Miracles done by the Hand of God; which is the principal Thing here aimed at. Now that the Miracles of later Date, such as those of (*b*) *Elijah, Elishah* and others, should not be Counterfeit, there is this further Argument; that in those Times *Judaea* was become more known, and because of the Difference of Religion, was hated by the Neighbours, who could very easily confute the first <69> Rise of a Lie. The History of *Jonah's* being three Days in the Whale's Belly, is in (*c*) *Lycophron,* and

---

Josephus in his Second Book against *Appion,* puts amongst the *Jewish* Precepts, and *Philostratus,* amongst the *Pythagoreans. Jamblicus* says, *A tender and fruitful Tree ought not to be corrupted or hurt,* which he had out of *Deuteronomy* xx. 19. The forementioned *Hermippus* ascribes this to *Pythagoras,* not to pass by a Place where an Ass has set upon his Knees: The Foundation of which is the Story in *Numb.* xxii. 27. *Porphyry* acknowledges that *Plato* took many things from the *Hebrews,* as *Theodoret* observes in his first Discourse against the *Greeks.* You will see Part of them in *Eusebius's* Preparation. (I suspect that *Hermippus,* or *Josephus,* instead of *Jews,* should have said *Idaeans,* that is, the Priests of *Jupiter Idaeus* in *Crete,* whom *Pythagoras* envied. See Sir *John Marsham's* Collection of these, in his Tenth Age of the *Egyptian* Affairs. *Le Clerc.*

a. *Strabo* and *Justin,* &c.] *Strabo* in his XIVth Book, after the History of *Moses,* says, *That his Followers for a considerable time kept his Precepts, and were truly righteous and godly.* And a little after he says, that those who believed in *Moses, worshipped God, and were lovers of Equity.* And *Justin* says thus, Book XXXVI. Chap. 2. *Whose Righteousness, (viz.* the Kings and Priests*) mixed with Religion, increased beyond Belief. Aristotle* also (witness *Clearchus* in his Second Book of Sleep, which *Josephus* transcribed) gives a great Character of a *Jew* whom he had seen, for his Wisdom and Learning. *Tacitus,* amongst his many Falsities, says this one Truth, that the *Jews* worshipped *that Supreme* and *Eternal Being, who was immutable, and could not perish;* that is, God, (*as Dion Cassius* speaks, treating of the same *Jews) who is ineffable and invisible.*

b. *Elijah,* &c.] Concerning whose Prophecy, *Eusebius* says, *Praep.* Book IX. Chap. 30. that *Eupolemus* wrote a Book. In the 39th Chapter of the same Book, *Eusebius* quotes a Place of his concerning the Prophecies of *Jeremiah.*

c. *Lycophron,* &c.] The Verses are these.

Of that three-nighted Lyon, whom of old
Triton's fierce Dog with furious Jaws devour'd,
Within whose Bowels, tearing of his Liver,

Aeneas Gazaeus, only under the Name of *Hercules,* to advance whose Fame, every thing that was great and noble used to be related of him, as (*a*) *Tacitus* observes. Certainly nothing but the manifest Evidence of the History could compel *Julian* (who was as great an Enemy to the *Jews* as to the Christians) to confess (*b*) that there were some Men inspired by the Divine Spirit amongst the *Jews,* (*c*) and that Fire descended from Heaven, and consumed the Sacrifices of *Moses* and *Elias.* And here it is worthy of Ob-<70>servation, that there was not only very (*d*) severe Punishments threatned amongst the *Hebrews,* to any who should falsely assume the Gift of Prophecy; (*e*) but very many Kings, who by that means might have procured great Authority to themselves; and many learned men, (*f*) such as *Esdras* and others, dared not to assume this Honour to themselves; (*g*) nay, some Ages before Christ's Time, no body dared to do it. Much

---

He rolled, burning with Heat, though without Fire,
His Head with Drops of Sweat bedew'd all o'er.

Upon which Place *Tzetzes* says, "Because he was three Days within the Whale." And *Aeneas Gazaeus* in *Theophrastus:* "According to the Story of *Hercules,* who was saved by a Whale swallowing him up, when the Ship in which he sailed was wrecked."

a. *Tacitus, &c.*] And *Servius,* as *Varro* and *Verrius Flaccus* affirm.

b. *That there were some, &c.*] Book III. in *Cyril.*

c. *That Fire descended, &c.*] *Julian* in the Xth Book of *Cyril.* "Ye refuse to bring Sacrifices to the Altar and offer them, because the Fire does not descend from Heaven and consume the Sacrifices, as it did in *Moses's* Time: This happened once to *Moses,* and again long after to *Elijah* the *Tishbite.*" See what follows concerning the Fire from Heaven. *Cyprian* in III of his Testimonies, says, "That in the Sacrifices, all those that God accepted of, Fire came down from Heaven, and consumed the Things sacrificed." *Menander* also in his *Phoenician* History mentions that great Drought which happened in the Time of *Elias,* that is, when *Ithobalus* reigned amongst the *Tyrians.* See *Josephus* in his Ancient History, Book VIII. Chap. 7.

d. *Severe Punishments, &c.*] Deut. XIII. 5. XVIII. 20. and the following.

e. *But very many Kings, &c.*] No body dared to do it after *David.*

f. *Such as Esdras, &c.*] The *Hebrews* used to remark upon those Times, *Hitherto the Prophets, now begin the Wise Men.*

g. *Nay, some Ages before Christ's Time, &c.*] Therefore in the Ist Book of *Maccabees,* IV. 46. we read that the Stones of the Altar which was defiled were laid aside, *until there should come a Prophet to shew what should be done with them.* And in the IXth Chap. *ver.* 27. of the same Book. "So was there a great Affliction in *Israel* the like whereof had never been, since the Time that there were no Prophets amongst them." The same we find in the *Talmud,* in the Title concerning the Council.

less could so many thousand People be imposed upon, in avouching a constant and publick Miracle, I mean (*a*) <71> that of the Oracle, (*b*) which shined on the High Priest's Breast, which is so firmly believed by all the *Jews* to have remained till the Destruction of the first Temple, that their Ancestors must of necessity be well assured of the Truth of it.

SECT. XVII. *The same proved also from Predictions.*

There is another Argument to prove the Providence of God, very like to this of Miracles, and no less powerful, drawn from the foretelling of future Events, which was very often and very expressly done amongst the *Hebrews;* such as the (*c*) Man's being childless who should rebuild

a. *That of the Oracle,* &c.] See *Exodus* XXVIII. 30. *Levit.* VIII. 8. *Numb.* XXVII. 21. *Deut.* XXXIII. 8. 1 *Sam.* XXI. 11. XXII. 10, 13, 15. XXIII. 2, 5, 9, 10, 11, 12. XXVIII. 6. Add *Nehem.* VII. 65. and *Josephus's* Book III. 9. This is what is meant by the Words ἐρώτημα δύλων, *the consulting* (an Oracle) *where you will have an Answer as clear as Light itself:* In the Son of Syrach XXXIII. 4. For the Word δηλα *clear,* answers to the *Hebrew* אורים *Urim,* and so the Seventy translate it in the forecited Places, *Numb.* XXVII. 21. 1 *Sam.* XXVIII. 6. and elsewhere δηλωσω *making clear,* as *Exod.* XXVIII. 26. *Lev.* VIII. 8. They also translate תמם *Thumim,* ἀλήθεια *Truth;* The *Egyptians* imitated this, just as Children do men. *Diodorus,* Book I. relating the Affairs of the *Egyptians,* says of *the Chief Judge, that He had Truth hanging about his Neck.* And again afterwards "The King commands that all Things necessary and fitting should be provided for the Subsistence of the Judges, and that the Chief Judge should have great Plenty. This Man carries about his Neck an Image of precious Stones hanging on a golden Chain, which they call Truth, and they then begin to hear Cases when the Chief Judge has fixed this Image of Truth." And *Aelian,* Book XIV. Ch. 24. of his various History. "The Judges in old Time amongst the *Egyptians* were Priests, the oldest of which was Chief Priest, who judged every one; and he ought to be a very just Man, and one that spared no body. He wore an Ornament about his Neck made of Saphire Stone, which was called Truth." The Babylonish *Gemara,* Ch. I. of the Book called *Joma* says, that some Things in the first Temple were wanting in the second, as the Ark with the Mercy Seat, and the *Cherubims,* the Fire coming from Heaven, the *Schecinab,* the Holy Ghost, and the *Urim* and *Thumim.*

b. *Which shined on the High Priest's Breast,* &c.] This is a Conjecture of the *Rabbins,* without any Foundation from Scripture. It is much more credible that the Priest pronounced the Oracle with his Mouth. See our Observat. on *Exod.* XXVIII. 30. *Numb.* XXVII. 31. *Le Clerc.*

c. *The Man's being childless,* &c.] Compare *Josuah* VI. 26. with 1 *Kings* XVI. 34.

Jericho; the destroying the Altar of *Bethel,* by King *Josiah* by Name, (*a*) above three hundred Years be-<72>fore it came to pass; so also *Isaiah* foretold the (*b*) very Name and principal Acts of *Cyrus;* and *Jeremiah* the Event of the Siege of *Jerusalem,* after it was surrounded by the *Chaldaeans;* and *Daniel* (*c*) the Translation of the Empire from the *Assyrians,* to the *Medes* and *Persians,* and (*d*) from them to *Alexander* of *Macedon,* (*e*) whose Successors to part of his Kingdom should be the Posterity of *Lagus* and *Seleucus,* and what Evils the *Hebrews* should undergo from all these, particularly (*f*) the famous *Antiochus,* so very plainly, (*g*) that *Porphyry,* who compared the *Graecian* Histories extant in his Time with the Prophecies, could not make it out any other way, but by saying, that the Things ascribed to *Daniel,* were wrote after they came to pass; which is the same as if any one should deny that what is now extant under the Name of *Virgil,* and was always thought to be his, <73> was writ by him in *Augustus's* Time. For there was never any more doubt amongst the *Hebrews* concerning the one, than there was amongst the *Romans* concerning the other. To all which may be added the many and express Oracles (*h*) amongst those

a. *Above three hunded Years,* &c.] CCCLXI.[9] as *Josephus* thinks in his Antient History, Book X. Ch. 5.

9. 361.

b. *The very Name,* &c.] Chap. XXXVII, XXXVIII. For the fulfilling, see Chap. XXXIX. and LII. *Eusebius,* Book IX. ch. 39. of his Praepar. brings a Testimony out of *Eupolemus,* both of the Prophecy and the fulfilling of it.

c. *The Translation of the Empire,* &c.] *Daniel* I. 32, 39. V. 28. VII. 5. VIII. 3, 20. X. 20. XI. 2.

d. *From them to* Alexander, &c.] In the forecited[10] Chap. II. 32, and 39. VII. 6. VIII. 5, 6, 7, 8, 21. X. 20. XI. 3, 4.

10. Book of Daniel.

e. *Whose Successors,* &c.] Chap. II. 33, 40, VII. 7, 19, 23, 24. VIII. 22. X. 5, 6, 7, 8, 9, 10, 11, 12, 13, 14, 15, 16, 17, 18, 19, 20.

f. *The famous* Antiochus, &c.] VII. 8, 11, 20, 24, 25, VIII. 9, 10, 11, 12, 13, 14, 23, 24, 25, 26, XI. 21, 22, 23, 24, 25, 26, 27, 28, 29, 30, 31, 32, 33, 34, 35, 36, 37, 38, 39, 40, 41, 42, 43, 44, 45. XII. 1, 2, 3, 11. *Josephus* explains these Places as we do, Book X. Ch. 12; and Book XII. Ch. 11. and Book I. Ch. 1. of his *Jewish* War. *Chrysostom* II. against the *Jews;* making use of the Testimony of *Josephus,* and *Polychronius,* and other *Greek* Writers.

g. *That Porphyry,* &c.] See *Hieronymus,* upon *Daniel* throughout.

h. *Amongst those of* Mexico, &c.] (*Garcilazzo de la Vega*) Inca, Acosta, Herrera, and others, relate strange Things of these Oracles. See *Peter Cieza,* Tome II. of the *Indian* Affairs.

of *Mexico* and *Peru,* which foretold the coming of the *Spaniards* into those Parts, and the Calamities that would follow.

And by other Arguments.

(*a*) To this may be referred very many Dreams exactly agreeing with the Events, which both as to themselves and their Causes, were so utterly unknown to those that dreamed them, that they cannot without great Shamelessness be attributed to natural Causes; of which kind the best Writers afford us eminent Examples. (*b*) *Tertullian* has <74> made a Collection of them in his Book of the Soul; and (*c*) Ghosts have not only

a. *To this may be referred,* &c.] What is here said, does not so much prove the Existence of God, who takes care of the Affairs of Men; as that there are present with them some invisible Beings, more powerful than Men, which whoever believes, will easily believe that there is a God. For there is no necessity that all Things which come to pass different from the common Course of Nature should be ascribed to God himself; as if whatever cannot be affected by Men, or the Power of corporeal Things, must be done by him himself. *Le Clerc.*

b. *Tertullian has made a Collection,* &c.] Chap. XLVI. where he relates the remarkable Dreams of *Astyages,* of *Philip* of *Macedon,* of the *Himerraean* Woman of *Laodice,* of *Mithridates,* of *Illyrian Balaris,* of *M. Tully,* of *Artorius,* of the Daughter of *Polycrates Samius,* whom *Cicero* calls his Nurse, of *Cleonomus Picta,* of *Sophocles,* of *Neoptolemus* the Tragedian. Some of these we find in *Valerius Maximus,* Book I. Ch. 7. besides that of *Calpurnia* concerning *Caesar,* of *P. Decius* and *T. Manlius* the Consuls, *T. Atinius, M. Tully* in his Banishment, *Hannibal, Alexander the Great, Simonides, Craesus* the Mother of *Dionysius* the Tyrant. *C. Sempronius Gracchus, Cassius* of *Parmenia, Aterius Rufus* the *Roman* Knight, *Hamilcar* the *Carthaginian, Alcibiades* the *Athenian,* and a certain *Arcadian.* There are many remarkable things in *Tully's* Books of Divination; neither ought we to forget that of *Pliny,* Book XXV. Chap. 2. concerning the Mother of one that was fighting in *Lusitania.* Add also those of *Antigonus* and *Artucules,* who was the first of the Race of the *Osmanidae* in the *Lipsian Monita,* Book I. Chap. 5. and others collected by the industrious *Theodore Zuinger,* Vol. V. Book IV. the Title of which is *Concerning Dreams.*

c. *And Ghosts have not only,* &c.] See *Plutarch* in the Life of *Dion* and *Brutus,* and *Appion* of the same *Brutus,* in the fourth of his *Civilia,* and *Florus,* Book IV. Chap. 7. Add to these, *Tacitus* concerning *Curtius Rufus,* Annal. XI. which same History is in *Pliny,* Epist. XXVII. Book VII. together with another; concerning that which that wise and couragious Philosopher *Athenodorus* saw at *Athens.* And those in *Valerius Maximus,* Book I. Chap. 8. especially that of *Cassius* the *Epicuraean,* who was frighted with the sight of *Caesar* whom he had killed; which is in *Lipsius,* Book I. Chap. 5. of his *Warnings.* Many such Histories are collected by *Crysippus, Plutarch* in his Book of the Soul,

been seen, but also heard to speak, as we are told by those Historians who have been far from superstitious Credulity; and by Witnesses in our own Age, who lived in *Sina, Mexico,* and other Parts of *America;* neither ought we to pass by (*a*) that com-<75>mon Method of examining Persons Innocence by walking over red hot Plow-shares, *viz. Fire Ordeal,* mentioned in so many Histories of the *German* Nation, and in their very Laws.

SECT. XVIII. *The Objection of Miracles not being seen now, answered.*

Neither is there any Reason why any one should object against what has been said, because no such Miracles are now seen, nor no such Predictions heard. For it is sufficient to prove a Divine Providence, that there ever have been such. Which being once established, it will follow, that we ought to think God Almighty forbears them now, for as wise and prudent Reasons, as he before did them. Nor is it fit that the Laws given to the Universe for the natural Course of Things, and that what is future might be uncertain, should always, or without good Reason be suspended, but then only, when there was a sufficient Cause; as there was at that time when the Worship of the true God was banished almost out of the World,

---

and *Numenius* in his second Book of the Soul's Immortality, mentioned by *Origen* in his fifth Book against *Celsus.*

a. *That common Method,* &c.] See the Testimonies of this Matter collected by *Francis Juret,* to the 74th Epistle of *Ivon* Bishop of *Chartres. Sophocles's Antigone* tells us how old this is, where the *Theban* Relations of *Oedipus* speak thus.

> We are prepared with Hands to touch the Iron,
> And snatch the Fire, or to invoke the Gods,
> That we are innocent and did not do it.

Which we learn also from the Report of *Strabo,* Book V. and *Pliny's* Natural Hist. Book VII. Chap. 2. and *Servius* upon *Virgil's* XIth *Aeneid.* Also those Things which were seen of old in *Feronia's* Grove upon the Mountain *Soracte.* To these Things which happened contrary to the common Course of Nature, we may add, I think, those we find made use of to preserve Mens Bodies from being wounded by Arrows. See also the certain Testimonies, concerning those who have spoke after their Tongues were cut out for the sake of Religion, such as *Justinian,* Book I. C. of the *Praetorian* Office, of a Praefect in *Africa. Procopius* in the Ist of his *Vandalicks. Victor Uticensis* in his Book of Persecutions, and *Aeneas Gaza* in *Theophrastus.*

being confined only to a small Corner of it, *viz. Judaea;* and was to be defended from that Wickedness which surrounded it, by frequent Assistance. Or when the Christian Religion, con-<76>cerning which we shall afterwards particularly treat, was, by the Determination of God, to be spread all over the World.

Sect XIX. *And of there being so much Wickedness.*

Some Men are apt to doubt of a Divine Providence, because they see so much Wickedness practised, that the World is in a manner overwhelmed with it like a Deluge: Which they contend should be the Business of Divine Providence, if there were any, to hinder or suppress. But the Answer to such, is very easy. When God made Man a free agent, and at liberty to do well or ill, (reserving to himself alone a necessary and immutable Goodness) (*a*) it was not fit that he should put such a Restraint upon evil Actions, as was in-<77>consistent with this Liberty. But whatever Means of hindering them, were not repugnant to such Liberty; as establishing and promulging a Law, external and internal Warnings, together with Threatnings and Promises; none of these were neglected by God: Neither would he suffer the Effects of Wickedness to spread to the furthest;

a. *It was not fit,* &c.] Thus *Tertullian* against *Marcion* II. "An entire Liberty of the Will, is granted him on each side, that he may always appear to be Master of himself, by doing of his own accord that which is good, and avoiding of his own accord that which is evil. Because Man, who is in other Respects subject to the Determination of God, ought to do that which is just out of the good pleasure of his own free Will. But neither the Wages of that which is good or evil, can justly be paid to him who is found to be good or evil out of Necessity, and not out of Choice. And for this Reason was the Law appointed, not to exclude but to prove Liberty, by voluntarily performing Obedience to it, or by voluntarily transgressing it, so that in either Event the Liberty of the Will is manifest." And again afterwards. "Then the Consequence would have been, that God would have withdrawn that Liberty which was once granted to Man, that is, would have retained within himself his Fore-knowledge and exceeding Power, whereby he could have interposed to hinder Man from falling into Danger by attempting to make an ill Use of his Liberty. For if he had interposed, he would then have taken away that Liberty which his Reason and Goodness had given them." *Origen* in his IVth Book against *Celsus,* handles this Matter, as he uses to do others, very learnedly; where amongst other things, he says, *That you destroy the Nature of Virtue, if you take away Liberty.*

so that Government was never utterly subverted, nor the Knowledge of the Divine Laws entirely extinguished. And even those Crimes that were permitted, as we hinted before, were not without their Advantages, when made use of either to punish those who were equally wicked, or to chastise those who were slipt out of the way of Virtue, or else to procure some eminent Example of Patience and Constancy in those who had made a great Progress in Virtue. (*a*) *Lastly,* Even they themselves whose Crimes seemed to be overlooked for a time, were for the most part punished with a proportionable Punishment, that the Will of God might be executed against them, who acted contrary to his Will.

Sect. XX. *And that so great, as to oppress good Men.*

And if at any time Vice should go unpunished, or, which is wont to offend many weak Persons, some good Men, oppressed by the Fury of the Wicked, should not only lead a troublesome Life, but also undergo an infamous Death; we must not presently from hence conclude against a Divine Providence, which, as we have before ob-<78>served, is established by such strong Arguments; but rather, with the wisest Men, draw this following Inference:

Sect. XXI. *This may be turned upon them, so as to prove that Souls survive Bodies.*

That since God has a Regard to humane Actions, who is himself just; and yet these things come to pass in the mean time; we ought to expect a Judgment after this Life, lest either remarkable Wickedness should continue unpunished, or eminent Virtue go unrewarded and fail of Happiness.

---

a. *Lastly, Even they themselves,* &c.] Concerning this whole Matter, See the Note at Sect. VIII.

SECT. XXII. *Which is confirmed by Tradition.*

In (*a*) order to establish this, we must first shew that Souls remain after they are separated from their Bodies; which is a most ancient Tradition, derived from our first Parents (whence else could it come?) to almost all civilized People; as appears (*b*) from *Homer's* Verses, (*c*) and from the Philosophers, not only the *Greek*, but also the ancient *Gauls* (*d*) which were called *Druids*, <79> (*e*) and the *Indians* called *Brachmans*, and from those Things which many Writers have related (*f*) concerning the *Egyptians* (*g*) and *Thracians*, and also of the *Germans*. And moreover concerning a Divine Judgment after this Life, we find many Things extant, not only

a. *In order to establish this*, &c.] Whoever has a mind to read this Argument more largely handled, I refer him to *Chrysostom* on the Ild. Cor. Chap. 18. and to his *Ethicks* Tome VI. against those who say that humane Affairs are regulated by *Daemons:* And to his IVth Discourse upon Providence.

b. *From* Homer's *Verses*, &c.] Especially in that Part called νεκυῖα *concerning those that are departed:* To which may be added the like in *Virgil*, in *Seneca's Oedipus, Lucan, Statius*, and that in *Samuel*, 1 *Sam.* XXVIII.

c. *And from the Philosophers*, &c.] *Pherecydes, Pythagoras*, and *Plato*, and all the Disciples of them. To these *Justin* adds *Empedocles*, and many Oracles in his IId. Apologetick; and *Xenocrates*.

d. *Which were called* Druids, &c.] These taught that Souls did not die. See *Caesar*, Book VI. of the War with the *Gauls*, and *Strabo*, Book IV. of the same. *These and others say, that souls are incorruptible;* (see also *Lucan*, Book I. 455.)

e. *And the* Indians *called* Brachmans, &c.] Whose Opinion *Strabo* explains to us thus, Book XV. "We are to think of this Life, as of the State of a Child before it be born, and of Death as a Birth to that which is truly Life and Happiness to wise Men." See also a remarkable place concerning this Matter, in *Porphyry's* IVth Book against eating Living Creatures.

f. *Concerning the* Egyptians, &c.] *Herodotus* in his *Euterpe* says, that it was the Opinion of the *Egyptians, That the Soul of Man was immortal.* The same is reported of them by *Diogenes Laertius*, in his Preface, and by *Tacitus*, Book. V. of his History of the *Jews. They buried rather than burnt their Bodies, after the Manner of the* Aegyptians; *they having the same Regard and Persuasion concerning the Dead.* See *Diodorus Siculus*, concerning the Soul of *Osiris;* and *Servius* on the VIth *Aenead*, most of which is taken from the *Aegyptians.*

g. *And* Thracians, &c.] See again here the Places of *Hermippus*, concerning *Pythagoras*, which we before quoted out of *Josephus. Mela*, Book II. concerning the *Thracians*, says, "Some think that the Souls of those who die, return again; others, that though they do not return, yet they do not die, but go to a more happy Place." And *Solinus* concerning the same, Ch. X. "Some of them think that the Souls of those who die,

among the *Greeks*, (*a*) but <80> also among the *Egyptians* (*b*) and *Indians, as Strabo, Diogenes, Laertius*, and (*c*) *Plutarch* tell us: To which we may add a Tradition that the World should be burnt, which was found of Old (*d*) in *Hystaspes* and the *Sybils*, and now also (*e*) in *Ovid* (*f*) and

---

return again; others, that they do not die, but are made more happy." Hence arose that Custom of attending the Funerals with great Joy, mentioned by these Writers, and by *Valerius Max*. Book I. Chap. V. 12. That which we before quoted out of the Scholiast upon *Aristophanes*, makes this the more credible, *viz.* that some of the *Hebrews* of old came into *Thrace*.

a. *But also among the* Egyptians, &c.] *Diodorus Siculus*, Book I. says, that what *Orpheus* delivered concerning Souls departed, was taken from the *Egyptians*. Repeat what we now quoted out of *Tacitus*.

b. *And* Indians, &c.] Amongst whose Opinions *Strabo*, Book XV. reckons that *concerning the Judgments that are exercised amongst the Souls departed.*

c. *And* Plutarch, &c.] Concerning those whose Punishment is deferred by the Gods, and concerning the Face of the Moon's Orb. See a famous Place of his, quoted by *Eusebius*, Book XI. Ch. 38. of his Gospel Preparat. out of the Dialogue concerning the Soul.

d. *In* Hystaspes *and the* Sybils, &c.] See *Justin's* IId Apologetick, and *Clemens, Strom.* VI. whence is quoted that from the Tragoedian.

> For certainly the Day will come, 'twill come,
> When the bright Sky shall from his Treasure send
> A liquid Fire, whose all-devouring Flames,
> By Laws unbounded shall destroy the Earth,
> And what's above it; all shall vanish then.
> The Water of the Deep shall turn to Smoke,
> The Earth shall cease to nourish Trees; the Air,
> Instead of bearing up the Birds, shall burn.

e. *In* Ovid, &c.] *Metamorphosis*, Book I.

> For he remembred 'twas by Fate decreed
> To future times, that Sea, and Earth, and Heaven
> Should burn, and this vast Frame of Nature fail.

f. *And* Lucan, &c.] Book I.

> So when this Frame of Nature is dissolv'd,
> And the last Hour in future Times approach,
> All to its antient Chaos shall return;
> The Stars confounded tumble into Sea,
> The Earth refuse its Banks, and try to throw
> The Ocean off. The Moon attack the Sun,
> Driving Her Chariot through the burning Sky,

<81> *Lucan,* and amongst (*a*) the *Indians* in *Siam;* a Token of which, is the Sun's approaching nearer to the Earth, (*b*) observed by Astronomers. So likewise upon the first going into the *Canary Islands* and *America,* and other distant Places, the same Opinion, concerning Souls and Judgment, was found there.

SECT. XXIII. *And no way repugnant to Reason.*

(*c*) Neither can we find any Argument drawn from Nature, which over-throws this an an-<82>cient and extensive Tradition: For all those Things which seem to us to be destroyed, are either destroyed by the Opposition of something more powerful than themselves, as Cold is destroyed by the greater Force of Heat; or by taking away the Subject upon which they depend, as the Magnitude of a Glass, by breaking it; or by the Defect of the <83> efficient Cause, as Light by the Absence of the Sun. But none of these can be applied to the Mind; not the first, because nothing can be conceived contrary to the Mind; nay, such is the peculiar Nature of it, that it is capable equally, and at the same time, of contrary Things in its

---

Enrag'd, and challenges to rule the Day.
The Order of the World's disturb'd throughout.

Lucan was preceeded by his Uncle *Seneca,* in the end of his Book to *Marcia; The Stars shall run upon each other; and every thing being on a Flame, that which now shines regularly, shall then burn in one Fire.*

a. *The* Indians *in* Siam, &c.] See *Ferdinand Mendesius.*

b. *Observed by Astronomers,* &c.] See *Copernicus's* Revolutions, Book III. Ch. 16. *Joachim Rhaeticus* on *Copernicus,* and *Gemma Frisius.* See also *Ptolemy,* Book III. Ch. 4. of his *Mathematick Syntax.* That the World is not now upheld by that Power it was formerly, as itself declares, *and that its Ruin is evidenced by the Proof how the Things in it fail,* says *Cyprian* to *Demetrius.* The Earth is nearer to the Sun in its *Perihelion's,* that is, when it is in the extreme Parts of the lesser *Axis* of its *Parabola,* though the Earth always approaches at the same Distances; yet it is manifest from hence, that at the Will of God, it may approach still nearer, and if it so pleases Him, be set on Fire by the Sun, as it happens to Comets. *Le Clerc.* "It were to be wished that the learned Remarker had left out this and some other Notes of this Kind, unless he had studied such sort of Things more."

c. *Neither can we find any Argument,* &c.] This Matter might be handled more exactly, and upon better Principles of Philosophy, if our Room would allow it. I. We

own, that is, in an intellectual Manner. Not the second, because there is no Subject upon which the Nature of the Soul depends; (*a*) for if there were any, it would be a Humane Body; and that it is not so, appears from hence, that when the Strength of the Body fails by Action, the Mind only

---

ought to define what we mean by the *Death of the Soul,* which would happen, if either the Substance of the Soul were reduced to nothing, or if there were so great a Change made in it, that it were deprived of the Use of all its Faculties; thus Material Things are said to be destroyed, if either their Substance ceases to be, or if their Form be so altered, that they are no longer of the same Species; as when Plants are burnt or putrifyed; the like to which befalls Brute Creatures. II. It cannot be proved that the Substance of the Soul perishes: For Bodies are not entirely destroyed, but only divided, and their Parts separated from each other. Neither can any Man prove, that the Soul ceases to think, which is the Life of the Soul, after the Death of the Man; for it does not follow that when the Body is destroyed, the mind is destroyed too, it having never yet been proved that it is a Material Substance. III. Nor has the contrary yet been made appear by certain Philosophick Arguments drawn from the Nature of the Soul; because we are ignorant of it. It is true indeed, that the Soul is not, by its own Nature, reduced to nothing; neither is the Body; this must be done by the particular Act of their Creator. But it may possibly be without any Thought or Memory; which State, as I before said, may be called the Death of it. But IV. If the Soul, after the Dissolution of the Body, should remain for ever in that State, and never return to its Thought or Memory again, then there can be no Account given of Divine Providence, which has been proved to be, by the foregoing Arguments. God's Goodness and Justice, the Love of Virtue, and Hatred to Vice; which every one acknowledges in him, would be only empty Names; if he should confine his Benefits to the short and fading good Things of this Life, and make no Distinction betwixt Virtue and Vice; both good and bad men equally perishing for ever, without seeing in this Life any Rewards or Punishments, dispensed to those who have done well or ill: And hereby God would cease to be God, that is, the most perfect Being; which if we take away, we cannot give any Account of almost any other Thing, as *Grotius* has sufficiently shown by those Arguments, whereby he has demonstrated that all Things were created by God. Since therefore there is a God, who loves Virtue and abhors Vice; the Souls of Men must be Immortal, and reserved for Rewards or Punishments in another Life. But this requires further Enlargement. *Le Clerc.* The Proof of the Soul's Immortality, drawn from the Consideration of the Nature of it, may be seen in its full Force in Dr. *Clarke*'s Letter to Mr. *Dodwell* and the Defences of it.[11]

11. Added by John Clarke.

a. *For if there were any,* &c.] That there is none, *Aristotle* proves very well from Old men, Book I. Ch. IV. concerning the Soul. Also Book III. Chap. IV. he commends *Anaxagoras,* for saying that the Mind was simple and unmixt, that it might distinguish other Things.

does not contract any Weariness by acting. (*a*) Also the Powers of the Body suffer by the too great Power of the Things, which are the Objects of them, as Sight by the Light of the Sun, (*b*) But the Mind is <84> rendred the more perfect, by how much the more excellent the Things are, about which it is conversant; as about Figures abstracted from Matter, and about universal Propositions. The Powers of the Body are exercised about those Things which are limited by Time and Place, but the Mind about that which is Infinite and Eternal. Therefore, since the Mind in its Operations does not depend upon the Body, so neither does its Existence depend upon it; for we cannot judge of the Nature of those Things which we do not see, but from their Operations. Neither has the third Method of being destroyed, any Place here: For there is no Efficient Cause from which the Mind continually flows: Not the Parents, because the Children live after they are dead. If we allow any Cause at all from whence the Mind flows, it can be no other than the first and universal Cause, which, as to its Power, can never fail; and as to its Will, that That should fail, that is, that God should will the Soul to be destroyed, this can never be proved by any Arguments.

a. *Also the Powers of the Body,* &c.] *Aristotle,* Book III. of the Soul says: "That there is not the like Weakness in the Intellectual Part, that there is in the Sensitive, is evident from the Organs of Sense, and from Sensation it self; for there can be no Sensation, where the Object of such Sensation is too strong; that is, where the Sound is too loud, there is no Sound; and where the Smell is too strong, or the Colours too bright, they cannot be smelt nor seen. But the Mind, when it considers Things most excellent to the Understanding, it is not hindred by them from thinking, any more than it is by meaner Things, but rather excited by them; because the Sensitive Part cannot be separated from the Body, but the Mind may." Add to this, the famous Place of *Plotinus,* quoted by *Eusebius,* in his *Prepar.* Book XV. Ch. 22. Add also, that the Mind can overcome those Passions which arise from the Body, by its own Power; and can chuse the greatest Pains and even the Death of it.

b. *But the Mind is rendred,* &c.] And those are the most excellent Actions of the Mind, which call it off most from the Body.

Sect. XXIV. *But many Things favour it.*

Nay, there are many not inconsiderable Arguments for the contrary; such as (*a*) the absolute Power every Man has over his own Actions; a <85> natural Desire of Immortality; the Power of Conscience, which comforts him when he has performed any good Actions, though never so difficult; and, on the contrary, (*b*) torments him when he has done any bad Thing, especially at the Approach of Death, as it were with a Sense of impending Judgment; (*c*) the Force of which, many times could not be extinguished by the worst of Tyrants, tho' they have endeavoured it never so much; as appears by many Examples.

a. *The absolute Powers every Man has over his own Actions,* &c.] And over all other Living Creatures. To which may be added, the Knowledge of God, and of Immortal Beings. *An Immortal Creature is not known by any mortal one,* says *Sallust* the Philosopher. One remarkable Token of this Knowledge is, that there is nothing so grievous, which the Mind will not despise for the sake of God. Beside, the Power of Understanding and Acting, is not limited as it is in other Creatures, but unwearied, and extends it self infinitely, and is by this means like unto God; which Difference of Man from other Creatures, was taken Notice of by *Galen*.

b. *Torments him when he has done,* &c.] See *Plato*'s Ist Book of his Common-wealth: "When Death seems to approach any one, Fear and Sollicitude comes upon him, about those Things which before he did not think of."

c. *The Force of which,* &c.] Witness that Epistle of *Tiberius* to the Senate. "What I should write to you, O Senators, or how I should write, or what I should not write at this Time, let the Gods and Goddesses destroy me worse than I now feel myself to perish, if I know." Which Words, after *Tacitus* had recited in the VIth of his Annals, he adds. "So far did his Crimes and Wickedness turn to his Punishment; So true is that Assertion of the Wisest of Men, that if the Breasts of Tyrants were laid open, we might behold the Gnawings and Stingings of them, for as the Body is bruised with Stripes, so the Mind is torn with Rage and Lust and evil Designs." The Person which *Tacitus* here means, is *Plato*, who says of a Tyrant, in Book IX. of his Common-wealth: "He would appear to be in reality a Beggar, if any one could but see into his whole Soul; full of Fears all his Life long, full of Uneasiness and Torment." The same Philosopher has something like this in his *Gorgias. Suetonius,* Ch. 67, being about to recite the forementioned Epistle of *Tiberius,* introduces it thus. "At last, when he was quite wearied out, in the Beginning of such an Epistle as this, he confesses almost all his Evils." *Claudian* had an Eye to this place of *Plato,* when he describes *Rufinus* in his second Poem.

———— Stains within
Deform his Breast, which bears the Stamp of Vice.

Sect. XXV. *From whence it follows, that the End of Man is Happiness after this Life.*

If then the Soul be of such a Nature, as contains in it no Principles of Corruption; and God has given us many Tokens, by which we ought to <86> understand, that his Will is, it should remain after the Body; there can be no End of Man proposed more worthy of Him, than the Happiness of that State; and this is what *Plato* and the *Pythagoreans* said, (*a*) that the End of Man was to be made most like to God. Thus what Happiness is, and how to be secured, Men may make some Conjectures; but if there be any thing concerning it, revealed from God, that ought to be esteemed, most true and most certain.

Sect. XXVI. *Which we must secure, by finding out the true Religion.*

Now since the Christian Religion recommends itself above all others, whether we ought to give Credit to it or no, shall be the Business of the second Part of this Work to examine. <87>

a. *That the End of Man was,* &c.] Which the *Stoicks* had from *Plato,* as *Clemens* remarks. *Strom.* V.

Sect. I. *That the Christian Religion is true.*

The Design then of this second Book (after having put up our Petitions to Christ the King of Heaven, that he would afford us such Assistances of his holy Spirit, as may render us sufficient for so great a Business) is not to treat particularly of all the Opinions in Christianity; but only to show that the Christian Religion it self is most true and certain; which we attempt thus.

Sect. II. *The Proof that there was such a Person as Jesus.*

That Jesus of *Nazareth* formerly lived in *Judaea* in the Reign of *Tiberius* the *Roman* Emperor, is constantly acknowledged, not only by Christians dispersed all over the World, but also by all the Jews which now are, or have ever wrote since that time; the same is also testified by Heathens, that is, such as did not write either of the Jewish, or of the Christian Religion, (*a*) *Suetonius*, (*b*) <88> *Tacitus*, (*c*) *Pliny* the Younger, and many after these.

a. *Suetonius*, &c.] In his *Claudius*, Chap. 25. where *Chresto* is put for *Christo*, because that Name was more known to the *Greeks* and *Latins*.

b. *Tacitus*, &c.] Book XV. where he is speaking of the Punishment of the Christians. *The Author of that Name was Christ, who in the Reign of* Tiberius, *suffered Punishment under his Procurator* Pontius Pilate. Where the great Crimes and Hatred to humane kind they are charged with, is nothing else but their Contempt of False Gods; which same Reason *Tacitus* had to curse the *Jews;* and *Pliny* the Elder, when he calls the *Jews, a People remarkable for Contempt of the Gods.* That is, very many of the *Romans* were come to this, that their Consciences were not affected by that Part of their Theology which was Civil (which *Seneca* commends) but they feigned it in their outward Actions, and kept it as a Command of the Law, looking upon Worship as a Thing of Custom, more than in Reality. See the Opinion of *Varro* and *Seneca* about this matter, which is the same with that of *Tacitus;* in *Augustin,* Book V. Ch. 33. and

That he died an ignominious Death.

That the same Jesus was crucified by *Pontius Pilate,* the President of *Judaea,* is acknowledged by all the same Christians, notwithstanding it might seem dishonourable to them who worship such a <89> Lord. (*a*) It is also acknowledged by the *Jews,* though they are not ignorant how much they lie under the Displeasure of the Christians, under whose Government they every where live, upon this Account, because their Ancestors were the Cause of *Pilate*'s doing it. Likewise the Heathen Writers we mentioned, have recorded the same to Posterity; (*b*) and a long Time after, the Acts of *Pilate* were extant, to which the Christians sometimes appealed. Neither did *Julian,* or other Opposers of Christianity, ever call it in Question. So that no History can be imagined more certain than this; which is confirmed by the Testimonies, I don't say of so many Men, but of so many People, which differed from each other. (*c*) Notwithstanding

---

Book VI. Chap. 10. of his City of God. In the mean Time it is worth observing, that *Jesus,* who was punished by *Pontius Pilate,* was acknowledged by many at *Rome* in *Nero's* Time, to be the Christ. Compare that of *Justin* in his IId Apologetick concerning this History, where he addresses himself to the Emperors and *Roman* Senate, who might know those Things from the Acts.

c. Pliny *the Younger,* &c.] The Epistle is obvious to every one, *viz.* Book X. Chap. 97. which *Tertullian* mentions in his Apologetick, and *Eusebius* in his *Chronicon;* where we find that the Christians were used to say a Hymn to Christ as God, and to bind themselves not to perform any wicked Thing, but to forbear committing Theft, Robbery or Adultery; to be true to their Word, and strictly perform their Trust. *Pliny* blames their Stubbornness and inflexible Obstinacy in this one Thing, that they would not invoke the Gods, nor do Homage with Frankincense and Wine before the Shrines of Deities, nor curse Christ, nor could they be compelled to do it by any Torments whatsoever. The Epistle in answer to that of *Trajan,* says, that He openly declares himself to be no Christian, who supplicates the *Roman* Gods. *Origen* in his IVth Book against *Celsus,* tells us, there was a certain History of Jesus extant in *Numenius* the *Pythagoraean.*

a. *It is also acknowledged,* &c.] Who call him תלוי, that is, hanged. *Benjaminis Tudelensis* in his *Itinerary,* acknowledges that *Jesus* was slain at *Jerusalem.*

b. *And a long Time after,* &c.] See *Epiphanius* in his *Tessarescadocatitae.* (It were better to have omitted this Argument, because some imprudent Christians might appeal to some spurious Acts; for it does not appear there was any genuine. *Le Clerc.*)

c. *Notwithstanding which,* &c.] *Chrysostom* handles this Matter at large, upon 2 *Cor.* V. 7.

which we find Him worshipped as Lord, throughout the most distant Countries of the World.

Sect. III. *And yet, after his Death, was worshipped by wise Men.*

And that, not only in our Age, or those immediately foregoing; but also even in the first, the Age next to that in which it was done, in the Reign of the Emperor *Nero;* at which time the forementioned *Tacitus,* and others attest, that very many were punished because they professed the Worship of Christ. <90>

Sect. IV. *The Cause of which could be no other, but those Miracles which were done by him.*

And there were always very many amongst the Worshippers of Christ, who were Men of good Judgment, and of no small Learning; such as (not to mention *Jews*) (*a*) *Sergius* the President of *Cyprus,* (*b*) *Dionysius* the Areopagite, (*c*) *Polycarp,* (*d*) *Justin,* (*e*) *Irenaeus,* (*f*) *Athenagoras,* (*g*) *Origen,* (*h*) *Tertullian,* (*i*) *Clemens Alexandrinus,* and others: Who being

a. Sergius *the President,* &c.] *Acts* XIII. 12.

b. Dionysius the *Areopagite,* &c.] *Acts* XVII. 34.

c. *Polycarp,* &c.] Who suffered Martyrdom in *Asia,* in the CLXIXth[1] Year of Christ, according to *Eusebius.*

1. 169th.

d. *Justin,* &c.] Who published Writings in Defence of the Christians, in the CXLIId[2] Year of Christ. See the same *Eusebius.*

2. 142nd.

e. *Irenaeus,* &c.] He flourished at *Lyons,* in the CLXXXIIId.[3] Year of Christ.

3. 183rd.

f. *Athenagoras,* &c.] This Man was an *Athenian.* He flourished about the CLXXXth[4] Year of Christ, as appears from the inscription of his Book.

4. 180th.

g. *Origen,* &c.] He flourished about the CCXXXth[5] Year of Christ.

5. 230th.

h. *Tertullian,* &c.] Who was famous in the CCVIIIth[6] Year of Christ.

6. 208th.

i. *Clemens Alexandrinus,* &c.] About the same time. See *Eusebius.*

such Men; why they should themselves be Worshippers of a Man that was put to an ignominious Death, especially when almost all of them were brought up in other Religions, and there was neither Honour nor Profit to be had by the Christian Religion: Why, I say, they should do thus, there can be no Reason given but this one, that upon a diligent enquiry, such as becomes prudent Men to make in a matter of the highest Concern to them, they found that the Report which was spread abroad concerning the Miracles that were done by him, was true, and founded upon suffi-cient Testi-<91>mony: Such as healing sore Diseases, and those of a long Continuance, only by a Word, and this publickly; restoring Sight to him that was born blind; increasing Bread for the feeding of many thousands, who were all Witnesses of it; restoring the Dead to Life again, and many other such like.

Sect. V. *Which Miracles cannot be ascribed to any Natural or Diabolical Power, but must be from God.*

Which Report had so certain and undoubted a Foundation, that neither (*a*) *Celsus,* nor (*b*) *Julian,* when they wrote against the Christians, dared to deny that some Miracles were done by Christ; (*c*) the *Hebrews* also con-fess it openly in the Books of the *Talmud.* That they were not performed by any natural Power, sufficiently appears from hence, that they are called Wonders or Miracles; nor can it ever be, that grievous Distempers should be healed immediately, only by a Word speaking, or a Touch, by the Power of Nature. If those Works could have been accounted for by any natural Efficacy, it would have been said so at first by those, who either professed themselves Enemies of Christ when he was upon Earth, or of his Gospel. By the like Argument we gather, that they were not juggling

a. *Celsus,* &c.] Whose Words, in Book II. of *Origen* are: "You think he is the Son of God, because he healed the Lame and the Blind."

b. *Julian,* &c.] Nay, he plainly confesses the thing, when he says in the Words re-cited by *Cyril,* Book VI. "Unless any one will reckon amongst the most difficult things, healing the Lame and the Blind, and casting out of Devils in *Bethsaida* and *Bethany.*"

c. *The Hebrews also,* &c.] In the Title *Abuda Zara.*

Tricks, because very many of the Works were done openly, (*a*) the People looking on; and <92> amongst the People many learned Men, who bore no good Will to Christ, who observed all his Works. To which we may add, that the like Works were often repeated, and the Effects were not of a short Continuance, but lasting. All which rightly considered, as it ought to be, it will plainly follow, according to the *Jews* own Confession, that these Works were done by some Power more than humane, that is, by some good or bad Spirit: That these Works were not the Effects of any bad Spirit, is from hence evident, that this Doctrine of Christ, for the Proof of which these Works were performed, was opposite to those evil Spirits: For it forbids the Worship of evil Spirits; it draws Men off from all Immorality, in which such Spirits delight. It appears also from the things themselves, that wherever this Doctrine has been received, the Worship of Daemons and (*b*) Magical Arts have ceased; and the one God has been worshipped, with an Abhorrence of Daemons; whose Strength and Power (*c*) *Porphyry* acknowledges were broken upon the coming of Christ. And it is not at all credible, that any evil Spirits should be so imprudent, as to do those things, and that very often, from which no Honour or Advantage could arise to them, but on the contrary, great Loss and Disgrace. Neither is it any way consistent with the Goodness or Wisdom of God, that he should be thought to suffer Men, who were free from all wicked Designs, and who feared him, to be de-<93>ceived by the Cunning of Devils; and such were the first Disciples of Christ, as is manifest from their unblameable Life, and their suffering very many Calamities for Conscience-sake. If any one should say, that these Works were done by good Beings, who yet are inferior to God; this is to confess, that they were well-pleasing to God, and redounded to his Honour; because good Beings do nothing but what is acceptable to God, and for his Glory. Not to mention, that some of the Works of Christ were such as seem to declare

a. *The People looking on,* &c.] *Acts* XXVI. 26. *Luke* XII.

b. *Magical Arts,* &c.] The Books about which, were burnt by the Advice of the Disciples of Christ, *Acts* XIX. 19.

c. Porphyry *acknowledges,* &c.] The Place is in *Eusebius's Praep.* Book V. Chap. 3. "After Christ was worshipped, no Body experienced any publick Benefit from the Gods."

God himself to be the Author of them, such as the raising more than one of those that were dead, to Life. Moreover, God neither does, nor suffers Miracles to be done, without a Reason; for it does not become a wise Lawgiver to depart from his Laws, without a Reason, and that a weighty one. Now no other Reason can be given, why these things were done, but that which is alledged by Christ, *viz.* (*a*) to give Credit to his Doctrine; nor could they who beheld them, conceive any other Reason in their Minds: Amongst whom, since there were many of a pious Disposition, as was said before, it would be prophane to think God should do them to impose upon such. And this was the sole Reason why many of the *Jews,* who lived near the time of Jesus, (*b*) who yet could <94> not be brought to depart from any thing of the Law given by *Moses,* (such as they who were called *Nazarens* and *Ebionites,*) nevertheless owned Jesus to be a Teacher sent from Heaven.

Sect. VI. *The Resurrection of Christ proved from credible Testimony.*

Christ's coming to Life again in a wonderful Manner, after his Crucifixion, Death and Burial, affords us no less good an Argument for those Miracles that were done by him. For the Christians of all times and places, assert this not only for a Truth, but as the principal Foundation of their

a. *To give Credit to his Doctrine,* &c.] We may add that the Event itself, in that so great a Part of Mankind embraced the Christian Religion, shows that it was a thing so worthy of God, as for him to confirm it with Miracles at the Beginning. If he did so many for the Sake of one Nation, and that no very great one, I mean, the *Jewish;* how much more agreeable to his Goodness was it, to bestow this heavenly Light, to so great a Part of Mankind, who laid in the thickest Darkness. *Le Clerc.*

b. *Who yet could not be brought,* &c.] See *Acts* XV. *Rom.* XIV. *Hieronymus* in the *Eusebian Chronicon,* for the Year of Christ CXXV,[7] after he had named fifteen Christian Bishops of *Jerusalem,* adds, "These were all Bishops of the Circumcision, who governed till the Destruction of *Jerusalem* under the Emperor *Adrian.*" *Severus Sulpitius,* concerning the Christians of those Times and Places, says, "They believed Christ to be God, whilst they observed also the Law; and the Church had a Priest out of those of the Circumcision." See *Epiphanius,* where he treats of the *Nazarens* and *Ebionites. Nazarens* was a Name not for any particular Part, but all the Christians in *Palestine* were so called, because their Master was a *Nazarene.*

7. 125.

Faith: Which could not be, unless they who first taught the Christian Faith, had fully persuaded their Hearers, that the thing did come to pass. Now they could not fully persuade Men of any Judgment of this, unless they affirmed themselves to be Eye-witnesses of it; for without such an Affirmation, no Man in his Senses would have believed them, especially at that time when such a Belief was attended with so many Evils and Dangers. That this was affirmed by them with great Constancy, their own Books, (*a*) and the Books <95> of others, tell us; nay, it appears from those Books, that they appealed to (*b*) five hundred Witnesses, who saw Jesus after he was risen from the Dead. Now it is not usual for those that speak Untruths, to appeal to so many Witnesses. Nor is it possible so many Men should agree to bear a false Testimony. And if there had been no other Witnesses, but those twelve known first Propagators of the Christian Doctrine, it had been sufficient. No Body has any ill Design for nothing. They could not hope for any Honour from saying what was not true, because all the Honours were in the Power of the Heathens and *Jews,* by whom they were reproached and contemptuously treated: Nor for Riches, because, on the contrary, this Profession was often attended with the Loss of their Goods, if they had any; and if it had been otherwise, yet the Gospel could not have been taught by them, but with the Neglect of their temporal Goods. Nor could any other Advantages of this Life provoke them to speak a Falsity, when the very preaching of the Gospel exposed them to Hardship, to Hunger and Thirst, to Stripes and Imprisonment. Fame amongst themselves only was not so great, that for the sake thereof, Men of upright Intentions, whose Lives and Tenets were free from Pride and Ambition, should undergo so many Evils. Nor had they any Ground to hope, that their Opinion, which was so repugnant to Nature, (which is wholly bent upon its own <96> Advantages,)

a. *And the Books of others,* &c.] Even of *Celsus,* who wrote against the Christians. See *Origen,* Book II.

b. *Five hundred Witnesses,* &c.] *Paul,* 1 *Cor.* XV. 6. He says, some of them were dead at that time, but their Children and Friends were alive, who might be hearkened to, and testify what they had heard. But the greater Part of them were alive when *Paul* wrote this. This Appearance was in a Mountain in *Galilee.*

and to the Authority which every where governed, could make so great a Progress, but from a Divine Promise. Further, they could not promise to themselves that this Fame, whatever it was, would be lasting, because, (God on purpose concealing] his Intention in this Matter from them) they expected that (*a*) the End of the whole World was just at hand, as is plain from their own Writings, and those of the Christians that came after them. It remains therefore, that they must be said to have uttered a Falsity, for the sake of defending their Religion; which, if we consider the thing aright, can never be said of them; for either they believed from their Heart that their Religion was true, or they did not believe it. If they had not believed it to have been the best, they would never have chosen it from all other Religions, which were more safe and honourable. Nay, though they believed it to be true, they would not have made Profession of it, unless they had believed such a Profession necessary; especially when they could easily foresee, and they quickly learnt by experience, that such a Profession would be attended with the Death of a vast Number; and they would have been guilty of the highest Wickedness, to have given such Occasion, without a just Reason. If they believed their Religion to be true, nay, that it was the best, and ought to be professed by all means, and this after the Death of their Master; it was impossible this should be, if their Master's Promise concerning his Resurrection had failed <97> them; (*b*) for this had been sufficient to any Man in his Senses to have overthrown that Belief which he had before entertained. Again, all Religion, but particularly the Christian Religion, forbids (*c*) Lying and False Witness, especially in Divine Matters: They could not therefore be moved to tell a Lye, out of Love to Religion, especially such a Religion. To all which may be added, that they were Men who led such a Life, as was not blamed even by their Adversaries; and who had no Objection made

a. *The End of the whole World,* &c.] See 1. *Thess.* IV. 15, 16. 1 *Cor.* XV. 52. *Tertullian* of having but one Wife: *Now the Time is very short.* Hieronymus *to* Gerontias: *What is that to us, upon whom the Ends of the World are come?*

b. *For this had been sufficient,* &c.] *Chrysostom* handles this Argument at large, upon 1 *Cor.* I. towards the end.

c. *Lying and false Witness,* &c.] *Matt.* XII. 36. *Joh.* VIII. 44, 55. *Eph* IV. 25 *Rom.* IX. 1. 2 *Cor.* VII. 19 XI. 31. *Gal.* I. 20. *Col.* III. 9. 1 *Tim.* I. 10. and II. 7. *Jam.* III. 14. *Matt.* XXII. 16. *Mark* XII. 14. *Luke* XX. 21. *John* XIV. 16. *Eph.* V. 9. and elsewhere.

against them, (*a*) but only their Simplicity, the Nature of which is the most distant that can be from forging a Lie. And there was none of them who did not undergo even the most grievous things, for their Profession of the Resurrection of Jesus. Many of them endured the most exquisite Death for this Testimony. Now, suppose it possible that any Man in his Wits could undergo such things for an Opinion he had entertained in his Mind; yet for a Falsity, and which is known to be a Falsity; that not only one Man, but very many, should be willing to endure such Hardships, is a thing plainly incredible. And that they were not mad, both their Lives and their Writings sufficiently testify. What has been said of these first, the same may also be said of *Paul,* (*b*) who openly declared that he saw <98> Christ reigning in Heaven, (*c*) and he did not want the Learning of the *Jews,* but had great Prospect of Honour, if he had trod in the Paths of his Fathers. But on the contrary, he thought it his Duty for this Profession, to expose himself to the Hatred of his Relations; and to undertake difficult, dangerous and troublesome Voyages all over the World, and at last to suffer an ignominious Death.

Sect. VII. *The Objection drawn from the seeming Impossibility of a Resurrection, answered.*

Indeed, no Body can withstand the Credibility of so many and so great Testimonies, without saying that a thing of this Nature is impossible to be, such as we say all things that imply a Contradiction are. (*d*) But this

a. *But only their Simplicity,* &c.] Even *Celsus.* See *Origen,* Book I.

b. *Who openly declared,* &c.] 1 *Cor.* XV. 9. 2 *Cor.* XII. 4. Add to this what *Luke* the Disciple of *Paul* writes, *Acts* IX. 4, 5, 6. and XXII. 6, 7, 8.

c. *And he did not want the Learning,* &c.] *Acts* XXII. 3. There were two *Gamaliels* famous amongst the *Hebrews,* on account of their Learning: *Paul* was the Disciple of one of them, who was very skilful not only in the Law, but also in those things that were delivered by the Doctors. See *Epiphanius.*

d. *But this cannot be said of it,* &c.] See the seventh Answer to the Objections, concerning the Resurrection, in the Works of *Justin* "An Impossibility in itself, is one thing; and an Impossibility in any Particular, is another; an Impossibility in itself is, that the Diagonal of a Square should be commensurate with the Side; a particular Impossibility is, that Nature should produce an Animal without Seed. To which of these two kinds of Impossibles do Unbelievers compare the Resurrection; if to the first, their cannot be said of it. It <99> might indeed, if any one should affirm, that the same Person was alive and dead at the same time: But that a dead Man should be restored to Life, by the Power of him who first gave Life to Man, (*a*) there is no Reason why this should be thought impossible. Neither did wise Men believe it to be impossible: For *Plato* relates it of (*b*) *Er* the *Armenian;* (*c*) *Heraclides Ponticus,* of a certain Woman; (*d*) *Herodotus,* of *Aristaeus;* and (*e*) *Plu-*<100>*tarch,* out of another; which, whether they were true or false, shows the Opinion of learned Men, concerning the Possibility of the thing.

Reasoning is false; for a new Creation is not like making the Diagonal commensurate with the Side; but they that rise again, rise by a new Creation. If they mean a particular Impossibility; surely all things are possible with God, though they may be impossible to any else." Concerning this Difference of Impossibilities, see the learned Notes of *Maimonides,* in his Guide to the Doubting, Part III. Chap. 15.

a. *There is no Reason why,* &c.] All those who are skilful in the true Philosophy, acknowledge that it is as hard to understand, how the *Foetus* is formed in the Mother's Womb, as how the Dead should be raised to Life. But ignorant Men are not at all surprised at the things which they commonly see, nor do they account them difficult, though they know not the Reason of them: But they think those things which they never saw, are impossible to be done, though they are not at all more difficult than those things they see every Day. *Le Clerc.*

b. Er *the* Armenian, *&c.*] The Place of *Plato* concerning this thing, is extant in his tenth Book of Republicks, transcribed by *Eusebius,* in his Gospel *Preparat.* Book XI. Chap. 35. The Report of which History, is in *Valerius Maximus,* Book I. Chap 8. the first foreign Example. In the Hortatory Discourse among the Works of *Justin;* in *Clemens, Strom.* V. in *Origen,* Book II. against *Celsus;* in *Plutarch Symposiac* IX. 5. and in *Macrobius* in the Beginning, upon *Scipio's* Dream.

c. *Heraclides Ponticus,* &c.] There was a Book of his *Concerning the Dead,* mentioned by *Diogenes Laertius* in his Preface, and in his *Empedocles;* and by *Galen,* in the VIth concerning the Parts that are affected. *Pliny* speaks thus of him, Book VII. Chap. 32. *That noble Volume of* Heraclides *amongst the* Greeks, *of a Woman's being restored to Life, after she had been dead seven Days.* And *Diogenes Laertius,* in the latter Place, assign her thirty Days.

d. *Herodotus,* &c.] In his *Melpomene.* See *Pliny's* Natural History, Book VII. Chap. 52. *Plutarch's Romulus,* and *Hesychius* concerning the Philosophers.

e. *Plutarch,* &c.] Of *Thespesius* Plutarch has this, in his Discourse of God's deferring Punishment. And *Antyllus,* concerning whom *Eusebius* has preserved that Place of *Plutarch,* from his first Book of the Soul, in his *Prepar.* Book XI. Chap. 38. and *Theodoret, Serm.* XI.

The Truth of Jesus's Doctrine proved from his Resurrection.

If it be not impossible that Christ should return to Life again, and if it be proved from sufficient Testimonies, such as convinced (*a*) *Bechai* a Teacher of the *Jews,* so far as to acknowledge the Truth of it; and Christ himself (as both his own Disciples and Strangers confess) declared a new Doctrine as by a Divine Command: it will certainly follow that this Doctrine is true; because it is repugnant to the Justice and Wisdom of God to bestow such Endowments upon him who had been guilty of a Falsity in a Matter of so great Moment. Especially when he had before his Death declared to his Disciples that he should die, and what Manner of Death; and that he should return to Life again; (*b*) and that these things should therefore come to pass, that they might confirm the Truth of his Doctrine.

Sect. VIII. *That the Christian Religion exceeds all others.*

These Arguments are drawn from Matters of Fact; we come now to those which are drawn from the Nature of the Doctrine. Certainly all manner of Worship of God must be rejected; (which can never enter into any Man's Mind, <101> who has any Sense of the Existence of God, and of his Government of the Creation; and who considers the Excellency of Man's Understanding, and the Power of chusing moral Good or Evil, with which he is endued, and consequently that the Cause, as of Reward, so of Punishment, is in himself;) or else he must receive this Religion, not only upon the Testimony of the Facts, which we have now treated of; but likewise for the sake of those Things that are intrinsical in Religion; since there cannot be Any produced, in any Age or Nation, whose Rewards are more excellent, or whose Precepts are more perfect, or the Method in which it was commanded to be propagated, more wonderful.

a. *Bechai,* &c.] It were to be wished that *Grotius* had quoted the Place; for though his Reasoning drawn from the Resurrection of Christ, does not want the Approbation of *R. Bechai,* yet perhaps the *Jews* might be affected with his Authority. *Le Clerc.*

b. *And that these things,* &c.] See *John* XVII. *Luke* XXIV. 46, 47.

Sect. IX. *The Excellency of the Reward proposed.*

To begin with the Reward, that is, with the End proposed to Man; because, as we are used to say, that which is the Last in Execution, is the First in Intention; (*a*) *Moses,* in his Institution of the *Jewish* Religion, if we regard the express Condition of the Law, made no Promises beyond the good Things of this Life; such as a fruitful Land, abundance of Riches, Victory over their Enemies, long Life and Health, and Hope of their Posterities surviving them. And if there be any thing more, it is only obscurely hinted, and must be collected from wise and strong Arguing; Which is the Reason why many who professed to follow the Law of *Moses* ((*b*) as the *Sadducees*) cast off all <102> Hope of enjoying any Good after this Life. The *Greeks,* who derived their Learning from the *Chaldeans* and *Egyptians,* and who had some Hope of another Life after this, (*c*) spoke very doubtfully concerning it, as is evident (*d*) from the Disputes of *Socrates,* and from the Writings of (*e*) *Tully,* (*f*) *Seneca,* (*g*) and others.

a. Moses, *In his Institution,* &c.] *Deut.* XI. and XXVIII. *Heb.* VIII. 6.

b. *As the* Sadducees, &c.] *Mat.* XXII. 23. *Luke* in *Acts* XXIII. 8. Josephus: "The Sadducees argue that the Soul perishes with the Body." And in another Place, "They deny the Soul's Immortality, and Rewards and Punishments in another Life." *Hieronymus* says of them, "That they believe the Soul perishes with the Body."

c. *Spoke very doubtfully,* &c.] This is observed by *Chrysostom,* on 1 *Cor.* Ch. 1. 25.

d. *From the Disputes of* Socrates, &c.] "In *Plato's Phaedon.* Now I would have you to understand, that I hope to go amongst good Men; but I will not be too positive in affirming it." And afterwards, "If those Things I am speaking of, should prove true, it is very well to be thus persuaded concerning them; but if there be nothing after Death, yet I shall always be the less concerned for the present Things of this Life; and this my Ignorance will not continue long (for that would be bad,) but will shortly vanish." And *Tertullian* concerning the Soul. "From such a firm Steddiness and Goodness of Mind, did that Wisdom of *Socrates* proceed, and not from any certain Discovery of the Truth." The same is observed of *Socrates,* in the Exhortation among the Works of *Justin.*

e. *Tully,* &c.] In his first *Tusculan* Question. "Shew me first, if you can, and it be not too troublesome, that Souls remain after Death; or if you cannot prove this, (for it is difficult,) declare how there is no Evil in Death." And a little after, "I know not what mighty Thing they have got by it, who teach, that when the Time of Death comes, they shall entirely *perish;* which if it should be, (for I don't say any thing to the contrary,) what Ground of Joy or Glorying does it afford." And again, "Now suppose the Soul should perish with the Body, can there be any Pain, or can there be any Sense at all in the Body after Death? No Body will say so." *Lactantius,* Book VII. Ch. 8. cites the

And tho' they searched <103> diligently for Arguments to prove it, they could offer nothing of Certainty. For those which they alledge, (*a*) hold generally as strong for Beasts as they do for Men. Which when some of them considered, it is no wonder, that they imagined that Souls (*b*) passed out of Men into Beasts, and out of Beasts into Men. Again, because this could not be proved by any Testimonies, nor by any certain Arguments, and yet it could not be denied but that there must be some End proposed for Man; therefore others were led to say, (*c*) that Virtue was its own Reward, and that a wise Man was very happy, though in *Phalaris's* Bull. But others disliked this, and not without Reason; for they saw very well, that Happiness, especially in the highest Degree (unless we regard only the Sound of Words, without any Meaning) could not (*d*) consist in that which is <104> attended with Danger, Loss, Torment, and Death: And therefore they placed the chief Good and End of Man, in sensual Pleasure. And this Opinion likewise was solidly confuted by very many, as a Thing which overthrew all Virtue, the Seeds of which are planted

---

following Passage out of the same *Cicero,* spoken after a Dispute about the Soul: *Which of these Opinions is True, God only knows.*

f. *Seneca,* &c.] Epistle LXIV. "And perhaps, (if the Report of wise Men be true, and any Place receives us,) that which we think perishes, is only sent before."

g. *And others,* &c.] *Justin Martyr* says in general, in his Dialogue with *Trypho:* "The Philosophers knew nothing of these Things, nor can they tell what the Soul is."

a. *Hold generally as strong for Beasts,* &c.] As, that Argument *of Socrates* to *Plato,* that *That which moves of itself is Eternal.* See *Lactantius* in the forementioned Place.

b. *Passed out of Men into Beasts,* &c.] As the *Brachmans* of old, and now also; From whom *Pythagoras* and his Scholars had it.

c. *That Virtue was its own Reward,* &c.] See *Tully's* IId *Tusc. Quaest.* And *Lactantius's* Institutions, Book III. Ch. 27. where He strenuously disputes against this Opinion; and *Augustin, Epist.* III.

d. *Consist in that,* &c.] *Lactantius.* Book III. Ch. 12. "Virtue is not its own Happiness, because the whole Power of it consists, as I said, in bearing Evils." And a little after, when he had quoted a Place of *Seneca's,* he adds: "But the *Stoicks,* whom he follows, deny that any one can be happy without Virtue. Therefore the Reward of Virtue is a happy Life; if Virtue, as is rightly said, makes Life happy. Virtue therefore is not to be desired for its own sake, as they affirm, but for the sake of a happy Life, which necessarily attends Virtue; Which Argument might instruct them what is the chief Good. But this present Bodily Life cannot be happy, because it is subject to Evils, by means of the Body." *Pliny,* in his Natural History, Book VII. Ch. 7. says well, *That no Mortal Man is happy.*

in the Mind; and degraded Man, who was made for nobler Purposes, to the Rank of Brute Creatures, who look no further than the Earth. In so many Doubts and Uncertainties did Mankind at that time wander, till Christ discovered the true Knowledge of their End, promising to his Disciples and Followers another Life after this, in which there should be no more Death, Pain, or Sorrow, but accompanied with the highest Joy; And this not only to one Part of Man, that is, his Soul, of whose Happiness after this Life there was some Hope, partly from Conjecture, and partly from Tradition; but also to the Body, and that very justly, that the Body which oftentimes ought to endure great Losses, Torments and Death, for the sake of the Divine Law, might not go without a Recompense. And the Joys which are promised, are not such mean Things (*a*) as those Feasts, which the duller *Jews* hoped for after this Life, (*b*) and the Embraces which the *Mahometans* promise to themselves; for these are only proper Remedies for the Mortality of this frail Life; the former for the Preservation of particular Animals, and the latter for the Continuance of their Species: But the Body will be in a perpetual Vigour, and its Brightness will exceed the Stars. The Mind will have a <105> Knowledge of God, and of Divine Providence, and of whatever is now hidden from it, without any Mistake: The Will will be calm, employed in Wonder and Praises, in beholding God; in a Word, all Things will be much greater and better, than can be conceived by comparing them with the greatest and best here.

Sect. X. *A Solution of the Objection, taken from hence, that the Bodies after their Dissolution cannot be restored.*

Besides the Objection which we have now answered, it is commonly alledged, that the Bodies of Men, after their Dissolution, cannot be restored to the same Frame again; but this is said without the least

---

a. *As those Feasts,* &c.] The Places are quoted beneath, in the Vth Book.
b. *And the Embraces,* &c.] See the *Alcoran Azoara,* II, V, XLVII, LIV, LXV, LXVI.

Foundation. (*a*) For most Philosophers agree, that tho' the Things be never so much changed, the Matter of them still remains capable of being formed into different Shapes; and who will affirm, that God does not know in what Places, tho' never so far distant, the Parts of that Matter are, which goes to the making up of a humane <106> Body? Or, that he has not Power to bring them back, and reunite them? And do the same in the Universe, that we see Chymists do in their Furnaces and Vessels, collect those Particles which are of the same Kind, tho' separated from one another. And there are Examples in Nature, which show, that though the Shape of Things be never so much changed, yet the Things themselves return to their original Form; as in Seeds of Trees and Plants. Neither is that Knot which is objected by so many, such as cannot be loosed; *viz.* concerning humane Bodies passing into Nourishment of wild Beasts and Cattle; who, after they are thus fed, are eaten again by Men. For the greatest Part of what is eaten by us, is not converted into any Part of our Body, but goes into Excrements or Superfluities, such as Spittle and Choler: And much of that which has Nourishment in it, is consumed by Diseases, internal Heat, and the ambient Air. Which being thus; God, who takes such Care of all Kinds even of dumb Creatures, may have such a particular Regard to humane Bodies, that if any Part of them should come to be Food for other Men, it should no more be converted into their Substance, than Poison or Physick is; and so much the rather, because human Flesh was not given to be Food for Men. And, if it were otherwise; and that something which does not belong to the latter Body, must be

---

a. *For most Philosophers agree,* &c.] If any one be not satisfied with this Account of *Grotius,* he may be answered, that it is not at all necessary, that the Matter which is Raised, should be Numerically the same with that which the Dying Man carried to the Grave with him: For he will be as much the same Man, though his Soul were joined to Matter which it was never before joined to, provided it be the same Soul; as a Decrepit Old Man is the same as he was when a Child crying in the Cradle, though perhaps there is not in the Old Man one Particle of that Matter there was in the Infant, by reason of the continual *Effluvia* which fly from the Body. It may very well be called *A Resurrection of the Body,* when a like one is formed by God out of the Earth, and joined to the Mind; therefore there is no need of reducing ourselves to so great Streights, in order to defend too stiffly the *Sameness* of the Matter. *Le Clerc.*

taken from it; this will not make it a different Body; (*a*) for there happens a <107> greater change of its Particles in this Life: (*b*) Nay, <108> a Butterfly is contained in a Worm; and the Substance of Herbs or of Wine, (*c*) in some very little Thing, from whence they are again restored to

a. *For there happens a greater Change,* &c.] See *Alfenus,* in *l. Proponebatur. D. de Officiis:* "If any one should think that by altering the Parts, any thing is made different from what it was before: according to such Reasoning, we ourselves should be different from what we were a Year since: Because, as Philosophers say, those small Parts of which we consist, continually fly off from our Bodies, and other Foreign ones come in their room." And *Seneca,* Epist. LVIII. "Our Bodies are in a continual Flux, like a River; all that we behold, runs away as Time does: None of those Things we see, are durable. I myself am changed, while I am speaking of their Change." See *Methodius's* excellent Dissertation upon this Subject, whose Words *Epiphanius* has preserved in his Confutation of the *Origenists,* Numb. XII, XIII, XVI, XV.

b. *Nay, a Butterfly,* &c.] See *Ovid* in the last Book of his *Metamorphosis.*

> Wild Moths (a Thing by Country Men observ'd)
> Betwixt the Leaves in tender Threads involv'd,
> Transform their Shape into a Butterfly.

We may add something out of *Pliny's* Natural History, Book X. Ch. 5. concerning Frogs: He says, "For half a Year of their Life, they are turned into Mud, and cannot be seen; and by the Waters in the Spring, those which were formerly bred, are bred again afresh." And in the same Book, ch. 9. "The Cuckow seems to be made of a Hawk, changing his Shape in the Time of Year." And Book XI. ch. 20. "There are who think, that some Creatures which are dead, if they be kept in the House in Winter, will come to Life again, after the Sun shines hot upon them in the Spring, and they be kept warm all Day in Wood Ashes." And again, ch. 23. speaking of Silk-Worms, "Another Original of them may be from a larger sort of Worm, which shoots forth a double Kind of Horns; these are called Canker-Worms, and afterwards become what they call the Humble Bee; from whence comes another sort of Insect, termed *Necydalus,* which in six Months Time turns into a Silk-Worm." And again, ch. 23. speaking of the Silk-Worm of *Coos,* he says, "They were first small and naked Butterflies." And ch. 26. Concerning the Grashopper: "It is first a small Worm, but afterwards comes out of what they call *Tettygometra,* whose Shell being broke, they fly away about Mid-summer." ch. 30. "Flies drowned in Liquor, if they be buried in Ashes, return to Life again." And Ch. 32. Many Insects are bred in another Manner. "And first the Horse-Fly, out of the Dew: In the Beginning of the Spring, it sticks to a Radish-Leaf, and being stiffned by the Sun, it gathers into the Bigness of a Millet. Out of this springs a small Worm, and in three Days after a Canker-Worm, which increases in a few Days, having a hard Shell about it, and moves at the touch of a Spider; this Canker-worm, which they call a Chrysalis, when the Shell is broken, flies away a Butter-Fly."

c. *In some very little Thing,* &c.] If *Grotius* had lived till our Days, he would have spoke more fully; since it is evident that all Animals of what ever kind, spring from an Egg, in which they are formed, as all Plants do from Seeds, tho' never so small. But this

their true Bigness. Certainly, since these, and many other such like Suppositions, may be made without any Absurdity; there is no Reason why the restoring of a Body, after it is dissolved, should be reckoned amongst the Things that are impossible: Especially since learned Men, (*a*) such as *Zoroaster* among the *Chaldaeans,* (*b*) almost all the Stoicks, <109> (*c*) and *Theopompus* among the Peripateticks, believed that it could be, and that it would be.

Sect. XI. *The exceeding Purity of its Precepts; with respect to the Worship of God.*

Another Thing, in which the Christian Religion exceeds all other Religions, that ever were, are, or can be imagined; is the exceeding Purity and Holiness of its Precepts, both in those Things which concern the Worship of God, and also in all other Particulars. The Rites of the Heathens, almost all over the World, were full of Cruelty; (*d*) as *Porphyry* has largely shown; and as we are convinced by those in our Age, who have sailed to

---

is nothing to the Resurrection, for Bodies will not rise again out of such Principles. *Le Clerc.*

a. *Such as* Zoroaster, &c.] See *Clemens,* Strom. V.

b. *Almost all the* Stoicks, &c.] Clemens, Strom. V. "He (*Heraclitus*) knew, having learnt it from the *Barbarian* Philosophy, that Men who lived Wickedly, should be purified by Fire, which the *Stoicks* call ἐκπύρωσον, whereby they imagine every one shall rise again such an One as he really is; thus they treat of the Resurrection." And *Origen,* Book IV. against *Celsus,* "The *Stoicks* say, that after a certain Period of Time, the Universe shall be burnt, and after that shall be a Renovation, in which all Things shall continue unchangeable." And afterwards: "They have not the Name of the Resurrection, but they have the Thing." *Origen* here adds the *Egyptians. Chrysippus* concerning Providence, quoted by *Lactantius,* Book VI. of his Institutions, has these Words, "Which being thus, there is evidently no Impossibility, but that we also, when we are dead, after a certain Period of Time is past, may be restored again to the same State in which we now are." He that is at leisure, may look into *Nathaniel Carpenter's* XVIth Exercise of free Philosophy.

c. *And* Theopompus, &c.] Concerning whom, see *Diogenes Laertius* in the Beginning of his Book. "And *Theopompus* in his VIIIth *Philippick* relates, as the Opinion of the Wise Men, that Men shall live again, and become Immortal, and every Thing shall continue what it is."

d. *As* Porphyry, &c.] In his Book prohibiting eating Living Creatures; whence *Cyril* took many Things, in his IVth against *Julian.*

those Places. For it is an established Principle, almost every where, that the Gods are to be pacified with humane Blood; which Custom neither the *Greek* Learning, nor the *Roman* Laws, abolished: As appears from what we read concerning (*a*) Sacrifices offered up to *Bacchus Omesta,* amongst the *Greeks;* concerning a *Grecian* Man and a *Grecian* Woman, and concerning (*b*) a Man and Wo-<110>man amongst the *Gauls,* that were sacrificed to *Jupiter Latialis.* And the most holy Mysteries both of *Ceres,* and of *Bacchus,* were full of Lewdness; as was plain, when once the Secrets of their Religion began to be publickly discovered; as is at large declared by (*c*) *Clemens Alexandrinus,* (*d*) and others. And there was such Sights shown upon those Days, that were consecrated to the Honour of their Gods; that (*e*) *Cato* was ashamed to be present at them. In the *Jewish Religion* indeed there was nothing unlawful or immoral; but to prevent that People, (*f*) who were prone to Idolatry, from re-<111>volting from the

a. *Sacrifices offered up to* Bacchus, &c.] *Plutarch* mentions them in his *Themistocles,* and also *Pausanias.* The like Rites of the *Messenians, Pellaeans, Lictyans* in *Crete, Lesbians, Phocaeensians,* you have in the Hortatory Discourse in *Clemens.*

b. *A Man and Woman amongst the* Gauls, &c.] *Dionysius Halicarnassensis* tells us in his Ist Book, that it was a very antient Custom in *Italy,* to sacrifice Men. How long it remained, *Pliny* says, Book XXVIII. Ch. 1. "Our Age hath seen in the Beast Market, a *Graecian* Man and Woman Slain, or those of some other Nation with whom they dealt." This Custom remained till *Justin's* and *Tatian's* Time: For *Justin* in his Ist Apologetick, addresses the *Romans* thus: "That Idol which you worship; to whom not only the Blood of irrational Creatures is poured out, but also Humane Blood; which Blood of Slain Men, is poured out by the most Noble and Eminent Person amongst you." *And* Tatian: *I find among the* Romans, *that* Jupiter Latialis *was delighted with Humane Blood; and with that which flows from Men that are slain.* Porphyry tells us that these Rites remained till *Adrian's* Time. That there was a very antient Custom amongst the *Gauls,* of offering Humane Sacrifices, we learn from *Tully's* Oration in Defence of M. *Fonteius;* and out of *Plutarch,* concerning Superstition. *Tiberius* abolished it, as we find in *Pliny,* Book XXX. Ch. 1. See the same *Pliny* there, concerning the *Britains,* and *Dion* in *Nero,* and *Solinus;* also *Hermoldus* concerning the *Sclavonians,* Book I. ch. 3. *Porphyry* in his second Book against eating Living Creatures, says that it remained till his Time in *Arcadia* in *Carthage,* and *in the great City,* that is *Rome,* where he instances in the Rite of *Jupiter Latialis.*

c. *Clemens Alexandrinus,* &c.] In his Hortatory Discourse.

d. *And others,* &c.] Especially *Arnobius.*

e. *That* Cato *was ashamed,* &c.] See *Martial* in the Beginning of his Epigrams. *Gellius* X. 13. and *Valerius Maximus,* Book XI. ch. 10.

f. *Who were prone to Idolatry,* &c.] This is the Reason given for such Precepts by *Maimonides,* whom *Josephus Albo* follows.

true Religion, it was burthened with many Precepts, concerning Things that were in themselves neither good nor bad: Such as the Sacrifices of Beasts, Circumcision, strict Rest on the Sabbath Day, and the forbidding many sorts of Meats; some of which the *Mahometans* have borrowed, and added to them a Prohibition of Wine. But the Christian Religion teaches us to worship God, who is a most holy Being, (*a*) with a pure Mind, (*b*) and with such Actions as are in their own Nature virtuous, if they had not been commanded. Thus it does not bid us to (*c*) circumcise our Flesh, but our Desires and Affections; not to abstain (*d*) from all sorts of Works, but only from all such as are unlawful: Not to offer the Blood and Fat of Beasts in Sacrifice to God; but, if there be a just Occasion, (*e*) to offer our own Blood for a Testimony of the Truth; And (*f*) whatever Share of our Goods we give to the Poor, we are to look upon as given to God: Not to forbear certain Kinds of Meat or Drink, (*g*) but to use both of them with such Temperance as may most secure our Health; (*h*) and sometimes by Fasting to render our Bodies more subservient to the Mind, that it may with more Freedom advance it self towards <112> higher Objects. But the chief Part of Religion is every where declared to consist in such (*i*) a godly Faith, by which we may be framed to such (*j*) a sincere Obedience, as to (*k*) trust wholly upon God, and have (*l*) a firm Belief of his Promises; (*m*) whence arises Hope, (*n*) and a true Love both of God and of our

a. *With a pure Mind,* &c.] *John* IV. 24.

b. *And with such Actions,* &c.] Whence it is called a reasonable Service, *Rom.* XII. 1. *Phil.* IV. 8.

c. *Circumcise our Flesh,* &c.] *Rom.* II. 28, 29. *Phil.* III. 3.

d. *From all sorts,* &c.] 1 *Cor.* V. 8.

e. *To offer our own Blood,* &c.] 1 *Cor.* X. 16. *Heb.* XII. 4. 1 *Pet.* II. 21.

f. *Whatever Share of our Goods,* &c.] *Matth.* VI. 4. *Luke* XII. 33. 2 *Cor.* IX. 7. *Heb.* III. 6.

g. *But to use both of them,* &c.] *Luke* XXI. 34. *Rom.* XIII. 13. *Eph.* V. 18. *Gal* V. 21. 1 *Tim.* V. 3. 1 *Pet.* IV. 3.

h. *And sometimes by Fasting,* &c.] *Mat.* VI. 18. XVII. 21, 1 *Cor.* VII. 5.

i. *A Godly Faith,* &c.] *John* XII. 44.

j. *A sincere Obedience,* &c.] *Luke* XI. 28. *John* XIII. 7. and the following Verses; 1 *Cor.* VII. 19. 1 *Pet.* I. 2.

k. *Trust wholly upon God,* &c.] *Mat.* XXI. 21. 2 *Tim.* I. 12.

l. *A firm Belief of his Promises,* &c.] *Rom.* IV. 20. 2 *Cor.* VII. 1. *Gal.* III. 29.

m. *Whence arises Hope,* &c.] *Heb.* VI. 2. *Rom.* VIII. 24. XV. 4.

n. *And a true Love both of God,* &c.] *Gal.* V. 6. 1 *Thes.* III. 6.

Neighbour, which causes Obedience to his Commands; (*a*) not a servile Obedience proceeding from the Fear of Punishment, (*b*) but because it is well-pleasing to him, (*c*) and because he is our Father, (*d*) and Rewarder, out of his exceeding Goodness towards us. (*e*) And we are commanded to pray, not to obtain Riches or Honours, and such other Things, which many have desired to their own Hurt; but, in the first Place, for such Things as are for the Glory of God; and so much only for our selves, of those <113> perishable things, as Nature requires, permitting the rest to Divine Providence; being contented, which way soever they happen: But for those things that lead to Eternity, we are to pray with all Earnestness, *viz.* for Pardon of our past Sins, and for the Assistance of the Spirit for the future; that being established firmly against all Threats and Temptations, we may continue on in a godly Course. This is the Worship of God required by the Christian Religion, than which certainly nothing can be conceived more worthy of him.

Sect. XII. *Concerning those Duties of Humanity, which we owe to our Neighbour, though he has injured us.*

The Duties towards our Neighbour, required of us, are also of the like sort. The *Mahometan* Religion, which was bred in Arms, breathes nothing else; and is propagated by such Means only. (*f*) Thus *Aristotle* takes

a. *Not a servile Obedience,* &c.] *Rom.* VIII. 15.

b. *But because it is well pleasing,* &c.] *Heb.* XII. 28.

c. *And because He is our Father,* &c.] *Rom.* VIII.

d. *And Rewarder,* &c.] *Colos.* III. 24. 2 *Thes.* I. 6. (To which we may add; that we can easily apprehend that his Precepts are most worthy of him, and so exactly suited to our Nature, that better or more agreeable cannot be conceived by any one; therefore we ought to render our selves Obedient to Him, out of a grateful Sense of his Commands, because they are the best and most excellent that can be; and this, though there were no Punishment to be inflicted on the Disobedient, beside the Baseness of the Fact it self, this is to Obey God like Sons; and not like Servants. *Le Clerc.*)

e. *And we are commanded to Pray,* &c.] *Mat.* VI. 10.

f. *Thus* Aristotle, &c.] "*Polit.* VII. Chap. 14. Like unto these are some who afterwards declared their Opinions in their Writings. For in praising the Government of the *Lacedaemonians,* they commend the Design of the Lawgiver, because the whole Establishment tended to Power and War: Which may easily be confuted by Reason, and is now confuted by Fact." *Euripides* in *Andromacha,* said it before *Aristotle.*

notice of, and blames the Laws of the *Laconians* (which were so highly commended above any other in *Greece,* even by the Oracle of *Apollo,*) because they tended directly to Force of Arms. But the same Philosopher affirms, that War against Barbarians was lawful; whereas the contrary is true amongst Men, who <114> were designed by Nature for Friendship and Society. (*a*) For what greater Iniquity can there be, than to punish single Murders; but expose to publick View, in their Triumphs, whole Nations they had slain, as a glorious Exploit? And yet that most celebrated City of *Rome,* how did it procure that Title, but by Wars, and those (*b*) many times very unjust; as they themselves confess concerning (*c*) the Wars against *Sardinia* (*d*) and *Cyprus?* And in general, as the most famous Compilers of Annals have related, very many Nations did not account it infamous, (*e*) to commit Robberies out of <115> their own Bounds.

> —— If War, and Glory,
> If the Sword, were from the *Spartans* taken,
> There's nothing excellent that would remain.

a. *For what greater Iniquity,* &c.] To this Purpose is the 96th Epistle of *Seneca,* and Book II. Chap. 8. concerning Anger; and the IId Epistle of *Cyprian.*

b. *Many times very unjust,* &c.]

> —— If any secret Holes,
> If any Land did shining Gold contain,
> They War proclaim.
>   Petronius.

c. *The Wars against* Sardinia, &c.] See *Polybius,* Hist. III.

d. *And* Cyprus, *&c.*] *Florus,* Book III. Chap. 9. "So great was the Report, and that very justly, of its Riches, that though they were a People that conquered Nations, and were accustomed to bestow Kingdoms, yet at the Instance of *Publius Clodius* the Tribune, it was given in Charge to confiscate the King, though alive, and their Ally." *Plutarch* mentions the same thing, in his Life of *Cato,* and *Appion,* Book II. of his Politicks; and *Dion,* Book XXXVIII. See the same *Florus,* in his War of *Numantia* and *Crete.*

e. *To commit Robberies,* &c.] Thucydides, Book I. "Formerly the *Greeks,* as well as the *Barbarians,* whether they lived on the Continent near the Sea-shore, or whether they inhabited the Islands, after they began to hold Correspondence with one another by Sailing, fell to robbing, led on by great Men, either for the sake of Gain to themselves, or to procure Victuals for them that wanted. And happening upon Cities which were not walled, but inhabited like Villages, they plundered them, and the greatest Part made their Advantage of them, being not ashamed as yet of doing thus, but rather accounting it glorious. This is evidently the Practice of some that dwell upon the Continent now, who account it honourable to do thus; and amongst the ancient Poets, it is

(*a*) Executing of Revenge, is by *Aristotle* and *Cicero,* made a Part of Virtue. (*b*) The Gladiators tearing one another to pieces, was one of the publick Entertainments amongst the Heathens; (*c*) and to expose their Children <116> was a daily Practice. The *Hebrews* indeed had a better Law, a more holy Discipline; but yet there were some things overlooked or allowed in that People, whose Passion was ungovernable; (*d*) such as the giving up to their Power seven Nations, though indeed they deserved it: With which they not being contented, (*e*) persecuted with cruel Hatred, all that differed from them; (*f*) the Marks of which remain even to this

---

very frequent for them who met Sailors, to ask them if they were Pirates; knowing that they who were so asked, would not disown it; nor they who asked them, think it any Reproach. Nay they robbed one another upon the very Continent; and a great many of the *Greeks* live now in this ancient manner, as the *Ozolan Locrians,* the *Aetolians,* the *Acarnanians,* and those of the adjoining Continent." The Question *Thucydides* here mentions, is in *Homer's Odysses* T'. Upon which the Scholiast says, "To plunder, was not accounted infamous, but glorious by the Ancients." *Justin,* Book XLIII. Chap. 3. concerning the *Phocensians. They were more diligent in occupying the Sea, than the Land, in Fishing, and Trading; and very often they spent their Lives in plundering,* (which at that time was looked upon as honourable.) Concerning the *Spaniards,* see *Plutarch* in *Marius;* and *Diodorus,* Book V. concerning the *Tyrrhenians. Servius* on the VIIIth and Xth *Aenead; Caesar, Tacitus,* and *Saxo Grammaticus,* concerning the *Germans.*

a. *Executing of Revenge,* &c.] *Aristotle's* Ethicks to *Nichomachus,* IV. II. *Such an one seems to be no ways affected or concerned, nor to revenge himself, unless provoked; but it shews a mean Spirit, to bear contemptuous Treatment.* And *Tully,* in his second Book of Invention, places Revenge amongst the Duties that belong to the Law of Nature: "Whereby either in our own Defence, or by Way of Revenge, we keep off Force or Reproach." And to *Atticus:* "I hate the Man, and will hate him: I wish I could revenge myself upon him." And against *Antony:* "I would revenge every single Crime, according to the Degree of Provocation in each."

b. *The Gladiators,* &c.] See *Lactantius,* Book II. and *Tertullian* concerning Shews, Ch. 19.

c. *And to expose their Children,* &c.] See *Justin's* IId Apologetick, Chap. 9. and *Lactantius's* Institution, Chap. 20, and *Terence's Hecyra.*

d. *Such as the giving,* &c.] *Exodus* XXXIV. 11, 12. *Deut.* VII. 1, 2.

e. *Persecuted with cruel Hatred,* &c.] *R. Levi Ben Gerson* tells us, they were to endeavour to injure them any manner of way. *Bechai* says, that what was taken from them by Theft, was not to be restored.

f. *The Marks of which,* &c.] See a little Book of Prayers put out at *Venice,* in a small Volume, *page* 8. and a *German* Book of *Antonius Margarita,* and *Maimonides* on the XIII Articles, where he says, they are to be destroyed, who do not believe them. And

Day, in their Prayers uttered against Christians: And the Law itself allowed a Man (*a*) to revenge an Injury by the Punishments of Retaliation, and that a Man-slayer might be killed by the private Hand of the next Relation. But the Law of Christ (*b*) forbids requiting any Injury that hath been done us, either by Word or Deed; lest by imitating that Malice we condemn in others, we should on the contrary approve it. It would have us do Good in the first Place, to those that are good; and then to the bad also, (*c*) after the Example of God, from whom we receive Gifts in common with all other Men; such as the Sun, the Stars, the Air, the Winds, and the Rain. <117>

Sect. XIII. *About the Conjunction of Male and Female.*

The Conjunction of Man and Woman, whereby Mankind is propagated, is a thing that highly deserves to be taken care of by Law; which that the Heathen neglected, is no wonder, when they relate (*d*) Stories of the

---

it is a frequent Saying in the Mouths of the *Jews: Let all Sectaries suddenly perish.* The like Saying we find in *R. Isaac's Bereschith Rabba,* and the *Talmud* in *Baba Kama,* and *Baba Bathra.*

a. *To revenge an Injury,* &c.] *Levit.* XXIV. 20. *Deut.* XIX. 21.
b. *Forbids requiting any Injury,* &c.] *Matt.* V. 38, 44.
c. *After the Example of God,* &c.] *Matt.* V. 45.
d. *Stories of the Whoredoms,* &c.] See *Euripides's Ione.*

    —— I can't forbear
The Lewdness of *Apollo* to reprove,
Who forces Virgins to his Nuptial Bed,
And murders his own Children privately:
Is this to practise Virtue you enjoin?
If Mortals sin, you Gods revenge the Wrong;
And is it just that you, who Laws prescribe
To all Mankind, should live by none yourselves?
Though it will never be, yet I must speak;
If *Phoebus, Neptune,* and the King of Gods,
Should punish all unlawful Marriages,
None would remain to worship at their Shrines.

See this Matter fully handled by *Clemens,* in his hortatory Discourse; by *Athanagoras, Tatian, Arnobius,* Book IV. *Nazianzen* in his Ist against *Julian,* and *Theodoret,* Discourse III.

Whoredoms and Adulteries of those Gods which they worshipped. And which is worse, (*a*) the Conjunction of Males with one another, is defended by the Examples of their Gods: In the Number of which, *Ganymedes* of old, (*b*) and *Antinous* afterwards were reckoned, upon this Account; which horrid Crime is also <118> often esteemed lawful amongst the *Mahometans, Chinese,* and other Nations. The *Greek* Philosophers seem to take great Pains (*c*) to put a virtuous Name upon a vicious thing. The most eminent of which same *Greek* Philosophers, (*d*) commending the Company of Women; what did they do else but turn a whole City into one common Stew, (*e*) when even Brute Creatures observe some sort of Conjugal League? How much more reasonable is it then, that Man, who is the most divine Creature, should not be born from an uncertain Original, whereby the mutual Affections betwixt Parents and <119> Children

a. *The Conjunction of Males,* &c.] See this also, in the forementioned Places of *Clemens* and *Theodoret.*

b. *And* Antinous *afterwards,* &c.] Mentioned by *Justin,* in his IId Apologetick; by *Clemens,* in his hortatory Discourse; by *Origen,* in his IId and VIIIth Books against *Celsus;* by *Eusebius,* in his Ecclesiastical History, IV. 8. by *Theodoret,* 8. and the Historians of those Times.

c. *To put a virtuous Name,* &c.] So indeed it was thought, not only by *Lucian,* in his little Book concerning Love; but by *Gregory Nazianzen,* Orat. III. against *Julian;* and by *Elias Cretensis,* and *Nonnus* upon him. And also by *Cyril,* in his VIth Book against *Julian;* and by *Theodoret,* very largely, in his XIIIth Book to the *Greeks.* I cannot omit a Place of *Philo's,* who had a great Opinion of *Plato,* out of his Book concerning a contemplative Life. "*Plato's* Feast is spent almost wholly upon Love, not only of Men running mad for the Women, and the Women for the Men; for such Desires may be satisfied by the Law of Nature, but of Men for Males, differing from them only in Age; and if any thing be speciously said concerning Love and heavenly *Venus,* those Names are used only for a Cover." *Tertullian* concerning the Soul, preferring the Christian Wisdom to that of *Socrates,* adds. "Not bringing in new *Daemons,* but driving out the old; not corrupting Youth, but instructing them in all the Goodness of Modesty."

d. *Commending the Company of Women,* &c.] See *Plato,* as in other Places, so more particularly in his IVth Republick.

e. *When even Brute Creatures,* &c.] See *Pliny,* Book X. Chap. 33. "The Actions of Doves are mightily taken notice of by these, upon the same Account; their Customs are the same, but the highest Degree of Modesty belongs specially to them; Adulteries are not known to either of them, they do not violate the Fidelity of Wedlock." Concerning the conjugal Chastity of Ring-Doves, see *Porphyry* in his IIId Book against eating living Creatures.

is destroyed? The *Hebrew* Law indeed forbad all Uncleanness, (*a*) but a Man was allowed to have more Wives than one at a time, and the Husband had a Power (*b*) to put away his Wife for any Cause whatsoever; which is the Custom at this Day among the *Mahometans:* And formerly the *Greeks* and *Latins* took so great a Liberty, that (*c*) the *Laconians* and *Cato* permitted others to have their Wives for a time. But the Law of Christ, which is most perfect, strikes at the very Root of Vice, and (*d*) accounts him guilty before God (who can see into and judge the Hearts of Men,) that lusts after, though he has not committed the Crime; or that attempts the Chastity of any Woman, or looks upon her with such Desires. And because all true Friendship is lasting, and not to be broke; he would, with very good Reason, have *That* to be so (*e*) which contains the Union of their Bodies, as well as the Agreement of their Minds; and which, without doubt, is more convenient for a right Education of their Children. Among the Heathen, some few Nations were content with one Wife, as the *Germans* and *Romans;* and in this they are (*f*) followed by the Christians: Namely, <120> that the Wife having resigned herself entirely to her Husband, may be (*g*) recompensed with a like Return;

---

a. *But a Man was allowed,* &c.] This appears from *Deut.* XVII. 16, 17. XXI. 15. 2 *Sam.* XII. 8. So the *Hebrews* understood the Law; and *Chrysostom* 1 *Cor.* XI. and *Augustine,* Book III. Chap. 12. concerning the Christian Doctrine; and others of the Ancients. *Josephus,* who best understood the Law, says in the XVth of his Antiquities, *It was the Custom of our Fathers to have many Wives.*

b. *To put away his Wife,* &c.] *Deut.* XXIV. 1, 2, 3, 4. *Levit.* XXI. 14.

c. *The* Laconians *and* Cato, &c.] See *Herodotus* Book VI. and *Plutarch* in his *Cato Uticensis,* and *Lycurgus.*

d. *Accounts him guilty before God,* &c.] *Matt.* V. 28.

e. *Which contains the Union,* &c.] *Matt.* V. 3. XIX. 9.

f. *Followed by the Christians,* &c.] *Paul* the Apostle, 1 *Cor.* VII. 4. *Lactantius's* Institutions VI. 23. *Hieronymus* against *Oceanus.*

g. *Recompensed with a like Return,* &c.] *Salust* well expresses it, in his *Jugurthine* War. "Amongst those that have many Wives, there is but little Affection, because the Mind is distracted with a Multitude, so as to have none for an intimate Companion; but they are all equally esteemed of no Value." *Ammianus* concerning the *Persians,* Book XXIII. *By means of various Lusts, divided Love groves faint.* And *Claudian,* in his *Gildonick* War.

——— They have a thousand Marriages,
For they regard no Ties, no sacred Pledge,
But their Affection is in Number lost.

(*a*) that the Government of the Family may be better managed by one Governor, and that different Mothers might not bring a Disturbance in amongst the Children.

Sect. XIV. *About the Use of temporal Goods.*

To come now to the Use of those things which are commonly called Goods; we find Theft allowed by some heathen Nations, (*b*) as the *Egyptians,* (*c*) and *Spartans;* and they who did not allow it in private Persons, did scarce any thing else in the publick; as the *Romans,* of whom the *Roman* Orator said, (*d*) if every one should have his Due restored to him, they must go back to the very Cottages. Indeed, there was no such thing amongst the *Hebrews;* but they were permitted (*e*) to take <121> Usury of Strangers, that the Law might in some Measure be fitted to their Disposition; and therefore, amongst other things, (*f*) it promised Riches to them that obeyed it. But the Christian Law not only forbids (*g*) all kind of Injustice towards any Persons; but also forbids us (*h*) setting our Affections upon perishing things; because our Mind is of such a Nature that it cannot diligently attend to the Care of two things, each of which requires the whole Man, and which oftentimes draw him contrary ways: And besides, (*i*) Sollicitousness in procuring and preserving Riches, is attended with a certain Slavery and Uneasiness, which spoils that very Pleasure which is expected from Riches; (*j*) but Nature is satisfied with a very few things, and those such as can easily be procured, without any great

a. *That the Government,* &c.] *Euripides* in his *Andromacha,* rightly apprehends and expresses them both.

b. *As the* Egyptians, &c.] See *Diodorus Siculus's* History, Book I.

c. *And* Spartans, &c.] See *Plutarch* in his *Lycurgus.*

d. *If every one should have,* &c.] *Lactantius,* in his Epitome, Chap. 1. cites the Words of *Tully* to this Purpose, out of his IIId Republick.

e. *To take Usury of Strangers,* &c.] *Deut.* XXIII. 19.

f. *It promised Riches,* &c.] *Levit.* XXVI. 5. *Deut* XXVIII. 4, 5, 6, 7, 8, 11, 12.

g. *All kind of Injustice,* &c.] *Matt.* VII. 12. *Ephes.* V. 3.

h. *Setting our Affections,* &c.] *Matt.* VI. 24. and the following Verses, XIII. 22. *Luke* VIII. 14. 1 *Tim.* VI. 9.

i. *Sollicitousness in procuring,* &c.] *Matt.* VI. 34. *Philip* IV. 6.

j. *But Nature is satisfied,* &c.] 1 *Tim.* VI. 7, 8.

Labour or Charge. And, if God has granted us something beyond this, we are not commanded to cast it into the Sea, (*a*) as some Philosophers imprudently did; nor to let it lie useless by us, nor yet to lavish it away: But out of it to supply the Wants of other Men, (*b*) either by giving (*c*) or lending to those that ask it; (*d*) as becomes those who believe themselves not to be Proprietors of these things, but only Stewards and Deputies of the Most High God their Parent; <122> for a Kindness well bestowed, (*e*) is a Treasure full of good Hope, against which neither the Wickedness of Thieves, nor Variety of Accidents, can prevail any thing. An admirable Example of which sincere and undissembled Charity, the first Christians afford us, when things were sent from so great a Distance as (*f*) *Macedonia* and *Achaia,* in order to supply the want of those in *Palaestine;* as if the whole World had been but one Family. And here this Caution is added also in the Law of Christ; (*g*) that no Hope of Recompence or Honour, ought to diminish from our Liberality; because, if we have regard to any thing else but God, (*h*) it takes away his Acceptance. And, lest any one should pretend, as is commonly done, to cloak his Sparingness, as if he were afraid he should want what he has, when he comes to be an old Man, or if any Misfortune should befal him; the Law promises, (*i*) that a particular Care shall be taken of those who keep these Precepts: And, that they may the more rely upon it, reminds them of (*j*) the remarkable Providence of God, in providing for wild Beasts and Cattle, in adorning Herbs and Flowers; and that it would be an unworthy thing in us, not to believe so good, so powerful a God, nor to trust him any further than we

a. *As some Philosophers,* &c.] *Laertius* and *Suidas* affirm this of *Aristippus,* and *Philostratus* of *Crates.*

b. *Either by giving,* &c.] *Matt.* V. 42.

c. *Or lending,* &c.] In the same *Matt. Luke* VI. 35.

d. *As becomes those,* &c.] 1 *Tim.* VI, 17, 18.

e. *Is a Treasure,* &c.] *Matt.* VI. 20.

f. *Macedonia* and *Achaia,* &c.] *Rom.* XV. 25, 26. and the following Verses. 2 *Cor.* IX. 1, 2, 3, 4. *Philip* IV. 18.

g. *That no Hope of Recompense,* &c.] *Matt.* VI. 1, 2. *Luke* XIV. 12.

h. *It takes away his Acceptance,* &c.] See the forecited Place in *Matt.*

i. *That a particular Care,* &c.] *Matt.* VI. 32. *Luke* XII. 7. XXI. 8.

j. *The remarkable Providence of God,* &c.] *Matt.* VI. 26, 28.

would do a bad Debtor, of whom we never think ourselves secure without a Pledge. <123>

Sect. XV. *Concerning Oaths.*

Other Laws forbid Perjury; (*a*) but this would have us entirely to abstain from Oaths, except upon Necessity; and to have so great Regard to Truth in our common Conversation, (*b*) that there should be no need of requiring an Oath of us.

Sect. XVI. *Concerning other Actions.*

And indeed there is nothing excellent to be found in the Philosophick Writings of the *Greeks,* or in the Opinions of the *Hebrews,* or of any other Nation, which is not contained here, and moreover ratified by divine Authority. For instance; concerning (*c*) Modesty, (*d*) Temperance, (*e*) Goodness, (*f*) Moral Virtue, (*g*) Prudence, (*h*) the Duty of Governors and Subjects, (*i*) Parents and Children, (*j*) Masters and Servants, (*k*) Husbands and Wives; and particularly, abstaining from those Vices, which under a Shew of Virtue deceived many of the *Greeks* and *Romans,* viz. (*l*) the De-<124>sire of Honour and Glory. The Sum of it, is wonderful

a. *But this would have us,* &c.] *Matt.* V. 33, 34, 35, 36, 37. *Jam.* V. 12.
b. *That there should be no need,* &c.] See the forementioned Place of *Matth.*
c. *Modesty,* &c.] 1 *Pet.* III. 3.
d. *Temperance,* &c.] *Tit.* II. 12. 1 *Tim.* II. 19.
e. *Goodness,* &c.] 2 *Cor.* VI. 6. *Gal.* V. 22. *Colos.* III. 12. 1 *Cor.* XIII. 4.
f. *Moral Virtue,* &c.] *Phil.* IV. 8. 1 *Tim.* II. 2. III. 4. *Tit.* II. 7.
g. *Prudence,* &c.] *Matt.* X. 16. *Ephes.* I. 8.
h. *The Duty of Governors,* &c.] 1 *Tim.* II. 2. *Rom.* XIII. 1 *Pet.* II. 13, 17.
i. *Parents and Children,* &c.] *Colos.* III. 20, 21. *Ephes.* VI. 1, 2, 3, 4.
j. *Masters and Servants,* &c.] *Ephes.* VI. 5, 6, 7, 8, 9, 10. *Colos.* III. 22, 23, 24, 25.
k. *Husbands and Wives,* &c.] *Ephes.* V. 22, 23, 24, 25, 28, 33. *Colos.* III. 18, 19. 1 *Tim.* II. 2.
l. *The Desire of Honour,* &c.] *Matt.* XVIII. 4. XXIII. 12. *Luke* XIV. 11. XVIII. 14. *John* V. 44. *Ephes.* IV. 2. *Colos.* II. 18. III. 23. 1 *John* II. 16. *Phil.* II. 3. 1 *Thess.* II. 6. 1 *Pet.* I. 24. V. 5.

for its substantial Brevity; (*a*) that we should love God above all things, and our Neighbour as ourselves, that is, (*b*) we should do to others, as we would have them do to us. Perhaps some may object against what we have now said of the Excellency of Christ's Commands; the great Difference of Opinions amongst Christians, from whence have arisen so many various Sects.

Sect. XVII. *An Answer to the Objection, drawn from the many Controversies amongst Christians.*

But the Answer to this is evident: There are scarce any Arts but the same thing happens to them, partly through the Weakness of human Nature, and partly because Men's Judgment is hindered by Prejudices: But for the most part, this Variety of Opinions is limited within certain Bounds, in which Men are agreed; and whereby they determine Doubts: As in the Mathematicks, it is a Dispute whether the Circle can be squared or no; but whether, if you take Equals from Equals, the Remainder will be equal, this admits of no Dispute: And thus it is in natural Philosophy, Physick, and other Arts. So the Difference of Opinions that is amongst Christians, cannot hinder their Agreement in the principal things, that is, (*c*) those <125> Commands, by which we have now recommended the Christian Religion: And the Certainty of these appears from hence, that those who being highly enraged against one another, have sought for Matter of Disagreement, never ventured to go so far as to deny, that these were the Precepts of Christ; no, not even they who would not direct their Lives according to this Rule. And if any should attempt to contradict

---

a. *That we should love God,* &c.] *Matt.* IX. 18. XXII. 37, 39. *Luke* X. 27. *Rom.* XIII. 9, 10, 11. *Gal.* V. 14. *James* II. 8.

b. *We should do to others,* &c.] *Matt.* VII. 12. *Luke* VI. 31. This was commanded by the Emperor *Alexander;* see *Dion,* and he that wrote the Life of this Emperor in *Latin.*

c. *Those Commands,* &c.] We may add also in those Opinions that are necessary, and upon which the Observation of Commands depends, such as are mentioned in the most ancient Creeds which are extant in *Irenaeus* and *Tertullian,* and what we now call the *Apostles Creed,* as I have somewhat more fully shown in that little Piece annexed hereto, concerning the Choice of our Opinion, *&c. Sect.* IV. *Le Clerc.*

these, he ought to be looked upon to be like those Philosophers who denied that Snow was white. For as These were confuted by their Senses, so are They by the Consent of all Christian Nations, and by those Books which were wrote by the first Christians, and those after them, who were followed by Learned Men, and such who bore Testimony to the Faith of Christ by their Death. For that which all these acknowledge to be the Doctrine of Christ, ought to be accounted so by all fair and equal Judges; for the same Reason that we believe *Plato, Xenophon,* and other Disciples of *Socrates,* concerning the Opinions of *Socrates;* and the Schools of the Stoicks, for what *Zeno* delivered.

Sect. XVIII. *The Excellency of the Christian Religion, further proved from the Excellency of its Teacher.*

The third Thing wherein we said the Christian Religion exceeds all other Religions that are, or can be imagined, in the Manner in which it was delivered and propagated: In the Consideration of which Particular, the first Thing that offers it self, <126> is the Author of this Doctrine. The Authors of the *Graecian* Wisdom and Knowledge, themselves confessed that they alledged scarce any Thing for Certainty, because Truth was sunk, as it were, (*a*) to the Bottom of a Well; (*b*) and the Mind, as dim-sighted in regard to Divine Things, as the Eyes of an Owl in the Sun-shine. Beside, there was hardly any of them but was addicted to (*c*) some particular Vice: Some were (*d*) Flatterers of Princes, others devoted to (*e*)

---

a. *To the Bottom of a Well,* &c.] It was a Saying of *Democritus, That Truth laid at the Bottom of a Well,* as we find in *Tully's* Academical Questions, and in other Writers.

b. *And the Mind as dim-sighted,* &c.] See *Aristotle's* Metaphysicks, Book II. ch. 1. "As the Eyes of a Batt are dazled at the Light in the Day-time; so is the Understanding in our Soul, confounded at the plainest Things in the World."

c. *Some particular Vice,* &c.] *Socrates* is most commended by the Consent of all; yet *Cyril* in his VIth Book against *Julian,* sets before us, in the Words of *Porphyry,* the great degree of Anger he discovered in his Words and Sayings.

d. *Flatterers of Princes,* &c.] *Plato* and *Aristippus.*

e. *The Embraces of Harlots,* &c.] *Zeno* the chief of the *Stoicks,* was addicted to the Love of Men; and *Plato, Aristotle, Epicurus, Aristippus,* and almost all of them to the Love of Women; witness *Athenaeus's* Books, III and XIII. *Laertius* and *Lactantius. Theognis* mentions it of himself in many Places.

the Embraces of Harlots, others to (*a*) snarling Impudence; and one great Argument of the Envy and Hatred they all had against one another, is their (*b*) quarrelling about <127> Words, or Things of no Moment; and as good an Argument of their Coldness and Indifferency in the Worship of God, did yet lay him aside, and paid Divine Worship to others whom they believed to be no Gods; (*c*) making that the Rule of their Religion, which was publickly received. And, as for the Reward of Piety, they could affirm nothing for certain; as appears from (*d*) the last Dispute of *Socrates* a little before his Death. *Mahomet,* the Author of that Religion, which has

a. *To snarling Impudence,* &c.] Whence they were called *Cynicks.*
b. *Quarrelling about Words,* &c.] This is well observed by *Timon Phliasius.*

> O wretched Mortals, nought but Sin and Flesh,
> Always deceived with Words and fierce Contests;
> Vain Men, like empty Bladders, puff'd with Wind.

And again,

> Sharp Contest walks about with mighty Noise,
> Sister of Mortal Hatred and Confusion;
> 'Till wandring to and fro, at last She fix
> Her self in Humane Breasts, and raise their Hopes.

And again,

> Who has inflamed them with such deadly Strife?
> The Noisy Multitude, who Silence hate,
> From whom the Plague of Tattle has its Rise.

You will find these Verses in *Clemens, Strom.* V. in *Eusebius* at the end of his Preparation, and in *Theodoret*'s IId Discourse.

c. *Making that the Rule,* &c.] *Xenophon* in his VIth *Memorab.* recites the Oracle by which the Gods are commanded to be worshipped according to the Laws of every City. Here we may repeat the Words of *Seneca,* before quoted out of *Augustine;* after which *Augustine* adds these: *He worshipped that which he blamed; he did that which he condemned, and that which he found Fault with, he paid Adoration to.* According to what *Plato* says in his *Timaeus,* and other Places; and *Porphyry* in that Place of *Eusebius*'s *Preparat.* Book IV. ch. 8. that it is dangerous to speak the Truth in Divine Matters before the Vulgar. The Fear of which Danger, both in the *Greek* and *Latin,* and *Barbarian* Philosophers, prevailed over the sincere Profession of the Truth; which Thing alone, is sufficient to hinder any one from thinking that such Men were to be followed in every Thing. *Justin Martyr,* in his Exhortation to the *Greeks,* observes this of *Plato.*

d. *The last Dispute of* Socrates, &c.] See what we have before quoted concerning him.

spread itself so far, (*a*) abandoned himself to Lust <128> all his Life long, which his Friends themselves do not deny. Neither did he give any Assurance whereby it might appear, that those Rewards he promised, which consisted in Feasts and Women, would ever really be; since they do not pretend to say, that he is restored to Life again in his Body; so far from that, that it now lies buried in *Medina*. But *Moses,* the *Hebrew* Lawgiver, was an excellent Person, however not entirely free from Faults; for with great Reluctance he would scarce (*b*) undertake an Embassy to the king of *Egypt,* though at the Command of God; and he discovered some (*c*) Distrust of God's Promise concerning striking Water out of the Rock, as the *Hebrews* acknowledge. And he partook of scarce any of those Rewards which he promised to his People by the Law, (*d*) being driven to and fro in Desart Places by continual Tumults, (*e*) and never entering the happy Land. But Christ is described by his Disciples, (*f*) to be without any manner of Sin: (*g*) nor could he ever be proved to have committed any, by the Testimonies of others: And whatever he commanded others, (*h*) he performed himself; <129> for he faithfully fulfilled all Things that God commanded him; (*i*) he was most sincere in the whole Course of his Life; he was the (*j*) most patient of Injuries and Torments, as is evident from his Punishment on the Cross; he was so great a Lover of Mankind, of his Enemies, even of those by whom he was led to Death, (*k*) that he prayed to God for them. And the Reward that he promised to his Followers,

a. *Abandoned himself to Lust,* &c.] See what is said in the VIth Book.

b. *Undertake an Embassy,* &c.] *Exodus* IV. 2, 10, 13, 14.

c. *Distrust of God's Promise,* &c.] *Numb.* XX. 12.

d. *Being driven to and fro,* &c.] *Exodus* XXII. *Numb.* XI. XII. XIV. XVI. XX. XXV.

e. *And never entering the happy Land,* &c.] *Numb.* XX. 12. *Deut.* XXXIV. 4.

f. *To be without any manner of Sin,* &c.] *John* VIII. 46. X. 32. 2 *Cor.* V. 21. 1 *Pet.* II. 22. *Heb.* IV. That his Piety was commended by the Oracle among the Gentiles, we shall show in the VIth Book.

g. *Nor could he ever be proved,* &c.] *Origen* observes this in his IIId Book against *Celsus.*

h. *He performed himself,* &c.] *Lactantius* in the end of his Institutions well observes: *That he not only showed the Way, but walked before in it, lest any one should dread the Path of Virtue on the account of its Difficulty.*

i. *He was most sincere,* &c.] 1 *Pet.* II. 22.

j. *Most patient of Injuries,* &c.] *Mat.* XXVI. 50, 52. *John* VIII. 23. *Acts* VIII. 32.

k. *That he prayed to God for them,* &c.] *Luke* XXIII. 34.

he was possessed of himself, in a most eminent manner; as is declared and proved by certain Testimony. (*a*) Many saw, heard, and handled him after he was returned to Life again: (*b*) He was taken up into Heaven in the Sight of Twelve; And that he there obtained the highest Power, is manifest from hence; that he endued his Disciples with a (*c*) Power to speak those Languages which they had never learned; and (*d*) with other miraculous Gifts (*e*) as he promised them, when he departed from them: All which <130> put together show, that there is no reason to doubt of his Faithfulness, or of his Power to recompense us with that Reward he has promised. And hence it is we collect, that this Religion exceeds all others in this Particular also; that the Author of it performed himself, what he commanded; and was possessed of what he promised.

From the wonderful Propagation of this Religion.

We come now to the Effects of the Doctrine by him delivered; which indeed, if rightly considered, are such, that if God has any Regard or Care of humane Affairs, this Doctrine cannot possibly but be thought Divine. It was agreeable to Divine Providence, to cause That to spread the furthest which is in it self best. And this has happened to the Christian Religion, which, we our selves see, is taught all over *Europe;* (*f*) even the further Corners of the *North* not exempted; (*g*) and no less throughout,

a. *Many saw, heard, and handled him,* &c.] *John* XX. 27, 28, 29. *John* I. *Epist.* I. *Mat.* XXVII. *Mark* XVI. *Luke* XXIV. 1 *Cor.* XV. 3, 4, 5, 6, 7, 8.

b. *He was taken up into Heaven,* &c.] *Mark* XVI. 19. *Luke* XXIV. 51, 52. *Acts* I. 9, 10, 11. also *Acts* VII. 55. IX. 3, 4, 5. XXII. 6. 1 *Cor.* XV. 8.

c. *A Power to speak those Languages,* &c.] *Acts* II. 3, 4. X. 46. XX. 6. 1 *Cor.* XII. 10, 28, 30. XIII. 1, 8. XIV. 2, 4, 5, 6, 9, 13, 14, 18, 19–22, 23, 27, 39.

d. *And with other Miraculous Gifts,* &c.] *Acts* III. V. III. IX. X. XI. XIII. XIV. XVI. XIX. XX. XXI. XXXVII. *Rom.* XV. 19. 2 *Cor.* XII. 12. *Heb.* II. 4. The Truth hereof is shown by *Justin* in his Dispute with *Trypho;* by *Irenaeus,* Book II. by *Tertullian,* in his Apology; by *Origen,* in his VIIth Book against *Celsus;* by *Lactantius* and others.

e. *As he promised them,* &c.] *John* XIV. 12. XVII. 21. *Mark* XVI. 17.

f. *Even the further Corners of the North,* &c.] See *Adam Bremensis* and *Helmoldus,* and the Writers concerning *Iceland.*

g. *And no less throughout all* Asia, &c.] See the Acts of the general Councils.

all *Asia,* (*a*) even in the Islands in the Sea belonging to it, (*b*) thro' *Egypt*
also (*c*) and *Ethiopia,* (*d*) and some other Parts of *Africa,* (*e*) and at last
through *America.* Nor is this done <131> now only, but was so of old, as
the History of all Ages testify, the Books of the Christians, and the Acts
of Synods; and at this Day there is a Tradition preserved amongst the *Barbarians,* (*f*) of the Journies and Miracles of *Thomas* (*g*) and *Andrew,* and the
other Apostles. And (*h*) *Clemens,* (*i*) *Tertullian,* <132> (*j*) and others have

a. *Even the Islands in the Sea,* &c.] See *Osorius* in his Lusitanicks.

b. *Through* Egypt *also,* &c.] This appears from the Acts of the General Councils;
from the antient Ecclesiastical Histories, and particularly *Eusebius,* VI. 34. out of the
Coptick Liturgy.

c. *And* Ethiopia, &c.] See *Franciscus Alvaresius.*

d. *And some other Parts of* Africa, &c.] See *Tertullian, Cyprian, Augustin,* and the
Acts of the *African* Councils; especially that Council, which is subjoined to the Works
of *Cyprian.*

e. *And at last through* America, &c.] See *Acosta* and others who have wrote about
the Affairs of *America.*

f. *Of the Journies and Miracles of* Thomas, &c.] See *Abdias,* Book IX. *Eusebius's*
Ecclesiastical History, Book I. towards the end; and Book II. ch. 1. and the beginning
of Book III. *Ruffinus,* Book X. ch. 9. Add to these, *Osorius* and *Linschotius,* concerning
the Affairs of *East-India;* and *Freita* concerning the Empire of the *Lusitanians* in *Asia:*
The Sepulchre of this Apostle is now to be seen in the Country of *Coromandel.*

g. *And Andrew,* &c.] See *Eusebius* in the Beginning of his forementioned IIId Book,
and *Origen* upon *Genesis.*

h. *Clemens,* &c.] He says, *Strom.* V. That Christ was known in all Nations.

i. *Tertullian,* &c.] In his Ist Book against the *Jews.* "In whom else have all Nations
believed, but in Christ, who lately came? In whom have all these Nations believed,
Parthians, Medes, Elamites, and the Dwellers in *Mesopotamia, Armenia, Phrygia, Cappadocia;* the Inhabitants of *Pontus* and *Asia,* and *Pamphylia;* they that dwell in *Egypt,* and
they who live in the Country of *Africa,* beyond *Cyrene; Romans* and Strangers; *Jews* and
other Nations in *Jerusalem;* the different sorts of People in *Getulia;* the many Countries
of the *Moors;* all the Borders of *Spain;* the different Nations of *Gaul;* and those Places
of *Britain,* which the *Romans* could not come at, are yet subject to Christ; the *Sarma-
tae,* and *Daeci,* and *Germans* and *Scythians;* and many other obscure Nations, and many
Provinces and Islands unknown to us, so many that they cannot be reckoned? in all
which Places, the Name of Christ, who lately came, reigns." Presently after, he shews
how much larger the Kingdom of Christ was in his Time, that is, the end of the second
Century, than those of Old. *Nebuchadnezzar's, Alexander's,* or the *Romans:* "The Kingdom of Christ overspreads all Places, is received every where, in all the above-named
Nations (he had mentioned the *Babylonians, Parthians, Indians, Ethiopia, Asia, Germany, Britain,* the *Moors, Getulians* and *Romans*) it is in great Esteem: He reigns every
where, is adored in all Places, is divided equally amongst them all."

j. *And others,* &c.] *Irenaeus,* who was ancienter than *Tertullian,* Book I. Chap. 3.
"For though there be different Languages, the Power of Tradition is the same; neither

the Churches founded in *Germany*, have any other Belief, or any other Tradition: Nor yet those in *Iberia*, nor those among the *Celtae*, nor those which are in the *East*, nor those in *Egypt*, nor those in *Lybia*, nor those that are established in the Middle of the World: But like the Sun which God created, and is one and the same throughout the whole World: So the Light, the preaching of the Truth, shines every where, and enlightens all Men, who are willing to come to the Knowledge of the Truth." And *Origen's* Homily upon the IVth of *Ezekiel.* "The miserable *Jews* confess that these things were foretold of the Presence of Christ; but they are foolishly ignorant of his Person, though they see what is said of him fulfilled; for when did the *British* Land, before the coming of Christ, agree in the Worship of one God? When did the Country of the *Moors*, when did the whole World together do so?" And *Arnobius*, Book II. "The Powers which they saw with their Eyes, and those unheard-of Effects which were openly produced, either by him, or which were proclaimed by his Disciples throughout the whole World, subdued those violent Appetites, and caused Nations and People, and those whose Manners were very different, to consent with one Mind to the same Belief; For we might enumerate, and take into our Account, those things which were done in *India* among the *Serae, Persians* and *Medes*, in *Arabia, Egypt*, in *Asia, Syria*, among the *Galatians, Parthians, Phrygians*, in *Achaia, Macedonia, Epirus;* in those Islands and Provinces surveyed by the East and Western Sun; and lastly in *Rome*, the Mistress of the World." And *Athanasius*, in his Synodical Epistle, which we find in *Theodoret*, Book IV. Chap. 3. mentions the Christian Churches in *Spain, Britain, Gaul, Italy, Dalmatia, Mysia, Macedonia, Greece, Africa, Sardinia, Cyprus, Crete, Pamphylia, Lysia, Isauria, Egypt, Lybia, Pontus* and *Cappadocia*. And *Theodoret* in his VIIIth Discourse against the *Greeks*, speaks thus concerning the Apostles: "When they were conversant in the Body, they went about sometimes to one sort, and sometimes to another; sometimes they discoursed to the *Romans*, sometimes to the *Spaniards*, and sometimes to the *Celtans;* but after they returned to him that sent them, all enjoyed their Labours without exception; not only the *Romans*, and they that loved the *Roman* Yoke, and were subject to their Government, but also the *Persians*, and *Scythians*, and *Massegatae*, and *Sauromatae*, and *Indians*, and *Ethiopians;* and to speak in one Word, the Borders of the whole World." And again in his IXth Book, amongst the converted Nations, he reckons the *Persians*, the *Massagetae*, the *Tibareni*, the *Hyrcani*, the *Caspians* and *Scythians*. *Hieronymus* in the Epitaph of *Nepotian*, reckons among the Christians, the *Indians, Persians, Goths, Egyptians, Bessians*, and the People clothed with Skins: In his Epistle to *Laeta*, he reckons up the *Indians, Persians, Aethiopians, Armenians, Hunns, Scythians* and *Getans:* And in his Dialogue between an Orthodox Man and a *Luciferian*, he mentions the *Britains, Gauls*, the East, the People of *India*, the *Iberians*, the *Celtiberians*, and the *Aethiopians*. And *Chrysostom* in his VIth Homily upon 1 *Cor.* says, "If they were not worthy to be believed in what they said, how should their Writings have spread all over barbarous Countries, even to the *Indians*, and those Countries beyond the Sea?" And again, in his last Homily upon Pentecost. "The Holy Spirit descended in the Shape of Tongues, divided its Doctrine among the several Climates of the World; and by this Gift of Tongues as it were by a particular Commission, made known to every one the Limits of that Command and Doctrine that was committed to him." And again in his famous Oration, concerning Christ's being God: "We must say then, that a mere Man, could not in so short time have overspread the World, both Sea and Land; nor have so observed, how far the Name <133> of Christ was famous in their times amongst the *Britains, Germans,* and other distant Nations. What Religion is there that can compare with it, for the Extent of its Possession? If you answer, Heathenism: That indeed has but one Name, but is not one Religion: For they do not all worship the same thing; for some worship the Stars, others <134> the Elements, others Beasts, others things that have no Existence; neither are they governed by the same Law, nor under one common Master. The *Jews* indeed, though very much scattered, are but one Nation; however, their Religion has received no remarkable Increase since Christ: Nay, their own Law is made more known by the Christians than by themselves. Mahometanism is settled in very many Countries, but not alone; for the Christian Religion is cultivated in those same Countries, and in some Places by a greater Number: Whereas, on the contrary, there are no Mahometans to be found in many Parts where the Christian Religion is.

Considering the Weakness and Simplicity of those who taught it in the first Ages.

We come next to examine, in what manner the Christian Religion made such a Progress, that in this Particular also it may be compared with others. We see most Men are disposed to comply with the Examples of Kings and Rulers, especially if they be obliged to it by Law, or compelled by Force. To these the Religions of the Pagans, and that of the Mahometans, owe their Increase. But they who first taught the Christian Religion, were not only Men without any Authority, but of low Fortune, Fishers, Tentmakers, and the like: And yet by the Industry of these Men, that Doctrine, within thirty Years, or thereabouts, spread not only through (*a*) all Parts of the *Roman* Empire, but as far as the *Parthians* and *Indians.* And

---

called Men to such things, who were with-held by evil Customs, nay, possessed with Wickedness: Yet he was sufficient to deliver Mankind from all these, not only *Romans,* but also *Persians,* and all barbarous Nations." See also what follows, which is highly worth reading.

a. *All Parts of the* Roman *Empire,* &c.] *Rom.* XV. 19.

not only in the very Beginning, but for almost three hundred Years, by the Industry of private Persons, without any Threats, without any <135> Enticements, nay, opposed as much as possible by the Power of those who were in Authority, this Religion was propagated so far, that it became the greatest Part of the *Roman* Empire, (*a*) before *Constantine* professed Christianity. They among the *Greeks* who delivered Precepts of Morality, at the same time rendered themselves acceptable by other Arts; as the Platonicks, by the Study of Geometry; the Peripateticks, by the History of Plants and Animals; the Stoicks by Logical Subtilty; the Pythagoreans, by the Knowledge of Numbers and Harmony. Many of them were endued with admirable Eloquence, as *Plato, Zenophon* and *Theophrastus.* But the first Teachers of Christianity had no such Art. (*b*) Their Speech was very plain without any Enticements; they declared only the Precepts, Promises and Threats in bare Words; wherefore, since they had not in themselves any Power answerable to such a Progress, we must of Necessity allow that they were attended with Miracles; or that the secret Influence of God favoured their Undertaking, or both.

Sect. XIX. *And the great Impediments that hindred Men from embracing it, or deterred them from professing it.*

To which Consideration we may add this, that the Minds of those who embraced the Christian <136> Religion taught by these Men, were not entirely free and unprejudiced from any established Rule of Religion, and consequently very pliable; as they were who first embraced the Heathen Rites, and the Law of *Mahomet:* And much less were they prepared by any foregoing Institution; as the *Hebrews* were rendered fit for the Reception of the Law of *Moses,* by Circumcision, and the Knowledge of one

a. *Before* Constantine *professed Christianity,* &c.] *Tertullian* said in his time, Apology II. "We are but of Yesterday, and have filled all Places belonging to you, your Cities, Islands, Castles, Towns, Councils, your very Camps, Tribes, Companies, the Palace, Senate and *Forum;* we have left you only your Temples."

b. *Their Speech was very plain,* &c.] This was wisely observed by *Chrysostom,* on 1 *Col.* I. 17. and by *Theodoret,* after the Words now quoted.

God. But, on the contrary, their Minds were filled with Opinions, and had acquired Habits, which are a second Nature, repugnant to these new Instructions; having been educated and confirmed by the Authority of Laws, and of their Parents, in the Heathen Mysteries, and *Jewish* Rites. And besides this, there was another Obstacle as great, namely the most grievous Sufferings, which it was certain they who professed Christianity must endure, or be in fear of, upon that Account: For since such Sufferings are highly disagreeable to humane Nature, it follows, that those things which are the Cause of such Sufferings, cannot be received without great Difficulty. The Christians, for a long time, were kept out of all Places of Honour, and were moreover fined, had their Goods confiscated, and were banished: But these were small things; they were condemned to the Mines, had the most cruel Torments that it was possible to invent, inflicted upon them; and the Punishments of Death were so common, that the Writers of those times relate that no Famine, no Pestilence, no War, ever consumed more Men at a time. Neither were they the ordinary kinds of Death: (*a*) But burning of <137> them alive, crucifying them, and such like Punishments, which one cannot read or think of without the greatest Horror: And this Cruelty, which, without any long Interruption, and that not every where, continued in the *Roman* Empire almost till the time of *Constantine,* and in other Places longer; was so far from diminishing them, that on the contrary, their Blood was called the Seed of the Church, they so increased as they were cut off. Here therefore let us compare other Religions with Christianity. The *Greeks* and other Heathens, who are wont to magnify their own Matters, reckon a very few that suffered Death for their Opinions; some *Indian* Philosophers, *Socrates,* and not many more; and it can hardly be denied, but that in these famous Men, there was some Desire of transmitting their Fame to Posterity. But there were very many of the common People, scarce known to their Neighbours, among the Christians, who suffered Death for their Opinion; Women, Virgins, young Men, who had no Desire nor probable

a. *But burning of them alive,* &c.] *Domitius Ulpianus* a famous Lawyer, wrote seven Books about the Punishments that Christians ought to have inflicted on them. *Lactantius* mentions them, Book V. Chap. 7.

Hopes that their Name would continue; and indeed there are but a few whose Names remain in the Martyrologies, in comparison of the Number of them that suffered for this Cause, and are (a) reckoned only by the Heap. Further, very many of them might have escaped this Punishment by some small Dissimulation, such as throwing a little Frankincense upon the Altar; <138> which cannot be affirmed of them, who, whatever private Opinions they had in their Minds, yet in their outward Actions, conformed themselves to the Customs of the Vulgar. So that to suffer Death for the Honour of God, could scarce be allowed to any but the *Jews* and Christians; and not to the *Jews* after Christ's time; and before, only to a very few, compared with the Christians; more of which suffered Punishment for the Law of Christ in one Province, than ever there did *Jews;* all whose Sufferings of this kind may almost be reduced to the times of *Manesses* and *Antiochus.* Wherefore, seeing the Christian Religion, in this particular also, infinitely exceeds others; it ought justly to be preferred before them. It must be inferred from such a Multitude of every Age and Sex, in so many different Places and Times, who refused not to die for this Religion; that there was some great Reason for such a constant Resolution, which cannot be imagined to be any other, but the Light of Truth, and the Spirit of God.

An Answer to those who require more and stronger Arguments.

If there be any one who is not satisfied with the Arguments hitherto alledged for the Truth of the Christian Religion, but desires more powerful ones; he ought to know, (b) that different things <139> must have

a. *Reckoned only by the Heap,* &c.] As the innocent Company of three hundred at *Carthage,* mentioned in the XXIVth *Roman* Martyrology of *Augustus;* very many in *Africa,* under *Severus;* under *Valerian,* at *Antioch;* and in *Arabia, Cappadocia* and *Mesopotamia,* in *Phrygia,* in *Pontus,* under *Maximin,* at *Nicomedia,* in *Numidia,* at *Rome,* in *Thebais, Tyre, Trevers* under *Dioclesian,* in *Persis* under *Cabada* and *Sapores.* All which are mentioned in the Martyrology, without any Names.

b. *That different things,* &c.] See *Aristotle's* Ethicks to *Nicomachus* Book I. "It is sufficient if a thing be made appear according to the subject matter of it, for the same Evidence is not to be expected in all things." And in the latter part of his first *Metaphys.*

different kinds of Proof; one sort in Mathematicks, another in the Properties of Bodies, another in doubtful Matters, and another in Matters of Fact. And we are to abide by that, whose Testimonies are void of all Suspicion: Which if it be not admitted, not only all History is of no further Use, and a great Part of Physick; but all that natural Affection, which is betwixt Parents and Children, is lost, (*a*) who can be known no other way. (*b*) And it is the Will of God, that those things which he would have us believe, so that that Faith should be accepted from us as Obedience, should not so evidently appear, as those things we perceive by our Senses, and by Demon-<140>stration; but only so far as is sufficient to procure the Belief, and persuade a Man of the thing, who is not obstinately bent against it: So that the Gospel is, as it were, a Touch-stone, to try Mens honest Dispositions by. For since those Arguments, which we have brought, have gained the Assent of so many good and wise Men; it is very manifest, that the Cause of Infidelity in others, is not from the

---

the last Chap. "Mathematical Certainty is not to be met with in all things." And *Chalcidius* on the *Timaeus,* according to the Opinion of *Plato.* "A Disposition to believe, precedes all Doctrines; especially if they be asserted, not by common, but by great and almost divine Men."

a. *Who can be known no other way,* &c.] Thus *Homer,*

For no Man knows of whom it is he's born.

That is, with the most exact kind of Knowledge.

b. *And it is the Will of God,* &c.] There are two sorts of Propositions in the Christian Religion; one sort of which may be philosophically demonstrated, the other cannot. Of the former are such as these: The Existence of God, the Creation of the World, a Divine Providence; the Goodness and Advantage of the Precepts of Religion; all which are capable of a Demonstration, and are actually demonstrated by *Grotius* and others, so that a Man must renounce his Reason or else admit them. But those Passions which are contrary to them, hinder Unbelievers from receiving them, because if they should own them to be true, they must subdue those Passions, which they are unwilling to do, because they have been so long accustomed to them. Of the latter Sort, are the historical Facts upon which the Truth of the Gospel depends, and which are explained by *Grotius,* and proved by historical Arguments. Which same Arguments would be allowed to be good by Unbelievers, in the same manner as they do the Proofs of all those Histories which they believe, though they did not see the Facts; if they were not hindered by the Prevalence of their Passions, and which they must entirely subdue, if such Arguments came once to take place. See a little Book of mine in *French concerning Infidelity. Le Clerc.*

want of Proof, but from hence, (*a*) that they would not have that seem true, which contradicts their Passions and Affections. It is a hard thing for them lightly to esteem of Honours and other Advantages; which they must do, if they would receive what is related concerning Christ, and for that Reason think themselves bound to obey the Precepts of Christ. And this is to be discovered by this one thing, that they receive many other historical Relations as true, the Truth of which is established only upon Authorities, of which there are no Marks remaining at this time: As there is in the History of Christ, partly by the Confession of the *Jews,* which are now left; partly by the Congregation of Christians, every where to be found; for which there must of Necessity have been some Cause. And since the long Continuance of the Christian Religion, and the Propagation of it so far, cannot be attributed to any human Power, it follows, that it must be attributed to Miracles: Or if any one should deny it to have been done by Miracles; this very thing, <141> that (*b*) it should without a Miracle gather so much Strength and Power, ought to be looked upon as greater than any Miracle. <142>

a. *That they would not have that seem true,* &c.] *Chrysostom* treats very handsomely of this in the Beginning of 1 *Cor.* Chap. 3. And to *Demetrius* he says, *that they do not believe the Commandments, proceeds from their Unwillingness to keep them.*

b. *It should without a Miracle,* &c.] *Chrysostom* handles this Argument on 1 *Cor.* Ch. I. towards the End; and *Augustin* concerning the City of God. Book XXII. Chap. 5.

BOOK III

SECT. I. *Of the Authority of the Books of the New Testament.*

He who is perswaded of the Truth and Excellency of that Religion which Christians profess, having been convinced either by the Arguments before offered, or by any other besides them; in order to understand all the several Parts of it, he must go to the most antient Books, which contain this Religion; and they are what we call the Books of the New Testament, or rather Covenant: For it is unreasonable for any one to deny that That Religion is contained in those Books, as all Christians affirm; since it is fit that every Sect, good or bad, should be believed in this Assertion, that their Opinions are contained in this or that Book; as we believe the Mahometans, that the Religion of *Mahomet* is contained in the *Alcoran:* Wherefore, since the Truth of the Christian Religion has been proved before, and at the same Time it was evident that it was contained in these Books; the Authority of these Books is sufficiently established by this single Thing: However, if any one desire to have it more particularly made appear to him, he will first lay down that common Rule amongst all fair Judges, (*a*) That He who would disprove any Writing which has been received for many Ages, is obliged to bring Argu-<143>ments that may diminish the Credibility of such a Writing; which, if he cannot, the Book is to be defended, as in Possession of its own Authority.

---

a. *That he who would,* &c.] See *Baldus* in his Rubrick concerning the Credibility of Writings, and *Gailus,* Book II. *Obs.* CXLIX. *Numb.* 6 and 7, and those he there cites.

SECT. II. *The Books that have any Names affixed to them, were writ by those Persons whose Names they bear.*

We say then, that the Writings, about which there is no Dispute amongst Christians, and which have any particular Person's Name affixed to them, are that Author's whose Title they are mark'd with; because the first Writers, such as *Justin, Irenaeus,* (*a*) *Clemens,* and others after them, quote these Books under those Names: And besides, (*b*) *Tertullian* says that in his Time some of the Original Copies of those Books were extant. And because all the Churches received them as such, before there were any publick Councils held: Neither did any Heathens or *Jews* raise any Controversy, as if they were not the Works of those whose they were said to be. And (*c*) *Julian* openly confesses, that those were *Peter's, Paul's, Matthew's, Mark's* and <144> *Luke's*, which were read by the Christians under those Names. No Body in his Senses makes any Doubt of *Homer's* or *Virgil's* Works being theirs, by reason of the constant Testimony of the *Greeks* concerning the one, and of the *Latins* concerning the other; how much more then ought we to stand by the Testimony of almost all the Nations in the World, for the Authors of these Books?

a. *Clemens,* &c.] There is only *Clemens's* Epistle to the *Corinthians* extant, in which he quotes Places of the New Testament, but does not name the Writers; wherefore *Clemens's* Name might have been omitted; and so might *Justin's,* who is not used to add the Names. *Le Clerc.*

b. *Tertullian* says, &c.] In his Prescription against the Hereticks, *Let any one who would exercise his Curiosity rather in the Affair of his Salvation, let him run over the Apostolical Churches, over which the Seats of the Apostles have now the Rule in their respective Places, in which the Authentick Letters themselves are recited.* And why might not the Hand of the Apostles be then extant, when *Quintilian* says that in his Time *Cicero's* Hand was extant; and *Gellius* says the same of *Virgil's* in his?

c. Julian *openly confesses,* &c.] The Place is to be seen in *Cyril's* Xth Book. (See also our Annotations, in the Dissertation on the IV Evangelists, added to the Harmony of the Gospels, *Le Clerc.*)

SECT. III. *The Doubt of those Books that were formerly doubtful, taken away.*

There are indeed in the Volume we now use, some Books which were not equally received from the Beginning; (*a*) as the Second of *Peter,* that of *James,* and *Jude,* two under the Name of *John* the Presbyter, the *Revelations,* and the Epistle to the *Hebrews:* However, they were acknowledged by many Churches, as is evident from the ancient Christians, who use their Testimony as sacred; which makes it credible, that those Churches, which had not those Books from the Beginning, did not know of them at that Time, or else were doubtful concerning them; but having afterwards learned the Truth of the Thing, they began to use those Books after the Example of the rest; as we now see done in almost all Places: Nor can there be a sufficient Reason imagined, why any one should counterfeit those Books, when nothing can be gathered from them, but what is abundantly contained in the other Books that are undoubted. <145>

SECT. IV. *The Authority of those Books which have no Name to them, evident from the Nature of the Writings.*

There is no Reason why any one should detract from the Credibility of the Epistle to the *Hebrews,* upon this Account only, because we do not know who wrote it; and so likewise of the two Epistles of *John,* and the *Revelation;* because some have doubted whether *John* the Apostle wrote them, or another of the same Name. (*b*) For in Writers, the Nature of the Writings is more to be regarded than the Name. Wherefore we receive many

---

a. *As the Second of* Peter, &c.] However, *Grotius* himself doubted of this; the Reasons of which Doubt, he himself gives us in the Beginning of his Annotations upon this Epistle. But though one or two Epistles could be called in Question, this would not render the rest doubtful; nor would any Part of the Christian Faith be defective, because it is abundantly delivered in other Places. *Le Clerc.*

b. *For in Writers,* &c.] It had been more proper to say *in Writings,* or Books, which is the Meaning of *Grotius,* as appears from what follows. *Le Clerc.*

Historical Books, whose Authors we are ignorant of, as that of *Cesar's Alexandrian* War; *viz.* because we see, that whoever the Author was, he lived in those Times and was present at those Matters: So likewise ought we to be satisfied, when those who wrote the Books we are now speaking of, testify that they lived in the first Age, and were endued with the Apostolical Gifts. And if any one should object against this, that these Qualities may be feigned, as may the Names in other Writings; he would say a Thing that is by no means credible, *viz.* that they who every where press the Study of Truth and Piety, should without any Reason bring themselves under the Guilt of a Lie; which is not only abhorred by all good Men, (*a*) but was punished with Death by the *Roman* Laws. <146>

Sect. V. *That these Authors wrote what was true, because they knew the Things they wrote about.*

It is certain therefore, that the Books of the New Testament were wrote by those whose Names they bear, or by such Persons as they profess themselves to be; and it is moreover evident, that they had a Knowledge of Things they wrote about, and had no Desire to say what was false; whence it follows, that what they wrote must be true, because every Falsity preceeds either from Ignorance, or from an ill Intention. *Matthew, John, Peter* and *Jude,* were of the Company of those Twelve, which Jesus chose to be Witnesses of his Life and Doctrines: (*b*) So that they could not want the Knowledge of those Things they relate: The same may be said of *James,* who either was an Apostle, or as others would have it, (*c*) a near

---

a. *But was punished with Death,* &c.] See *L.*[1] *Falsi Nominis, D.*[2] *de Lege Cornelia;* and *Paul,* Book V. *Sent. Tit.* XXV. *Sect.* 10 and 11. See Examples of this Punishment, at the end of the Books of *Valerius Maximus,* and in *Capitolinus* in *Pertinax.*

1. Lex (law).

2. Decretum (decree, ordinance).

b. *So that they could not want the Knowledge,* &c.] *John* XV. 27. also 1 *Epist.* I. *Acts* I. 21, 22.

c. *A near Relation of Jesus,* &c.] So others, and they not a few, think; and St. *Chrysostom* every where. See *Josephus* also. (Add to these *Eusebius, H. E.* Book II. Ch. 1 and 23.)

Relation of Jesus, and made Bishop of *Jerusalem* by the Apostles. Neither could *Paul* be deceived through Ignorance, concerning those Doctrines which he professes were revealed to him by Jesus himself reigning in Heaven; neither could he be deceived in the Things which he performed himself; no more could *Luke,* who was his (*a*) inseparable Companion in his Travels. This same *Luke* could easily know what he wrote concerning the Life and Death of Jesus, because he was born in a neighbouring Place, and had travelled through *Palestine,* <147> where he says (*b*) he spake with them who were Eye-Witnesses of these Things. Without doubt there were many others (besides the Apostles with whom he was acquainted,) who were then alive, having been healed by Jesus, and who had seen him die, and come to Life again. If we believe *Tacitus* and *Suetonius,* concerning those Things which happened long before they were born, because we rely upon their diligent Enquiry; how much more reasonable is it to believe this Author, who says he had every Thing from Eye-Witnesses? (*c*) It is a constant Tradition that *Mark* was a continual Companion of *Peter;* so that what he wrote, is to be esteemed as if *Peter* himself, who could not be ignorant of those Things, had dictated it: Besides, almost every Thing which he wrote, is to be found in the Writings of the Apostles. Neither could the Writer of the *Revelations* be deceived in those Visions which he says (*d*) were caused from Heaven; (*e*) nor he to the *Hebrews,* in those Things which he professes he was taught, either by the Spirit of God, or by the Apostles themselves.

a. *Inseparable Companion,* &c.] See *Acts* XX. and the following, *Colos.* IV. 14. 2. *Tim.* IV. 11. *Philem.* 24.

b. *He spake with them,* &c.] In the Preface of his Gospel History.

c. *It is a constant Tradition,* &c.] *Irenaeus,* Book III. ch. 1. and *Clemens* in his Hypotyposes, cited in *Eusebius's* Ecclesiastical History.

d. *Were caused from Heaven,* &c.] *Rev.* I. 1, 2. IV. 1. and the following XXII. 18, 19, 20, 21.

e. *Nor he to the* Hebrews, &c.] *Heb.* II. 4. V. 14. XIII. 7, 8, 23.

Sect. VI. *And because they would not say what was false.*

The other Thing we affirmed, *viz.* that they would not speak an Untruth; belongs to what was before treated of, when we shewed the Credibility <148> of the Christian Religion in general, and of the History of Christ's Resurrection. They who would disprove Witnesses in this Particular relating to their Disposition and Will, must of necessity allege something to make it credible, that they set their Mind against the Truth. But this cannot be said here; For if any one should object that their own Cause was concerned; he ought to examine upon what Account it was their Cause; Certainly not for the sake of getting any Advantage, or shunning any Danger; when, on the Account of this Profession, they lost all Advantages, and there was no Dangers which they did not expose themselves to. It was not therefore their own Cause, unless out of Reverence to God, which certainly does not induce any Man to tell a Lie, especially in a Matter of such Moment, upon which the Eternal Salvation of Mankind depends. We are hindred from believing such a wicked Thing of them, both by their Doctrines, which are in every part (*a*) full of Piety; and by their Life, which was never accused of any evil Fact, no, not by their Enemies, who only objected their Unskilfulness against them, which is not at all apt to produce a Falsity. If there had been in them the least Dishonesty, they would not have set down their own Faults to be eternally remembered; (*b*) as in <149> the Flight of them all, when Christ was in Danger; and (*c*) in *Peter*'s thrice denying him.

a. *Full of Piety,* &c.] And abhor Lying. *John* XIV. 17. XV. 26. XVI. 13. XVII. 17, 19. XVIII. 37. *Acts* XXVI. 25. *Rom.* I. 25. 2 *Thes.* II. 20. 1 *John* I. 6, 8. II. 4, 21. 2 *Cor.* VI. 8. *Eph.* IV. 15, 25. *Colos.* III. 9. *Rev.* XXII. 15. 2 *Cor.* II. 31. *Gal.* I. 20. Observe how industriously St. *Paul* distinguishes those Things which are his own, and those which are the Lord's, 1 *Cor.* VII. 10, 12, how cautious in speaking of what he saw, whether he saw them in the Body, or out of the Body, 2 *Cor.* XII. 2.

b. *As in the Flight of them all,* &c.] *Mat.* XXVI. 34, 56.

c. *In* Peter's *thrice denying Him,* &c.] *Mat.* XXVI. 69. and the following; *Mark* XIV. 66. and the following; *Luke* XXII. 54. and the following.

Sect. VII. *The Credibility of these Writers further confirmed, from their being famous for Miracles.*

But on the contrary, God himself gave remarkable Testimonies to the Sincerity of them; by working Miracles, which they themselves and their Disciples (*a*) publickly avouched with the highest Assurance; adding the Names of the Persons and Places, and other Circumstances; the Truth or Falsity of which Assertion might easily have been discovered by the Magistrates Enquiry; amongst which Miracles, this is worthy Observation, (*b*) which they constantly affirmed, of their speaking Languages they had never learned, before many thousand People; and healing in a Moment Bodies that were diseased, in the Sight of the Multitude; nor were they at all afraid, tho' they knew at that Time, that the Jewish Magistrates were violently set against them; and the Roman Magistrates very partial; who would not overlook any Thing that afforded Matter of traducing them as Criminals, and Authors of a new Religion; nor did any of the Jews or Heathens in those nearest Times, dare to deny that Miracles were done by these Men: Nay, *Phlegon,* who was a Slave of the Emperor *Adrian,* (*c*) mentions the Miracles of *Peter* in his Annals: <150> And the Christians themselves in those Books, wherein they give an Account of the Grounds of their Faith, before the Emperors, Senate, and Rulers (*d*) speak of these Facts, as things known to every Body, and about which there could be no Doubt: Moreover, they openly declare that the wonderful Power of them (*e*) remained in their Graves for some Ages; when they could

a. *Publickly avouched,* &c.] See the Acts of the Apostles throughout, and 2 *Cor.* XII. 12.

b. *Which they constantly affirmed,* &c.] The Places are quoted before.

c. *Mentions the Miracles of* Peter, &c.] Book XIII. As *Origen* says in his IId Book against *Celsus.* This is that *Phlegon* whose Remains we have yet, concerning Miracles, and long-lived Men.

d. *Speak of these Facts as things,* &c.] The Places are very many, especially in *Origen.* See the whole VIIIth Chap. of *Augustine's* XXIId Book of the City of God.

e. *Remained in their Graves,* &c.] The Miracles at the Sepulchres of holy Men, then began to be boasted of, when the Christians having the Power in their Hands, began to make an Advantage of the Martyrs and other dead Bodies in those Churches in which

not but know, if it were false, that they could easily be disproved by the Magistrates to their Shame and Punishment. And these Miracles, now mentioned at their Sepulchres, were so common, and had so many Witnesses, (*a*) that they forced *Porphyry* to confess the Truth <151> of them. These things which we have now alleged, ought to satisfy us: But there are abundance more Arguments, which recommend to us the Credibility of these Books.

SECT. VIII. *And of their Writings; because in them are contained many things which the Event proved to be revealed by a Divine Power.*

For we find in them many Predictions concerning things which Men could not possibly know of themselves, and which were wonderfully confirmed by the Event; (*b*) such as the sudden and universal Propagation of this Religion; (*c*) the perpetual Continuance of it; (*d*) that it should

---

they were buried. Wherefore I would not have this Argument made use of, lest we diminish from the Credibility of certain Miracles, by these doubtful or fictitious ones. Every one knows how many Stories are related after the IVth Century, about this Matter. But *Origen* does not mention any such Miracles: but in his VIIth Book against *Celsus* says, *Very many Miracles of the Holy Spirit were manifested at the Beginning of Jesus's Doctrine, and after his Ascension, but afterwards they were fewer; however there are now some Footsteps of them in some few, whose Minds are purified by Reason, and their Actions agreeable thereto.* Who can believe that so many Miracles should be done in one or two Centuries after *Origen*, when there was less need of them? Certainly it is as reasonable to derogate from the Credibility of the Miracles of the IVth and Vth Centuries, as it would be impudent to deny the Miracles of Christ and his Apostles. These Miracles could not be asserted without Danger; those could not be rejected without Danger, nor be believed without Profit to those who perhaps forged them; which is a great Difference. *Le Clerc.*

a. *That they forced* Porphyry, &c.] See *Cyril's* Xth Book against *Julian*, and *Hieronymus* against a Book of *Vigilantius*.

b. *Such as the sudden,* &c.] *Matt.* XIII. 33. and following Verses. *Luke* X. 18. *John* XII. 32.

c. *The perpetual Continuance of it,* &c.] *Luke* I. 33. *Matt.* XXVIII. 20. *John* XIV. 16.

d. *That it should be rejected,* &c.] *Matt.* XXI. 33. and following Verses; XXII. at the Beginning. *Luke* XV. 11. and following Verses.

be rejected by very many of the *Jews,* (*a*) and embraced by Strangers; (*b*) the Hatred of the *Jews* against those who professed this Religion; (*c*) the severe Punishments they should undergo upon the Account of it; (*d*) the Siege and Destruction of *Jerusalem* and the Temple, and (*e*) the sore Calamities of the *Jews.*

SECT. IX. *And also from the Care that it was fit God should take, that false Writings should not be forged.*

To what has been said may be added, that if it be granted, that God takes care of human Af-<152>fairs, and especially those that concern his own Honour and Worship; it is impossible he should suffer such a Multitude of Men, who had no other Design than to worship him with Sincerity, to be deceived by false Books. And, after there did arise several Sects in Christianity, there was scarce any found, who did not receive either all, or most of these Books, except a few which do not contain any thing particular in them; which is a very good Argument why we should think that nothing in these Books could be contradicted; because those Sects were so inflamed with Hatred against each other, that whatsoever pleased one, for that very Reason displeased another.

SECT. X. *A Solution of that Objection, that many Books were rejected by some.*

There were indeed amongst those who were willing to be called Christians, a very few who rejected all those Books which seemed to contradict their particular Opinion; such as they who out of Hatred to the *Jews,*

---

a. *And embraced by Strangers,* &c.] In the same Places, and also *Matt.* VIII. 2. XII. 21. XXI. 43.

b. *The Hatred of the* Jews, &c.] *Matt.* X. 17.

c *The severe Punishments,* &c.] *Matt.* X. 21, 39. XXIII. 34.

d. *The Siege and Destruction* &c.] *Mat.* XXIII. 38. XXIV. 16. *Luke* XIII. 34. XXI. 24.

e. *And the sore Calamities of the Jews,* &c.] *Matt.* XXI. 33. and following Verses. XXIII. 34. XXIV. 20.

(*a*) spoke ill of the God of the *Jews,* of the Maker of the World, and of the Law: Or, on the contrary, out of fear of the Hardships that the Christians were to undergo, (*b*) sheltered themselves under the Name of *Jews,* (*c*) who might profess their Religion with-<153>out Punishment. (*d*) But these very Men were disowned by all other Christians every where, (*e*) in those times, when all pious Persons that differed from one another, were very patiently born with, according to the Command of the Apostles. The first sort of these Corrupters of Christianity are, I think, sufficiently confuted above, where we have shewn that there is but one true God, whose Workmanship the World is: And indeed it is sufficiently evident from those very Books which they, that they might in some measure appear to be Christians, receive; (*f*) such as the Gospel of St. *Luke* in particular: It is, I say, evident, that Christ preached the same God, which *Moses* and the *Hebrews* worshipped. We shall have a better Opportunity to confute the other sort, when we come to oppose those who are *Jews,* and willing to be called so. In the mean time I shall add only this, that the Impudence of those Men is very surprising, who undervalue the Authority of *Paul,* when there was not any one of the Apostles who founded more Churches; nor of whom there were so many Miracles related, at that time when, as was before observed, the Facts might be easily inquired into. And if we

a. *Spoke ill of the God of the Jews,* &c.] See *Irenaeus,* Book I. Chap. 29. *Tertullian* against *Marcion,* and *Epiphanius* concerning the same.

b. *Sheltered themselves under the Name,* &c.] See *Gal.* II. 2. VI. 13, 14. *Philip.* III. 18. *Irenaeus* Book III. Chap. 28. *Epiphanius* concerning the *Ebionites.*

c. *Who might profess their Religion,* &c.] *Acts* IX. 20. XIII. and many times in that Book. *Philo,* against *Flaccus,* and concerning the *Embassy, Josephus* every where. To which may be added *L. Generaliter, D. de Decurionibus,* and *Lib.* I. *C. de Judaeis. Tertullian,* in his Apology, says, *But the Jews read openly; they generally purchase Leave by a Tribute, which they gather upon all Sabbath-Days.*

d. *But these very Men were disowned,* &c.] *Tertullian,* in his Ist against *Marcion,* says, *You cannot find any Church of Apostolical Order, who are not Christians out of regard to the Creator.*

e. *In those times,* &c.] See what will be said of this Matter at the End of the VIth Book. Add also *Iraeneus*'s Epistle to the *Victor,* and what *Hieronymus* writes concerning it in his Catalogue; and *Cyprian* in his *African* Council. *Judging no Man, nor removing any one from the Right of Communion, for his differing in Opinion.*

f. *Such as the Gospel of St.* Luke, &c.] *Tertullian* in his VIth Book against *Marcion,* makes it appear very plainly.

believe his Miracles, <154> what Reason is there why we should not believe him in his heavenly Visions, and in his receiving his Instructions
from Christ? If he was so beloved of Christ, it cannot possibly be, that
he should teach any thing disagreeable to Christ, that is, any thing false;
and that one thing which they find fault with in him, namely his Opinion
concerning the Freedom procured to the *Hebrews* from the Rites formerly
injoined by *Moses,* there could be no Reason for his teaching it, but the
Truth; (*a*) for he was circumcised himself, (*b*) and observed most of the
Law of his own accord: And for the sake of the Christian Religion, (*c*)
he performed things much more difficult, and underwent things much
harder than the Law commanded, or that he had Reason to expect upon
the Account of it; (*d*) and he was the Cause of his Disciples doing and
bearing the same things: Whence it is evident, he did not deliver any thing
to please the Ears of his Hearers, or for their Profit, when he taught them,
(*e*) instead of the *Jewish* Sabbath, to spend every Day in Divine Worship;
instead of the small Expence the Law put them to, (*f*) to bear the Loss
of all their Goods; (*g*) and instead of offering Beasts to God, to offer their
own Blood <155> to him. And *Paul* himself openly assures us, (*h*) that
Peter, John and *James* gave him their right Hands, in Token of their Fel-
lowship with him; which, if it had not been true, he would not have ventured to say so, when they were alive, and could have convicted him of an
Untruth. Except only those therefore, which I have now mentioned, who
scarce deserve the Name of Christians; the manifest Consent of all other
Assemblies, in receiving these Books, beside what has been already said
concerning the Miracles which were done by the Writers of them, and the

a. *For he was circumcised,* &c.] *Philip* III. 5.

b. *And observed most of the Law,* &c.] *Acts* XVI. 3. XX. 6. XXI. and the following
Chap.

c. *He performed things,* &c.] 2 *Cor.* XI. 23. and the following Verses; and every where
in the *Acts.* See also 1 *Cor.* XI. 3. 2 *Cor.* XI, 30. XII. 10.

d. *And he was the Cause,* &c.] *Acts* XX. 29. *Rom.* V. 3. VIII. XII. 12. 2 *Cor.* I. 4, 8. II.
4. VI. 4. 1 *Thess.* I. 6. 2 *Thess.* I. 6.

e. *Instead of the* Jewish *Sabbath,* &c.] *Acts* II. 46. V. 42. 1 *Tim.* V. 5. 2 *Tim.* I. 3.

f. *To bear the Loss of all,* &c.] 2 *Cor.* VI. 4. XII. 10.

g. *And instead of offering Beasts,* &c.] *Rom.* VIII. 36. 2 *Cor.* IV. 11. *Phil.* I. 20.

h. *That* Peter, John, *and* James, &c.] *Gal.* II. 9. And 1 *Cor.* XV. 11. 2 *Cor.* XI. 5. XII.
11.

particular Care of God about things of this Nature; is sufficient to induce all impartial Men, to give Credit to these Relations; because they are used to believe many other historical Books, which have not any Testimonies of this kind; unless very good Reason can be given to the contrary, which cannot be done here.

Sect. XI. *An Answer to the Objection, of some things being contained in these Books, that are impossible.*

For if any one should say, that there are some things related in these Books, that are impossible to be done; (*a*) we have before shown, that there are some things which are impossible to be done by Men, but are possible with God; that is, such as do not include any Contradiction in themselves; amongst which things, are to be reckoned those which we account most wonderful, the Power of working Miracles, and calling the Dead to Life again; so that this Objection is of no Force. <156>

Sect. XII. *Or disagreeable to Reason.*

Nor is there more Heed to be given to them, who say, that there are some Doctrines to be found in these Books, which are inconsistent with right Reason. For first, this may be disproved by that great Multitude of ingenious, learned and wise Men, who have relied on the Authority of these Books from the very Beginning: Also every thing that has been shewn in the first Book to be agreeable to right Reason, *viz.* that there is a God, and but one, a most perfect Being, all-powerful, loving, wise, and good; that all things which are, were made by him; that his Care is over all his Works, particularly over Men; that he can reward those that obey him, after this Life; that we are to bridle sensual Appetites; that there is a natural Relation betwixt Men, and therefore they ought to love one another: All these we may find plainly delivered in these Books. To affirm any thing more than this for certain, either concerning the Nature of God, or concerning his Will, (*b*) by the mere Direction of human Reason, is an

a. *We have before shewn,* &c.] Book II.
b. *By the mere Direction of,* &c.] *Matt* XI. 27. *Rom.* XI. 33, 34, 35. 1 *Cor.* II. 11, 16.

unsafe and fallible thing, as we may learn from the many Opinions of the Schools different from one another, and of all the Philosophers. Nor is this at all to be wondered at; for if they who dispute (*a*) about the Nature of their own Minds, fall into such widely different Opinions; must it not necessarily be much more so with them, who would determine any thing concerning the Supreme Mind, which is placed so much out of our Reach? If <157> they who understand human Affairs, affirm it dangerous (*b*) to pry into the Councils of Princes, and that therefore we ought not to attempt it; who is sagacious enough to hope, by his own Conjectures to find out *which* it is, that God will determine of the various kinds of those things that he can freely *will?* Therefore *Plato* said very well, that (*c*) none of these things could be known without a Revelation: And there can be no Revelation produced, which can be proved truly to be such, by greater Testimonies than those contained in the Books of the New Testament. There is so far from being any Proof, that it has never yet been asserted, that God ever declared any thing to Man concerning his Nature, that was contradictory to these Books; nor can there be any later Declaration of his Will produced, that is credible. And if any thing was commanded or allowed, before Christ's time, of those sort of things which are plainly indifferent, or certainly not at all obligatory of themselves, nor plainly evil; this does not oppose these Books; (*d*) because in such things the former Laws are nulled by the latter. <158>

a. *About the Nature of their own Minds,* &c.] See *Plutarch*'s Works, Book IV. or the Opinions of the Philosophers. And *Stobaeus*'s Physicks, Chap. XI.

b. *To pry into the Councils of Princes,* &c.] *Tacitus* has it in the VIth of his Annals.

c. *None of these things could be known,* &c.] The Place is in his *Phaedon,* and also in *Timaeus.* It was well said by *Ambrose. Who should I rather believe concerning God, than God himself?*

d. *Because in such things,* &c.] *The latter Constitutions are more valid than the former.* It is a Saying of *Modestinus, L. Ultima, D. de Constitutionibus Principum.* Tertullian, *I think,* says he, *that in human Constitutions and Decrees, the latter are more binding than the former.* And in his Apology: *Ye lop and hew down the ancient and foul Wood of the Laws, by the new Axes of the Decrees and Edicts of the Princes.* And concerning Baptism. *In all Things we are determined by the latter; the latter things are more binding than those that went before.* Plutarch, Sympos. IX. *In Decrees and Laws, in Compacts and Bargains, the latter are esteemed stronger and firmer than the former.*

SECT. XIII. *An Answer to this Objection,*
that some Things are contained in these Books
which are inconsistent with one another.

It is objected by some, that the Sense of these Books, is sometimes very different: But whoever fairly examines this Matter, will find that on the contrary this is an Addition to the other Arguments for the Authority of these Books; that in those Places which contain any Thing of Moment, whether in Doctrine or History, there is every where such a manifest Agreement, as is not to be found in any other Writers of a Sect; (a) whether they be *Jews,* (b) or *Greek* Philosophers, (c) or Physicians, (d) or *Roman* Lawyers; in all which we very often find, that not only they of the same Sect contradict one another, (e) as *Plato* and *Xenophon* do, (f) but very often the same Writer sometimes asserts one Thing, and sometimes another; as <159> if he had forgot himself, or did not know which to affirm: But these Writers, of whom we are speaking, all urge the same Things to be believed, deliver the same Precepts, concerning the Life of Christ, his Death, and Return to Life again; The main and principal Things are every where the same. And as to some very minute Circumstances, which make nothing towards the main Thing, we are not wholly at such a Loss for a fair Reconciliation of them, but that it may easily be made; tho' we are ignorant of some Things, by reason of the

a. *Whether they be* Jews, &c.] The different Opinions amongst whom, as they are to be seen in other Places, so likewise in *Manasses* the Son of *Israel,* a very learned Man in this sort of Learning, in his Books of the Creation and Resurrection.

b. *Or* Greek *Philosophers,* &c.] See the forecited Book of the Opinion of the Philosophers.

c. *Or Physicians,* &c.] See *Galen* of Sects, and of the best Sect; and *Celsus* of Physick, in the Beginning; to which the *Spagirici* may be added.

d. *Or* Roman *Lawyers,* &c.] There was a remarkable Difference of Old, between the *Sabiniani* and *Proculiani;* and now betwixt those who follow *Bariolus* and his Followers, and those who follow *Cujacius* and others who were more learned. See *Gabriel's* Common, more Common, and most Common Sentences.

e. *As* Plato *and* Xenophon *do,* &c.] See *Xenophon's* Epistle to *Aeschines,* the Disciple of *Socrates Athaeneus* I. *Laertius's* Life of *Plato;* and *Gellius,* Book XIV.

f. *But very often the same Writer,* &c.] Many have shewn this of *Aristotle;* and others of the *Roman* Lawyers.

Similitude of Things that were done at different Times, the Ambiguity of Names, one Man's or Place's having many Names, and such like. Nay, this very Thing ought to acquit these Writers of all Suspicion of Deceit; because they who bear Testimony to that which is false, (*a*) are used to relate all Things so by Agreement, that there should not be any Appearance of Difference. And, if, upon the Account of some small Difference, which cannot be reconciled, we must immediately disbelieve whole Books; then there is no Book, especially of History, to be believed; and yet *Polybius, Halicarnassensis, Livy,* and *Plutarch,* in whom such Things are to be found, keep up their Authority amongst us in the principal Things; how much more reasonable then is it, that no such Thing should destroy the Credibility of those, whom we see, from their own Writings, to have always a <160> very great Regard to Piety and Truth? There remains another Way of confuting Testimonies, from contrary external Testimonies.

SECT. XIV. *An Answer to the Objection from external Testimonies: Where it is shown they make more for these Books.*

But I confidently affirm, that there are no such Things to be found; unless any one will reckon amongst these, what is said by those who were born a long while after, and they such who professed themselves Enemies to the Name of Christ, and who therefore ought not to be looked upon as Witnesses. Nay, on the contrary, though there is no need of them, we have many Testimonies, which confirm some Parts of the History delivered in these Books. Thus that Jesus was crucified, that Miracles were done by him and his Disciples, both *Hebrews* and Heathens relate. Most clear Testimonies of *Josephus,* published a little more than forty Years after Christ's Death, are now extant, concerning *Herod, Pilate, Festus, Felix, John* the

a. *Are used to relate all Things,* &c.] This is what the Emperor *Adrian* affirms; in Witnesses we are to examine whether they offer one and the same praemeditated Speech: *L. Testium D. de Testibus. Speculator, lib.* I. *parte* IV. *de Tege in pr. n.* 81. A very exact Knowledge of all Circumstances, is not necessary in a Witness. See *Luke* I. 56. III. 23 *John* II. 6. VI. 10, 19. XIX. 14.

Baptist, *Gamaliel,* and the Destruction of *Jerusalem;* which are exactly agreeable to what we find amongst the Writers of the *Talmud* concerning those Times: The Cruelty of *Nero* towards the Christians is mentioned by *Tacitus:* And formerly there were extant Books of private Persons, (*a*) such as *Phlegon,* <161> (*b*) and publick Acts, to which the Christians appealed; (*c*) wherein they agreed about the Star that appeared after the Birth of Christ; about the Earthquake, and the preternatural Eclipse of the Sun at full Moon, about the Time that Christ was crucified.

Sect. XV. *An Answer to the Objection of the Scriptures being altered.*

I see no other Objection can be made against these Books; unless it be that they have not continued to be the same, as they were at the Beginning. It must be owned, that as in other Books, so in these, it might happen, and has happened, that through Carelesness or Perverseness in the Transcribers, some Letters, Syllables, or Words, may be changed, omitted, or added. (*d*) But it is very <162> unreasonable, that because of such

---

a. *Such as* Phlegon, &c.] Book XIII. of his *Chronicon* or *Olympiads,* in these Words, "In the fourth Year of the CCIId Olympiad there happened the greatest Eclipse of the Sun that ever was known; there was such a dark Night at the Sixth Hour of the Day, that the Stars were seen in the Heavens; and there was a great Earthquake in *Bithynia,* which overturned a great Part of *Nicaea.*" These Words are to be seen in *Eusebius's* and *Hieronymus's Chronicon.* And *Origen* mentions *the same Thing,* Tract. XXXV. upon *Mat.* and in his IId against *Celsus.*

b. *And publick Acts,* &c.] See *Tertullian's* Apology, CXXI. *This Misfortune which has befallen the World, you find related in your Mystical Books.*

c. *Wherein they agreed,* &c.] *Chalcidius* the Platonist, in his Commentary on *Timaeus.* "There is another more Holy and more Venerable History, which relates the Appearance of a new Star, not to foretell Diseases and Death, but the Descent of a venerable God, who was to preserve Mankind, and to show Favour to the Affairs of Mortals; which Star the Wise Men of *Chaldaea* observing as they travelled in the Night, and being very well skilled in viewing the Heavenly Bodies, they are said to have sought after the New Birth of this God; and having found that Majesty in a Child, they paid him Worship, and made such Vows as were agreeable to so great a God."

d. *But it is very unreasonable,* &c.] This is now very manifest, from the most accurate Collection of the various Readings of the New Testament, and especially from the Edition of Dr. *Mills.* Tho' there is a great Variety, yet no new Doctrine can be raised from thence, nor no received one confuted; no History of any Moment, in regard to a Difference of Copies, which could not but happen in so long time, there should arise any Controversy about the Testament or Book itself; because both Custom and Reason requires, that *that* should be preferred before the rest, which is to be found in the most antient Copies. But it can never be proved, that all the Copies are corrupted by Fraud, or any other way, especially in those Places which contain any Doctrine, or remarkable Point of History; for there are no Records that tell us that they were so, nor any Witnesses in those Times: And if, as we before observed, any thing be alleged by those who lived a long Time after, and who shew the most cruel Hatred against those who were Defenders of these Books; this is to be looked upon as Reproach, and not Testimony. And this which we have now said, may suffice in Answer to those who object that the Scripture may have been altered: Because he that affirms this, especially against a Writing which has been received so long and in so many Places, (*a*) ought himself to prove that which he presumes. But that the Folly of this Objection may more plainly appear, we will show that *That* which they imagine to be, neither is, nor can be done. We have before proved these Books to have been wrote by those whose Names they bear; which being granted, it follows that one Book is not forged for the sake of another. Neither is any remarkable Passage altered; for such an Alteration must have <163> something designed by it, and then that Part would plainly differ from those other Parts and Books which are not altered, which is no where to be seen; nay, as we observed, there is a wonderful Harmony in the Sense every where. Moreover, as soon as any of the Apostles or Apostolical Men, published any Thing; doubtless the Christians took great Care to have many Copies of it, as became pious Persons and such as were desirous of preserving and propagating the Truth to Posterity; and these were therefore dispersed, as far as the Name of Christ extended itself, through *Europe, Asia,* and *Egypt,* in which Places the *Greek* Language flourished; and, as we before observed, some of the original Copies

---

the Truth of the Christian Religion, which was before believed from the Books of the New Testament, is from thence to be rejected; nor any that was before unknown, to be collected from the various Readings. And what is said of the Books of the New Testament, the same we are to conceive said of the Old Testament. *Le Clerc.*

  a. *Ought himself to prove,* &c.] *L. ult. C. de Edicto Divi Adriani tollendo.*

were preserved for two hundred Years. Now no Book, of which so many Copies had been taken, that were kept not by some few private Persons, but by the Care of whole Churches, (*a*) can be corrupted. To which we may add, that in the very next Ages, these Books were translated into the *Syriac, Aethiopic,* and *Latin* Tongues, which Versions are now extant, and do not any where differ from the *Greek* Books in any Thing of Moment. And we have the Writings of those who were taught by the Apostles themselves, or their Disciples, who quote a great many Places of these Books in that Sense which we now understand them. Nor was there at that Time, any one in the Church of so great Authority, as to have been obeyed, if he had designed to alter any Thing; as <164> is sufficiently manifest from the Liberty taken by *Irenaeus, Tertullian,* and *Cyprian,* to differ from those who were of the highest Rank in the Church. And after the Times now mentioned, many others followed, who were Men of great Learning, and as great Judgment; who, after a diligent Enquiry, received those Books, as retaining their original Purity. And further, what we now said concerning the different Sects of Christians, may be applied here also; that all of them, at least all that own God to be the Creator of the World, and Christ to be a new Lawgiver, make use of these Books as we now have them. If any attempted to put in any Thing, they were accused of Forgery by the rest. And that no Sect was allowed the Liberty to alter these Books according to their own Pleasure, is sufficiently evident from hence, that all Sects fetched their Arguments against the rest from hence. And what we hinted concerning the Divine Providence, relates as much to the principal Parts, as to the whole Books; that it is not agreeable thereto, that God should suffer so many thousand Men, who were regardful of Piety, and sought after eternal Life with a sincere Intention, to fall into an Error that they could not possibly avoid. And thus much may suffice for the Books of the New Testament, which if they were alone extant, were sufficient to teach us the True Religion.

a. *Can be corrupted,* &c.] That is, so as that it should run through all the Copies, and corrupt all the Versions; for otherwise wicked Men, who are obstinately bent on their own Opinions, may here and there corrupt their own Copies; as not only *Marcion* did, but also some Library-keepers, who had a better Apprehension; as we have shown in our *Ars Critica,* Part III. Sect. 1. C. XIV. *Le Clerc.*

SECT. XVI. *The Authority of the Books of the Old Testament.*

But since God has been pleased to leave us the Records of the *Jewish* Religion, which was True of Old, and affords no small Testimony to the Christian Religion; it is not foreign to our Purpose, to see upon what Foundation the Credibility of these is built. That these Books are theirs to whom they <165> are ascribed, appears in the same Manner as we have proved of Our Books. And they whose Names they bear, were either Prophets, or Men worthy to be credited; such as *Esdras,* who is supposed to have collected them into one Volume, at that Time when the Prophets *Haggai, Malachi,* and *Zacharias* were yet alive. I will not here repeat what was said before, in Commendation of *Moses.* And not only that first Part delivered by *Moses,* as we have shewn in the first Book, but the later History is confirmed by many *Pagans.* (*a*) Thus the *Phoenician* Annals mention the <166>

a. *Thus the* Phoenician *Annals,* &c.] See what *Josephus* cites out of them, Book VIII. Ch. 2. of his Antient History; where he adds, that if any one would see the Copies of those Epistles, which *Solomon* and *Hirom* wrote to each other, they may be procured of the publick Keepers of the Records at *Tyrus,* (we must be cautious how we believe this; however see what I have said upon 1 *Kings* V. 3.) There is a remarkable Place concerning *David,* quoted by *Josephus,* Book VII. Ch. 6. of his Antient History, out of the IVth of *Damascenus's* History. "A long while after this, there was a certain Man of that Country, who was very powerful, his Name was *Adadus,* who reigned in *Damascus,* and the other Parts of *Syria,* except *Phoenice:* He waged War with *David* King of *Judaea,* and having fought many Battles, the last was at *Euphrates,* where he was overcome: He was accounted one of the best of Kings for Strength and Valour: After his Death, his Children reigned for Ten Generations, each of them continuing his Father's Government and Name; in the same Manner as the *Egyptian* Kings are called *Ptolemy's.* The Third being the most potent of them all, being willing to recover the Victory his Grandfather had lost, made War upon the *Jews,* and laid waste that which is now called *Samaria.*" The first Part of this History we have in 2 *Sam.* VIII. 5. 1 *Chron.* XVIII. and the latter Part in 1 *Kings* XX. where see *Josephus.* This *Adadus* is called by *Josephus, Adar;* and *Adores* by *Justin,* out of *Trogus. Eusebius* in his Gospel Prepar. Book IV. Ch. 30. tells us more Things concerning *David,* out of *Eupolemus.* And the forementioned *Josephus* in the same Chap. and in his Ist against *Appion,* brings this Place out of *Dius's* Phoenician History. "After *Abibalus's* Death, his Son *Hirom* reigned; this Man increased the *Eastern* Part of the City; and much enlarged the City; and he joined *Jupiter Olympius's* Temple to the City, which before stood by itself in an Island, by filling up the Space between; and he adorn'd it with the Gifts of Gold offered to the Gods; he also went up to *Libanus,* and cut down Wood to adorn the Temple with. And they say that *Solomon,* who reigned in *Jerusalem,* sent Riddles to *Hirom,* and received some from him; and he that could not resolve the Riddles, was to pay a large Sum of Money. Afterwards *Abdemonus,* a Man of *Tyrus,* resolved the Riddles that were proposed, and sent others, which *Solomon* not resolving, paid a large Sum of Money to *Hirom.*" He afterwards adds a famous Place of *Menander,* the *Ephesian,* who wrote the Affairs of the *Greeks* and *Barbarians.* "After *Abibalus's* Death, his Son *Hirom* succeeded in the Government; he liv'd thirty-four Years, and inclosed the large Country, and erected the Golden Pillar in *Jupiter's* Temple. He afterwards cut down Wood from the Mountain call'd *Libanus,* Cedar-Trees for the Roof of the Temple, and pulled down the Old Temples, and built New. He consecrated the Grove of *Hercules* and *Astarte.* He first laid the Foundation of *Hercules's,* in the Month *Peritius,* and afterwards *Astarte's* about the Time that he invaded the *Tityans* for not paying Tribute, and returned after having reduced them. About this Time there was one *Abdemonus* a young Man, who overcame in explaining the Riddles proposed by *Solomon,* the King of *Jerusalem.* The Time from this King, to the Building of *Carthage,* is reckoned thus. After *Hirom's* Death; *Beleazar* his Son succeeded in the Kingdom; who lived forty-three Years, and reigned seven. After him was his Son *Abdastratus,* who lived twenty-nine Years, and reigned nine. This Man was slain by the four Children of his Nurse, who laid in Ambush for him; the eldest of which reigned twelve Years. After these, was *Astartas,* the Son of *Delaestartus,* who lived fifty-four Years, and reigned twelve. After him came his Brother *Asergmus,* who lived fifty-four Years, and reigned nine: This Man was killed by his Brother *Pheletes,* who seized the Kingdom, and reigned eight Months; he lived fifty Years; He was slain by *Ithobalus,* the Priest of *Astarte,* who reigned thirty-two Years, and lived sixty-eight. He was succeeded by his Son *Badezorus,* who lived forty-five Years, and reigned six. His Successor was *Matgemus* his Son, who lived thirty-two Years, and reigned nine: He was succeeded by *Pygmalion,* who lived fifty-six Years, and reigned forty-seven. In his seventh Year, his Sister, who fled from him, built the City of *Carthage* in *Lybia.*" *Theophilus Antiochenus,* in his IIId Book to *Antolychus,* has set down this Place of *Menander,* but has contracted it. *Tertullian* in his Apology, *ch.* 19. says, *We must look into the Records of the most Antient Nations,* Egyptians, Chaldaeans, Phoenicians, *by whom we are supplied with Knowledge.* Such as *Manethon* the *Egyptian,* or *Berosus* the *Chaldaean,* or *Hirom* the *Phoenician, King of* Tyre; *and their Followers,* Mendesus, Ptolomaeus, *and* Menander *the* Ephesian, *and* Demetrius Phalereus, *and King* Juba, *and* Appion *and* Thallus. This *Hirom,* and *Solomon,* who was Cotemporary with him, are mentioned also by *Alexander Polyhistor, Menander, Pergamenus,* and *Laetus* in the *Phoenician* Accounts, as *Clemens* affirms, *Strom.* I. whence we may correct *Tatian,* who wrote Χαῖτος, *Chaetus,* for Λαῖτος, *Laetus,* who is reported to have translated into *Greek,* what *Theodotus, Hypsicrates,* and *Mochus* wrote about *Phoenicia.* The Memory of *Hazael* King of *Syria,* whose Name is in 1 *Kings* XIX. 15. 2 *Kings* VIII. 11. XII. 17. XIII. 3, 24. is preserved at *Damascus,* with Divine Worship, as *Josephus* relates, Book IX. ch. 2. of his Antient History. The same Name is in *Justin,* out of *Trogus.* Concerning *Salmanasar,* who carried the Ten Tribes into Captivity, as it is related in 2 *Kings* XVIII. 3, etc., and who took *Samaria,* 2 *Kings* XVIII. 9. there is a Place of *Menander the Ephesian,* which I mentioned before, in *Josephus,* Book IX. Ch. 14. "*Elulaeus* reigned thirty-six Years; this Man with a Fleet reduced the *Cittaeans,* who revolted from him. But the King

Names of *David* and *Solomon,* and the League <167> they made with the
Tyrians. And *Berosus,* as <168> well as the *Hebrew* Books mention, (*a*)

---

of *Assyria* sent an Army against them, and brought War upon all *Phoenicia;* and having
made Peace with them all, returned back again. But *Sidon, Arce, Palaetyrus,* and many
other Cities who had yielded themselves to the King of *Assyria,* revolted from the *Tyrian* Government; yet the *Tyrians* not submitting, the King of *Assyria* returned upon
them again, after he had received from the *Phoenicians* sixty Ships and eight hundred
Rowers. Against which, the *Tyrians* coming out with twelve Ships, broke their Enemies
Ships in Pieces, and took five hundred Men Prisoners, hereupon the Price of every
Thing was raised in *Tyrus.* Then the King of *Assyria* departed, and placed Guards upon
the River, and upon the Water-Pipes, that they might hinder the *Tyrians* from drawing
any; and this they did for five Years, and they were forced to drink out of Wells which
they digged." *Josephus* adds in the same Place, that *Salmanasar,* the Name of this King,
remained till his Time in the *Tyrian* Records. *Senacherib,* who subdued almost all *Judea,*
except *Jerusalem,* as it is related, 2 *Kings* XVIII. 13. 2 *Chron.* XXXII. I. *Isaiah* XXXVI. 1.
his Name and Expeditions into *Asia,* and *Egypt* are found in *Berosus's Chaldaicks,* as
the same *Josephus* testifies, Book X. ch. 1. and *Herodotus* in his IId Book mentions,
the same *Senacherib,* and calls him King of the *Arabians* and *Assyrians. Baladan,* King
of *Babylon* is mentioned in 2 *Kings* XX. 12. and *Isaiah* XXXIX. And the same Name
is in *Berosus's Babylonicks,* as *Josephus* testifies in his Antient History, Book X. Ch. 3.
Herodotus mentions the Battle in *Mageddo,* in which *Nechao* King of *Egypt* overcame
the *Jews;* (which History is in 2 *Chron.* XXXV. 22. *Zach.* XII. 1.) in the foresaid IId
Book, in these Words. *And* Necho *encountred the* Syrians, (for so *Herodotus* always
calls the *Jews,* as do others also,) *in a Land Battle, and overcame them in* Magdolus.
     a. *Nabuchadonosor,* &c.] Concerning him, *Josephus* has preserved us a Place of
Berosus in the Xth of his Ancient History, and in his first Book against *Appion;* which
may be compared with *Eusebius,* who in his *Chronicon* about these Times, and in his
Prepar. Book IX. ch. 40, and 41, produces this and the following Place of *Abydenus.*
"*Nabopallasarus* his Father hearing that he who was appointed Governor over *Egypt,*
and the Places about *Coelo Syria* and *Phoenice,* had revolted, being himself unable to
bear Hardships, he invested his Son *Nabuchadonosor,* who was a Young Man, with Part
of his Power, and sent Him against him. And *Nabuchadonsor* coming to a Battle with
the Rebel, smote him, and took him, and reduced the whole Land to his Subjection
again. It happened about this Time, that his Father *Nabopallasurus* fell sick, and died,
in the City of *Babylon,* after he had reigned twenty-nine Years. *Nabuchadonosor* in a
little Time hearing of the Death of his Father, after he had put in order his Affairs in
Egypt, and the rest of the Country, and committed to some of his Friends the Power
over the Captives of the *Jews, Phoenicians, Syrians,* and the People about *Egypt,* and ordered every thing that was left of any Use, to be conveyed to *Babylon,* he himself with
a few, came through the Wilderness to *Babylon;* where he found Affairs settled by the
Chaldaeans, and the Government maintained under one of the most eminent amongst
them, so that he inherited his Father's Kingdom entire; and having taken a View of the
Captives, he ordered them to be dispersed by Colonies, throughout all the proper

Places in the Country about *Babylon*. And he richly adorned the Temple of *Belus* and others, with the Spoils of the War; and he renewed the ancient City of *Babylon*, by adding another to it; so as that afterwards in a Siege, the River might never be turned out of its Course, to assault the City. He also encompassed the City with three Walls within, and three without, some made of Tile and Pitch, others of Tile alone. The City being thus well walled, and the Gates beautifully adorned, he added to his Father's Palace, a new one, far exceeding it in Heighth and Costliness; to relate the Particulars of which would be tedious. However, as exceeding great and beautiful as it was, it was finished in fifteen Days; on this Palace he built very high Walks of Stone, which to the Sight appeared like Mountains, and planted them with all sorts of Trees, and made what they call a Pensile Garden for his Wife, who was brought up in *Media*, to delight herself with the Prospect of the mountainous Country. After he had begun the forementioned Wall, he fell sick and died, having reigned forty three Years." This Wife of *Nabuchadonosor*, is *Nitocris*, according to *Herodotus* in his Ist Book, as we learn from the great *Scaliger*, in his famous Appendix to the Emendation of time. These things are explained by *Curtius*, in his Vth Book, to which I refer you; and partly by *Strabo*, Book XV. and *Diodorus* Book II. *Berosus*, out of whom we have quoted these things and those before, was the Priest of *Belus*, after *Alexander* the Great's time; to whom the *Athenians* erected a Statue with a golden Tongue, in the publick Gaming Place, for his Divine Predictions. This is mentioned by *Pliny*, Book VII. Chap. 37. of his Natural History. *Athenaeus* in his XVth, calls his Book *Babylonica*. *Tatian* (who himself also affirms that *Berosus* mentions *Nabuchadonosor*,) and *Clemens* call it *Chaldaica*. King *Juba* confesses that he took out hence what he wrote concerning the Affairs of *Syria*, as *Tatian* observes. He is also mentioned by *Vitruvius*, and by *Tertullian* in his Apology, and by the Writer of the *Alexandrian Chronicon*. *Eusebius*, both in his *Chronicon*, and in the End of the IXth of his *Praeparatio*, tells us that *Nabuchadonosor* is mentioned also in *Abydenus*, who wrote of the *Assyrians:* The Words are these. "*Meghasthenes* says, that *Nabuchodrosorus* was stronger than *Hercules*, and waged War against *Lybia* and *Iberia*, and having overcome them, he planted them in several Colonies on the right Shore of the Sea. And the *Chaldaeans* relate moreover concerning him, that as he was going into his Palace on a certain time, he was inspired by a God, and spake the following Words. I *Nabuchodrosorus* foretel a sad Calamity that will befal you, O *Babylonians;* which neither *Belus*, our Forefather, nor Queen *Beltis* could persuade the Fates to avert: There shall come a *Persian* Mule, who assisted by your Gods, shall bring Slavery upon you; *Medus*, the Glory of the *Assyrians*, will also help to do this. I wish that before he betrays his Countrymen, some *Charybdis*, or Sea, would swallow him up and destroy him; or that he were directed another way, through the Wilderness, where there are no Cities, or Footsteps of Men, where the wild Beasts feed, and the Birds fly about: That he might wander solitary amongst the Rocks and Dens, and that a happy End had overtaken me, before these things were put into my Mind. Having prophesied this, he suddenly disappeared." Compare this last with that which is said of this *Nabuchadonosor*, in the Book of *Daniel;* the first out of *Megasthenes*, we have also in *Josephus*, Book X. Chap. II. of his Ancient History; and he says it is in the IVth of his *Indian* History. *Eusebius* likewise has this concerning *Nabuchadonosor*, out of *Abydenus*. "It is reported (*of the Place where* Babylon *stands*) that at first it was all Water, called Sea, but *Belus*

Na-<169> <170> <171>*buchadonosor, (a)* and other *Chaldeans.* <172> <173>

---

drained it, and allotted to every one his Portion of Land, and incompassed *Babylon* with a Wall, which Time has worn out. But *Nabuchadonosor* walled it again, which remained till the *Macedonian* Empire; and it had brazen Gates." And a little after: "When *Nabuchadonosor* came to the Government, in fifteen Days time he walled *Babylon* with a triple Wall, and he turned out of their Course the Rivers *Armacale* and *Acracanus,* which is an Arm of *Euphrates.* And for the City of the *Sipparenians,* he digged a Pool forty Furlongs round, and twenty Fathom deep; and made Sluices to open, and water the Fields: They call them Guides to the *Aquaeducts.* He also built up a Wall to exclude the Red Sea; and he rebuilt *Teredon,* to hinder the Incursions of the *Arabians;* and he planted his Palace with Trees, called the Pensile Gardens." Compare this with *Dan.* IV. 27. And *Strabo,* Book XV. quotes these Words also out of the same *Magasthenes.* "*Nabuchadonosor,* whose Fame amongst the *Chaldaeans* is greater than *Hercules,* went as far as the Pillars." There were others who touched upon the History of this King, but we have only the Names of them remaining. *Diocles* in the IId of his *Persian* History, and *Philostratus* in that of the *Indians* and *Phoenicians,* who says that *Tyrus* was besieged by him XIII Years, as *Josephus* tells us in the forecited Place of his Ancient History, and in his Ist Book against *Appion,* where he quotes the following Words out of the publick Acts of the *Phoenicians.* "When *Ithobalus* was King, *Nabuchadonosor* besieged *Tyrus* thirteen Years. After him, *Baal* reigned ten Years; after him, Judges were appointed to govern *Tyrus. Eccibalus,* the Son of *Baslacus,* two Months; *Chelbes* the Son of *Abdaius* ten Months; *Abbarus* the High Priest three Months; *Mutgonus,* and *Gerastratus,* the Sons of *Abdelinus,* were Judges six Years; betwixt whom, *Balatorus* reigned one. After his Death they sent and fetched *Cerbalus* from *Babylon;* he reigned four Years. After his Death, they sent for his Brother *Hirom,* who reigned twenty Years. In his time, *Cyrus* the *Persian* flourished." For the exact Agreement of this Computation with the Sacred Books, see *Josephus* in the forecited Book against *Appion:* Where follows in *Josephus,* these Words concerning *Hecataeus.* "The *Persians,* says he, drew many Millions of us to *Babylon.*" And concerning the War of *Senacherib,* and *Nabuchadonosor's* Captivity, see the Place of *Demetrius* in *Clemens, Strom.* I.[3] *Hecataeus's* authority is very little to the Purpose, because he is a spurious Writer. See *Ger. John Vossius* upon the *Greek* Historians. *Le Clerc.*

3. Up to this point, the note is by Grotius.

a. *And other* Chaldeans, &c.] After the forecited Words of *Berosus,* follow these, according to *Josephus,* in both the Places now mentioned. "His Son *Evilmaradoch* was made Head of the Kingdom; he managed Affairs unjustly and wantonly; after he had reigned two Years, he was treacherously slain by *Neriglissoroorus,* who married his Sister; after his Death, *Neriglissoroorus,* who thus killed him, possessed the Government, and reigned four Years. His Son *Laborosoarchodus* a Youth reigned nine Months; but because there appeared in him many evil Dispositions, he was slain by the Treachery of his Friends. After his Death, they who killed him, agreed to devolve the Government upon *Nabonnedus,* a certain *Babylonian,* who was also one of the Conspirators. In this Reign, the Walls of the City *Babylon* along the River were beautified with burnt

Vaphres (*a*), the King of *Egypt* in *Jeremiah*, (*b*) is the same with *Apries* in *Herodotus*. And the *Greek* Books (*c*) are filled with *Cyrus* and his Successors (*d*) down to *Darius; and Josephus* in his Book against *Appion*, quotes

---

Brick and Pitch. In the seventeenth Year of his Reign, *Cyrus* came out of *Persia* with a great Army, and having subdued all the rest of *Asia,* he came as far as *Babylon; Nebonnidus* hearing of his coming, met him with a great Army also, but he was overcome in the Battle, and fled away with a few, and shut up himself in the City of the *Borsippeni*. Then *Cyrus* having taken *Babylon,* ordered the outward Walls of the City to be razed, because the People appeared to be very much given to change, and the Town hard to be taken; and went from thence to *Borsippus,* to besiege *Nabonnidus;* but he not enduring the Siege, yielded himself immediately; whereupon *Cyrus* treated him kindly, and giving him *Carmania* to dwell in, he sent him out of *Babylonia;* and *Nabonnidus* passed the Remainder of his Days in that Country, and died there." *Eusebius,* in the forementioned Place, has preserved the following Words of *Abydenus,* immediately after those now quoted concerning *Nabuchadonosor.* "After him reigned his Son *Evilmaruebus:* His Wife's Brother *Neriglasarus,* who slew him, left a Son, whose Name was *Labossoarascus.* He dying by a violent Death, they made *Nabannidachus* King, who was not related to him. *Cyrus,* when he took *Babylon,* made this Man Governor of *Carmenia.*" This *Evilmerodach* is mentioned by Name in 2 *Kings* XXV. 27. Concerning the rest, see *Scaliger.* That of *Cyrus*'s taking *Babylon,* agrees with this of *Herodotus.* "So *Cyrus* made an Irruption as far as *Babylon;* and the *Babylonians* having provided an Army, expected him: As soon as he approached the City, the *Babylonians* fought with him; but to save themselves from being beaten, they shut themselves up in the City." Compare this with the LIst of *Jeremiah,* 20, 30, 31. Concerning the Flight at *Borsippe,* see *Jeremiah,* LI. 39. Concerning the drying up the Rivers Channel, *Herodotus* agrees with *Jeremiah,* LI. 39. The Words of *Herodotus* are, *He divided the River, bringing it to a standing Lake, so that he made the ancient Current passable, having diverted the River.* It is worth considering, whether what *Diodorus* relates in his second Book concerning *Belesis* the *Chaldaean,* may not have respect to *Daniel,* whose Name in *Chaldee* was *Beltashazzar, Dan.* I. 7.[4] The Truth of which we read in Scripture concerning the *Chaldaean* Kings is strongly confirmed by the Chronology of the Astronomical Canon of *Nabonassar,* as you may see in Sir *John Marsham*'s Chronological Canon. *Le Clerc.*

4. Up to this point, the note is by Grotius.

a. Vaphres *the King of* Egypt, &c.] So the Seventy and *Eusebius* translate the *Hebrew* Word חפרע *Chephre.* He was Contemporary with *Nabuchadonosor.*

b. *Is the same with* Apries *in* Herodotus, &c.] Book II.

c. *Are filled with* Cyrus, &c.] See the Places already quoted, and *Diodorus Siculus,* Book II. and *Ctesias* in his *Persicks;* and *Justin,* Book IV. Chap. 5. and the following. The Foundation of the Temple of *Jerusalem* was laid in *Cyrus*'s time, and was finished in *Darius*'s, according to *Berosus,* as *Theophilus Antiochenus* proves.

d. *Down to* Darius, &c.] *Cadomannus.* See the forementioned Persons, and *Aeschylus*'s Account of *Persia,* and the Writers of the Affairs of *Alexander.* In the time of this *Darius, Jaddus* was the High Priest of the *Hebrews, Nehem.* XII. 22. the same that went

many other things relating to the *Jewish* Nation: To which may be added that what we above took (*a*) out of *Strabo* and *Trogus.* But there is no Reason for us Christians to doubt of the Credibility of these Books, because there are Testimonies in our Books, out of almost every one of them, the same as they are found in the *Hebrew.* Nor did Christ, when he <174> reproved many things in the Teachers of the Law, and in the Pharisees of his time, ever accuse them of falsifying the Books of *Moses* and the Prophets, or of using supposititious or altered Books. And it can never be proved or made credible, that after Christ's time the Scripture should be corrupted in any thing of Moment, if we do but consider how far and wide the *Jewish* Nation, who every where kept those Books, was dispersed over the whole World. For first the ten Tribes were carried into *Media* by the *Assyrians,* and afterwards the other two. And many of these fixed themselves in foreign Countries, after they had a Permission from *Cyrus* to return; (*b*) the *Macedonians* invited them into *Alexandria* with great Advantages; the Cruelty of *Antiochus,* the Civil War of the *Asmonaei,* and the foreign Wars of *Pompey* and *Sossius,* scattered a great many; (*c*) the Country of *Cyrene*

---

out to meet *Alexander* the Great, according to the Relation of *Josephus,* in his Ancient History, Book XI. 8. At this time lived *Hecataeus Abderita,* so famous in *Plutarch,* in his Book concerning *Isis,* and *Laertius* in *Pyrrho;* he wrote a single Book concerning the *Jews,* whence *Josephus* in Book II. against *Appion,* took a famous Description of the City and Temple of *Jerusalem;* which Place we find in *Eusebius,* Book IX. Chap. 9. of his Gospel Preparation; and in each of them there is a Place of *Clearchus,* who commends the *Jewish* Wisdom in the Words of *Aristotle.* And *Josephus* in the same Book names *Theophilus, Theodoret, Mnaseas, Aristophanes, Hermogenes, Enemerus, Conoron, Zopyrion* and others, as Persons who commended the *Jews* and gave Testimony concerning the *Jewish* Affairs.

a. *Out of* Strabo *and* Trogus, &c.] Book I.

b. *The* Macedonians *invited them,* &c.] *Hecataeus* transcribed by *Josephus,* in his Ist Book against *Appion,* speaking of the *Jews. Not a few,* (viz *thousands,* as appears from the foregoing Words) *after the Death of* Alexander, *went into* Egypt *and* Phoenicia, *by reason of the Commotions in* Syria. To which we may add that of *Philo* against *Flaccus. There are no less than ten hundred thousand* Jews *Inhabitants of* Alexandria, *and the Country about it, from the lower Parts of* Lybia, *to the Borders of* Aethiopia. See moreover *Josephus,* Book XII. Chap. 2, 3. and the following Book XIII. Chap. 4, 5, 6, 7, 8. XVIII. 10. And the *Jews* were free of *Alexandria, Josephus* XIV. 1.

c. *The Country of* Cyrene *was filled with* Jews, &c.] See *Josephus,* Book XVI. 10. of his Ancient History. *Acts* VI. 9. XI. 20.

was filled with *Jews;* (*a*) the Cities of *Asia,* (*b*) *Macedonia,* (*c*) *Lycaonia,* (*d*) and the Isles of *Cyprus,* <175> (*e*) and *Crete,* and others were full of them; and that there was a vast Number of them (*f*) in *Rome* we learn from (*g*) *Horace,* (*h*) *Juvenal,* and (*i*) *Martial.* It is impossible that such distant

a. *The Cities of* Asia, &c.] *Josephus* XII. 3. XIV. 17. XVI. 4. *Acts* XIX.

b. *Macedonia,* &c.] *Acts* XVII.

c. *Lycaonia,* &c.] *Acts* XIV. 18.

d. *And the Isles of* Cyprus, &c.] *Acts* XIII. 5.

e. *And* Crete, &c.] *Acts* II. 11.

f. *In* Rome, &c.] *Josephus* XVIII. 5. of his Ancient History. *Acts* XVIII. 2. XXVIII. 17.

g. *Horace,* &c.] Book I. Sat. IV.

——— For we are many,
And like the *Jews* will force you to our Side,

And Sat. V.

——— Let circumcised Jews believe it.

And Sat. IX.

——— This is the thirtieth Sabbath, &c.

h. *Juvenal,* &c.] Sat. IX.

Some are of Parents born, who Sabbaths keep.

And what follows, Sat. XIV.

i. *Martial,* &c.] III. 4.

The Sabbath-keepers Fasts.

And in other Places; as VII. 29, and 34. XI. 97. XII. 57. To which we may add that of *Rutilius,* Book I. of his *Itinerary.*

I wish *Judaea* ne'er had been subdu'd
By *Pompey*'s War, or *Titus*'s Command.
The more suppress'd, the dire Contagion spreads,
The conquered Nation crush the Conqueror.

Which is taken out of *Seneca,* who said of the same *Jews; The Customs of the most wicked Nation have prevailed so far, that they are embraced all the World over, so that the Conquered give Laws to the Conquerors.* The Place is in *Augustin,* Book IV. Chap. II. of his City of God: He calls them the most wicked Nation only for this Reason, because their Laws condemned the Neglect of the Worship of one God, as we observed before; upon which Account, *Cato Major* blamed *Socrates.* To which may be added the Testimony of *Philo* in his Embassy, of the vast Extent of the *Jewish* Nation. "That

Bodies of <176> Men should be imposed upon by any Art whatsoever, or that they should agree in a Falsity. We may add further, (*a*) that almost three hundred Years before Christ, by the Care of the *Egyptian* Kings, the *Hebrew* Books were translated into *Greek,* by those who are called the *Seventy;* that the *Greeks* might have them in another Language, but the Sense the same in the main; upon which Account they were the less liable to be altered. And the same Books were translated into *Chaldee,* and into the *Jerusalem* Language; that is, half *Syriac;* (*b*) partly a little before, (*c*) and partly a little after Christ's time. After which followed other *Greek* Versions, that of *Aquila, Symmachus,* and *Theodotion,* which *Origen,* and others after him, compared with the seventy Interpreters, and found no Difference in the History, or in any weighty Matters. *Philo* flourished in *Caligula's* time, and *Josephus* lived till *Vespasian's.* Each of them quote out of the *Hebrew* Books the same things that we find at this Day. By this time the Christian Re-<177>ligion began to be more and more spread, (*d*) and many of its Professors were *Hebrews:* (*e*) Many had studied the *Hebrew* Learning, who could very easily have perceived and discovered it, if the *Jews* had received any thing that was false, in any remarkable Subject, I mean, by comparing it with more ancient Books. But they not only do this, but they bring very many Testimonies out of the Old Testament, plainly in that Sense in which they are received amongst the *Hebrews;* which *Hebrews* may be convicted of any Crime, sooner than (I will not say of Falsity, but) of Negligence, in

––––––––––

Nation consists of so great a Number of Men, that it does not, like other Nations, take up one Country only, and confine itself to that; but possesses almost the whole World; for it overspreads every Continent and Island, that they seem not to be much fewer than the Inhabitants themselves." *Dion Cassius,* Book XXXVI. concerning the *Jewish* Nation, says, "that though it has been often suppressed, it has increased so much the more, so as to procure the Liberty of establishing its Laws."

a. *That almost three hundred Years,* &c.] See *Aristaeus* and *Josephus,* Book XII. 2.

b. *Partly a little before,* &c.] By *Onkelos,* and perhaps by *Jonathan.*

c. *And partly a little after,* &c.] By the Writer of the *Jerusalem Targum,* and by *Josephus Caecus,* or by him, whoever he was, one Man or many, who translated *Job, Psalms, Proverbs,* and what they call the *Hagiography.*

d. *And many of its Professors were* Hebrews, &c.] Or next to *Hebrews,* as *Justin,* who was a *Samaritan.*

e. *Many had studied the* Hebrew *Learning,* &c.] As *Origen, Epiphanius,* and especially *Hieronymus.*

relation to these Books; (*a*) because they used to transcribe and compare them so very scrupulously, that they could tell how often every Letter came over. We may add, in the first Place, an Argument, and that no mean one, why the *Jews* did not alter the Scripture designedly; because the Christians prove, and as they think very strongly, <178> that their Master Jesus was that very Messiah who was of old promised to the Forefathers of the *Jews;* and this from those very Books, which were read by the *Jews.* Which the *Jews* would have taken the greatest Care should never have been, after there arose a Controversy between them and the Christians; if it had ever been in their Power to have altered what they would. <179>

a. *Because they used to transcribe,* &c.] *Josephus* in his Ist Book against *Appion.* "It is very manifest by our Deeds how much Credit we give to our own Writings; for after so many Ages past, no one has presumed to add, take away, or change any thing." See the Law, *Deut.* IV. 1. and the *Talmud,* inscribed *Shebnoth.* (We are to understand this of the time after the *Masora;* for it was otherwise before, in the time of their Commonwealth; and after it was overturned by the *Chaldaeans,* they were not so accurate as is commonly thought. This is evident from *Lud. Capellus*'s Criticks upon the Bible, and from the Commentaries of learned Men upon the Old Testament, and likewise from *Grotius*'s own Annotations. And we also have shewn it to be so on the historical Books of the Old Testament. *Le Clerc.*)

BOOK IV

Sect. I. *A particular Confutation of the Religions that differ from Christianity.*

The fourth Book, (beginning with that Pleasure Men for the most Part take at the Sight of other Mens Danger, when they themselves are placed out of the Reach of it;) shows that the principal Aim of a Christian ought to be, not only a Satisfaction upon his having found out the Truth himself, but also an Endeavour to assist others, who wander in various crooked Paths of Error, and to make them Partakers of the same Happiness. And this we have in some measure attempted to do in the foregoing Books, because the Demonstration of the Truth, contains in it the Confutation of Error. But however, since the particular sorts of Religion, which are opposed to Christianity; as Paganism, Judaism, or Mahometanism, for instance; besides that which is common to all, have some particular Errors, and some special Arguments, which they use to oppose us with; I think it may not be foreign to our present Purpose, to attempt a particular Examination of every one of them; in the mean time beseeching our Readers to free their Judgment from all Passion and Prejudice, which clogg the Understanding; that they may the more impartially determine concerning what is to be said. <180>

Sect. II. *And first of Paganism. That there is but one God. That created Beings are either good or bad. That the Good are not to be worshipped without the Command of the Supreme God.*

And first against the Heathens, we say, if they suppose many Gods eternal and equal, this is sufficiently confuted in the first Book, where we have shewn that there is but one God the Cause of all things. If by Gods they mean created Beings superior to Man, these are either good or bad; if they say they are good, they ought in the first Place to be very well assured of this, (*a*) lest they fall into great Danger, by entertain-<181>ing Enemies instead of Friends, Deserters instead of Ambassadors. And Reason also demands that there should be some manifest Difference in the Worship, betwixt the Supreme God and these Beings: And further, we ought to know of what Rank these Beings are, what Benefit we may expect from any of them, and what Honour the Supreme King would have us pay to them. All which things being wanting in their Religion, it sufficiently appears from thence, that there is nothing of Certainty in it; and it would be much safer for them to betake themselves to the Worship of the one Supreme God; (*b*) which even *Plato* owned to be the Duty of a wise Man; because as good Beings are the Ministers of the Supreme God, (*c*) they cannot but be assisting to such as are in favour with him.

a. *Lest they fall into great Danger,* &c.] 2 *Cor.* XII. 14. *Porphyry* in his second Book about abstaining from eating Animals, says, that "By those who are opposite (*to the Gods,*) all Witchcraft is performed; for both these and their Chief is worshipped by all such as work evil upon Mens Fancies by Inchantments; for they have a Power to deceive by working strange things: By them evil Spirits prepare Philtres, and Love-Potions; all Incontinence and Love of Riches and Honour, and especially Deceit, proceed from them; for it is natural to them to lie; they are willing to be thought Gods; and the highest in Power of them, to be esteemed God." And afterwards concerning the *Egyptian* Priests; "These put it past all Dispute that there are a Kind of Beings, who give themselves up to deceive; of various Shapes and Sorts; Dissemblers, sometimes assuming the Form of Gods or *Daemons,* or of Souls of dead Men; and by this Means they can effect any seeming Good or Evil: But as to things really good in themselves, such as those belonging to the Soul; of producing these they have no Power, neither have they any Knowledge of them; but they abuse their Leisure, mock others, and hinder those who walk in the way of Virtue, they are filled with Pride, and delight in Perfumes and Sacrifice." And *Arnobius* Book IV. against the Gentiles. "Thus the Magicians, Brethren to the Soothsayers in their Actions, mention certain Beings opposite to God, who often impose upon Men for true Gods. And these are certain Spirits of grosser Matter, who feign themselves to be Gods." Not to transcribe too much, we find something to the same Purpose in *Jamblichus,* concerning the *Egyptian* Mysteries, Book III. Chap. 33. and Book IV. Chap 17.

b. *Which even* Plato *owned,* &c.] Jupiter *is worshipped by us, and other Gods by others.* The Words are quoted by *Origen,* in his VIIIth Book against *Celsus.*

c. *They cannot but be assisting,* &c.] This is very well prosecuted by *Arnobius,* Book III.

SECT. III. *A Proof that evil Spirits were worshipped by the Heathen, and the Unworthiness of it shown.*

But that the Spirits, to which the Heathen paid their Worship, were evil, and not good, appears from many substantial Arguments. First, (*a*) because they did not direct their Worshippers to <182> the Worship of the Supreme God; but did as much as they could to suppress such Worship, or at least were willing in every thing to be equalled with the Supreme God in Worship. Secondly, because they were the Cause of the greatest Mischiefs coming upon the Worshippers of the one Supreme God, provoking the Magistrates and the People to inflict Punishments upon them: For, though they allowed their Poets the Liberty to celebrate the Murders and Adulteries of their Gods; and the *Epicureans* to banish the Divine Providence out of the World; nor was there any other Religion so disagreeable in its Rites, but they admitted it into their Society, as the *Egyptian, Phrygian, Greek,* and *Thuscan* Rites at *Rome;* (*b*) yet the *Jews* were every where ridiculed, as appears from their Satyrs and Epigrams, (*c*) and were sometimes banished; (*d*) and the Christians had moreover the most cruel Punishments inflicted upon them: for which there can be no other Reason assigned, but because these two Sects worshipped one God, whose Honour their received Gods opposed, being more jealous of him than of one another. Thirdly, from the manner of their Worship, such as is unworthy of a good and virtuous Mind; <183> (*e*) by human

a. *Because they did not direct,* &c.] This is very well treated of by *Augustin,* Book X. Chap. 14, 16, 19. of his City of God.

b. *Yet the Jews were every where ridiculed,* &c.] "As being cropt, circumcised, Sabbath-keepers, Worshippers of the Clouds and Heavens, merciful to Swine."

c. *And were sometimes banished,* &c.] *Josephus* XVIII. 5. *Tacitus,* Annal. II. *Seneca,* Epist. CIX. *Acts* XVIII. 1. *Suetonius* in *Tiberius;* Chap. XXVI.

d. *And the Christians had moreover,* &c.] *Tacitus,* Annal XV. to which that of *Juvenal* relates.

—— You like a Torch shall burn,
As they who flaming stand stifled with Smoke,
And with their Body's Print have mark'd the Ground.

e. *By human Blood,* &c.] See what was said of this Book II.

Blood, (*a*) by Mens running naked about their Temples, (*b*) by Games and Dancings filled with Uncleanness; such are now to be seen amongst the People of *America* and *Africa,* overwhelmed in the Darkness of Heathenism. Nay, more than this, there were of old, and still are, People, who worship evil Spirits, which they know and own to be such; (*c*) as the *Arimanes* of the *Persians,* the *Cacodaemons* of the *Greeks,* (*d*) and the *Vejoves* of the *Latins;* and some of the *Ethiopians* and *Indians* now have others; than which nothing can be imagined more impious. For what else is religious Worship, but a Testimony of the exceeding Goodness which you acknowledge to be in him whom you worship; which, if it be paid to an evil Spirit, is false and counterfeit, and comprehends in it the Sin of Rebellion; because the Honour due to the King is not only taken from him, but transferred to a Deserter and his Enemy. And it is a foolish Opinion to imagine that a good God will not revenge this, because that is not agreeable to his Goodness; (*e*) for Clemency, if it be reasonable, hath its proper Bounds; and where the <184> Crimes are very great, Justice itself forces Punishment, as it were necessarily. Nor are they less blameable, who say that they are driven by Fear to pay Obedience to evil Spirits; for he who is infinitely Good, is also in the highest Degree ready to communicate; and therefore all other Beings were produced by him. And if it be so, it will follow that he has an absolute Right over all Creatures as his own Workmanship; so that nothing can be done by any of them, if he desires to hinder it: Which being granted, we may easily collect, that evil Spirits cannot hurt him who is in Favour with the most High God, who

a. *By Mens running naked about,* &c.] As in their Rites dedicated to *Pan.* See *Livy,* Book I. *Plutarch* in *Antoninus,* and others.

b. *By Games* and *Dancings,* &c.] As in the Rites of *Flora.* See *Ovid's Fasti,* Book IV. and *Tatian,* and *Origen* in his VIIIth against *Celsus.*

c. *As the* Arimanes *of the* Persians, &c.] See *Plutarch's Isis* and *Osiris,* and *Diogenes Laertius* in his Preface. (See also *Thomas Stanley,* of the Philosophy of the *Persians;* and our Observations upon the Word *Arimanes* in the Index. *Le Clerc.*)

d. *And the* Vejoves *of the* Latins, &c.] *Cicero,* Book III. of the Nature of the Gods.

e. *For Clemency, if it be reasonable,* &c.] *How can you love, unless you be afraid not to love? Tertullian* I. against *Marcion.*

is infinitely Good; any further than That God suffers it to be done for the sake of some Good. Nor can any thing be obtained of evil Spirits, but what ought to be refused; (*a*) because a bad Being when he counterfeits one that is good, is then worst; and (*b*) the Presents of Enemies are only Snares.

Sect. IV. *Against the Heathen Worship paid to departed Men.*

There have been, and now are, Heathens, who say that they pay Worship to the Souls of Men departed this Life. But here in the first Place, this Worship is also to be distinguished, by manifest Tokens, from the Worship of the Supreme God. Besides, our Prayers to them are to no Purpose, if those Souls cannot assist us in any thing; and their Worshippers are not assured of this, nor is there any more Reason to affirm that they can, than that they cannot: And what is worst of all, <185> is, that those Men who are thus had in Honour, are found to have been Men remarkable for very great Vices. A drunken *Bacchus,* an effeminate *Hercules,* a *Romulus* unnatural to his Brother, and a *Jupiter* as unnatural to his Father. So that their Honour is a Reproach to the true God, and that Goodness which is well-pleasing to him; (*c*) because it adds a Commendation from Religion, to those Vices which are sufficiently flattering of themselves.

a. *Because a bad Being,* &c.] See the Verses of *Syrus* the Mimick.

b. *The Presents of Enemies are only Snares,* &c.]

Enemies Gifts are no Gifts, no Advantage.
Sophocles.

c. *Because it adds a Commendation,* &c.] See an Example hereof in *Terence's* Eunuch, Act. III. Scene V. *Cyprian,* Epist. II. "They imitate those Gods they worship; those Wretches commit Religious Crimes. *Augustine Epist.* CLII. Nothing renders Men so unsociable by perverseness of Life, as the Imitation of those whom they commend and describe in their Writings. *Chalcidius* in *Timaeus;* So it comes to pass, that instead of that Gratitude that is due to Divine Providence from Men, for their Original and Birth; they return Sacrilege." See the whole Place.

Sect. V. *Against the Worship given to the Stars and Elements.*

(*a*) More antient than this, was the Worship of the Stars, and what we call the Elements, Fire, Water, Air, and Earth; Which was indeed a very great Error. For Prayers are a principal Part of Religious Worship, which to put up to any but Beings that have Understanding, is very foolish; and that what we call the Elements are not such, is evident in a good Measure from Experience. If any one affirms otherwise of the Stars, he has no Proof of it, because no such Thing can be gathered <186> from their Operations, which are the only Signs to judge of Beings by. But the contrary may be sufficiently collected from the Motion of them, which is not various, like that of Creatures endued with Freedom of Will, (*b*) but certain and determinate. We have elsewhere shown, that the Course of the Stars is adapted to the Use of Man; whence Man ought to acknowledge, that he in his better Part, bears a nearer Resemblance to God, and is dearer to him; and therefore ought not to derogate so much from his own high Birth, as to place himself below those Things which God has given him; and he ought to give God Thanks for them, which is more than they can do for themselves, or at least more than we are assured of.

Sect. VI. *Against the Worship given to Brute Creatures.*

But that which is of all Things most abominable, is, that some Men, particularly the *Egyptians,* (*c*) fell into the Worship even of Beasts. For, though in some of them there do appear, as it were, some Shadow of Understanding, yet it is nothing compared with Man: for they cannot express

a. *More antient than this,* &c.] There are Reasons to persuade us that Idolatry began with the Worship of Angels and the Souls of Men, as you may see in the Index to the Oriental Philosophy, at the Word *Idolotatria. Le Clerc.*

b. *But certain and determinate,* &c.] By which Argument, a certain King of *Peru,* was perswaded to deny that the Sun could be a God. See the History of the *Incha's.*

c. *Fell into the Worship even of Beasts,* &c.] Concerning whom, *Philo* in his Embassy says, *They esteem Dogs, Wolves, Lions, Crocodiles, and many other wild Creatures in the Water and on the Land, and Birds, as Gods.* To which may be added a long Discourse of this Matter, in the Ist Book of *Diodorus Siculus.*

their inward Conceptions, either by distinct Words or Writings; nor do they perform Actions of different Kinds, nor those of the same Kind in a different Manner; and much less can they attain to the <187> Knowledge of Number, Magnitude, and of the Coelestial Motions. But on the other Hand, (*a*) Man by his Cunning and Subtilty can catch the strongest Creatures, wild Beasts, Birds, or Fishes; and can in some measure bring them under Rules, as Elephants, Lions, Horses, and Oxen; he can draw Advantage to himself out of those that are most hurtful, as Physick from Vipers; and this <188> Use may be made of them all, which themselves are ignorant of, that by viewing the Structure and Situation of the Parts of their Bodies, and comparing together their several Species and Kinds, he learns his own Excellency, and how much more perfect and noble the Frame of humane Body is than others; which, if rightly consider'd, is so

a. *Man by his Cunning and Subtilty,* &c.]

> Man has but little Strength,
> Yet can, by various Arts,
> Tame the wildest Creatures
> In Sea, or Earth, or Air.
>> Euripides in Aeolus.

And *Antiphon:*

> They us in Strength, we them in Art, exceed.

Which affords us no bad Explication of *Genesis* I. 26. and *Psalm* VIII. 8. He that desires a larger Discourse of this Matter, may look into *Oppianus* in the Beginning of his Vth Book of Fishing, and *Basil's* Xth Homily on the Six Days Creation. *Origen* in his IVth Book against *Celsus,* has these Words. "And hence you may learn, for how great a Help our Understanding was given us, and how far it exceeds all the Weapons of wild Beasts; for our Bodies are much weaker than those of other Creatures, and vastly less than some of them; yet by our Understanding, we bring wild Beasts under our Power, and hunt huge Elephants: and those whose Nature is such, that they may be tamed, we make subject to us; and those that are of a different Nature, or the Taming of which seems to be of no Use to us, we manage these wild Beasts with such Safety, that as we will, we keep them shut up, or, if we want their Flesh for Meat, we kill them as we do other Creatures that are not wild. Whence it appears, that the Creator made all living Creatures subject to Him who is endued with Reason, and a Nature capable of understanding him." *Claudius Neapolitanus,* in *Porphyry's* Ist Book against eating living Creatures, speaks thus concerning Man. "He is Lord over all Creatures void of Reason, as God is over Men."

far from inclining him to worship other Creatures, that he should rather think himself appointed their God in a manner, under the Supreme God.

Sect. VII. *Against the Worship given to those Things which have no real Existence.*

We read that the *Greeks* and *Latins,* and others likewise, worshipped Things, which had no real Existence, but were only the Accidents of other Things. For, not to mention those mad Things, (*a*) Fever, Impudence, and such like; Health is nothing else but a just Temperature of the Parts of the Body; and good Fortune, a Correspondence of Events with the Wishes of Men: And the Affections, such as Love, Fear, Anger, Hope, and the like, arising from the Consideration of the Goodness or Badness, the Easiness or Difficulty of a Thing; are certain Motions in that Part of the Mind, which is most closely connected with the Body, by Means of the Blood; and they have no Power of their own, but are subject to the Command of the Will, which is Mistress of them, at least as far as respects their Continuance and Direction. So likewise the Virtues, which have different Names. Prudence, which consists in the Choice of what is profitable; Fortitude, in under-<189>going Dangers; Justice, in abstaining from what is not our own; Temperance, in moderating Pleasure, and the like: There is also a certain Disposition or Inclination towards that which is right, which grows upon the Mind by long Exercise, which, as it may be increased, so it may be diminished by Neglect, nay, it may entirely be destroyed in a Man. (*b*) And Honour, to which we read of Temples being dedicated, is only the Judgment of one concerning another, as endued with Virtue; which often happens to the Bad, and not to the Good, thro' the natural Aptness of Mankind to mistake. (*c*) Since therefore

---

a. *Fever, Impudence, and such like,* &c.] See *Tully's* IIId Book of the Laws.

b. *And Honour, to which we read,* &c.] *Tully* in the forementioned Place; and *Livy,* Book XXVII.

c. *Since therefore these Things have no real Existence,* &c.] Perhaps some may explain this Worship of the Heathens in this Manner, as to say, that it was not so much the Things which were commonly signified by those Words, that they worshipped, as a certain Divine Power, from which they flowed, or certain Ideas in the Divine

these Things have no real Existence, and cannot be compared in Excellence with those that have <190> a real Existence; nor have any Knowledge of our Prayers or Veneration of them, it is most disagreeable to right Reason, to worship them as God; and He is rather to be worshipped upon their Account, who can give us them, and preserve them for us.

SECT. VIII. *An Answer to the Objection of the Heathen, taken from the Miracles done amongst them.*

The Heathens used to recommend their Religion by Miracles; but they were such as were liable to many Exceptions. For the wisest Men amongst the Heathens themselves, rejected many of them, (*a*) as not supported by the Testimony of sufficient Witnesses, (*b*) but plainly counterfeit: And those that seem to have been done, came to pass in some secret Place, in

---

Understanding. Thus they might be said to worship *a Fever,* not the Disease itself which is seated in the Humane Body; but that Power, which is in God, of sending or abating a Fever, to worship *Impudence,* not that Vice which is seated in the Minds of Men; but the Will of God, which sometimes allows Men's *Impudence* to go on, which he can restrain and punish: And the same may be said of the rest, as Love, Fear, Anger, Hope, which are *Passions* which God can either excite or restrain: or of *Virtues* which are perfect in the Divine Nature, and of which we see only some faint Resemblances in Men, arising from the Ideas of those Virtues which are most compleat in God. And of *Honour,* which does not consist so much in the Esteem of Men, as in the Will of God, who would have Virtue honourable amongst Men. But the Heathens themselves never interpreted this Matter thus, and it is absurd to worship the Attributes and Ideas of God as real Persons, under obscure Names, such as may deceive the common People. It is much more sincere and honest to worship the Deity himself without any Perplexities. *Le Clerc.*

a. *As not supported by the Testimony,* &c.] So *Livy,* in the Beginning. "I do not design either to affirm or deny those Things related before, or upon the Building of the City; as fitter for Poetick Fables, than the Sincere Memorials of Affairs that were transacted; Thus much must be allowed Antiquity, that by mixing Humane Things with Divine, the Original of Cities was rendred the more venerable."

b. *But plainly counterfeit,* &c.] It were much better to acquiesce in this Answer than to allow of their Miracles, or that such Things were done as Men could not commonly distinguish from Miracles; such as Oracles, Wonders, Curing of Diseases, which if they were done, could scarce be distinguished from true Miracles, at least by the Common People. See what I have said upon this Matter in the *Prolegomena to my Ecclesiastical History.* Sect. II. c. 1. *Le Clerc.*

the Night, before one or two Persons, whose Eyes might easily be deceived with a false Appearance of Things, by the Cunning of the Priests. There were some which only caused the People, who did not understand the Nature of Things, especially their occult Quali-<191>ties to wonder at them; much in the same Manner, as if any one should draw Iron with a Loadstone, before People who knew nothing of it; and it is related by many (*a*) that these were the Arts in which *Simon* and *Apollonius Tyanaeus* were so skilful. I do not deny, but that some greater than these were seen, which could not be the Effect of natural Causes by humane Power alone; but they were such as did not require a Power truly Divine, that is, Omnipotent; for these Spirits who were inferior to God, and superior to Man, were sufficient for these Things; because by their Swiftness, Strength and Cunning, they could easily remove distant Things, and so to compound different Sorts of Things, as to produce Effects which should be very surprizing to Men. But the Spirits by whom this was effected, were not good, and consequently neither was their Religion good; as is evident from what was said before, and from this Consideration also, because they said that they were compelled (*b*) by certain <192> Inchantments against their

a. *That these were the Arts,* &c.] Tatian. "There are certain Diseases and Contrarieties of the Matter of which we are compounded; when these happen, the *Daemons* ascribe the Causes of them to themselves."

b. *By certain Inchantments,* &c.] Thus the Oracle of *Hecate* in *Porphyry.*

> I come, invoked by well consulted Prayers,
> Such as the Gods have to Mankind reveal'd.

And again,

> Why have you call'd the Goddess *Hecate*
> From Heaven; and forc'd her by a Charm Divine;

And that of *Apollo* in the same Writer,

> Hear me, for I am forced to speak against my Will.

These are the Rites of their secret Arts, by which they address themselves to I know not what Powers, as *Arnobius* expresses it, as if they compelled them by Charms to be their Servants; so *Clemens* explains it. There is a Form of their Threats in *Jamblichus,* Book IV. Chap. 5, 6, 7. of his *Egyptian* Mysteries. The same we meet with in *Lucan,* Book IX, in the Words of *Pompey* the Less, and in *Eusebius,* out of *Porphyry,* Book V. Chap 10. of his Gospel Praeparat. Other Forms of Threatnings, you have in *Lucan,* where he speaks of *Erichthon;* and in *Papinius* about *Tiresias.*

Will: And yet the wisest Heathens agreed that there could not possibly be any such Force in Words, but that they could only persuade, and this according to the Manner of their Interpretation. And a further Sign of their Wickedness is, that they would undertake many times (*a*) to entice some to the Love of others, notwithstanding their own Endeavours against it, either by false Promises, or by doing them some Hurt; (*b*) which Things were forbidden by human Laws, as Witchcraft. Neither ought any one to wonder, that the Supreme God should suffer some Miracles to be done by evil Spirits; because they who were already fallen from the Worship of the true God, (*c*) deserved to be deluded by such Deceits. But this is an Argument of their Weakness, that their Works were not attended with any remarkable Good; for if any seemed to be called to Life again, they did not continue long in it, nor exercise the Functions of living Persons. If at any <193> time any thing proceeding from a Divine Power, appeared in the Sight of the Heathen; yet it was not foretold, that that would come to pass in order to prove the truth of their Religion; so that nothing hinders but the Divine Power might propose to itself some other End widely different from this. For instance; suppose it true, that a blind Man was restored to his Sight by *Vespasian;* it might be done (*d*) to render him more venerable

a. *To entice some to the Love of others,* &c.] See the *Pharmacentria* of *Theocritus* and *Virgil,* and the Confession of *Porphyry* in *Eusebius,* Book V. Chap. 17. of his Praeparat. and *Augustin,* Book X. Chap. 11. of his City of God. And the same *Porphyry* against eating living Creatures, Book II. and *Origen* against *Celsus,* Book VII.

b. *Which things were forbidden by human Laws,* &c.] L. *Ejusdem.* Sect. *Adjectio D. ad Legem Corneliam de Sicariis & Veneficis. L. si quis sect. qui abortionis. D. de poenis. Paulus Sententiarum* lib. V. Tit. XXIII.

c. *Deserved to be deluded by such Deceits,* &c.] *Deut.* XIII. 3. 2 *Thess.* II. 9, 10. *Ephes.* II. 2, 3.

d. *To render him more venerable,* &c.] *Tacitus,* Hist. IV. "Many Miracles were done, whereby the Favour of Heaven, and the good Disposition of the Gods towards *Vespasian,* appeared." He had said before in Hist. I. "We believe that after previous good Luck, the Empire was decreed to *Vespasian* and his Children, by the secret Law of Fate, and by Wonders and Oracles." *Suetonius* ushers in his Relation of the same Miracles thus, Ch. 7. "There was a certain Authority and Majesty wanting, *viz.* in a new and unthought of Prince; to which this was added." See the same *Suetonius* a little before, Chap. 5. *Josephus* says of the same *Vespasian,* Book III. Chap. 27. of the Wars of the *Jews;* "That God raised him up to the Government, and foretold him of the Scepter by other Signs."

upon this Account; and that he might thereby the more easily obtain the *Roman* Empire; and was therefore chosen by God, to be the Executioner of his Judgments upon the *Jews;* and other like Reasons there might be, for other Wonders, (*a*) which had no Relation at all to Religion.

SECT. IX. *And from Oracles.*

And almost all the same things may be applied to solve that which they alledge concerning Oracles; especially what was before said, that such Men deserved to be imposed upon, who despised <194> that Knowledge which Reason and ancient Tradition suggested to every Man. Moreover, the Words of the Oracles (*b*) were for the most part ambiguous, and such as might be interpreted of the Event, be it what it would. And if any thing was more particularly foretold by them, there is no Necessity of its proceeding from an Omniscient Being; because either they were such as might be perceived beforehand from natural Causes then appearing, (*c*) as some Physicians foretel future Diseases; or they might with Probability be conjectured from what we usually see come to pass; which we

a. *Which had no Relation,* &c.] But see the Examination of Miracles feigned to be done in favour of *Vespasian* and *Adrian,* in my *Ecclesiastical History. Century* II. 138th Year. *Le Clerc.*

b. *Were for the most Part ambiguous,* &c.] See the Places of *Oenomaus,* concerning this Subject, in *Eusebius* Book IV. Chap. 20, 21, 22, 23, 24, 25, 26. Hence *Apollo* was by the *Greeks* called Λοξίας, *Ambiguous. Cicero,* in his second Book of Divination, says the Oracles of *Apollo* were ambiguous and obscure. *Which soever of them came to pass* (says he) *the Oracle was true.*[1] (Perhaps many of the Oracles were counterfeited after the Event: And there are many Reasons to suspect, that abundance of Frauds were used by Diviners; concerning which, *D. de Fontenelle* has wrote an excellent Book in *French,* which I refer you to, and what is said in Defence of it, Vol. XIII. of the *Choice Library;* and what *Antony Van Dale* has wrote of this Matter above all others, in his Book of Oracles.)

1. Up to this point, the note is by Grotius. The following part is by Le Clerc.

c. *As some Physicians foretel future Diseases,* &c.] *Chalcidius* on *Timaeus.* "Men are forewarned either by the flying of Birds, or by Entrails, or by Oracles, some propitious *Daemons* foretelling, who know all things that will afterwards come to pass: just as a Physician, according to the Rules of Physick, declares either Death or Health, and as *Anaximander* and *Pherecydes* did an Earthquake." *Pliny,* Book II. Chap. 79.

read was often done (*a*) by those who <195> were skilful in civil Matters. And if at any time God made use of any of those Works, done by the Diviners among the Heathen, to foretel such things as could have no other real Foundation but the Will of God; it did not tend to confirm the Heathen Religion, but rather to overthrow it; such as those things we find (*b*) in *Virgil's* fourth Eclogue, taken out of the *Sibylline* Verses; (*c*) in <196> which, though unknown to himself, he describes the Coming of Christ, and the Benefits we should receive from him. Thus in the same

a. *By those who were skilful in civil Matters,* &c.] See the Writers of the Life of *Atticus.* "A plain Evidence of this thing, besides those Books wherein he (*Cicero*) mentions it expressly, (which are published among the common People,) are sixteen Volumes of Epistles sent to *Atticus,* from his Consulship to the End of his Days; which whoever reads, will not think that he wants a compleat and regular History of those Times; there is such a full Description of the Inclinations of Princes, of the Vices of great Men, and of the Alterations in the Republick, that there is nothing which is not laid open; so that one would easily be led to think Prudence to be a kind of Divination. For *Cicero* did not only foretel future things that would happen in his own Lifetime, but like a Diviner declared those also that come to pass now." *Cicero* affirms truly of himself, in his sixth Epistle of his sixteenth Book. "In that War nothing happened ill, which I did not foretel. Wherefore, since I who am a publick Augur, like other Augurs and Astrologers, by my former Predictions have confirmed you in the Authority of Augury and Divination; you ought to believe what I foretel. I do not make my Conjecture from the flying of Birds, nor from the manner of their Chirping, as our Art teaches us, nor from the rebounding of the Corn that falls from the Chickens Mouths, nor from Dreams; but I have other Signs, which I observe." Thus *Solon* foretold that great Calamities would come upon *Athens,* from *Munichia.* And *Thales,* that the *Forum* of the *Milesii* would one time be in a Place then despised. *Plutarch* in *Solon.*

b. *In* Virgil's *fourth Eclogue,* &c.] See *Augustine's* City of God, Book X. Chap 27.

c. *In which, though unknown,* &c.] It is now sufficiently evident, that all the Prophecies of the *Sibyls* are either doubtful or forged; wherefore I would not have *Virgil,* an Interpreter of the *Sibyl,* be thought to have declared a kind of Prophecy, without any Design, like *Caiaphas* who was ignorant of what he prophesied; I know not what *Sibyl,* or rather Person under the Disguise of such a one, predicted that the Golden Age was a coming, from the Opinion of those who thought that there would be a Renovation of all things, and that the same things would come to pass again. See what *Grotius* has said of this Matter, Book II. *Sect.* 10. and the Notes upon that Place. Wherefore in this the *Sibyl* was not a Prophetess, nor did *Virgil* write thence any Prophecies of Christ; see *Servius* upon the Place, and *Isaac Vossius's* Interpretation of that Eclogue. *Le Clerc.*

Sibyls, that (*a*) he was to be acknowledged as King, who was to be truly our King; (*b*) who was to rise out of the East, and be Lord of all things. (*c*) The Ora-<197>cle of *Apollo* is to be seen (*d*) in *Porphyry,* in which he says, the other Gods were Aerial Spirits, and that the one God of the *Hebrews* was to be worshipped: Which Words, if the Worshippers of *Apollo* obeyed, they ceased to be his Worshippers; if they did not obey him, they accused their God of a Lie. To which may be added, that if these Spirits would in their Oracles have consulted the Good of Mankind, they would above all things have proposed to them a general Rule of Life,

a. *He was to be acknowledged as King,* &c.] *Cicero* mentions him in his IId Book of Divination.

b. *Who was to rise out of the East,* &c.] *Suetonius* of *Vespasian,* Chap. 4. *Tacitus,* Hist. 4.

c. *The Oracle of* Apollo, &c.] See *Augustine* of the City of God, Book XX. Chap. 23. and *Eusebius's Praeparat.* Book IV. Chap. 4. And the same *Porphyry* in his Book of Oracles says, *The God* (Apollo) *testifies that the* Egyptians, Chaldaeans, Phoenicians, Lydians *and* Hebrews, *are they who have found out the Truth.* He that wrote the Exhortation to the *Greeks,* amongst the Works of *Justin,* quotes this Oracle.

> The *Hebrews* only and *Chaldees* are wise.
> Who worship God the eternal King, sincere.

And this.

> Who the first Mortal form'd, and called him *Adam.*

There are two Oracles of *Cato's*[2] concerning Jesus, which *Eusebius* in his Gospel Demonstration transcribed out of *Porphyry.*

> Souls of their Bodies stript, immortal are,
> This wise Men know; and that which is endued
> With greatest Piety, excels the rest.
> The Souls of pious Men to Heaven ascend,
> Though various Torments do their Bodies vex.

The same are mentioned by *Augustine,* Book XXIX. Chap. 23. of his City of God, out of the same *Porphyry;* where he brings another Oracle, in which *Apollo* said, that the Father whom the pious *Hebrews* worshipped, was a Law to all the Gods.

2. The text should read, "There are two Oracles of *Hecate's,*" not Cato's.

d. *In* Porphyry, &c.] This is justly enough said upon *Porphyry,* and those who are of the same Opinion with him concerning those Oracles, and may be brought as an Argument *ad hominem,* as Logicians call it; but since it does not appear that these Oracles were not feigned, nay there are very good Reasons to think they were fictitious, they ought to be of no Weight amongst Christians. *Le Clerc.*

and assured them of a Reward, which they who so lived might expect: But they did neither of them. On the contrary, (*a*) they many times in their Verses applauded Kings, though never so wicked; (*b*) decreed Divine Honours to Champions, (*c*) enticed Men to unlawful Embraces, (*d*) to catch at unjust Gain, (*e*) and to commit Murder; which may be evidenced by many Instances. <198>

Sect. X. *The Heathen Religion rejected, because it failed of its own Accord, as soon as human Assistance was wanting.*

Besides those things already alleged, the Heathen Religion affords us a very strong Argument against itself, in that wheresoever human Force was wanting, it immediately fell, as if its only Support were then taken away. For if you turn your Eyes towards all the Christian or Mahometan Empires, you will find Heathenism no where mentioned but in Books: Nay, History informs us, that in those times when the Emperors made use of Force and Punishment, as the first Emperors did; or of Learning and Cunning, as *Julian* did, to support the Heathen Religion; even then it continually decreased; no Force being made use of against it, no Greatness of Family, (for it was commonly believed that Jesus was the Son of a Carpenter,) no Flourish of Words, no Bribes (for they were poor;) no Flattery, for they on the contrary despised all Advantages, and said there was no Adversity but they ought to undergo upon Account of their Law. And now how weak must the Heathen Religion be, to be overthrown by such Forces? Nor did the vain Credulity of the Heathens only vanish at this Doctrine, (*f*) but Spirits themselves came out of Men at the Name

a. *They many times in their Verses,* &c.] See those alleged by *Oenomaus,* in *Eusebius's* Gospel Preparat. Book V. Chap. 23. and 35.

b. *Decreed divine Honours to Champions,* &c.] See the same Author, Chap. 32. of *Cleomedes;* which we find also in *Origen's* IIId Book against *Celsus.*

c. *Enticed Men to unlawful Embraces,* &c.] This was shown before.

d. *To catch at unjust Gain,* &c.] See *Eusebius's* Gospel Preparat. Book V. Chap. 22.

e. *And to commit Murder,* &c.] *Oenomaus* recites Oracles of this kind, which you may find in the forementioned Book of *Eusebius,* Chap. 19. and 27.

f. *But Spirits themselves came out of Men,* &c.] *Acts* V. 16. VIII. 7. XVI. 18.

of Christ; were silenced; and being asked the Reason of their Silence, (*a*) were forced to own, that they could do nothing when Christ was invoked. <199>

SECT. XI. *An Answer to this, that the Rise and Decay of Religion is owing to the Stars.*

There were some Philosophers who ascribed the Rise and Decay of all Religion to the Stars. But this starry Science, which they profess to know and understand, is delivered in such different Rules, (*b*) that there is nothing certain to be found in it, but this one thing, that there is no Certainty in it. I do not speak of those Effects which naturally follow from necessary Causes; (*c*) but of such as proceed from the Will of Man, which is in its own Nature so far free, as that no external Necessity can be laid upon it: For if the Act of Willing flowed from such a necessary Impression, (*d*) that Power which we experience in the Soul of deliberating and chusing, would be given us to no Purpose; (*e*) and the Justice of all Laws, and of Rewards and Punishments, would be entirely taken away; because there is neither Blame nor Desert due to <200> that which is plainly unavoidable. Further, since some Actions of the Will are evil: If they are

a. *Were forced to own,* &c.] *Tertullian,* in his Apology. See also *Lucan* against false Diviners. *Apollo* in *Daphne. This Place,* Daphne, *is filled with dead Bodies, which hinder the Oracles. Babylas* and other Christian Martyrs died there. See *Chrysostom* against the Gentiles.

b. *That there is nothing certain to be found in it,* &c.] See the excellent Dissertation of *Bardesanes* the *Syrian,* concerning this Matter, which you may find in the *Philocalia* collected from *Origen,* and in *Eusebius's Praeparat.* Book VI. Chap. 10.

c. *But of such as proceed from the Will of Man,* &c.] See *Alexander Aphrodisaeus's* Book concerning this Matter.

d. *That Power which we experience,* &c.] See *Eusebius's* Gospel *Praeparat.* Book VI. Chap 6.

e. *And the Justice of all Laws,* &c.] See *Justin's* Apology II. "If Mankind be not endued with a Power of chusing freely, to avoid that which is bad, and to comply with that which is good; the Cause of either of them cannot be said to be from himself." See also what follows. And thus *Tatian;* "the Freedom of the Will consists in this; that a wicked Man is justly punished, because his Wickedness is from himself; and a good Man is rewarded, because he has not voluntarily transgressed the Will of God." To this may be added *Chalcidius's* Disputation concerning this Matter in *Timaeus.*

caused by a certain Necessity of the Heavens, and because God has given such a Power to the Heavens and the heavenly Bodies; it will follow, that God, who is perfectly good, (*a*) is the true Cause of moral Evil; and at the same Time that he professes his utter Abhorrence of Wickedness in his positive Law, He has planted the efficient and inevitable Cause of it in the Nature of Things; therefore he wills two Things contrary to each other, *viz.* that the same thing should be, and not be; and that *that* should be a Sin, which is done by a Divine Impulse. (*b*) It is said by others with a greater Shew of Probability, that first the Air, and afterwards our Bodies are affected by the Influence of the Stars, and so suck in certain Qualities, which for the most Part excite in the Soul Desires answerable to them; that by these the Will is enticed, and oftentimes yields to them. But, if this be granted, it makes nothing to the Question in hand. For the Religion of Christ could not possibly have its Rise from the Affections of the Body, nor consequently from the Power of the Stars; which, as was said, act upon the Mind no otherwise than by such Affections; because this Religion, in the highest Degree, draws Men off from those Things that are <201> pleasing to the Body. The wisest Astrologers do, (*c*) except truly knowing and good Men from the Laws of the Stars; and such were they who first proposed the Christian Religion, as their Lives plainly show. And, if We allow a Power in Learning and Knowledge, to hinder their Bodies from being thus infected; there always were amongst Christians some who might be commended upon this Account. Further, the Effects of the Stars, as the most Learned confess, respect only particular Parts of the World, and are temporary: But this Religion has continued already for above sixteen hundred Years, not only in one, but in very

a. *Is the true Cause of Moral Evil*, &c.] *Plato* speaks against this in his IId *Republick*, *The Cause is from him that choses, God is not the Cause.* Thus *Chalcidius* translates it in *Timaeus*, which *Justin*, in the forementioned Place, says agrees with *Moses*.

b. *It is said by others with a greater Shew of Probability*, &c.] But they speak most truly, who deny any such Influences at all; and acknowledge nothing else in the Stars but Heat and Light, to which we may add their Weight resulting from their Bigness; but these have, properly speaking, no relation to the Mind. *Le Clerc.*

c. *Except truly knowing and good Men*, &c.] Thus *Zoroaster. Do not increase your Fate. And* Ptolomaeus: *A wise Man may avoid many Influences of the Stars.*

distant Parts of the World, and such as are under very different Positions of the Stars.

Sect XII. *The principal Things of the Christian Religion, were approved of by the wisest Heathens: And if there be any Thing in it hard to be believed, the like is to be found amongst the Heathen.*

There is the less Reason for the Heathens to oppose the Christian Religion, because all the Parts of it are so agreeable to the Rules of Virtue, that by their own Light they do in a Manner convince the Mind; insomuch that there have not been wanting some amongst the Heathen, who have said those Things singly, which in our Religion are all put together. For instance; (*a*) that Religion does <202><203> not consist in Ceremo-

---

a. *That Religion does not consist in Ceremonies,* &c.]

> With a clean Mind do Sacrifice to God,
> Not so much neat in Cloaths, as pure in Heart.
> > Menander.

Cicero in his IId Book of the Nature of the Gods. "The best Worship of the Gods, which is also the most innocent, the most holy, and the most full of Piety; is to reverence them always with a pure, sincere, uncorrupted Mind and Expression." And again in his IId Book of Laws. "The Law commands us to approach the Gods sincerely; that is, with our Minds, which is all in all."

> This let us offer to the Gods (which blear'd
> *Messala's* Offspring can't with all their Cost.)
> Justice and Right in all our secret Thoughts,
> An undissembled Virtue from the Breast.
> Bring these, and what you please then sacrifice.
> > Persius, Satyr II.

These Verses seem to have respect to the *Pythian* Oracle, which we find in *Porphyry's* IId Book against eating living Creatures, where any Thing offered by a pious Man, is preferred to Hecatombs of another. In the same Book *Porphyry* has these Words to the like Purpose. "Now they esteem him not fit to offer Sacrifice worthily, whose Body is not cloathed with a white and clean Garment; but they do not think it any great Matter,

nies, but is in the Mind; (*a*) that he who has it in his Heart to commit Adultery, is an Adulterer; (*b*) that we ought not to return an <204>

---

if some go to Sacrifice, having their Bodies clean and also their Garments, though their Minds be not void of Evil: As if God were not most delighted with the Purity of that which in us is most Divine, and bears the nearest Resemblance to him. For it is written in the Temple of *Epidaurus.*

> Let all who come to offer at this Shrine
> Be Pure; so we command.

Now Purity consists in Holy Thoughts." And a little after. "No material Things ought to be offered or dedicated to God, who, as the Wise Man said, is above all; for every Thing material, is impure to him who is immaterial; wherefore Words are not proper to express ourselves by to him, not even Internal ones, if polluted by the Passions of the Mind:" And again: "For it is not reasonable, that in those Temples which are dedicated to the Gods by Men, they should wear clean Shoes without any Spots; and in the Temple of the Father, that is, in this World, not keep their inner Cloaths (which is the Body) neat, and converse with Purity in the Temple of their Father." Neither can I omit what follows out of the same Book. "Whoever is perswaded that the Gods have no need of these (*Sacrifices*) but look only to the Manners of these who approach them, esteeming right Notions of them and of Things, the best Sacrifices, how can such an one be otherwise than Sober, Godly, and Righteous?" Where we find these three known Words *of Paul, Tit.* II. 2. *Soberly, Righteously, and Godly. Charondas,* in his Preface to the Laws: "Let your Mind be void of all Evil; for the Gods delight not in the Sacrifices and Expences of wicked Men, but in the just and virtuous Actions of good Men. *Seneca* quoted by *Lactantius* in his Institutions, Book XI. ch. 24. Would you conceive God to be Great, Propitious, and to be reverenced as meek in Majesty, as a Friend, and always at hand? You must not worship him with Sacrifices, and abundance of Blood, but with a pure Mind, and an upright Intention." To the same Sense is that of *Dion Prusaeensis,* Orat. 3. *Thucydides,* Book I. *There is no other Festival, but a Man's doing his Duty.* Diogenes: *Does not a good Man think every Day a Festival?*

    a. *That he who has it in his Heart,* &c.] Thus *Ovid,*

> He who forbears, only because forbid,
> Does sin; his Body's free, his Mind is stain'd;
> Were he alone, he'd be an Adulterer.

Seneca the Father: *There is such a Thing as Incest, without the Act of Whoredom;* viz. *The Desire of it.* And in another Place, "She is reckoned amongst Sinners, and not without Reason, who is modest out of Fear, and not for Virtues Sake."

    b. *That we ought not to return an Injury,* &c.] See *Plato's Criton,* and *Maximus Tyrius's* IId Dissertation. *Menander,*

Injury; (*a*) that a Husband ought to have but one Wife; (*b*) that the Bands of Matrimony ought not to be dissolved; (*c*) that it is every Man's Duty to do good to another, (*d*) especially to him that is in Want; (*e*) that as

---

O *Gorgias,* he's the very best of Men.
Who can forgive the greatest Injuries.

Ariston Spartianus; "To a certan Person, who said that it was a princely Thing to do Good to Friends, and Evil to Enemies; rather, answered he, to do good to Friends, and to make Enemies Friends." And the same *Dion* the Deliverer of *Sicily,* in *Plutarch* says, that a true Demonstration of a Philosophical Disposition, consists not in any One's being kind to his Friends; but when he is injured, in being easily intreated, and merciful towards those who have offended him.

a. *That a Husband ought to have but one Wife,* &c.] See what is before quoted out of *Salust* and others, about this Matter. *Euripides* in his *Andromache.*

—— It is by no means fit
One Man should o'er two Women have the Rule;
One Nuptial Bed will a wise Man suffice,
Who would have all Things regulated well.

And more to the same Purpose, in the Chorus of the same Tragedy.

b. *That the Bands of Matrimony ought not to be dissolved,* &c.] So it was amongst the *Romans,* till the five hundred and twentieth Year of the City, as *Valerius Maximus* informs us, Book III. Ch. 1. *Anaxandrides* to the same Purpose.

'Tis shameful thus for Men to ebb and flow.

c. *That it is every Man's Duty to do Good to another,* &c.] *Terence's* Self-Tormentor.

I am a Man, and think every Thing humane belongs to me.

We are by Nature related to each other, says *Florentinus* the Lawyer, *L. ut vim. D. de Justitia.* And this is the Meaning of the Proverb, *One Man is a kind of God to another. Cicero,* in his Ist Book of Offices, says there is a mutual Society betwixt Men, all of them being related to one another.

d. *Especially to him that is in Want,* &c.] *Horace,* Book II.

Wretch, why should any want, when you are Rich?

In *Mimus.*

Mercy procures strong Security.

e. *That as much as possible, Men ought to abstain from Swearing,* &c.] Pythagoras. "We ought not to swear by the Gods, but endeavour to make ourselves believed without an Oath:" Which is largely explained by *Hierocles,* on his golden Verses. *Marcus Antoninus,* Book III. in his Description of a good Man, says, *such an one needs no Oath. Sophocles* in his *Oedipus Coloneus.*

much as possible Men ought <205> to abstain from Swearing; (*a*) that in Meat and Cloaths they ought to be content with what is necessary to supply Nature. And if there be any thing in the Christian Religion difficult to be believed, the like is to be found amongst the wisest of the Heathens, as we have before made appear, with respect to the Immortality of the Soul and Bodies being restored to Life again. Thus *Plato*, taught by the *Chaldaeans*, (*b*) distinguished the <206> Divine Nature into the Father; the Father's Mind, which he also calls a Branch of the Deity, the Maker of the World; and the Soul, which comprehends and contains all Things.

I would not have you swear, because 'tis bad.

Clinius the *Pythagorean*, would sooner lose three Talents in a Cause, than affirm the Truth with an Oath. The Story is related by *Basilius* concerning reading *Greek* Authors.
    a. *That in Meat and Cloaths*, &c.]

There are but two Things which Mankind do want,
A Crust of Bread, and Draught of Springing Water.
Both which are near, and will suffice for Life.
                       Euripides.

And *Lucan*.

There is enough of Bread and Drink for all.

And *Aristides*.

We want nothing but Cloaths, Houses, and Food.

    b. *Distinguished the Divine Nature*, &c.] See *Plato*'s Epistle to *Dionysius, Plato* calls the first Principle, the Father; the second Principle, the Cause or Governor of all Things, in his Epistle to *Hermias, Erastus*, and *Coriscus*. The same is called the *Mind* by *Plotinus*, in his Book *Of the three principal Substances*: *Numenius* calls it the Workman, and also the Son; and *Amelius* the *Word*, as you may see in *Eusebius*, Book XI. ch. 17, 18, 19. See also *Cyril*'s IIId, IVth, and VIIIth Books against *Julian, Chalcidius* on *Timaeus*, calls the first the Supreme God; the second, the Mind, or Providence; the third, the Soul of the World, or the Second Mind. In another Place, he distinguishes these three thus. The Contriver, the Commander, and the Effecter. He speaks thus of the second: *The Reason of God, is God consulting the Affairs of Men, which is the Cause of Mens living well and happily, if they do not neglect that Gift which the Supreme God has bestowed on them.* The Pythagoreans *assign to the Supreme God, the Number Three, as perfect*, says *Servius* on the seventh Eclogue. Not much differing from which, is that of *Aristotle*, concerning the same *Pythagoreans*, in the Beginning of his Ist Book of the Heavens. (This is more largely handled, by the very learned *R. Cudworth*, in his *English* Work of the Intellectual System of the World, Book I. ch. 4. which you will not repent consulting. *Le Clerc.*)

That the Divine Nature could be joined with the Humane, (*a*) *Julian,* that great Enemy to the Christians, believed, and gave an Example in *Aesculapius,* who he thought came from Heaven to deliver to Men the Art of Physick. Many are offended at the Cross of Christ; but what Stories are there which the Heathen Authors do not tell of their Gods? Some were Servants to Kings, others were struck with Thunder-Bolts, ripp'd up, wounded. And the wisest of them affirmed, that the more Virtue cost, the more delightful it was. (*b*) *Plato* in his IId Re-<207>publick, says in a manner prophetically, that for a Man to appear truly good, it is necessary that his Virtue be deprived of all its Ornaments, so that he may be looked upon by others as a wicked Man, may be derided, and at last hanged: And certainly to be an Example of eminent Patience, is no otherwise to be obtained. <208>

a. Julian, *that great Enemy to the Christians,* &c.] Book VI. "Amongst those Things which have Understanding, *Jupiter* produced *Aesculapius* from himself, and caused him to appear upon Earth, by means of the fruitful Life of the Sun; he taking his Journey from Heaven to Earth, appeared in one Form in *Epidaurus.*" Thus *Porphyry,* as *Cyril* relates his Words in his forementioned VIIIth Book: *There is a certain kind of Gods, which in a proper Season, are transformed into Men.* What the *Egyptians* Opinion of this Matter was, see *Plutarch Sympos.* VIII. *Quaest.* I. to which may be added that Place of *Acts* XIV. 10.

b. Plato *in his* IId *Republick,* &c.] The Words are these translated from the *Greek. He will be Scourged, Tormented, Bound, his Eyes Burnt out, and die by Crucifixion, after he has endured all those Evils.* Whence he had that which he relates in his IIId Book of Republick. "That good Man will be tormented, furiously treated, have his Hands cut off, his Eyes plucked out, will be bound, condemned, and burnt." *Lactantius* in his Institutions, Book VI. ch. 17. has preserved this Place of *Seneca.* "This is that virtuous Man, who though his Body suffer Torments in every Part; though the Flame enter into his Mouth, tho' his Hands be extended on a Cross; does not regard what he suffers, but how well." Such an one *Euripides* represents to us in these Verses.

> Burn, scald this tender Flesh; drink your full Glutt
> Of purple Blood. Sooner may Heaven and Earth
> Approach each other, and be join'd in one,
> Than I to you express a flattering Word.

To which that of *Aeschylus,* mentioned by *Plato* in the forecited Place, exactly agrees.

> He strives to be, not to be thought the best,
> Deep rooted in his Mind he bears a Stock
> Whence all his wiser Councils are derived.

SECT. I. *A Confutation of Judaism, beginning with an Address to the Jews.*

Now we are coming out of the thick Darkness of Heathenism; the *Jewish* Religion, which is a Part and the Beginning of Truth, appears to us much like Twilight to a Person gradually advancing out of a very dark Cave: Wherefore I desire the *Jews,* that they would not look upon us as Adversaries. We know very well, (*a*) that they are the Offspring of Holy Men, whom God often visited by his Prophets and his Angels; that the Messiah was born of their Nation, as were the first Teachers of Christianity: They were the Stock into which we were grafted; to them were commited the Oracles of God, which we respect as much as they, and with *Paul* put up our hearty Prayers to God for them, beseeching him that that Day may very speedily come, (*b*) when the Veil, which now hangs over their Faces, being taken off, they, together with us, may clearly perceive (*c*) the fulfilling of the Law; and when, according to the antient Prophecies, many of us, who are Strangers, shall lay hold of (*d*) the Skirt of a *Jew,* <209> praying him, that with equal Piety we may worship that One God, the God of *Abraham, Isaac* and *Jacob.*

a. *That they are the Offspring of Holy Men,* &c.] This, and what follows, is taken out of the IXth, Xth, and XIth of the *Romans;* to which may be added *Mat.* XV. 2.

b. *When the Veil,* &c.] 2 *Cor.* III. 14, 15, 16.

c. *The fulfilling of the Law,* &c.] *Rom.* III. 24. VIII. 14. X. 4. XIII. 8. *Gal.* III. 24.

d. *The Skirt of a Jew,* &c.] *Zachar.* VIII. 20. and following. *Isaiah* II. 2. XIX. 18. and 24. *Micah* IV. 2. *Hosea* III. 4. *Rom.* XI. 25.

Sect. II. *That the* Jews *ought to look upon the Miracles of Christ as sufficiently attested.*

First therefore, they are requested not to esteem that unjust in another's Cause, which they think just in their own: If any Heathen should ask them why they believe the Miracles done by *Moses;* they can give no other Answer, but that the Tradition of this Matter has been so continual and constant amongst them, that it could not proceed from any Thing else but the Testimony of those who saw them. Thus, (*a*) that the Widow's Oil was encreased by *Elisha,* (*b*) and the *Syrian* immediately healed of his Leprosy; (*c*) and the Son of her who entertained him, raised to Life again; with many others; are believed by the *Jews* for no other Reason, but because they were delivered to Posterity by credible Witnesses. And concerning (*d*) *Elijah's* being taken up into Heaven, they give Credit to the single Testimony of *Elisha,* as a Man beyond all Exception. But (*e*) we bring twelve Witnesses, whose Lives were unblameable, (*f*) of Christ's ascending into Heaven; and many more, of Christ's being seen upon Earth after his Death; which, if they be true, the Chri-<210>stian Doctrine must of necessity be true also; and it is plain that the *Jews* can say nothing for themselves, but what will hold as strong or stronger for us. But, to pass by Testimonies; (*g*) the Writers of the *Talmud,* and the *Jews* themselves, own the miraculous things done by Christ; which ought to satisfy them: For God cannot more effectually recommend the Authority of any Doctrine delivered by Man, than by working Miracles.

a. *That the Widow's Oil was increased,* &c.] 2 *Kings,* ch. IV.

b. *And the* Syrian *immediately healed,* &c.] Ch V.

c. *And the Son of her who entertained him,* &c.] In the forementioned IVth Ch.

d. *Elijah's being taken up into Heaven,* &c.] Ch. II. of the forecited Book.

e. *We bring twelve Witnesses,* &c.] *Mark* XVI. 19. *Luke* XXIV. 52. *Acts* I.

f. *Of Christ's ascending into Heaven.* &c.] *Mat.* XXVIII. *Mark* XVI. *Luke* XXIV. *John* XX, XXI. 1 *Cor.* XV.

g. *The Writers of the* Talmud, &c.] See what is quoted, Book II.

SECT. III. *An Answer to the Objection, that those Miracles were done by the Help of Devils.*

But some say, that these Wonders were done by the Help of Devils: But this Calumny has been already confuted from hence, that as soon as the Doctrine of Christ was made known, all the Power of the Devils was broken. What is added by some, that Jesus learned Magical Arts in *Egypt*, carries a much less Appearance of Truth than the like Objection of the Heathen against *Moses*, which we find in (*a*) *Pliny* and (*b*) *Apuleius*. For it does not appear, but from the Books of his Disciples, that Jesus ever was in *Egypt;* and they add, that he returned from thence a Child. But it is certain, that *Moses* spent a great Part of his Time, when he was grown up, in *Egypt*, both (*c*) from his own Account, (*d*) and the Relation of others. But the Law of each of them, strongly clears both *Moses* and *Jesus* from this Crime, (*e*) because they <211> expressly forbid such Arts, as odious in the Sight of God. And if in the times of Christ and his Disciples, there had been any such Magical Art any where, either in *Egypt,* or other Places, whereby those things, related of Christ, could be done; such as dumb Mens being suddenly healed, the Lame walking, and Sight given to the Blind; the Emperors, (*f*) *Tiberius,* (*g*) *Nero,* and others, who would not have spared any Cost in enquiring after such things, would undoubtedly

a. *In* Pliny, &c.] Book XXX. Chap. I.

b. *And* Apuleius, &c.] In his IId Apology.

c. *From his own,* &c.] *Exodus* II. 4. and following.

d. *And the Relation of others,* &c.] *Manethon, Chaeremon, Lysimachus* in *Josephus's* Ist Book against *Appion,* and *Justin* and *Tacitus.*

e. *Because they expressly forbid such Acts,* &c.] *Exod.* XXII. 28. *Levit.* XX. 6, 27. *Numb.* XXIII. 23. *Deut.* XVIII. 10. 1 *Sam.* XXVIII. 9. 2 *Kings* XVII. 17. XXI. 6. *Acts* XIII. 8, 9, 10. XVI. 18. XIX. 19.

f. *Tiberius,* &c.] *Tacitus,* Annal VI. *Suetonius* in his Life, Ch. LXIII and LXIX.

g. *Nero,* &c.] Concerning whom *Pliny,* Book XXX. Ch. XI. in his History of Magick says, *He had not a greater Desire after Musick and Tragical Singing.* And afterwards: *No Man favoured any Art with greater Cost; for these things he wanted neither Riches, Abilities, nor Disposition to learn.* Presently after, he relates how he was initiated into the Magical Suppers by King *Tiridates.*

have found it out. And if it be true, (*a*) what the *Jews* report, that the Counsellors of the great Council were skilled in Magical Arts, in order to convict the guilty; certainly they who were so great Enemies to Jesus, and so much envied his Reputation, which continually increased by his Miracles, would have done the like Works by some Art; or have made it plain by undeniable Arguments, that his Works could proceed from nothing else.

Sect. IV. *Or by the Power of Words.*

Some of the *Jews* ascribe the Miracles of *Jesus* to a certain secret Name, which was put into the Temple by *Solomon,* and kept by two Lions for above a thousand Years, but was conveyed thence by Jesus; which is not only false, but an impu-<212>dent Fiction. For, as to the Lions, so remarkable and wonderful a thing, neither the Books of the *Kings,* nor the *Chronicles,* nor *Josephus,* mention any thing of them: Nor did the *Romans,* who before the times of Jesus entered the Temple with *Pompey,* find any such thing.

Sect. V. *That the Miracles of Jesus were divine, proved from hence, because he taught the Worship of one God, the Maker of the World.*

Now, if it be granted, that Miracles were done by Christ, which the *Jews* acknowledge; we affirm that it follows from the Law of *Moses* itself, that we ought to give Credit to him: For God has said in the XVIIIth Chapter of *Deuteronomy,* that he would raise up other Prophets besides *Moses,* which the People were to hearken to, and threatens heavy Punishments if they did not. (*b*) Now the most certain Token of a Prophet, is Miracles; nor can any thing be conceived more flagrant. Yet it is said, *Deut.* XIII. that if any one declares himself to be a Prophet by working Wonders, he

a. *What the* Jews *report,* &c.] See the *Talmud* entitled, Concerning the Council; and concerning the Sabbath.

b. *Now the most certain Token,* &c.] And the foretelling future Events, which may justly be reckoned amongst Miracles, *Deut.* XVIII. 22.

is not to be hearkened to, if he intices the People to the Worship of new Gods: For God permits such Wonders to be done only to try whether his People be firmly established in the Worship of the true God. From which Places compared together, (*a*) the *Hebrew* Interpreters rightly collected, (*b*) that every one who worked Miracles was <213> to be believed, if he did not draw them off from the Worship of the true God; for in that Instance only it is declared, that no Credit is to be given to Miracles, though never so remarkable ones. Now Jesus did not only not teach the Worship of false Gods, but on the contrary (*c*) did expressly forbid it, as a grievous Sin; and taught us to reverence the Writings of *Moses,* and those Prophets which followed him: So that nothing can be objected against his Miracles; for what some object, that the Law of Jesus in some things differ from that of *Moses,* is not sufficient.

Sect. VI. *An Answer to the Objection drawn from the Difference betwixt the Law of* Moses, *and the Law of Christ, where it is shown, that there might be given a more perfect Law than that of* Moses.

For the *Hebrew* Doctors themselves lay down this Rule (*d*) for the Extent of a Prophet's Power, that is, of one that works Miracles; that he may securely violate any sort of Precept, except that of the Worship of one God. And indeed the Power of making Laws, which is in God, did not cease upon his giving Precepts by *Moses;* nor is any one, who has any Authority to give Laws, thereby hindered from giving others contrary to

a. *The* Hebrew *Interpreters,* &c.] See *Moses, Maimonides,* and others quoted in *Manasses's Conciliator, Quaest.* IV. on *Deut.*

b. *That every one who worked Miracles,* &c.] And whose Prophecies came to pass; this Argument is strongly urged in *Chrysostom's* Vth against the *Jews,* and in his Discourse concerning Christ's Divinity, VI. *Tom. Savil.*

c. *Did expressly forbid it,* &c.] *Matt.* XII. 29, 32. *John* XVII. 3. *Acts* XV. 28. 1 *Cor.* V. 10, 11, 18. VI. 9. X. 7. XII. 2. 2 *Cor.* VI. 16. 1 *Thess.* I. 9. 1 *John* V. 21.

d. *For the Extent of a Prophet's Power,* &c.] This Rule is laid down in the *Talmud,* entitled, *Concerning the Council.* Thus at the Command of *Joshua,* the Law of the Sabbath was broken, *Jos.* V. And the Prophets often sacrificed out of the Place appointed by the Law, as *Samuel,* 1 *Sam.* VII. 17. XIII. 8. and *Elijah,* 1 *Kings* XVIII. 38.

them. The Objection of God's Immutability is nothing to the Purpose; for we do not speak of the Nature and Essence of God, but of his Actions. Light is <214> turned into Darkness, Youth into Age, Summer into Winter, which are all the Acts of God. Formerly God allowed to *Adam* all other Fruit, (*a*) except that of one Tree, which he forbad him, *viz.* because it was his Pleasure. He forbad killing Men in general, (*b*) yet he commanded *Abraham* to slay his Son; (*c*) he forbad some, and accepted other Sacrifices, distant from the Tabernacle. Neither will it follow, that because the Law given by *Moses* was good, therefore a better could not be given. Parents are wont to lisp with their Children, to wink at the Faults of their Age, to tempt them to learn with a Cake: But as they grow up, their Speech is corrected, the Precepts of Virtue instilled into them, and they are shown the Beauty of Virtue, and what are its Rewards. (*d*) Now that the Precepts of the Law were not absolutely perfect, appears from hence, that some holy Men in those times led a Life more perfect than those Precepts required. *Moses,* who allowed revenging an Injury, partly by Force, and partly by demanding Judgment; when himself was afflicted with the worst of Injuries, (*e*) prayed for his Enemies. (*f*) Thus *David* was willing to have his rebellious Son spared, (*g*) and patiently bore the Curses thrown upon him. Good Men are no where found to have divorced their Wives, <215> though the Law allowed them to do it. (*h*) So that Laws are only accommodated to the greater Part of the

a. *Except that of one Tree,* &c.] *Gen.* II. 17.

b. *Yet he commanded* Abraham, &c.] *Gen.* XXII. 2.

c. *He forbad some, and accepted other,* &c.] As was said just before.

d. *Now that the Precepts of the Law,* &c.] *Heb.* VIII. 7.

e. *Prayed for his Enemies,* &c.] *Exod.* XXXII. 2. 12, 14, 31. *Numb.* XI. 2. XII. 13. XIV. 13. and following Verses, XXI. 7, 8. *Deut.* IX. 18, 26. XXXIII.

f. *Thus* David *was willing,* &c.] 2 *Sam.* XVIII. 5.

g. *And patiently bore the Curses,* &c.] 2 *Sam.* XXI. 10.

h. *So that Laws are only accommodated,* &c.] *Origen* against *Celsus,* Book III. "*As a certain Lawgiver said to one who asked him, if he gave to his Citizens the most perfect Laws, not, says he, the most perfect in themselves, but the best they can bear.*" *Porphyry,* Book I. against eating living Creatures, concerning Lawgivers, says thus. "If they have regard to the middle sort of Life, called Natural, and according to what is agreeable to most Men, who measure Good and Evil by external things which concern the Body: If, I say, with this View they make Laws; what Injury is done to Life, if any one adds something more excellent than this?"

People; and in that State it was reasonable some things should be over-looked, which were then to be reduced to a more perfect Rule, when God, by a greater Power of his Spirit, was to gather to himself a new People out of all Nations. And the Rewards which were expressly promised by the Law of *Moses,* do all regard this mortal Life only: Whence it must be confessed, (*a*) that a Law, better than this, might be given, which should propose everlasting Rewards, not under Types and Shadows, but plainly and openly, as we see the Law of Christ does.

SECT. VII. *The Law of* Moses *was observed by Jesus when on Earth, neither was any Part of it abolished afterwards, but only those Precepts which had no intrinsick Goodness in them.*

We may here observe, by the way, to shew the Wickedness of those *Jews,* who lived in our Saviour's time; that Jesus was very basely treated by them, and delivered up to Punishment, when they could not prove that he had done any thing contrary to the Law. (*b*) He was circum-<216>cised, (*c*) made use of the *Jewish* Meats, (*d*) was cloathed like them; (*e*) those who were cleansed from their Leprosy, he sent to the Priests, (*f*) he religiously observed the Passover, and other Festival Days. If he healed any on the Sabbath-Day, he made it appear, (*g*) not only from the Law, (*h*) but from their received Opinions, that such Works were not forbidden on the Sabbath. He then first began (*i*) to discover the abrogating some Laws, when he had overcome Death, was ascended into Heaven, and endued his Disciples with remarkable Gifts of the Holy Spirit, and had shown by

a. *That a Law better than this,* &c.] *Heb.* VII. 19, 22. VIII. 6. 2 *Tim.* I. 10.

b. *He was circumcised,* &c.] *Luke* II. 21.

c. *Made use of the* Jewish *Meats,* &c.] *Gal.* IV. 5.

d. *Was cloathed like them,* &c.] *Matt.* IX. 20.

e. *Those who were cleansed,* &c.] *Matt.* VIII. 4. *Mark* I. 44. *Luke* V. 14.

f. *He religiously observed the Passover,* &c.] *Luke* II. 41. *John* II. 13, 23. XI. 56. XII. 1. *John* VII. 2.

g. *Not only from the Law,* &c.] *Matt.* XII. 5.

h. *But from their received Opinions,* &c.] *Matt.* XII. 11.

i. *To discover the Abrogating,* &c.] *Acts* X. *Colos.* II. 14.

those things (*a*) that he had obtained a Kingly Power, (*b*) in which is included an Authority to make Laws, according to that Prophecy of *Daniel,* Chap. III and VIII, the VIII and XI, being compared together; who foretold that after the Overthrow of the Kingdoms of *Syria* and *Egypt,* (the latter of which came to pass under *Augustus*) God would give to a Man, (*c*) who should appear to be an ordinary Person, a Kingdom extending to the People of all Nations and Languages, and which should never have an End. Now that <217> Part of the Law, the Necessity of which was taken away by Christ, did not contain in it any thing in its own Nature virtuous; but consisted of things indifferent in themselves, and therefore not unalterable: For if there had been any thing in the Nature of those things, to inforce their Practice, God would have prescribed them (*d*) to all the World, and not to one People only; and that from the very Beginning, and two thousand Years and more after Mankind had been created. *Abel, Enoch, Noah, Melchisedech, Job, Abraham, Isaac, Jacob,* and all the eminently pious Men, who were so beloved of God, were ignorant of all, or almost all this Part of the Law; and yet nevertheless they received Testimony of their Faith towards God, and of his divine Love towards them. Neither did *Moses* advise his Father-in-Law *Jethro* to perform these Rites, nor *Jonas* the *Ninevites,* nor did the other Prophets reprove the *Chaldaeans, Egyptians, Sidonians, Tyrians, Idumaeans* and *Moabites,* to whom they wrote, for not embracing them, though they particularly enumerate their Crimes. These Precepts therefore were particular, and introduced either

a. *That he had obtained a Kingly Power,* &c.] *Acts* II. 36. *Rev.* I. 5.

b. *In which is included,* &c.] *James* I. 25.

c. *Who should appear to be an ordinary Person,* &c.] *Dan.* II. 45. VII. 13. For the Son of Man expresses in *Hebrew,* a certain *Meanness,* and so the Prophets are called, compared with Angels, as is observed by *Jachiades,* on *Dan.* X. 16.

d. *To all the World, and not to one People only,* &c.] So far from that, that some Laws, such as those of First Fruits, Tythes, Assembling upon Festivals, relate expressly to the Place of *Judaea* only, whither it is certain all Nations could not come. See *Exodus* XXXIII. 19. and XXXIV. 26. *Deut.* XXVI. 2. and what follows. Also *Deut.* XII. 5. and following, XIV. 23, and following. Also *Exodus* XXIII. 17. XXXIV. 2, 23, 24. *Deut.* XVI. 16. The most ancient Custom, interpreted the Law of Sacrifices, in the same Manner. The *Talmud* entitled, Concerning the Councils, and that entitled *Chagiga,* tells us that the Law of *Moses* was given to the *Hebrews* only, and not to Strangers. See *Maimonides,* on *Deut.* XXXIII. and *Bechai.*

to hinder some Evil, (*a*) to which <218> the *Jews* were especially inclined, or for a Trial of their Obedience, or to signify some future things. Wherefore there is no more Reason to wonder at their being abolished, than at a King's abrogating some municipal Laws, in order to establish the same Ordinances all over a Nation: Neither can there be any thing alleged to prove, that God had obliged himself to make no Alteration herein. For if it be said, that these Precepts are stiled perpetual; (*b*) Men very often make use of this Word, when they would signify only that what they command in this manner, is not limited for a Year's Continuance, (*c*) or to a certain time, suppose of War or Peace, accommodated to the Scarceness of Provision; now this does not hinder but that they may appoint new Laws concerning these Matters whenever the Publick Good requires it. Thus the Precepts which God gave to the *Hebrews,* were some of them temporary, (*d*) only during the Continuance of that People in the Wilderness; (*e*) others confined to their Dwelling in the Land of *Canaan.* That these might be distinguished from the other, they are called perpetual; by which may be meant, that they ought not to be neglected any where, nor at any time, unless God should signify his Will to the contrary. Which manner of speaking, as it is common to all People, the He-<219>*brews* ought the less to wonder at, because they know that in their Law, that is called (*f*) a perpetual Right, and a perpetual Servitude, which continued

a. *To which the* Jews *were especially inclined,* &c.] Being very much addicted to Rites, and, on that Account, prone to Idolatry. This the Prophets every where show, especially *Ezekiel* XVI.

b. *Men very often make use of this Word,* &c.] L. *Hac Edictali. Cod. de secundis Nuptiis.* L. *Hac in perpetuum. Cod. de diversis Praedus Libro* XI. and in many other Places.

c. *Or to a certain Time,* &c.] L. *Valerius* in *Livy,* XXXIV. "The Laws which particular times require, are liable to be abolished, and I find are changed with the times; those that are made in the time of Peace, are abrogated in War; and those made in War, abrogated in Peace."

d. *Only during the Continuance,* &c.] As *Exodus* XXVII. *Deut.* XXIII. 12.

e. *Others confined to their Dwelling,* &c.] *Deut.* XII. 1, 20. *Numb.* XXXIII. 52.

f. *A perpetual Right,* &c.] *Exodus* XXI. 6. 1 *Sam.* I. 22. And thus *Josephus Albo,* in his IIId Book of Foundations, Ch. 16. thinks the Word לעילם *Le-olam* in the Ritual Law, may be understood. And *Phinees's* Priesthood is called, *Ps.* CVI. 30, 31, עד־עילם *Ad-olam everlasting.* And by the Son of *Sirach,* XLV. 28, 29, 30, an everlasting Priesthood, and 1 *Mach.* II. 55.

only from Jubilee to Jubilee. (*a*) And the Coming of the Messiah is by themselves called the fulfilling of the Jubilee, or the Great Jubilee. And moreover, the Promise of entering into a new Covenant, is to be found amongst the old Prophets, (*b*) as *Jeremiah* XXXI; where God promises that he will make a new Covenant, which shall be writ upon their Hearts, and Men will have no need to learn Religion of each other, for it shall be evident to them all: And moreover, that he would pardon all their past Transgressions: Which is much the same as if a Prince, after his Subjects had been at great Enmity with each other; in order to establish a Peace, should take away their different Laws, and impose upon them all one common Law, and that a perfect one; and for the future, promise them pardon for all their past Transgressions, upon their Amendment. Tho' what has been said might suffice; yet we will go through every Part of the Law that is abolished, and shew that the things are not such as are in their own Nature well-pleasing to God, or such as ought to continue always. <220>

Sect. VIII. *As Sacrifices, which were never acceptable to God upon their own Account.*

The principal, and which first offer themselves to us, are Sacrifices; concerning which many *Hebrews* are of Opinion, (*c*) that they first proceeded from the Invention of Men, before they were commanded by God. Thus

a. *And the Coming of the Messiah,* &c.] In *Pereck Cheleck,* and elsewhere. And in *Isaiah* LXI. 2.[1] (*Pereck Cheleck* is the XIth Chap. of the *Talmud* concerning Councils; but what *Grotius* mentions, is not to be found there, at least in the *Mischna* Text; these Citations ought to have been more exact.)

1. Up to this point, the note is by Grotius. The following part is by Le Clerc.

b. *As* Jeremiah XXXI, &c.] V. 31. and following.

c. *That they first proceeded from the Invention of Men,* &c.] *Chrysostom* XII. concerning Statues, speaking of *Abel,* says, "that he offered Sacrifices, which he did not learn from any other Person, nor did he ever receive any Law that established any thing about First Fruits; but he had it from himself, and was moved to it by his own Conscience only." In the Answer to the Orthodox, in the Words of *Justin,* to the LXXXIIId Query: "None of those who sacrificed Beasts to God before the Law, sacrificed them at the Divine Command; though it is evident that God accepted them, and by such Acceptance discovered that the Sacrifices were well-pleasing to him." (This Matter is largely handled by Dr. *Spencer,* concerning the Ritual Law of the *Jews.* Book III. Dis. 2. to which I refer you. *Le Clerc.*)

much certainly is evident, that the *Hebrews* were desirous of very many Rites; (*a*) which was a sufficient Reason why God should enjoin them such a Number, upon this Account, lest the Memory of their Dwelling in *Egypt* <221> should cause them to return to the Worship of false Gods. But when their Posterity set a greater Value upon them than they ought, as if they were acceptable to God upon their own Account, and a Part of true Piety; they are reproved by the Prophets: (*b*) *As to Sacrifices,* says God in *David*'s Fiftieth Psalm, according to the *Hebrew, I will not speak to you at all concerning them,* viz. *that you shall slay Burnt-offerings upon Burnt-offerings, or that I will accept young Bullocks or Goats out of thy Fold: For all the living Creatures, which feed in the Forests, and wander upon the Mountains, are mine; I number both the Birds, and the wild Beasts; so that if I be hungry, I need not come to declare it to you; for the whole Universe, and every thing in it is mine. Do you think I will eat the Fat of Flesh, and drink the Blood of Goats? No: Sacrifice Thanksgiving, and offer thy Vows unto God.* There are some amongst the *Hebrews* who affirm that this was said, because they who offered these Sacrifices were unholy in their Hearts and Lives. But the Words themselves, which we have quoted, tell us the contrary, *viz.* that the thing was not at all acceptable to God in itself. And if we consider the whole Tenor of the Psalm, we shall find that God addresses himself to holy Men; for he had before said, *Gather my Saints together,* and afterwards, *Hear, O my People.* These are the Words of a Teacher; then having finished the Words before cited, he turns his Discourse, as is usual, to the Wicked: *But to the Wicked, said God;* and in other Places we find the same Sense. As Psalm LI. *To offer Sacrifices is not acceptable to thee, nei-*<222>*ther art thou delighted with Burnt-offerings:*

a. *Which was a sufficient Reason,* &c.] This very Reason for the Law of Sacrifices, is alleged by *Maimonides* in his Guide to the Doubting, Book III. Chap. 32. *Tertullian* against *Marcion,* Book II. "No Body should find Fault with the Labour and Burthen of Sacrifices, and the busy Scrupulousness of Oblations, as if God truly desired such things, when he so plainly exclaims against them: To what Purpose is the Multitude of your Sacrifices? And who hath required them at your Hands? But let such observe the Care God has taken to oblige a People prone to Idolatry and Sin, to be religigious, by such Duties, as that superstitious Age was most conversant in, that he might call them off from Superstition, by commanding those things to be done upon his Account, as if he desired it, lest they should fall to making Images."

b. *As to Sacrifices,* &c.] (This is *Grotius*'s Paraphrase upon *Psal.* L. not a literal Translation: And so are the following. *Le Clerc.*)

But the Sacrifice which thou truly delightest in, is a Mind humbled *by the Sense of its Faults; for thou, O God, wilt not despise a broken and contrite Heart:* The like to which is that of Psalm XL. *Sacrifices and Oblations thou dost not delight in, but thou securest me to thyself, (a) as if I were bored through the Ear; thou dost not require Burnt-sacrifices, or Trespass-offerings; therefore have I answered, Lo, I come; and I am as ready to do thy Will, as any Covenant can make me; for it is my Delight. For thy Law is fixed in my whole Heart; the Praises of thy Mercy I do not keep close in my Thoughts, but I declare thy Truth and Loving-kindness every where; but thy Compassion and Faithfulness do I particularly celebrate in the great Congregation.* In Chap. I. of *Isaiah,* God is introduced speaking in this manner. *What are so many Sacrifices to me? I am filled with the Burnt-offerings of Rams, and the Fat of fed Beasts; I do not love the Blood of young Bullocks, of Lambs, or of Goats, that you should appear with it before me: For who hath required this of you, that you should thus pollute my Courts?* And *Jeremiah* VII. which is a like Place, and may serve to explain this. *Thus saith the Lord of Angels, the God of Israel, ye heap up your Burnt-offerings with your Sacrifices, and yourselves eat the Flesh of them. For at the time when I first brought your Fathers up out of Egypt, I neither required nor commanded them any thing about Sacrifices, or Burnt-offerings. But that which I earnestly commanded them was, that they should be obedient to me; so would I be their God, and they should be my People; and that they should walk in the Way that I should teach them, so should all things succeed prospe-<223>rously to them.* And these are the Words of God in *Hosea,* Chap. VI. *Loving-kindness towards Men, (b) is much more acceptable to me than Sacrifice; to think aright of God, is above all Burnt-offerings.* And in *Micah,* when the Question was put, how any Man should render himself most acceptable to God, by a vast Number of Rams, by a huge Quantity of Oil, or by Calves of a Year old: God answers, *I will tell you what is truly good and acceptable to me,* viz. *(c) that you render to every Man his due, that you do Good to others,*

---

a. *As if I were bored,* &c.] A Mark of Servitude amongst the *Hebrews.*
b. *Is much more acceptable to me,* &c.] So the *Chaldee* Interpreter explains this Place.
c. *That you render to every Man his due,* &c.] Therefore the *Jews* say that the ICCII.[2] Precepts of the Law are by *Isaiah* contracted into six, Chap. XXXIII. 15. by *Micah* into

and that you become humble and lowly before God. Since therefore it appears from these Places, that Sacrifices are not reckoned amongst those things which are primarily, and of themselves acceptable to God; but the People, gradually, as is usual, falling into wicked Superstition, placed the principal Part of their Piety in them, and believed that their Sacrifices made a sufficient Compensation for their Sins: It is not to be wondered at, if God in time abolished a thing in its own Nature indifferent, but by use converted into evil; especially (*a*) when King *Hezekiah* broke the brazen Serpent erected by *Moses,* because the People began to worship it with religious Worship. Nor are there wanting prophecies, which foretold that those Sacrifices, about which the Controversy now is, should cease: Which any one will easily understand, who will but consider that according to the Law of *Moses,* <224> the sacrificing was committed entirely to the Posterity of *Aaron,* and that only in their own Country. Now in *Psalm* CX. according to the *Hebrew,* a King is promised, whose Kingdom should be exceeding large, who should begin his reign in *Sion,* and who should be a King and a Priest for ever, after the Order of *Melchisedech.* And *Isaiah,* Chap. XIX. saith, that an Altar should be seen in *Egypt,* where not only the *Egyptians,* but the *Assyrians* also and *Israelites* should worship God; and Chap. LXVI. he saith, that the most distant Nations, and People of all Languages, as well as the *Israelites,* should offer Gifts unto God, and out of them should be appointed Priests and *Levites;* all which could not be, (*b*) whilst the Law of *Moses* continued. To these we

---

three in this Place; by *Isaiah* into two, Chap. LVI. I. by *Habbakkuk* into one, Chap. II. 4. as also by *Amos,* V. 6.

2. 602.

a. *When King* Hezekiah, &c.] 2 *Kings* XVIII. 4.

b. *Whilst the Law of* Moses *continued,* &c.] Add this Place of *Jeremy,* Chap. III. 16. *In those Days, saith the Lord, they shall say no more, the Ark of the Covenant of the Lord, neither shall it come to mind, neither shall they remember it, neither shall they visit it, neither shall that be done any more.* (Even the *Jews* themselves could no longer observe their Law, after they were so much scattered. For it is impossible that all the Males should go up thrice in a Year to *Jerusalem,* according to the Law, *Exodus* XXIII. 17. from all those Countries which were inhabited by them. This Law could be given to no other, than a People not very great, nor much distant from the Tabernacle. *Le Clerc.*)

may add that Place in (*a*) *Malachi,* Chap. I. where God foretelling future Events, says, that the Offerings of the *Hebrews* would be an Abomination to him; that from the East to the West his Name should be celebrated among all Nations; and that Incense, and the purest things should be offered him; and *Daniel* in Chap. IX. relating the Prophecy of the Angel *Gabriel,* concerning Christ, says, *that he shall abolish Sacrifices* <225> *and Offerings:* And God has sufficiently signified, not only by Words but by the things themselves, that the Sacrifices prescribed by *Moses,* are no longer approved by him: Since he has suffered the *Jews* to be above sixteen hundred Years without a Temple, or Altar, or any Distinction of Families, whence they might know who those are, who ought to perform the sacred Rites.

SECT. IX. *And the Difference of Meats.*

What has been said concerning the Law of Sacrifices, the same may be affirmed of that, in which different kinds of Meat are prohibited. It is manifest, that after the universal Deluge, (*b*) God gave to *Noah* and his Posterity a Right to use any sort of Food; which Right descended, not only to *Japhet* and *Ham,* but also to *Shem* and his Posterity, *Abraham, Isaac* and *Jacob.* But afterwards, when the People in *Egypt* were tinctured with the vile Superstition of that Nation, then it was that God first prohibited the eating some sort of living Creatures, either because for the most part (*c*) such were <226> offered by the *Egyptians* to their Gods, and they

a. *Malachi,* Chap. I. &c.] See *Chrysostom's* excellent Paraphrase upon this Place, in his IId against the Gentiles.

b. *God gave to* Noah *and his Posterity,* &c.] The Mention of clean and unclean Creatures, seems to be an Objection against this, in the History of the Deluge; but either that was said by way of *Prolepsis* to those who knew the Law; or by unclean, ought to be understood those which Men naturally avoid for Food, such as *Tacitus* calls prophane, Hist. VI. Unless any one had rather understand by clean, those which are nourished by Herbs; and by unclean, those which feed on other living Creatures.

c. *Such were offered by the* Egyptians, &c.] *Origen,* in his IVth Book against *Celsus.* "Some wicked *Daemons,* and (as I may call them) Titanick or Gigantick ones, who were rebellious against the true God and the heavenly Angels, and fell from Heaven, and are continually moving about gross and unclean Bodies here on Earth, having some foresight of things to come, by reason of their Freedom from earthly Bodies, and being conversant in such things, and being desirous to draw off Mankind from the true God, made Divination by them; or because (*a*) in that <227> typical Law, the particular Vices of Men, were represented by certain Kinds of living Creatures. That these Precepts were not universal, appears from the Instance

---

they enter into living Creatures, especially those that are ravenous, wild and sagacious, and move them to what they will: Or else they stir up the Fancies of such living Creatures, to fly or move in such a manner, that Men taken by the Divination in these dumb Creatures, might not seek the God that comprehends the Universe, nor enquire after the pure Worship of God, but suffer their Reason to degenerate into earthly things, such as Birds and Dragons, Foxes and Wolves. For it is observed by those who are skilful in these things, that future Predictions are made by such living Creatures as these; the *Daemons* having no Power to effect that in tame Creatures, which by Reason of their Likeness in Wickedness, not real, but seeming Wickedness in such Creatures, they are able to effect in other Creatures. Whence, if any thing be wonderful in *Moses,* this particularly deserves our Admiration, that discerning the different Natures of living Creatures; and whether instructed by God concerning them, and the *Daemons* appropriated to every one of them; or whether he understood by his own Wisdom, the several ranks and sorts of them; he pronounced them unclean, which were esteemed by the *Egyptians,* and other Nations to cause Divination, and he declared the other to be clean." The like to which we find in *Theodoret,* Book VII. against the *Greeks:* And not very different from this, is that of *Manetho, Having established in the Law many other things, particularly such as were contrary to the Customs of the* Egyptians. And that which *Tacitus* says of the *Jews: All things are prophane amongst them, which are sacred amongst us.* And afterwards: *They slay a Ram in contempt of* Jupiter Ammon, *and sacrifice an Ox, which the* Egyptians *worshipped the God* Apis *by.*

a. *In that typical Law,* &c.] *Barnabas* in his *Epistle.* "*Moses* said, ye shall not eat a Swine, nor an Eagle, nor a Hawk, nor a Raven, nor any Fish which hath no Finns. By which he meant we should understand three things. What he aims at is evident from these Words in *Deuteronomy.* And my Judgments shall be established amongst my People. Now the Commandment of God, is not to prohibit eating; but *Moses* spake by the Spirit. He mentions Swine for this End, that they should not converse with Men who resemble Swine; for when they live in Luxury, they forget their Master; but when they want, they own their Master: Thus a Swine while he is eating, will not know his Master; when he is hungry, he cries out, and when he is full, he is quiet. Again, Thou shalt not, says he, eat the Eagle or the Hawk, or the Kite or the Raven. As much as to say, you shall not converse with such Men who know not how to get their Food by Labour and Pains, but unjustly steal it from others; and who walk about as if they were sincere, when they lie in wait for others. Thus these slothful Creatures contrive how they may devour the Flesh of others, being pestilent by their Wickedness. Again, Thou shalt not eat, says he, the Lamprey, nor the Pourcontrel, nor the Cuttle; that is to say, you shall not converse with those Men who are finally wicked, and condemned to Death: As these Sort of Fish alone, are doomed to swim at the Bottom of the Sea, not like others to hover on the Top of the Water, but to dwell on the Ground at the Bottom. Also he says, thou shalt not eat the Coney: Wherefore? That you may not be a Corrupter of Children, nor such like; for the Hare has a new Place to lay her Excrements in every Year; for so many Years as she lives, so many Holes has she under

of what is appointed concerning the Flesh of a Beast that died of it self, *Deut.* XIV. that it was not lawful for the *Is-*<228>*raelites* to eat it, (*a*) but it was lawful for Strangers, which Strangers the *Jews* were commanded to perform all good Offices to, as esteemed of God. And the antient *Hebrew* Teachers openly declare, (*b*) that in the Times of the Messiah, the Law of <229> the Prohibition of Meats could cease, and that Swines Flesh

---

Ground. Further, thou shalt not eat the *Hyaena,* that is, thou shalt not be an Adulterer, or unclean Person, or such like: For what Reason? Because this Creature changes its Nature every Year, and sometimes is a Male, and sometimes a Female. And he justly hated the Weasel; as much as to say, you shall not be like such Persons who, we have heard, have committed Iniquity in their Mouths by Uncleanness; neither shall you have Correspondence with such Workers of Iniquity; for this Animal conceives in its Mouth. Concerning Meats therefore, *Moses* meant three Things spiritually; but they, thro' fleshly Inclinations, understood him of Meats. But *David* knew these three Opinions, and therefore agreeably thereto he says, *Blessed is the Man that walketh not in the Council of the Ungodly,* as Fishes wander in Darkness at the Bottom of the Sea. *And hath not stood in the Way of Sinners,* viz. like them, who though they would seem to fear God, sin like Swine: *And hath not sat in the Seat of the Scornful;* like Birds watching for their Prey. Thus you have the End and the Meaning of them. But *Moses* commanded to eat every Creature that is cloven-footed, and that cheweth the Cud. And what does he mean by this? He that receiveth Meat, knoweth him that feeds him, and is satisfied with it and seems to rejoice: Which is very well said, if we consider the Command. What therefore is the Meaning of it? Why, converse with those who fear their Master; with those who meditate in their Hearts upon the Word they have received; with those who speak of, and keep the Judgments of their Master; with those who know that Meditation is a pleasant Work, and belongs to those who thoroughly consider their Master's Word. But what means cloven-footed; That a Man should walk uprightly in this World, in Expectation of another Life. See what excellent Laws are established by *Moses.*" *Clemens* commends this of *Barnabas,* in his Vth *Strome.* You may find also many Things partly like, and partly the same with these, in *Philo's* Book of Agriculture; and in the Book entitled, *The Wicked lay Snares for the Righteous;* which are too long to be transcribed. The like is to be seen in *Eusebius,* out of *Aristaeus,* Book VIII. ch. 9.

a. *But it was lawful for Strangers,* &c.] Holy Men, but not circumcised, which you find mentioned, *Levit.* XXII. 25. and XXV. 4, 7. and in the *Talmud,* chap. of the King, and of the Council; and in *Maimonides's* Book of Idolatry.

b. *That in the Times of the Messiah,* &c.] Thus *R. Samuel* in *Mechor Chaim.* The *Talmud* intitled *Nida,* says, the Law was to continue but till the Times of the Messiah. We may moreover observe, that some *Hebrew* Teachers, amongst whom is *Bechai,* were of Opinion, that the Laws concerning forbidden Meats, were peculiar to the Land of *Canaan,* nor was any one obliged to observe them out of the Bounds thereof. And beside, the *Jews* themselves are ignorant, or at least dispute about the Signification of many of the Names of those Animals; which we cannot think God would have permitted, if the Obligation to observe that Law, were to have continued till this Time.

should be as clean as that of an Ox. And certainly, since God designed to gather a People to himself out of all Nations, it was more reasonable, that he should make Liberty and not Bondage, in such Things, common to all. Now follows an Examination of Festival Days.

Sect. X. *And of Days.*

These were all instituted in Memory of the Benefit they had received from God, when they were delivered from the *Egyptian* Bondage, and brought into the Promised Land. Now the Prophet *Jeremiah* says, Chap. XVI, and XXIII, that the Time would come when new and much greater Benefits, should so eclipse the Memory of that Benefit, that there would scarce be any Mention made of it. And moreover, what we now said of Sacrifices, is as true of Festivals; the People began to put their Trust in them, so far, that if they rightly observed them, it was no great Matter how they offended in other Respects. Wherefore in *Isaiah,* Chap. I. God says, that he hated their New Moons and Feast-Days, they were such a Burden to him, that he was not able to bear them. Concerning the Sabbath, it uses particularly to be objected, that it is an universal and perpetual Precept, not given to one People only, but in the Beginning of the World, to *Adam* the Father of them all. To which <230> I answer, agreeably to the Opinions of the most learned *Hebrews,* that this Precept concerning the Sabbath is two-fold: (*a*) A Precept of Remembrance, *Exodus* XX. 8. and (*b*) Precept of Observation, *Exodus* XXXI. 31. The Precept of Remembrance is fulfilled, in a religious Memory of the Creation of the World; the Precept of Observation consists in an exact Abstinence from all manner of Labour. The first Precept was given from the Beginning, and without doubt (*c*) the pious Men before the Law obeyed it, as *Enoch, Noah, Abraham,*

---

a. *A Precept of Remembrance,* &c.] זכיר.

b. *A Precept of Observation* &c.] שמיר. Thus *Moses Gerundensis,* and *Isaac Aramas* distinguish. (*Observation* and *Remembrance* signify the same Thing in *Moses,* as to this Matter, as we have shown on *Deut.* V. 1. however, the Thing here treated of is true. *Le Clerc.*)

c. *The pious Men before the Law,* &c.] From whom a certain Veneration for the Seventh Day was derived to the *Greeks,* as *Clemens* observes. See what is said in relation to this, Book I.

Isaac, Jacob; the latter of whom, tho' we have a Relation of many of their Travels, (*a*) yet there is no Sign of their stopping their Journey on the Account of the Sabbath; which Thing we frequently meet with after their coming out of *Egypt.* For after the People were brought out of *Egypt,* and had safely passed through the Red Sea, they kept the first Day a Sabbath of Rest, and sung an Hymn to God, upon that Account; and from this Time, that exact Rest of the Sabbath was commanded, the first Mention of which is in the gathering of Manna, *Exodus* XXXV. 2. *Levit.* XXIII. 3. And in this Sense, the Reason alledged, *Deut.* V. <231> 21. For the Law of the Sabbath, is the Deliverance out of *Egypt.* And further, this Law had regard to Servants against the Severity of those Masters, who allowed them no Respite from their Labours, as you find it in the forecited Places. It is true indeed, (*b*) that Strangers were obliged by this Law, and that for this Reason, that there might be an universal Rest of all the People. But that this Law of perfect Rest was not given to other People, appears from hence, that in many Places it is called a Sign, and a particular Covenant between God and the *Israelites, Exodus* XXXI. 13, 16. And further, that those Things which were instituted in Memory of the coming out of *Egypt,* are not such as ought never to cease, we have before shown, from the Promise of much greater Benefits. To which may be added, that if the Law concerning Rest on the Sabbath had been given from the Beginning, and in such a Manner as never to be abolished, certainly that Law would have prevailed over all other Laws; the contrary to which we now find. For it is evident, (*c*) that Children were rightly circumcised on the Sabbath-Day; and while the Temple stood, (*d*) the Sacrifices were slain on the Sabbath-Day, as well as on other Days. The *Hebrew* Teachers themselves show, that this Law is changeable, when they say that Work may justly be done on the Sabbath, at the Command of a

a. *Yet there is no Sign,* &c.] That the pious Men of those Times did in this Sense σαββατίσαι, that is, observe the Sabbath, is denied by *Justin* in his Dialogue with *Tryphon,* and by *Tertullian* in two Places against the *Jews.*

b. *Strangers were obliged by this Law,* &c.] Not those others, who out of *Judaea* observed the Precepts given to the Posterity of *Noah.* This is the Opinion of the *Hebrews.*

c. *That Children were rightly Circumcised,* &c.] Thus the *Hebrew* Proverb, *The Sabbath gives Way to Circumcision.* See *John* VII. 22.

d. *The Sacrifices were slain,* &c.] *Numb.* XXVIII. 9.

Prophet, which they prove by the Example of the taking of *Jericho* on
<232> the Sabbath-Day by the Command of *Joshua.* And that in the
Time of the Messiah, the Difference of Days should be taken away, some
of them show very well, from that Place of *Isaiah* LXVI. 23. where it is
foretold, that there should be a continual Worship of God from Sabbath
to Sabbath, from New Moon to New Moon.

Sect. XI. *And Circumcision of the Flesh.*

We come now to Circumcision, which is indeed ancienter than *Moses,* as
being commanded to *Abraham* and his Posterity; but this very Precept
was the Beginning of the Covenant declared by *Moses.* Thus we find God
said to *Abraham, Genesis* XVII. *I will give unto thee, and to thy Seed after
thee, the Land wherein thou art a Stranger, even the Land of Canaan, for
an everlasting Possession; therefore keep my Covenant, thou and thy Seed for
ever; this is the Covenant betwixt me and thee and thy Seed, every Male shall
be circumcised.* But we have before seen, that there was to succeed a new
Covenant in the Room of this Covenant, such as should be common to
all People, for which Reason the Necessity of a Mark of Distinction must
cease. And this is further evident, that there was some mystical and higher
Signification, contained under this Precept of Circumcision; as appears
from the Prophets, when they command (*a*) the Heart to be circumcised,
to which all the Precepts of Christ tend. So likewise the Promises added
to Circumcision, must of Necessity relate to something further: Namely,
that of an Earthly Possession, (*b*) to the Revelation of an everlasting Possession, which is no <233> where made more manifest than by Jesus; (*c*)
and that of making *Abraham* a Father of many Nations; to the Time
when not only some few People, but innumerable of them, spread all over
the World, should imitate that memorable Faith of *Abraham* towards
God; which never yet came to pass, but by the Gospel. Now it is no Wonder, that when the Work is finished, the Shadow of the Work that was

a. *The Heart to be circumcised,* &c.] *Deut.* X. 16. XXX. 6. *Jer.* IV. 4.

b. *To the Revelation,* &c.] *Heb.* IV.

c. *And that of making* Abraham *a Father,* &c.] *Gen.* XVII. 5. *Rom.* IV. 11, 13, 16, 17.
Luke XIX. 9. *Gal.* III. 7.

designed, should be taken away. (*a*) And that God's Mercy was not confined to this Sign, is from hence manifest, that not only those who lived before *Abraham,* but even *Abraham* himself was acceptable to God before he was circumcised: And Circumcision was omitted by the *Hebrews* (*b*) all the while they journeyed through the Desarts of *Arabia,* without being reproved of God for it.

Sect. XII. *And yet the Apostles of Jesus easily allowed of those Things.*

There was certainly very good Reason why the *Hebrews* should return their hearty Thanks to Jesus and his Ambassadors, in that he freed them from that heavy Burden of Rites, and secured their Liberty to them (*c*) by Miracles and Gifts no way <234> inferior to those of *Moses.* But yet they who first delivered this Doctrine, did not require this of them, that they should acknowledge such their Happiness; but if they would perform the Precepts of Jesus, which were full of all Virtue, they easily allowed them, in indifferent Things, (*d*) to follow what Course of Life they would; (*e*) provided they did not impose the Observation of it, as necessary upon Strangers, to whom the Ritual Law was never given; which one Thing sufficiently shows that the *Jews* very unjustly reject the Doctrine of *Jesus,* under Pretence of the Ritual Law. Having answered this Objec-

a. *And that God's Mercy,* &c.] *Justin* in his Dialogue with *Trypho* says, "Circumcision was given for a Sign, and not for a Work of Righteousness." And *Irenaeus,* Book IV. ch. 30. "We learn from Scripture, that Circumcision is not that which perfects Righteousness; but God gave it, that *Abraham's* Posterities might continue distinguishable. For God said to *Abraham,* let every Male of you be circumcised, and circumcise the Flesh of your Foreskin, and it shall be for a Sign of a Covenant betwixt you and me."

b. *All the while they Journeyed,* &c.] *Josh.* V. 5, 6.

c. *By Miracles and Gifts no way inferior,* &c.] *R. Levi Ben Gerson* said, that the Miracles of the Messiah ought to be greater than those of *Moses,* which is most evident in the Dead restored to Life.

d. *To follow what Course of Life they would,* &c.] *Acts* XVI. 3. XXI. 24. *Rom.* XIV. 1. 1 *Cor.* IX. 17. *Gal.* V. 6. *Colos.* III. 2.

e. *Provided they did not impose,* &c.] *Acts* XV. *Gal.* I. 3, 6, 15. IV. 10. VI. 12.

tion, which is almost the only one commonly opposed to the Miracles of *Jesus,* we come now to other Arguments suited to convince the *Jews.*

SECT. XIII. *A Proof against the* Jews, *taken from their own Confession of the extraordinary Promise of the Messiah.*

Both they and we are agreed, that in the Predictions of the Prophets, there is a Promise, that amongst the many Persons who should make known to the *Jews,* from Heaven, very great Advantages; there should be One far exceeding the rest, whom they called the Messiah; which though a common Name, did more eminently agree to his Person. We assert, that he came long since; they expect that he is yet to come. It remains therefore that we put an End to the Controversy, from those Books, <235> the Authority of which is equally acknowledged by both.

SECT. XIV. *That he is already come, appears from the Time foretold.*

Daniel, (*a*) a Testimony of whose great Piety *Ezekiel* affords us, could neither deceive us, nor be deceived himself by the Angel *Gabriel:* And he, according to the Direction of the Angel, has left us upon Record, Chap. IX. that there should not pass above five hundred Years between the Publication of the Edict for rebuilding the City of *Jerusalem,* (*b*) and the Coming of the Messiah. But there is above two thousand Years passed since

a. *A Testimony of whose great Piety,* &c.] XIV. 14. XXXVIII. 3. *Josephus* concerning *Daniel,* at the End of the Xth Book says, "That the Spirit of God was with him." And afterwards: "That He was endued with every Thing in an incredible Manner, as being one of the greatest of the Prophets. In his Life-time, he was had in great Honour and Esteem, both by the Kings and the People: And after his Death, he was had in everlasting Remembrance; the Books wrote by him and left to us, we read at this Day, and their Testimony convinces us that he had a Communication with God."

b. *And the Coming of the Messiah,* &c.] The great *Hebrew* Doctors, such as *Solomon Jarchi, Rabbi Josue,* quoted by *Abenesdras,* and *Saaidias,* agree that the Son of Man in *Daniel,* is the Messiah: Thus *Rabbi Josue,* who saw the razing of the Temple, said that the Time of the Messiah was then past, as *R. Jacob* in *Caphthor* testifies.

that Time to this Day, and he, whom the *Jews* expect is not yet come; neither can they name any other, to whom that Time will agree. But it agrees so well to *Jesus,* that (*a*) a *Hebrew* Teacher *Nehemiah,* who lived five hundred Years before him, said <236> openly then, that the Time of the Messiah, signified by *Daniel,* could not be deferred above five hundred Years. There is another Mark before hinted at, which agrees with this of the Time; and that is, (*b*) that a Government over all Nations should be appointed from Heaven, after (*c*) the Posterity of *Seleucus* and *Lagus* should cease to reign; the latter of which ended in *Cleopatra,* not long before *Jesus* was born. A third Token is in the forementioned Chap. IX. of *Daniel,* that after the Coming of the Messiah the City of *Jerusalem* should be razed; which Prophecy of the Destruction of that City, (*d*) *Josephus* himself refers to his own Age. From whence it follows, that the Time limited for the Coming of the Messiah, was then past. To this may be referred that of *Haggai,* Chap. II. where God comforts *Zerubbabel,* a Heathen Prince, and *Joshua* the Son of *Josedech,* the High Priest, upon their Sorrow, because the Temple built by them did not answer the Greatness of <237> the former Temple, with this Promise, that there should be greater Honour done to that Temple, than to the former: Which could be

a. *A Hebrew* Teacher Nehemiah, &c.] *Grotius* ought to have told us whence he had this. If I remember right, in some Epistle of his to his Brother *William Grotius,* he says he received it from a *Jew. Le Clerc.*

b. *That a Government over all Nations,* &c.] *R. Levi Ben Gerson* tells us, that that Stone, by the Blow whereof that Image which represented the Empires, should be broken to Pieces, was the Messiah. *Rabbi Solomon, R. Abenesdras,* and *R. Saaida* say, that that Kingdom which would consume the rest of the Kingdoms, was the Kingdom of the Messiah. *R. Levi Ben Gerson* and *Saaida,* affirm the Son of Man in *Daniel,* to be the Messiah.

c. *The Posterity of* Seleucus *and* Lagus, &c.] See the Annotations upon this in the First Book.[3]

3. See above, Book I, Section 17, note d, p. 84 of the present volume.

d. Josephus *himself refers to his own Age,* &c.] Book X. ch. 12. "*Daniel* wrote concerning this Time, and concerning the *Roman* Empire, and that (our Nation) should be destroyed by it. God having discovered all these Things to him, he left them us in Writing; so that whoever reads them, and considers what has come to pass, cannot but admire the Honour God did to *Daniel.*" *Jaccides* also upon *Dan.* IX. 24. tells us that the seventy Weeks of Years were finished in the Destruction of *Jerusalem.*

said neither of the Bigness of the Work, nor of the Materials, nor of the Workmanship, nor of the Ornaments; as is very plain from the History of those Times in the sacred Writings, and in *Josephus,* compared with that of the Temple of *Solomon:* To which we may add; which is observed by the *Hebrew* Teachers, that there were wanting two very great Endowments in the latter Temple, which were in the former, *viz.* (*a*) a visible Light, as a Token of the Divine Majesty, and a Divine Inspiration. But wherein this latter Temple was to exceed the former, God briefly declares, when he says (*b*) that he would establish his Peace, that is, his Favour and Goodwill in that Temple, as it were by a firm Covenant: This is further prosecuted by *Malachi,* Chap. III. *Behold I will send my Messenger, who shall prepare my Way;* (*c*) *and the Lord whom ye seek, shall suddenly come to his Temple* (now *Malachi* lived after the latter Temple was built,) *even the Messenger of the Covenant whom ye delight in.* Therefore the Messiah ought to come while the second Temple stood, (*d*) in which Account is reckoned <238> by the *Hebrews* all the time from *Zerubbabel* to *Vespasian;* for the Temple in the time of *Herod* the Great, was not rebuilt from the Foundation, but only (*e*) gradually renewed by Parts; notwithstanding which Alteration, it might be called the same Temple. And indeed there was so firm an Expectation of the Messiah at that time amongst the

a. *A visible Light, as a Token,* &c.] In the Title, concerning Instruction, and the *Jerusalem Gemara,* ch. 3.

b. *That he would establish his Peace,* &c.] We must observe what goes before. *The Desire of all Nations shall come, and I will fill this House with Glory.* Which wonderfully agrees with what we have taken out of *Malachi;* so that these two Prophets may serve for Interpreters of each other. *Rabbi Akiba* and many others, as *Rabbi Solomon* testifies, were of Opinion that the Messiah ought to come in the second Temple.

c. *And the Lord whom ye seek,* &c.] This Place of *Malachi,* the *Jews* commonly explain of the Messiah.

d. *In which Account is reckoned,* &c.] As in the *Talmud,* ch. the last, concerning the Council; and that entitled *Joma,* and that entitled *Roch. Hasschana.*

e. *Gradually renewed by Parts,* &c.] *Philo* concerning the World. "That is not corruptible, all the Parts of which are corrupted; but that, all the Parts of which are destroyed together at the same time." Add to this, *L. proponebatur. D. de Judiciis. et L. quid tamen.* Sect. *in navis. D. quibus modis usus fructus amittatur.*

Hebrews, and their Neighbours, (*a*) that *Herod* was thought by some to be the Messiah, (*b*) *Judas Gaulonita* by others, (*c*) and some more by others, who lived about the time of our Saviour.

Sect. XV. (*With an Answer to what is alleged, that his Coming was deferred upon the Account of the Sins of the People.*)

The *Jews* see themselves put to Difficulties by these Arguments: That they may elude the Force of them therefore, some say that their Sins were <239> the Cause why he did not come at the promised time. Now not to mention, (*d*) that in the forecited Prophecies, what is determined by them has no Signs of being suspended upon any Conditions; how could his Coming be deferred on the Account of their Sins, when this also was foretold, that for the many and great Sins of the People, (*e*) the City should be destroyed a little after the time of the Messiah? Further, the Messiah was to come for this very Reason, (*f*) that he might bring a Remedy for the most corrupt Age, and together with the Rules of reforming

a. *That* Herod *was thought by some,* &c.] These were the *Herodians, Matt.* XII. 16. *Mark* III. 6. VIII. 15. XIII. 13. *Tertullian* in his Enumeration of Hereticks; *amongst these were the* Herodians, *who said that* Herod *was the Christ.* And *Epiphanius* says the same of them: Agreeable to which is that of the ancient Scholiast on *Persius;* "*Herod* reigned amongst the *Jews,* in the time of *Augustus,* in the Parts of *Syria;* therefore the *Herodians* keep the Birth day of *Herod,* as they do the Sabbath, upon which Day they put lighted Candles crowned with Violets on their Windows."

b. Judas Gaulonita *by others,* &c.] See *Josephus* XVIII. 1. *Acts* V. 36.

c. *And some more by others,* &c.] *Acts* XXI. 38. *Josephus* has many Instances in the time of *Felix,* and some after the Destruction of *Jerusalem.*

d. *That in the forecited Prophecies,* &c.] This is expressly affirmed by *R. Jochnaan* in *Schemoth Rabba,* and *R. David Kaimchi,* on *Psalm* CVIII. 5. *Josephus,* Book X. towards the End says well of *Daniel:* "That in his Prophecies he not only foretold what was to come, like the other Prophets, but he determined the time in which those things should come to pass." That the Decree of the Messiah's being sent at that time, was not suspended upon any Conditions, appears also from *Malachi* III. 1. Besides seeing that the Messiah was to be the Author of the New Covenant, as *Malachi* in that Place, and other Prophets shew, his coming could not be suspended on the Condition of observing that Covenant he came to abolish.

e. *The City should be destroyed,* &c.] *Dan.* IX. 24.

f. *That he might bring a Remedy,* &c.] *Isaiah* LIII. 4. and following Verses. *Jeremiah* XXXI. 31. and what follows, *Ezekiel* XI. 19, 21.

Sacrifice for Sin, (a) he shall see his Posterity, he shall live a long Life; and those Things which are acceptable to God, shall happily succeed through him; Seeing himself freed from Evil, says God, (b) He shall be satisfied with Pleasure, and that principally for this Reason, because by his Doctrine my righteous Servant shall acquit many, bearing himself their Sins. I will give him a large Portion (c) when the Spoil shall be divided amongst the Warriors; because he submitted himself to Death, and <251> was reckoned amongst the Wicked; and when he bore the Punishment of other Men's Crimes, he made himself a Petitioner for the Guilty. Which of the Kings or Prophets can be named, to whom these Things will agree? Certainly none of them. And as to what the modern *Jews* conceit, that the *Hebrew* People themselves are here spoken of, who being dispersed into all Nations, should by their Example and Discourse make Proselytes; this Sense, in the first Place, is inconsistent with many Testimonies of the sacred Writings, which declare, (d) that no Misfortunes should befall the *Jews,* which, and much greater than which, they have not deserved by their Actions. Further, the Order it self of the Prophetick Discourse, will not bear such an Interpretation. For the Prophet, or, which seems more agreeable to that Place, God says, *This Evil hath happened to him for the Sins of my People.* Now *Isaiah*'s People, or God's People, are the *Hebrew* People; wherefore he who is said by *Isaiah* to have endured such grievous Things, cannot be the same People. The ancient *Hebrew* Teachers more rightly confessed, that these Things were spoken of the Messiah; which when some of the

---

a. *He shall see his Posterity,* &c.] *Alseck* here says, that by the Word Seed in the *Hebrew,* is meant Disciples. Thus the Seed of the Serpent is by the *Hebrews* interpreted the *Canaanites;* and so some understand *their Sons, Isaiah* VIII. 18. as the *Jerusalem Talmud* observes, under the Title concerning the Council.

b. *He shall be satisfied with Pleasure,* &c.] *Abarbanel* refers these Words to a future Age.

c. *When the Spoil shall be divided,* &c.] The *Babylonish Gemara* entitled סוכה, tells us that these Words are to be understood in a spiritual Sense. *Alseck* upon this Place says, that by Spoils are to be understood the Honours and Rewards of wise Men.

d. *That no Misfortunes should befall the* Jews, &c.] This appears from those Places of the Prophets cited above, and from *Daniel* IX. and *Nehemiah* IX. To which we may add that he of whom *Isaiah* speaks, was to pray to God for the Heathens, which the *Jews* do not do.

latter saw, (*a*) they imagined two Messiahs; one of which they call the Son of *Joseph,* who endured many Evils, and a cruel Death; the other the Son of *David,* to whom all things succeeded prosperously; (*b*) tho' it is much easier, and more agree-<252>able to the Writings of the Prophets, to acknowledge one, who arrived at his Kingdom through Adversity and Death, which we believe concerning *Jesus,* and which the Thing itself shews us to be true.

Sect. XX. *And as though they were good Men, who delivered him to Death.*

Many are with-held from embracing the Doctrine of *Jesus,* out of a prejudiced Notion they have entertained of the Virtue and Goodness of their Forefathers, and especially of the Chief Priests; who condemned *Jesus,* and rejected his Doctrine, without any just Reason. But what sort of Persons their Forefathers often were, that they may not think I falsely slander them, let them hear in the very Words of their Law, and of the Prophets, by whom they are often called (*c*) Uncircumcised in Ears and Heart, (*d*) a People who honoured God with their Lips, and with costly Rites, but their Mind was far removed from him. It was their Forefathers (*e*) who were very near killing their Brother *Joseph,* and who actually sold him into Bondage; it was their Forefathers also, (*f*) who made *Moses,* their Captain and Deliverer, whom the Earth, Sea and Air obeyed, weary of his Life by their continual Rebellions; (*g*) who despised the Bread

a. *They imagined two Messiahs,* &c.] See the *Talmud* entitled *Succha, R. Solomon,* and *R. David Kimchi.*

b. *Though it is much easier,* &c.] Which *Abarbanel* follows, not in one Place only, on this Chap. of *Isaiah.*

c. *Uncircumcised in Ears and Heart,* &c.] *Jerem.* IV. 4. VI. 10.

d. *A People who honoured God with their Lips,* &c.] *Deut.* XXXII. 5, 6, 15, 28. *Isaiah* XXIX. 13. *Amos* V. 21. *Ezekiel* XVI. 3.

e. *Who were very near killing their Brother,* &c.] *Genes.* XXXVIII.

f. *Who made Moses,* &c.] The Places are observed before in the IId Book.

g. *Who despised the Bread,* &c.] *Numb.* XI. 6.

sent from Heaven; (*a*) who complained as if they were <253> in extreme Want, when they could scarce contain within them the Birds they had eaten. It was their Forefathers (*b*) who forsook the great and good King *David,* to follow his rebellious Son: It was their Forefathers, (*c*) who slew *Zacharias,* the Son of *Jehoiada,* in the most Holy Place, making the very Priest himself a Sacrifice of their Cruelty. (*d*) And as to the High Priests, they were such as treacherously designed the Death of *Jeremiah,* and had effected it, if they had not been hindered by the Authority of some of the Rulers; however, they extorted thus much, (*e*) that he should be held a Captive till the very Moment the City was taken. If any one think that they who lived in the Times of *Jesus* were better, *Josephus* can free them from this Mistake, who describes their most horrid Crimes, and their Punishments, which were heavier than any that were ever heard of; and yet, as he himself thinks, (*f*) beneath what they deserved. Neither are we to think better of the Council, especially when at that Time the Members of it were not admitted according to the ancient Custom by the Imposition of Hands, but were wont to be chosen (*g*) at the Will of great Men, as the Chief Priests also were, whose Dignity was not now perpetual, (*h*) but yearly, and oftentimes purchased. <254> So that we ought not to wonder that Men swelled with Pride, whose Avarice and Ambition was insatiable, should be enraged at the Sight of a Man, who urged the most Holy Precepts, and reproved their Lives by the Difference from his. Nor was he accused of any Thing, but what the best Men of old were;

a. *Who complained as if they were in extreme Want,* &c.] In the forecited XIth Chap. towards the End.

b. *Who forsook the great and good King* David, &c.] 2 *Sam.* XV.

c. *Who slew* Zacharias, &c.] 2 *Chron.* XXIV 21.

d. *And as to the High Priests,* &c.] *Jer.* XXVI.

e. *That he should be held a Captive,* &c.] *Jer.* XXXVIII.

f. *Beneath what they deserved,* &c.] He says no other City ever endured such Calamities, nor was there ever any Age so fruitful of all Kinds of Wickedness. The *Jews* brought greater Mischiefs upon themselves, than the *Romans* did, who came to expiate their Crimes.

g. *At the Will of great Men,* &c.] *Josephus* XIV. 9.

h. *But yearly, and oftentimes purchased,* &c.] *Josephus* XVIII. 3. and 6.

(*a*) Thus *Micaiah*, who lived in the Time of *Jehosaphat*, was delivered to Prison, for resolutely asserting the Truth against four hundred false Prophets. (*b*) *Ahab* charged *Elijah*, just as the Chief Priests did *Jesus*, with being a Disturber of the Peace of *Israel*. (*c*) And *Jeremiah* was accused, as *Jesus* was, of prophecying against the Temple. To which may be added what the antient *Hebrew* Teachers (*d*) have left us in Writing, that in the Times of the Messiah, Men would have the Impudence of Dogs, the Stubbornness of an Ass, and the Cruelty of a wild Beast. And God himself, who saw long before what sort of Men many of the *Jews* would be, in the Times of the <255> Messiah; foretold that they (*e*) who were not his People, should be admitted to be his People; (*f*) and that out of every City and Village of the *Jews,* not above one or two should go up to the Holy Mountain; but that what was wanting in their Number, should be filled up by Strangers. And also (*g*) that the Messiah should be the Destruction of the *Hebrews;* but that this Stone which was rejected by the Master-Builders, should be put in the Chief Place, to hold the whole Fabrick together.

a. *Thus* Micaiah, &c.] 2 *Kings* XXII.

b. *Ahab charged* Elijah, &c.] 1 *Kings* XVIII. 17. *Ahab* said to *Elijah, Art not thou he that troubles* Israel? And thus the High Priests said of *Jesus, Luke* XXIII. 2. *We found this Man a Troubler of* Israel.

c. *And* Jeremiah *was accused,* &c.] *Jer.* VII. 4. and following. XXVI. 6, 11.

d. *Have left us in Writing,* &c.] See the *Talmud* concerning the Council; *Kelmboth* and *Sota. R. Solomon* on the forementioned Title concerning the Council, *c. Helech;* and the *Talmud,* entitled concerning Weights. And also the Tradition of *Rabbi Judah,* in the *Gemara,* on the same Title concerning the Council *c. Helech.* "At that time when the Son of *David* shall come, the House that was appointed of God shall be made a Brothel-House." See *Jeremiah* X. 21. XIX. 14. (Here was a great Mistake, for the *Masoreth* was put instead of the *Gemara;* for these Words are to be found in the *Gemara,* ch. XI. entitled concerning the Council. *At that Time, when the Son of* David *shall come, the House of Assembling together,* בית הם יעד, *shall be made a Brothel-House,* Ed. *Cocceius.* Sect. 27. *Le Clerc.*)

e. *Who were not his People,* &c.] *Hosea* II. 24.

f. *And that out of every City,* &c.] *Jerom.* III. 14, 17. And *Isaiah* LIII.

g. *That the Messiah should be the Destruction,* &c.] *Isaiah* VIII. 14. *Psalm* CXVIII. 22.

SECT. XXI. *An Answer to the Objection of the Christians worshipping many Gods.*

It remains that we answer two Accusations, which the *Jews* assault the Doctrine and Worship of the Christians with. The first is this; they affirm that we worship many Gods: But this is no more than an odious Explication of another Ones Doctrine. For there is no more Reason why this should be objected against the Christians, (*a*) than against *Philo* the *Jew,* who often affirms, that there <256> are three Things in God; and calls the *Reason,* (*b*) or *Word of God,* the *Name of God,* (*c*) the Maker of the World, (*d*) not unbegotten, as is God the Father of all, nor yet begotten in like Manner as Men are: The same is likewise called (*e*) the Angel, or the

a. *Than against* Philo *the* Jew, &c.] Concerning the Sacrifices of *Abel* and *Cain.* "When God, attended with his two principal Powers, Government and Goodness; Himself, who is one only, being between them, he framed three Conceptions in the contemplative Soul; each of which can by no Means be comprehended, for his Powers are unlimited, for they each contain the Whole." Afterwards he calls *Government, Power;* and, *Goodness* he calls *Beneficence;* and says that they are not pronounced by a pious Mind, but kept in silent Secrecy. And the same we find in his Book of Cherubim, in the IId Book of the Husbandry of *Noah,* he mentions *Existence,* the *Governing Power, the Merciful Power. Maimonides,* in the Beginning of his Book of Fundamentals, and after him *Joseph Albo,* distinguish in God, *that which understandeth, that by which any Thing is understood, and the Understanding.* We find something belonging to this Matter in *Abenesdras,* on Gen. XVIII. and *Maimonides's* Guide to the Doubting, Part I. ch. 68.

b. *Or Word of God,* &c.] In his Allegories, and of the Confusion of Tongues.

c. *The Maker of the World,* &c.] In his Allegories: "His Word, by making use of which, as of an Instrument, he made the World." Concerning *Cain. The Word of God was the Instrument, by which it* (the World) *was made.* (The Word λόγος, might better be translated *Reason,* here in *Philo,* as I have abundantly shown in the Dissertation on the Beginning of St. *John. Le Clerc.*)

d. *Not unbegotten, as is God, the Father of all,* &c.] The Place is in the Book entitled, *Who shalt inherit Divine Things.* The same Word is called by *Philo,* the Image of God, in his Book of Monarchy, and in that of Dreams sent by God; sometimes ἀπεικόνιοσμα, *the Resemblance,* as in the Book, intitled, *The Wicked lay Snares for the Righteous.* Sometimes χάρακτήρ, *the Form,* as in Book II. of Agriculture. Compare *John* I. Heb. I. 3.

e. *The Angel, or the Ambassador,* &c.] He calls him ἄγγελος, *Angel,* in his Allegories, and in his Book of *Cherubin;* ἀρχάγγελος, *Archangel,* in his Book entitled, *Who shall inherit Divine good Things,* and in his Book *of the Confusion of Tongues.* And the same is called *Angel,* and יהוה *Jehovah,* by *R. Samuel* in *Mecor Chaim.*

Embassador, who takes Care of the Universe, by *Philo* himself, and by (*a*) *Moses* the Son <257> of *Nehemannus:* (*b*) Or against the *Cabalists*, who distinguish God into three Lights, and some of them by the same Names as the Christians do, of the Father, Son or Word, and Holy Ghost. And to take that which is chiefly allowed amongst all the *Hebrews;* That Spirit by which the Prophets were moved, is not any created Thing, and yet is distinguished from him that sent it; as is likewise that which is (*c*) commonly called the *Schechinah.*[8] Now <258> (*d*) many of the *Hebrews* have

---

a. Moses *the Son of* Nehemannus, &c.] The learned *Masius* has translated his Words thus, on the Vth ch. of *Joshua,* "That Angel, to speak the Truth, is the Angel, the Redeemer, of whom it is written; because my Name is in him. That Angel, I say, who said to *Jacob,* I am the God of *Bethel;* He of whom it is said, And God called *Moses* out of the Bush. And he is called an Angel, because he governs the World. For it is written, *Jehovah,* (*that is the Lord God*) brought us out of *Egypt;* and in other Places, he sent his Angel, and brought us out of *Egypt:* Besides it is written, And the Angel of his Presence hath made them safe. Namely, That Angel which is the Presence of God, concerning whom it is said, my Presence shall go before, and I will cause thee to rest. Lastly, this is that Angel of whom the Prophet said, And suddenly the Lord whom ye seek, shall come into his Temple, even the Angel of the Covenant whom ye desire." And again, other Words of the same Person to this Purpose: "Consider diligently what those Things mean; for *Moses* and the *Israelites* always desired the first Angel; but they could not rightly understand who he was. For they had it not from others, nor could they arrive fully at it by prophetick Knowledge. But the Presence of God, signifies God himself, as is confessed by all Interpreters; neither could any one understand those Things by Dreams, unless he were skilled in the Mysteries of the Law." And again: "My Presence shall go before, that is, the Angel of the Covenant whom ye desire, in whom my Presence will be seen. Of whom it is said, I will hear thee in an acceptable Time; for my Name is in him, and I will make thee to rest; or I will cause him to be kind and merciful to thee. Nor shall he guide thee by a rigid Law, but kindly and gently." Compare with this, what we find in *Manasses, Conciliator,* in the XIXth *Quest.* on *Genesis.*[7] (The Name of this *Rabbi's* Father, may better be pronounced *Nachman,* for it is written נחמן, *Nahhman.*)

7. Up to this point, the note is by Grotius. The following part is by Le Clerc.

b. *Or against the* Cabalists, &c.] See the Appendix to *Schindler's Hebrew Lexicon,* in the Characters אבז. And the Book called *Schep-tal* says, ספרית *Siperoth, Number* in God does not destroy his Unity.

c. *Commonly called the* Schechinah, &c.] And they distinguish it from the Holy Ghost. See the *Jerusalem Gemara,* entitled concerning Instructions, ch. 3. And the *Babylonish Gemara,* entitled *Jomach* 1. *R. Jonathan* in his Preface to *Ecka Rabthi* says, that the *Schechinah* remained three Years and a half upon Mount *Olivet,* expecting the Conversion of the *Jews;* which is very true, if we apprehend him right.

8. The Shekinah is the majestic presence or dwelling of God among men.

d. *Many of the* Hebrews *have this Tradition,* &c.] Rabbi *Solomon,* on *Genesis* XIX.

this Tradition, that that Divine Power which they call *Wisdom,* should dwell in the Messiah; (*a*) whence the *Chaldee* Paraphrast calls the Messiah the *Word of God,* as the Messiah is also called in *David, Messiah,* and others, (*b*) by that venerable Name of God, (*c*) and also of Lord.

SECT. XXII. *And that human Nature is worshipped by them.*

To the other Objection they make against us, namely, That we give the Worship due to God, to a Being made by God; the Answer is ready: For we say, that we pay no other Worship or Ho-<259>nour to the Messiah, (*d*) but what we are commanded in *Psalm* II. and CX. the former of which was fulfilled in *David* only in a loose Manner, and belong'd more eminently to the Messiah, (*e*) as *David Kimchi,* a great Enemy to the Christians, acknowledges; and the latter cannot be explained of any other but the Messiah. For the Fictions of the latter *Jews;* some of *Abraham,* some of *David,* and others of *Hezekiah;* are very trifling. The *Hebrew* Inscription shows us that it was a Psalm of *David*'s own. Therefore

---

18. acknowledges, that God can take upon him humane Nature, which he thinks was formerly done for a Time; to which agrees the *Talmud,* entituled, *Schebnoth* and *Sabbathoth.*

a. *Whence the* Chaldee *Paraphrast,* &c.] As *Hosea* XII. (But they are mistaken who think that the *Chaldee* Paraphrast means any Thing else by the *Name of God,* but God himself; as a very learned Man hath shewn, in the *Balance of Truth,* published in the Year 1700, a long Time after the Author's Death. *Le Clerc.*)

b. *By that venerable Name of God,* &c.] Namely, יהוה *Jehovah. Jonathan* and *David Kimchi* on *Jeremiah* XXIII. 6. with which agrees *Abba* in *Ecka Rabbathi.* צבאית יהוה *Jehovah Sabaoth, Zachariah* XIV. 16. The Talmud in *Taanith* from *Isaiah* XXV. 9. saith, in that Time God, ייהוה *Jehovah,* shall be shown as it were with the Finger.

c. *And also of Lord,* &c.] אלהים *Elohim, Psal.* XLV. 7. which *Psalm* the *Chaldee* Paraphrast there owns, treats of the Messiah, as he did before in that Place of *Isaiah* now cited. Also אדון *Adonai* in *Psalm* CX. which treats of the Messiah, as will presently appear.

d. *But what we are commanded,* &c.] The very learned Rabbi *Saadia* explains these Places, and *Zachariah* IX. 9. of the Messiah.

e. *As* David Kimchi, &c.] This same IId Psalm is expounded of the Messiah by *Abraham Esdras,* and *R. Jonathan* in *Beresith Rabba.*

what *David* says *was said to his Lord,* cannot agree to *David* himself, nor to *Hezekiah,* who was of the Posterity of *David,* and no Way more excellent than *David.* And *Abraham* had not a more excellent Priesthood; nay, *Melchisedec* gave him his Blessing, (*a*) as inferior to himself. But both this, and that which is added concerning (*b*) a Scepter's coming out of *Sion,* and extending to the most distant Places, plainly agrees to the Messiah, (*c*) as is clear from those Places which, without doubt, speak of the Messiah; neither did the ancient *Hebrews* and Paraphrasts understand them otherwise. Now that *Jesus* of *Nazareth* was truly the Person in whom these Things were fulfilled, I could believe upon the Affirmation of his Disciples only, upon the Account of their great Honesty, in the same Manner as the *Jews* believe *Moses,* without any other Witness, in those <260> Things which he says were delivered to him from God. (*d*) But there are very many and very strong Arguments besides this, of that exceeding Power which we affirm *Jesus* to have obtained. He himself was seen by many after he was restored to Life: He was seen to be taken up into Heaven: Moreover Devils were cast out, and Diseases healed, by his Name only; and the Gift of Tongues was given to his Disciples; which Things *Jesus* himself promised as Signs of his Kingdom. Add to this, that his Scepter, that is, the Word of the Gospel, came out of *Sion,* and, without any humane Assistance, extended itself to the utmost Limits of the Earth, by the Divine Power alone, and made Nations and Kings subject unto it, as the *Psalms* expressly foretold. The Cabalistical *Jews* (*e*)

a. *As inferior to himself,* &c.] And received the Tythe of him by a Sacerdotal Right, *Gen.* XIV. 19, 20.

b. *A Scepter's coming out of* Sion, &c.] *Psalm.* CX. 2.

c. *As is clear from those Places,* &c.] As *Genesis* XLIX. 10. and those before cited out of the Prophets.

d. *But there are very many,* &c.] See them handled before in the Second Book; and what is said in the Beginning of this Book.

e. *Made the Son of* Enoch, &c.] The Name which the *Hebrews* give him, is, מטטיר *Metator.* So the *Latins* call him, who prepares the Way for the King. Thus *Lucan.*

As Harbinger, to the *Hesperian* Fields, I boldly come.

Vegetius, Book II. says, They were called *Metatores, Harbingers in the Camps, who went before and chose a Place fit for the Camp.* And thus *Suidas:* Μεταταξ, *A Harbinger is a*

made the Son of *Enoch* a certain Middle Person betwixt God and Men, who had no Token of any such great Power. How much more reasonable then is it for us to do it to him, who gave us such Instructions? Neither does this at all tend to the lessening of God the Father, (*a*) from whom this Power of *Jesus* was <261> derived, (*b*) and to whom it will return, (*c*) and whose Honour it serves.

SECT. XXIII. *The Conclusion of this Part, with a Prayer for the Jews.*

It is not the Design of this Treatise to examine more nicely into these Things; nor had we treated of them at all, but to make it appear that there is nothing in the Christian Religion, either impious or absurd, which any Man can pretend against embracing a Religion recommended by so great Miracles, whose Precepts are so virtuous, and whose Promises are so excellent. For he who has once embrac'd it, ought to consult those Books which we have before shewn to contain the Doctrines of the Christian Religion, for particular Questions. Which that it may be done, let us beseech God that he would enlighten the Minds of the *Jews* with his own Light, and render those Prayers effectual, (*d*) which Christ put up for them, when he hung upon the Cross. <262>

Messenger who is sent before from the Prince.[9] (The Rabbis rather call it *Metatron* מטטרון concerning which see *John Buxtorf*'s Chaldee and Rabbinical Lexicon.)

9. Up to this point, the note is by Grotius. The following part is by Le Clerc.

a. *From whom this Power,* &c.] As himself confesses, *John* V. 19, 30, 36, 43. VI. 36, 57. VIII. 28, 43. X. 18, 29. XIV. 28, 31. XVI. 28. XX. 21. And the Apostle to the *Heb.* V. 5. *Rom.* VI. 4. *Cor.* XI. 4.

b. *And to whom it will return,* &c.] As the Apostle confesses, 1 *Cor.* XV. 24.

c. *And whose Honour it serves,* &c.] *John* XIII. 31. XIV. 13. *Rom.* XVI. 27. Therefore the *Talmud,* entituled, Concerning the Council, denies *Jesus* to be the Name of an Idol, seeing the Christians in honouring him have a Regard to God the Maker of the World.

d. *Which Christ put up for them,* &c.] *Luke* XXIII. 34.

Sect. I. *A Confutation of Mahometanism; the Original thereof.*

Instead of a Preface to this Sixth Book, which is designed against the Mahometans, it relates the Judgments of God against the Christians, down to the Original of Mahometanism; namely, (*a*) how that sincere and unfeigned Piety, which flourished amongst the Christians, who were most grievously afflicted and tormented, began by Degrees to abate; after *Constantine* and the following Emperors had made the Profession of the Christian Religion not only safe but honourable; but having as it were (*b*) thrust the World into the Church, first, (*c*) the Christian Princes <263> waged War without Measure, even when they might have enjoyed Peace. (*d*) The Bishops quar-<264>relled with each other most bitterly about the

a. *How that sincere and unfeigned Piety,* &c.] See *Ammianus Marcellinus,* at the End of the Twenty-first Book concerning *Constantius:* "And above all, he was very ready to take away what he had given; confounding the Christian Religion, which is perfect and sincere, with old Wives Fables, by more intricately searching into which, rather than seriously setling them, he caused a great many Differences; which spreading further, he kept up by quarrelling about Words, that the Body of Prelates, who were the publick Pack-horses running here and there in Synods, as they call them, might cut the Nerves of their Carriage, by endeavouring to make every Rite conformable to their own Opinion."

b. *Thrust the World into the Church,* &c.] See what is excellently said about this, in *Chrysostom's* second Moral Discourse on the XIIth Chapter of the 2 *Cor.* after *ver.* 10.

c. *The Christian Princes waged War,* &c.] It is a commendable Saying of *Marcian* in *Zonaras, That a King ought not to take up Arms, so long as he can maintain Peace.*

d. *The Bishops quarrelled with each other,* &c.] *Ammianus,* Book XXVII. "The cruel Seditions of the quarrelsome People, which gave Rise to this Business, frighted this Man also *(Viventius,* from chief Commissioner of the Palace.) *Damasus* and *Ursicinus,* being above all reasonable Measure desirous of seizing the Episcopal Chair, contended with each other most vehemently by different Interests, their Accomplices on each Side

highest Places: And, as of old, the (*a*) preferring the Tree of Knowledge to the Tree of Life, was the Occasion of the greatest Evils; so then nice Enquiries were esteemed more than Piety, (*b*) and <265> Religion was

carrying on their Differences as far as Death and Wounds; which *Viventius* not being able to correct or soften, being compelled by a great Force, retired into the Suburbs; and *Damasus* overcame in the Contest, the Party which favoured him, pressing hard. And it is evident, that in the Palace of *Sicininus,* where the Assemblies of the Christians used to be, there were found the dead Bodies of one hundred thirty seven slain in one Day; and it was a long time before the enraged common People could be appeased. Nor do I deny, when I consider the City's Pomp, but that they who are desirous of this thing, ought to contend by stretching their Lungs to the utmost, in order to obtain what they aim at: For when they are arrived at it, they will be so secure, that they may enrich themselves with the Gifts of Matrons, may sit and ride in their Chariots, be neatly dressed, have large Feasts provided, insomuch that their Banquets will exceed the Royal Tables; who might have been truly happy, if they had despised the Grandeur of the City, which flattered their Vices; and had lived after the Manner of some of the Provincial Bishops, whose Sparingness in Eating and Drinking moderately, and Meanness in Clothes, and Eyes fixed on the Ground continually, recommend them as pure and modest to the Deity, and to those that worship him." And a little after; "*Praetextatus,* whilst he takes care of the Government in a higher Degree, amongst other things, by manifold Acts of Integrity and Goodness, for which he has been famous from the Beginning of his Youth, has obtained that which seldom happens; that at the same time that he is feared, he does not lose the Love of his Subjects, which is seldom very strong towards those Judges they are afraid of. By whose Authority and just Determinations of Truth, the Tumult, raised by the Quarrels of the Christians, was appeased; and *Ursicinus* being driven away, the *Roman* Subjects grew into a firm Peace jointly, and with one Mind; which is the Glory of an eminent Ruler, regulating many and advantageous things." This was that *Praetextatus,* of whom *Hieronymus* tells a Story, not unworthy to be mentioned here; to *Pammachius,* against the Errors of *John* of *Jerusalem.* "*Praetexatus,* that died when he was designed for Consul, used to say jestingly to the holy Pope *Damasus;* Make me Bishop of the City of *Rome,* and I will be a Christian immediately." See also what the same *Ammianus* says, Book XV. The *African* Council did not without Reason admonish the Bishop of the City of *Rome* thus: "That we may not seem to bring the vain Arrogance of the Age into the Church of Christ; which affords the Light of Simplicity, and the Day of Humility, to them who desire to see God." To which we may add the noble Epistles of the *Roman* Bishop *Gregory,* truly stiled the Great, Book IV. 32, 34, 36. Book VI. 50. Book VII. Indict. 1. Epist. 30.

    a. *Preferring the Tree of Knowledge,* &c.] *Genesis* II. and III.

    b. *And Religion was made an Art,* &c.] See what was before quoted out of the 21st Book of *Ammianus.* The same Historian, Book XXIII. in the History of *Julian,* says, "And that his Disposition of things might produce a more certain Effect, having admitted the disagreeing Prelates of the Christians, together with the divided Multitude, into the Palace; he admonished them, that every one, laying aside their civil Discords, should apply himself without Fear to his Religion; which he urged the more earnestly, that their Differences might increase by the Liberty that was given them; so

made an Art. The Consequence of which was, that after the Example of them (*a*) who built the Tower of *Babel,* their rashly affecting lofty Matters, produced different Languages and Confusion; which the common People taking notice of, many times not knowing which way to turn themselves, cast all the Blame upon the Sacred Writings, and began to avoid them, as if they were infected. And Religion began every where <266> to be placed, not in Purity of Mind, but in Rites, as if *Judaism* were brought back again: And in those things which contained in them (*b*) more of bodily Exercise, than Improvement of the Mind; and also in a violent adhering to (*c*) the Party they had chosen; the final Event of which was, that there were every where a great many (*d*) Christians in

---

that he needed not afterwards to fear the common People would be all of a Mind; knowing that no Beasts are so mischievous to Mankind, as very many of the Christians were, who were so outrageous against one another." See also *Procopius* in the Ist of his Gothicks, to be read with some Abatement here, as in other Places. "Embassadors came from *Byzantium,* to the Bishop of *Rome,* when *Hypatius* was Bishop of *Ephesus,* and *Demetrius* of *Philippi* in *Macedonia,* concerning an Opinion which was controverted amongst the Christians; though I know what Opposition they made, yet I am very unwilling to relate it. For I think it the maddest Folly, to search nicely into the Nature of God, and wherein it consists. For, as I conceive, Man cannot fully comprehend human things, much less those that appertain to the Divine Nature. I may therefore securely pass by these things in Silence, and not disturb what they reverence. As for myself, I can say nothing more of God, but that he is every way good, and upholds all things by his Power; he that knows more, whether he be a Priest, or one of the common People, let him speak it." *Gregoras,* Book XII. cites the Saying of *Lysis* the *Pythagorean,* and afterwards of *Synesius; That talking Philosophy among the Vulgar, was the Cause of Mens so much contemning divine things.* So also Book the Xth, he much dissuades Men from such Disputes; and speaking of the *Latins* of his time, he says, "I blame and condemn the *Italians* highly, because they run into divine Matters with great Arrogance." Afterwards he adds: "Amongst them, the Mechanicks utter the Mysteries of Divinity, and they are all as eager of reasoning Syllogistically, as the Cattle are of Food and Grass. Both they who doubt of what they ought to believe rightly, and they who know not what they ought to believe, nor what they say they believe; these fill all the Theatres, *Forums,* and Walks with their Divinity, and are not ashamed to make the Sun a Witness of their *Impudence.*"

a. *Who built the Tower of* Babel, &c.] *Gen.* XI. *Mahomet* often reproaches these Controversies of the Christians, particularly in *Azoarae,* XXVI. XXXII.

b. *More of bodily Exercise,* &c.] 1 *Tim.* IV. 8. *Colos.* II. 23.

c. *The Party they had chosen,* &c.] *Rom.* X. 2. 1 *Cor.* I. 12, and following Verses.

d. *Christians in Name,* &c.] See *Salvian,* Book III. concerning the Government of God. "Excepting a very few who avoid Wickedness, what else is the whole Body of Christians but a Sink of Vice?"

Name, but very few in Reality. God did not overlook these Faults of his People; but from the furthest Corners (*a*) of *Scythia*, (*b*) and *Germany*, poured vast Armies like a Deluge upon the Christian World: And when the great Slaughter made by these, did not suffice to reform those which remained; by the just Permission of God, (*c*) *Mahomet* planted in *Arabia* a new Religion, directly opposite to the Christian Religion; yet such as did in a good Measure express in Words, the Life of a great Part of the Christians. This Religion was first embraced by the *Saracens*, who revolted from the Emperor *Heraclius;* whose Arms quickly subdued *Arabia, Syria, Palaestine, Egypt, Persia*, and afterwards they invaded *Africa*, and came over Sea into *Spain*. But the Power of the *Saracens* was derived to <267> others, (*d*) particularly to the *Turks*, a very war-like People, who after many long Engagements with the *Saracens*, being desired to enter into a League, they easily embraced a Religion agreeable to their Manners, and transferred the Imperial Power to themselves. Having taken the Cities of *Asia* and *Greece*, and the Success of their Arms increasing, they came into the Borders of *Hungary* and *Germany*.

Sᴇᴄᴛ. II. *The* Mahometans *Foundation overturned in that they do not examine into Religion.*

This Religion, which was plainly calculated for Bloodshed, delights much in Ceremonies; (*e*) and would be believed, without allowing Liberty to enquire into it: For which Reason the Vulgar are prohibited reading those Books which they account sacred; which is a manifest Sign of their Iniquity. For those Goods may justly be suspected, which are imposed upon us with this Condition, that they must not be looked into. It is true indeed,

a. *Of* Scythia, &c.] *Hunns, Avari, Sabiri, Alani, Enthalites* and *Turks.*

b. *And* Germany, &c.] *Goths, Eruli, Gepidae, Vandals, Franck, Burgundians, Swedes, Almains, Saxons, Varni* and *Lumbards.*

c. Mahomet *planted in* Arabia, &c.] Dr *Prideaux*'s Life of *Mahomet* wrote in *English*, is very well worth reading, published at *London, Anno* 1697. *Le Clerc.*

d. *Particularly to the* Turks, &c.] See *Leunclavius*'s History of *Turkey*, and *Laonicus Chalcocondilas.*

e. *And would be believed*, &c.] See the *Alcoran Azoara* XIII. according to the first *Latin* Edition, which for the Reader's sake, we here follow.

all Men have not like Capacities for understanding every thing; many are drawn into Error by Pride, others by Passion, and some by Custom: (*a*) But the Divine Goodness will not <268> allow us to believe, that the way to eternal Salvation cannot be known by those, who seek it without any Regard to Profit or Honour; submitting themselves, and all that belong to them, to God, and begging Assistance from him. And indeed, since God has planted in the Mind of Man a Power of judging; no Part of Truth is more worthy to employ it about, than that which they cannot be ignorant of, without being in danger of missing eternal Salvation.

SECT. III. *A Proof against the* Mahometans, *taken out of the sacred Books of the* Hebrews *and* Christians; *and that They are not corrupted.*

Mahomet and his Followers confess, (*b*) that both *Moses* (*c*) and *Jesus* were sent by God; and that they who first propagated the Institution of Jesus, (*d*) were holy Men. (*e*) But there are many things related in the *Alcoran,* which is the Law of *Mahomet,* directly contrary to what is delivered by *Moses,* and the Disciples of Jesus. To instance in one Example out of many. All the Apostles and <269> Disciples of Jesus, entirely agree

a. *But the Divine Goodness will not allow us,* &c.] See the Answer to the Orthodox, Question the IVth, among the Works of *Justin.* "That it is impossible for him not to find the Truth, who seeks it with all his Heart and Power; our Lord testifies, when he says, he that asks receives, he that seeks shall find, and to him that knocks it shall be opened." And *Origen* in his XIIIth Book against *Celsus.* "He ought to consider, that he who sees and hears all things, the common Parent and Maker of the Universe, judges, according to Mens Deserts, of the Disposition of every one that seeks him, and is willing to worship him, and he will render to every one of these the Fruit of his Piety."

b. *That both* Moses, &c.] *Azoara* V. XXI.

c. *And Jesus,* &c.] *Azoara* V. VII.

d. *Were holy Men,* &c.] *Azoara* V. LXXI.

e. *But there are many things related,* &c.] As the Temple of *Mecha,* built by *Abraham, Azoara* XI. and many other things of *Abraham, Azoara* XXXI. A confused History of *Gideon* and *Saul, Azoara* III. Many things in the History of *Exodus, Azoara* XVII. XXX. and XXXVIII. Many things in the History of *Joseph, Azoara* XII. concerning the Birds cut in Pieces by *Abraham,* and called to Life again, *Azoara* IV. concerning *Mary's* being brought up with *Zachariah, Azoara* V. concerning the Birds made of Clay by Jesus, *Ibid.* and XIII.

in this Testimony, that Jesus died upon the Cross, returned to Life upon the third Day, and was seen of many: On the contrary, *Mahomet* says, (*a*) that *Jesus* was privately taken up into Heaven, and that a certain Resemblance of him was fixed to the Cross, and consequently Jesus was not dead, but the Eyes of the *Jews* were deceived. This Objection cannot be evaded, unless *Mahomet* will say, as indeed he does, (*b*) that the Books both of *Moses,* and of the Disciples of Jesus, have not continued as they were, but are corrupted; but this Fiction we have already confuted in the third Book. Certainly, if any one should say that the *Alcoran* is corrupted, the *Mahometans* would deny it, and say, that that was a sufficient Answer to a thing which was not proved. But they cannot easily bring such Arguments for the Uncorruptedness of their Book, as we bring for ours, *viz.* that Copies of them were immediately dispersed all over the World; and that not like the *Alcoran* in one Language only; and were faithfully preserved, by so many Sects, who differed so much in other things. The *Mahometans* persuade themselves, that in the XIVth Chapter of St. *John,* which speaks of sending the Comforter, there was something written of *Mahomet,* which the Christians have put out: But here we may ask them, do they suppose this Alteration of the Scripture, to have been made after the coming of *Mahomet,* or before? It is plainly impossible to have been done after the coming of *Mahomet,* because at that time there were extant all over the World very many Copies, not only <270> *Greek,* but *Syriac, Arabic,* and in Places distant from *Arabia, Aethiopic* and *Latin,* of more Versions than one. Before the coming of *Mahomet* there was no Reason for such a Change; for no Body could know what *Mahomet* would teach: Further, if the Doctrine of *Mahomet* had nothing in it contrary to the Doctrine of Jesus, the Christians would as easily have received his Books, as they did the Books of *Moses* and the *Hebrew* Prophets. Let us suppose on each Side that there was nothing written either of the Doctrine of Jesus, or of that of *Mahomet;* Equity will tell us, that that is to be esteemed the Doctrine of Jesus, in which

a. *That Jesus was privately taken up into Heaven,* &c.] *Azoara* XI.
b. *That the Books both of* Moses, &c.] *Azoara* IX.

all Christians agree; and that the Doctrine of *Mahomet,* in which all *Mahometans* agree.

SECT. IV. *From comparing Mahomet with Christ.*

Let us now compare the Adjuncts and Circumstances of each Doctrine together, that we may see which is to be preferred to the other: And first let us examine their Authors. *Mahomet* himself confessed (*a*) that Jesus was the Messiah promised in the Law and the Prophets; he is called by *Mahomet* himself (*b*) the Word, (*c*) Mind and (*d*) Wisdom of God; he is also said by him (*e*) to have had no Father amongst Men. *Mahomet* is acknowledged by his own Disciples (*f*) to have been begotten according to the common Course <271> of Nature. Jesus led an innocent Life, against which no Objection can be made. *Mahomet* (*g*) was a long time a Robber, (*h*) and always effeminate. (*i*) Jesus was taken up into Heaven, by the Confession of *Mahomet;* but *Mahomet* remains in the Grave. And now can any one doubt which to follow?

SECT. V. *And the Works of each of them.*

Let us now proceed to the Works of each of them. (*j*) *Jesus* gave Sight to the Blind, made the Lame to walk, and recovered the Sick; nay, as

---

a. *That Jesus was the Messiah,* &c.] *Azoara* XXIX.

b. *The Word,* &c.] *Azoara* V, and XI. and in the Book of *Mahomet's* Doctrine *Euthymius Zigabenus* in his Disputations against the *Saracens,* says, that Jesus is called by *Mahomet, the Word and Spirit of God.*

c. *Mind,* &c.] *Azoara* IV. XI. XXIX. and in the forementioned Book.

d. *And Wisdom,* &c.] In the forecited Places.

e. *To have had no Father amongst Men,* &c.] *Azoara* XXXI.

f. *To have been begotten,* &c.] See the Book of *Mahomet's* Generation.

g. *Was a long time a Robber,* &c.] See *Mahomet's* Chronicon, translated out of *Arabick.* See the Dispute betwixt a *Saracen* and a *Christian,* published by *Peter Abbot* of *Clugny.*

h. *And always effeminate,* &c.] *Azoara* XLII, XLIII, LXXV, and LXXVI. See the forementioned Disputation.

i. *Jesus was taken up into Heaven,* &c.] *Azoara* XI.

j. *Jesus gave Sight to the Blind,* &c.] *Azoara* V. XII.

Mahomet confesses, he restored the Dead to Life. *Mahomet* says, (*a*) that he himself was not sent with Miracles, but with Arms; however there were some afterwards who ascribed Miracles to him, but what were they? None but such as might easily be the Effects of human Art, as that of the Dove flying to his Ear; or such as had no Witnesses, as that of the Camels speaking to him by Night; or else such as are confuted by their own Absurdity, (*b*) as that of a great Piece of the Moon falling into his Sleeve, and sent back again <272> by him to make the Planet round. Who is there that will not say but that in a doubtful Cause, we are to stick to that Law which has on its Side the most certain Testimony of the Divine Approbation? Let us also examine Them who first embraced each of these Laws.

Sect. VI. *And of those who first embraced each of these Religions.*

They who embrac'd the Law of Christ, were Men who feared God, and led innocent Lives; and it is not reasonable that God should suffer such Persons to be deceived with cunning Words, or with a Shew of Miracles. (*c*) But they who first embraced *Mahometanism,* were Robbers, and Men void of Humanity and Piety.

a. *That he himself was not sent with Miracles,* &c.] *Azoara* III. XIV. XVII. XXX. LXXI. Concerning this Matter, see the Life of *Mahomet* published in *English* by the learned Dr. *Prideaux,* p. 30. where he shows at large, that the false Prophet, dared not boast of any Miracles. *Le Clerc.*

b. *As that of a great Piece of the Moon,* &c.] *Azoara* LXIV. See this Fable more at large in the Chapter *Ceramuz,* in *Cantacuzenus*'s Oration against *Mahomet,* Sect. 23.

c. *But they who first embraced Mahometanism,* &c.] This the Word *Saracen* shows, which signifies *Robber,* See *Scaliger*'s Emendation of the times Book III. Ch. of the *Arabian* Period. (The first Followers of *Mahomet* were indeed truly Robbers; but the *Arabian* Word to which *Scaliger* refers, signifies *to steal privately,* not *to Rob;* nor is it credible that they would take upon themselves such an infamous Name; not to mention that this was more antient than *Mahomet,* for we find it in *Ptolemy* and *Philostorgius;* wherefore I rather follow the Opinion of those who deduce the Name *Saracen* from the Word שרק, *Schark,* which signifies *Eastern,* whence comes שרקיין, *Sharkiin, Saracens,* or *People dwelling in the East,* as the *Arabians* are called in Scripture. About which see *Edward Pocock* on the Specimen of the History of the *Arabians* in the Beginning. *Le Clerc.*)

SECT. VII. *And of the Methods by which each Law was propagated.*

Next let us show the Method by which each Religion was propagated. As for the Christian Religion, we have already said several Times, that its Increase was owing to the Miracles not only of <273> Christ, but of his Disciples and their Successors, and also to their patiently enduring of Hardships and Torments. But the Teachers of *Mahometanism* did not work any Miracles, did not endure any grievous Troubles, nor any severe kinds of Death for that Profession. (*a*) But that Religion follows where Arms lead the Way; it is the Companion of Arms; (*b*) nor do its Teachers bring any other Arguments for it, but the Success of War, and the Greatness of its Power; than which nothing is more fallacious. They themselves condemn the *Pagan* Rites, and yet we know how great the Victories of the *Persians, Macedonians,* and *Romans* were, and how far their Enemies extended themselves. Neither was the Event of War always prosperous to the *Mahometans;* (*c*) there are remarkable Slaughters which they have received in very many Places, both by Land and Sea. They were driven out of all *Spain.* That Thing cannot be a certain Mark of true Religion, which has such uncertain Turns, <274> and which may be common both to good and bad: And so much the less, because their Arms were unjust, (*d*) and often taken up against a People who no Ways disturbed them, nor were distinguished for any Injury they had done; so

a. *But that Religion follows where Arms lead the Way,* &c.] *Azoara* X, XVIII, XXVI.

b. *Nor do its Teachers bring any other Arguments,* &c.] *Azoara* XXXIII. XLVII.

c. *There are remarkable Slaughters,* &c.] And greater since the Time of *Grotius.* For they were driven, after many Slaughters, from the *Austrian* Dominions, from *Hungary, Transilvania,* and *Peloponnesus,* not many Years since. And since that Time, the *Turkish* Empire seems to decrease. In the Year 1715, after these short Notes were first published, the *Turks* recovered the *Morea,* which was poorly defended by the *Venetian* Governors; but in the following Year 1716. when they attempted to invade *Hungary* and the Island of *Corsica,* they were first overthrown in a great Fight by the *Germans* under the Command of Prince *Eugene* of *Savoy;* and lost *Temiswaer,* which was forced to yield after a stout Siege; then being repulsed by the Valour of Count *Schulembourg,* not without Loss, they retired to their Fleet. While I wrote this, *April* 1717, they threatned they would attempt the same again with new Forces, but the *Germans* did not seem to be much affected with it. *Le Clerc.*

d. *And often taken up against a People,* &c.] *Azoara* XIX.

that they could have no Pretence for their Arms, but Religion, which is the most profane Thing that can be; (*a*) for there is no Worship of God, but such as proceeds from a willing Mind. Now the Will is inclined only by Instruction and Perswasion, not by Threats and Force. He that is compelled to believe a Thing, does not believe it, but only pretends to believe it, that he may avoid some Evil. He that would extort Assent, from a Sense of Evil or from Fear; shows by that very Thing, that he distrusts Arguments. And again, they themselves destroy this very Pretence of Religion, when they suffer those who are reduced to their Obedience, to be of what Religion they please; nay, (*b*) and sometimes they openly acknowledge that Christians may be saved by their own Law.

Sect. VIII. *And of their Precepts compared with one another.*

Let us also compare their Precepts together. The one commands Patience, nay, Kindness towards those who wish ill to us: The other, Revenge. The one commands that the Bonds of Matrimony should be perpetual, that they should bear with <275> each other's Behaviour; (*c*) the other gives a Liberty of separating: Here the Husband does the same himself which he requires of his Wife; and shows by his own Example, that Love is to be fixed on one. (*d*) There Women upon Women are allowed, as being always new Incitements to Lust. Here Religion is reduced inwardly to the Mind, that being well cultivated there, it may bring forth Fruits, profitable to Mankind; there, almost the whole Force of it is spent (*e*) in Circumcision, (*f*) and Things indifferent in themselves. Here a moderate

---

a. *For there is no Worship of God,* &c.] *Lactantius* Book X. ch. 20. *For there is nothing so voluntary as Religion, in which if the Mind of the Sacrificer goes contrary, it is taken away, there remains none.*

b. *And sometimes openly acknowledge,* &c.] *Azoara* I, and XII. The Book of the Doctrine of *Mahomet,* see *Enthymius.*

c. *The other gives a Liberty of separating,* &c.] See *Enthymius,* and others who have wrote of the *Turkish* Affairs.

d. *There Women upon Women,* &c.] *Azoara* III. VIII. IX. XXX. LII.

e. *In Circumcision,* &c.] See also *Bartholomew Georgivitius* of the Rites of the *Turks.*

f. *And Things indifferent in themselves,* &c.] As Washings. *Azoara* IX. See also *Enthymius.*

Use of Wine and Meat is allowed; (*a*) There the eating Swines Flesh, (*b*) and drinking Wine is forbidden; which is the great Gift of God, for the Good of the Mind and Body, if taken moderately. And indeed it is no Wonder that childish Rudiments should precede the most perfect Law, such as that of Christ is; but it is very preposterous after the Publication thereof, to return to Figures and Types. Nor can any Reason be given why any other Religion ought to be published after the Christian Religion, which is far the best.

SECT. IX. *A Solution of the* Mahometans *Objection, concerning the Son of God.*

The *Mahometans* say, they are offended because we ascribe a Son to God, who makes no Use of a <276> Wife; as if the Word Son, as it refers to God, could not have a more Divine Signification. But *Mahomet* himself ascribes many Things to God, no less unworthy of him, than if it were said he had a Wife; for Instance, (*c*) that he has a cold Hand, and that himself experienced it by a Touch; (*d*) that he is carried about in a Chair, and the like. Now we, when we call *Jesus* the Son of God, mean the same Thing that He did, (*e*) when he calls him the Word of God; for the Word is in a peculiar Manner (*f*) produced from the Mind: To which we may add, that he was born of a Virgin, by the Help of God alone, who supplied the Power of a Father; that he was taken up into Heaven by the Power of God; which Things, and those that *Mahomet* confesses,

a. *There the eating Swines Flesh,* &c.] *Azoara* II. XXVI.

b. *And drinking Wine,* &c.] See *Enthymius,* and others who have wrote of the Affairs of the *Saracens.*

c. *That he has a cold Hand,* &c.] See the Place in *Richardus* against the *Mahometans,* ch. I. and XIV. and in *Cantacuzenus* in the IId Oration against *Mahomet,* Sect. XVIII. and in the IVth Oration not far from the Beginning.

d. *That he is carried about in a Chair,* &c.] In the same Place.

e. *When he calls him the Word of God,* &c.] See above.

f. *Produced from the Mind,* &c.] See *Plato* in his Banquet, and *Abarbanel* in his Dialogue, which is commonly called That of *Leo Hebraeus.* See *Enthymius* concerning this Matter, in the forementioned Dispute, where he says, *In like Manner as our Word proceeds from the Mind,* &c. And Cardinal *Cusan,* Book I. ch. XIII. etc. against the *Mahometans;* and *Richardus,* ch. IX. and XV.

show (*a*) that *Jesus* may, and ought to be called the Son of God, by a peculiar Right.

SECT. X. *There are many absurd Things in the* Mahometan *Books.*

But on the other Hand, it would be tedious to relate how many Things there are in the *Mahome-*<277>*tan* Writings, (*b*) that do not agree to the Truth of History; and how many that are very ridiculous. Such as (*c*) the Story of a beautiful Woman, who learnt a famous Song from Angels overtaken with Wine, by which she used to ascend up into Heaven, and to descend from thence; who when she was ascended very high into the Heavens, was apprehended by God, and fixed there, and that she is the Star *Venus*. Such another (*d*) is that of the Mouse in *Noah*'s Ark, that sprung out of the Dung of an Elephant; and on the contrary, (*e*) of a Cat bred out of the Breath of a Lion. And particularly that (*f*) of Death's being changed into a Ram, which was to stand in the middle Space betwixt Heaven and Hell; and (*g*) of getting rid of Banquets in the other Life by Sweat; and (*h*) of a Company of Women's being appointed to every one for sensual Pleasure. Which Things are really all of them such, that they

---

a. *That Jesus may, and ought to be called,* &c.] *Luke* I. 35. *John* X. 36. *Acts* III. 13, 14, 15. XIII. 33. *Heb.* I. 5. V. 5. In the forementioned Book of the Doctrine of *Mahomet,* Jesus is brought in, calling God his Father.

b. *That do not agree to the Truth of History,* &c.] As that of *Alexander* the Great, who came to a Fountain where the Sun stood still. *Azoara* XXVIII. concerning *Solomon, Azoara* XXXVII.

c. *The Story of a Beautiful Woman,* &c.] This Fable is in the Book of the Doctrine of *Mahomet,* taken out of the Book of *Enarrations.* See also *Cantacuzenus,* in his IId Oration against *Mahomet,* ch. 15.

d. *Is that of the Mouse,* &c.] This is in the forementioned Book of the Doctrine of *Mahomet.*

e. *Of a Cat,* &c.] In the same Book.

f. *Of Death's being changed into a Ram,* &c.] In the End of the forementioned Book of the Doctrine of *Mahomet.*

g. *Of getting rid of Banquets,* &c.] In the forecited Book of the Doctrine of *Mahomet.*

h. *Of a Company of Women's,* &c.] See what was above alledged on the second Book.

are deservedly given over to Senselessness, who can give any Credit to them, especially when the Light of the Gospel shines upon them. <278>

Sect. XI. *The Conclusion to the Christians; who are admonished of their Duty upon Occasion of the foregoing Things.*

Having finished this last Dispute, I come now to the Conclusion, which regards not Strangers, but Christians of all Sorts and Conditions; briefly showing the Use of those Things which have been hitherto said; that those which are right may be done, and those which are wrong may be avoided. First, (*a*) that they lift up undefiled Hands to that God (*b*) who made all Things visible and invisible out of nothing; (*c*) with a firm Perswasion that he takes care of Mankind, (*d*) since not a Sparrow falls to the Ground without his Leave: (*e*) And that they do not fear them who can only hurt the Body, before him who hath an equal Power over both Body and Soul: (*f*) That they should trust not only on God the Father, but also on *Jesus;* since there is (*g*) none other Name on Earth, by which we can be saved; (*h*) which they will rightly perform, if <279> they consider that not they, who call one by the Name of Father, and the other by the Name of Lord, shall live eternally; but they who conform their Lives to his Will. They are moreover exhorted carefully to preserve (*i*) the

a. *That they lift up undefiled Hands,* &c.] 1 *Tim.* II. *James* IV. 8. *Tertullian* in his Apology. "Thither the Christians direct their Eyes, with Hands extended, because Innocent; with Head uncovered, because we are not ashamed; without any Instructor, because from our Heart we pray for all Emperors, that they may enjoy a long Life, a secure Government, a safe House, couragious Armies, a faithful Senate, an honest People, and a peaceful Land."

b. *Who made all Things,* &c.] *Colos.* I. 16. *Heb.* XI. 3. *Acts* IV. 24. 2 *Mac.* VII. 28.

c. *With a firm Perswasion,* &c.] 1 *Pet.* III. 11. V. 7.

d. *Since not a Sparrow.* &c.] *Mat.* X. 29.

e. *And that they do not fear them,* &c.] *Mat.* X. 28. *Luke* XII. 4.

f. *That they should trust,* &c.] *John* XIV. 2. *Heb.* XIV. 15, 16. *Ephes.* III. 12. and 17.

g. *None other Name on Earth,* &c.] *Acts* IV. 12.

h. *Which they will rightly perform,* &c.] *John* VIII. 43. and following, *Mat.* VII. 21. *John* XV. 14. 1 *John* II. 3, 4.

i. *The Holy Doctrine of Christ,* &c.] *Mat.* XIII. 44, 45. 1 *Cor.* IV. 7. 1 *Tim.* VI. 20. 2 *Tim.* I. 14.

Holy Doctrine of Christ, as a most valuable Treasure; and to that End, (*a*) often to read the sacred Writings, by which no one can possibly be deceived, who has not first deceived himself. (*b*) For the Authors of them were more faithful, and more full of the Divine Influence, than either willingly to deceive us in any necessary Truth, or to hide it in Obscurity; but we must bring (*c*) a Mind prepared to obey, which if we do, (*d*) none of those Things will escape us, which we are to believe, hope, or do; and by this Means (*e*) that Spirit will be cherished and excited in us, which is given us as (*f*) a Pledge of future Happiness. Further, they are to be de-<280>terred from imitating the Heathen; First (*g*) in the Worship of false Gods, (*h*) which are nothing but empty Names, (*i*) which evil Angels make use of (*j*) to turn us from the Worship of the true God; wherefore (*k*) we cannot partake of their Rites, and at the same Time be profited by the Sacrifice of Christ. Secondly, (*l*) in a licentious Way of living, having no other Law but what Lust dictates, (*m*) which Christians ought to be the furthest from; because they ought not only (*n*) far to exceed the Heathen; (*o*) but also the Scribes and Pharisees among

a. *Often to read the sacred Writings*, &c.] *Colos.* III. 16. 1 *Thes.* V. 27. *Rev.* I. 3.

b. *For the Authors of them were more faithful*, &c.] *Tertullian* speaks thus concerning the Hereticks in his Prescription. "They are wont to say, that the Apostles did not know all Things; being acted by the same Madness, by which they again change, and say that the Apostles did indeed know all Things, but did not deliver all Things to all Men; in both of which they make Christ subject to Reproach, who sent Apostles either not well instructed, or not very honest." See what there follows, which is very useful.

c. *A Mind prepared to obey*, &c.] *John* VII. 17. V. 44. *Mat.* XI. 25. *Philip.* III. 15. 2 *Pet.* III. 16. *Hosea* XIV. 10.

d. *None of those Things will escape us*, &c.] 2 *Tim.* II. 15, 16. *John* XX. 31. 1 *Pet.* I. 23.

e. *That Spirit will be cherished*, &c.] 2 *Tim.* VI. 1 *Thes.* V. 19.

f. *A Pledge of future Happiness*, &c.] *Ephes.* I. 14. 2 *Cor.* I. 22. V. 3.

g. *In the Worship of false Gods*, &c.] 1 *Cor.* VIII. 5, 6.

h. *Which are nothing but empty Names*, &c.] In the same, V. 4. X. 19.

i. *Which evil Angels make use of*, &c.] 1 *Cor.* X. 20. *Rev.* IX. 2.

j. *To turn us from the Worship of the true God*, &c.] *Ephes.* II. 2. *Rev.* IX. 5. 2 *Thes.* II. 12.

k. *We cannot partake of their Rites*, &c.] 1 *Cor.* X. 20.

l. *In a licentious Way of living*, &c.] *Ephes.* II. 3. *Tit.* II. 14.

m. *Which Christians ought to be the furthest from*, &c.] 2 *Cor.* VI. 15.

n. *Far to exceed the Heathen*, &c.] *Mat.* V. 47. VI. 7, 32.

o. *But also the Scribes and Pharisees*, &c.] *Mat.* V. 20. XXIII. 23. *Rom.* III. 20. *Galat.* II. 16.

the *Jews,* whose Righteousness, which consisted in certain external Acts, was not sufficient to secure them a heavenly Kingdom. (*a*) The Circumcision made with Hands availeth nothing now, but that other internal Circumcision of the Heart, (*b*) Obedience to the Commands of God, (*c*) A new Creature, (*d*) Faith which is effectual by Love, (*e*) <281> by which the true *Israelites* are distinguished, (*f*) the Mystical *Jews,* that is, such as praise God. (*g*) The Difference of Meats, (*h*) Sabbaths, (*i*) Festival Days (*j*) were the Shadows of Things, which really are in Christ and Christians. *Mahometanism* gave Occasion for mentioning the following Admonitions; (*k*) it was foretold by our Lord Jesus, that after his Time there should come some who should falsely say they were sent of God; but though (*l*) an Angel should come from Heaven, we are not to receive any other Doctrine than that of Christ, (*m*) confirmed by so many Testimonies. In times past indeed, (*n*) God spake in many and various Manners, to the pious Men that then were; but last of all he was pleased to call us by his Son, (*o*) the Lord of all Things, (*p*) the Brightness of his Father's Glory, and the express Image of his Substance; (*q*) by whom

a. *The Circumcision made with Hands,* &c.] 1 *Cor.* VII. 19. *Galat.* V. 6. VI. 15. *Philip.* III. 3. *Ephes.* II. 11. *Colos.* II. 11. *Rom.* II. 29.

b. *Obedience to the Commands of God,* &c.] 1 *Cor.* VII. 19.

c. *A new Creature,* &c.] *Galat.* VI. 15.

d. *Faith which is effectual by Love,* &c.] *Galat.* V. 6.

e. *By which the true Israelites are distinguished,* &c.] *Rom.* IX. 6. 1 *Cor.* X. 18. *Galat.* VI. 16. *John* I. 47.

f. *The Mystical Jews,* &c.] *Rom.* II. 28. *Philo* concerning Allegories. Judas *was a Symbol of him that confesses (God.)*

g. *The Difference of Meats,* &c.] *Acts* X. 13, 14, 15. XV. 19, 20. 1 *Cor.* X. 15. *Colos.* II. 16, 21.

h. *Sabbaths,* &c.] In the forecited Place of the *Colossians.*

i. *Festival Days,* &c.] In the same Place, and *Rom.* XIV. 5.

j. *Were Shadows of Things,* &c.] *Colos.* II. 17. *Heb.* X. 1.

k. *It was foretold by our Lord Jesus,* &c.] *John* V. 34. 2 *Thes.* II. 9. *Mat.* VII. 15. XXIV. 11. *Mark* XIII. 22. 1 *John* IV. 1.

l. *An Angel should come from Heaven,* &c.] *Galat.* I. 8.

m. *Confirmed by so many Testimonies,* &c.] 1 *John* V. 7. 8. *Heb.* II. 4. XII. 1. *John* I. 7, 32. V. 32, 37, 39, 46. *Luke* XXIV. 27. *Acts* II. 22, 23. X. 43.

n. *God spake in many and various Manners,* &c.] *Heb.* I. 2.

o. *The Lord of all Things,* &c.] 1 *Cor.* XV. 27. *Heb.* II. 5.

p. *The Brightness of his Father's Glory,* &c.] *Heb.* I. 3.

q. *By whom all Things were made,* &c.] In the same ch. *Colos.* I. 16.

all Things were made, which <282> were or shall be; (*a*) who acts and upholds all Things by his Power; and who (*b*) having made Atonement for our Sins, is advanced to the Right Hand of God, having obtained (*c*) a higher Dignity than the Angels; and therefore nothing more noble can be expected, (*d*) than such a Lawgiver. They may also take Occasion from hence to remember, (*e*) that the Weapons appointed for the Soldiers of Christ, are not such as *Mahomet* depends upon, but proper to the Spirit, fitted for the pulling down of strong Holds erected against the Knowledge of God; (*f*) the Shield of Faith, which may repel the fiery Darts of the Devil; the Breast-plate of Righteousness, or Holiness of Life; for a Helmet which covers the weakest Part, the Hope of eternal Salvation; (*g*) and for a Sword, the Word delivered by the Spirit, which can enter into the innermost Parts of the Mind. Next follows an Exhortation (*h*) to mutual Agreement, which Christ seriously commended to his Disciples when he went <283> from them; (*i*) We ought not to have amongst us many Masters, but only *Jesus Christ:* (*j*) All Christians were baptized into the same Name, therefore there ought (*k*) to be no Sects or Divisions amongst them; To which that there may be some Remedy

a. *Who acts and upholds all Things,* &c.] *Heb.* I. 3. *Revel.* I. 5.

b. *Having made Atonement for our Sins,* &c.] *Heb.* I. 3. IX. 12. *Mat.* XX. 28. 1 *John* II. 2. IV. 10. *Mat.* XXVI. 64. *Mark* XVI. 19. *Acts* II. 33, 34. VII. 55, 56. *Rom.* VIII. 34. *Ephes.* I. 10. *Colos.* III. 1. *Heb.* VIII. 1. X. 12. XII. 5.

c. *A higher Dignity than the Angels,* &c.] 2 *Pet.* III. 22. *Heb.* I. 13. *Ephes.* I. 21.

d. *Than such a Lawgiver,* &c.] *Heb.* II. 3, 4, 5, 6, 7, 8. III. 3, 4, 5, 6.

e. *That the Weapons appointed for the Soldiers of Christ,* &c.] *Rom.* XIII. 12. 2 *Cor.* VI. 7. X. 4. *Ephes.* VI. 11, 12, 13, 14, 15, 16, 17, 18.

f. *The Shield of Faith,* &c.] See beside the aforecited Place to the *Ephesians,* 1 *Thes.* V. 8.

g. *And for a Sword,* &c.] See beside the forementioned Place, *Ephes.* VI. 17. *Heb.* IV. 12. *Revel.* I. 6.

h. *To mutual Agreement,* &c.] *John* XIV. 27. XIII. 34, 35. XV. 12, 17. XVII. 20. and following. XX. 19, 26. 1 *John* III. 23. Also *Ephes.* III. 14. and following. VI. 16. *Heb.* XIII. 20. *Mat.* V. 9.

i. *We ought not to have amongst us many Masters,* &c.] *Mat.* XXIII. 8. *James* III. 1.

j. *All Christians were baptized,* &c.] *Rom.* VI. 3, 4. 1 *Cor.* I. 13, 15. *Gal.* III. 27. *Ephes.* IV. 5. *Colos.* II. 12.

k. *To be no Sects or Divisions amongst them,* &c.] 1 *Cor.* I. 10. XI. 18. XII. 25.

applied, those Words of the Apostle are suggested, (*a*) to be temperate in our Wisdom, (*b*) according to the Measure of the Knowledge God has afforded us; (*c*) if any have not so good an Understanding of all Things, that we bear with their Infirmities, (*d*) that they may quietly, and without quarrelling, unite with us; (*e*) if any exceed the rest in Understanding, it is reasonable he should exceed in good Will towards them: And as to those (*f*) who in some Things think otherwise than we do, we are to wait till God shall make the hidden Truth manifest unto them: In the mean Time, (*g*) we are to hold fast, and fulfil those Things we are agreed in. (*h*) Now we know in Part; (*i*) the <284> Time will come, when all Things shall be most certainly known. But this is required of every one, (*j*) that they do not unprofitably keep by them the Talent committed to their Charge; (*k*) but use their utmost Endeavours to gain others unto Christ; (*l*) in order whereunto, we are not only to give them good and wholesome Advice, but to set before them (*m*) an Example of Reformation of Life; that Men may judge of the Goodness of the Master by the Servant, and of the Purity of the Law, by their Actions. In the last Place, we direct our Discourse, as we did in the Beginning, to common Readers, beseeching them to give God the Glory, (*n*) if they receive any good from what has

a. *To be temperate in our Wisdom,* &c.] *Rom.* XII. 8. 16. 1 *Cor.* IV. 6.

b. *According to the Measure of the Knowledge,* &c.] In the forecited Place to the *Romans,* and XII. 6. 2 *Cor.* X. 13. *Ephes.* IV. 7, 15, 16.

c. *If any have not so good an Understanding,* &c.] *Rom.* XIV. XV. 2. 1 *Cor.* VIII. 7.

d. *That they may quietly,* &c.] *Rom.* XIV. 1. 2 *Cor.* XII. 20. *Gal.* V. 20. *Philip.* I. 16. II. 3, 15. 1 *Cor.* XI. 16.

e. *If any exceed the rest,* &c.] *Rom.* VIII. 1, 2, 3, 9. XII. 8. XIII. 3, 14. 16. 1 *Cor.* XIII. 2. 2 *Cor.* VI. 6. VIII. 7. 2 *Pet.* I. 5, 9.

f. *Who in some Things think otherwise,* &c.] *Philip.* III. 15. *Ephes.* IV. 2. 1 *Cor.* XIII. 4, 7. 1 *Thes.* IV. 14. 2 *Cor.* VI. 6. *Gal.* V. 22. *Colos.* IV. 11. 2 *Tim.* IV. 2. *Luke* IX. 54, 55.

g. *We are to hold fast,* &c.] *Philip.* III. 16. *James* I. 22, 23, 24, 25.

h. *Now we know in Part,* &c.] 1 *Cor.* XIII. 9, 12.

i. *The Time will come,* &c.] The same V. 10, 12. 1 *John* III. 2. *Mat.* V. 8.

j. *That they do not unprofitably keep,* &c.] *Mat.* XXV. 15. and following.

k. *But use their utmost Endeavours,* &c.] 1 *Cor.* IX. 19. 20, 21, 22.

l. *In order whereunto,* &c.] *Gal.* VI. 6. *Ephes.* IV. 29. 2 *Tim.* I. 13. *Titus* II. 8.

m. *An Example of Reformation of Life,* &c.] 1 *Pet.* III. 1, 16. *Eph.* VI. 6. 2 *Tim.* II. 24. 1 *Pet.* II. 12. *Eph.* IV. 1. *Philip.* I. 27.

n. *If they receive any Good,* &c.] *James* I. 17. 2 *Thes.* I. 3. 1 *Cor.* I. 4.

been said; (*a*) and if there be any thing they dislike, let them impute it to the Errors all Mankind are prone to fall into; (*b*) and to the Place and Time, in which this was delivered, more according to Truth, than elaborately. <285>

a. *And if there be any thing they dislike,* &c.] *James* III. *Gal.* VI. 1, 2.

b. *And to the Place and Time,* &c.] Because this very excellent and learned Man, was kept in *Lipstadt* Prison,[1] to which he was condemned for Life; at which Time, and in which Place, he could never have taken so great Pains in accomplishing so many Pieces remarkable for great Learning, accurate Judgment, and singular Brightness; without incredible Firmness and Constancy of Mind, and unshaken Faith in God; for which Endowments bestowed upon him by God, for the Benefit of all *Christendom,* let every one who reads his other Works, or this, with a Mind intent upon Truth, give Thanks to God, as I do from the Bottom of my Heart. *Le Clerc.*

1. Loevestein Castle (see the introduction).

BOOK I

Concerning the Choice of Our Opinion Amongst the Different Sects of Christians.

Sect. I. *We must enquire, amongst what Christians the true Doctrine of Christ flourisheth most at this time.*

Whoever reads over the Books of the New Testament with a Desire to come at the Knowledge of the Truth, and does not want Judgment, will not be able to deny, but that every one of the Marks of Truth, alleged by *Hugo Grotius* in his IId and IIId Books, are to be found there. Wherefore if he has any Concern for a blessed Immortality, he will apprehend it to be his Duty to embrace what is proposed to him in those Books as Matter of Belief, to do what he is commanded, and to expect what he is there taught to hope for. Otherwise, if any one should deny that he doubts of the Truth of the Christian Religion, and at the same time thinks the Doctrines, Precepts, and Promises of it not fit to <288> be believed or obeyed in every Particular; such an one would be inconsistent with himself, and manifestly show that he is not a sincere Christian. (*a*) Now this is one of the Precepts of Christ and his Apostles, that we should profess ourselves the Disciples of Christ before Men, if we would have him own us for his, when he shall pass Sentence on the Quick and Dead at the last Day; and if we do not, as we have denied him to be our Master before Men, so he also, in that last Assembly of Mankind will deny us to be his

---

a. *Now this is one of the Precepts of Christ,* &c.] Thus Christ saith, *Matt.* X. 32. "Whosoever therefore shall confess me *(to be his Master)* before Men, him will I confess also *(to be my Disciple)* before my Father which is in Heaven. But whosoever shall deny me *(to be his Master)* before Men, him will I also deny *(to be my Disciple)* before my Father which is in Heaven." See also 2 *Tim.* II. 12. *Rev.* III. 5.

Disciples before God. (*a*) For Christ would not have those that believe on him, be his Disciples privately, as if they were ashamed of his Doctrine, or as if they valued the Kindnesses, Threats, or Punishments of Men more than his Precepts, and the Promises of eternal Life; but be Christians openly and before all the World, that they may invite other Men to embrace the true Religion, and render back to God (*b*) that Life which they received from him, in the <289> most exquisite Torments, if it so seem good to him, whilst they openly profess that they prefer his Precepts above all things. And thus St. *Paul* teaches us, that if we confess (*c*) with our Mouth the Lord Jesus, and believe in our Heart that God hath raised him from the Dead, we shall be saved; *For,* says he, *with the Heart Man believeth unto Righteousness, and with the Mouth Confession is made unto Salvation; for the Scripture saith, Whosoever believeth on him shall not be ashamed.* Which being thus, it is his Duty who thinks the Christian Religion to be true, to discover and profess boldly and without Fear this his sincere Opinion, upon all Occasions that offer themselves.

And it is further necessary for him to enquire, if there be any of the same Opinion with himself, and (*d*) to maintain a particular Peace and Friendship with them; for Christ tells us, this is one Mark his Disciples are to be known by, if they love one another, and perform all Acts of Love and Kindness towards each other. Moreover he exhorts them (*e*) to have

a. *For Christ would not have,* &c.] Therefore he says, *Mat.* V. 14. "That his Disciples are the Light of the World; that a City set on a Hill cannot be hid; neither is a Candle lighted to be put under a Bushel, but set in a Candlestick that it may give Light to all that are in the House, etc."

b. *That Life which they received from him,* &c.] *Luke* XII. 4. Christ bids us *not to be afraid of them that kill the Body, and after that have no more that they can do;* and commands us *to fear him, which after we are killed, can cast us into Hell Fire.* And moreover he foretels all manner of Evils to his Disciples, *Matt.* X. 29, and following; and says, *that he who shall lose his Life for his sake, shall find it* (again) &c. which Precepts were particularly observed by the primitive Christians, who for the Testimony they gave to the Doctrine of the Gospel, are called *Martyrs,* that is, Witnesses.

c. *Confess with our Mouth,* &c.] *Rom.* X. 9, 10, 11.

d. *To maintain a particular Peace,* &c.] *John* XIII. 34, 35. "A new Commandment give I unto you, that ye love one another, that as I have loved you, so ye love another; by this shall all Men know that ye are my Disciples, if ye have Love one towards another." See 1 *John* II 7. III. 11, 16, 23.

e. *To have Congregations,* &c.] *Matt.* XVIII. 19, 20.

Congregations *in his Name,* that is, such as should be called Christian; and promises that he would be present there where two or three are met together upon that <290> Account; by this means, beside the mutual Love, and strict Friendship of Christians united into one Society, there is also a Provision made (*a*) for preserving their Doctrines; which can hardly continue, if every one has a private Opinion to himself, and does not declare the Sense of his Mind to another, unless for his own Advantage; for those things that are concealed, are by Degrees forgotten, and come in time to be quite extinguished; but Christ would have his Doctrine, and the Churches which profess it, be perpetual, that it may not cease to be beneficial to Mankind.

Wherefore whoever derives his Knowledge of the Christian Religion from the New Testament, and thinks it true; such an one ought to make Profession of it, (*b*) and to join himself with those of the like Profession. But because there is not at this time (neither was there formerly) one sort of Men only, or one Congregation of such as are gathered together *in the Name of Christ;* we are not therefore presently to believe that he is a true Christian, who desires to be called by that holy Name; neither ought we to join ourselves, (*c*) without Examination, to any Assembly who <291> stile themselves Christians. We must consider, above all things, whether their Doctrines agree with that Form of sound Words, which we have entertained in our Mind from an attentive reading of the New Testament; otherwise it may happen that we may esteem that a Christian Congregation, which is no further Christian than in Name. It is therefore the Part of a prudent Man not to enter himself into any Congregation, at least

a. *For preserving their Doctrines,* &c.] Thus likewise all the Philosophers transmitted their Doctrine to Posterity by the Help of Schools in which it was taught; but the Christian Churches, which are united by a much firmer and stronger Bond, will with more Certainty and Ease, propagate the Doctrine they received from their Master, to the End of the World, which can hardly be done without Congregations. *Pythagoras* would have effected this, but in vain, because his Doctrine had nothing divine in it. See *Laertius* and *Jamblichus.*

b. *And to join himself with those,* &c.] See the Epistles to *Timothy* and *Titus,* where they are commanded to found Churches. And *Heb.* X. 25.

c. *Without Examination,* &c.] See 1 *Thess.* V. 21. But more expressly 1 *John* IV. 1. *Beloved* (says he) *believe not every Spirit, but try the Spirits whether they be of God; for many false Prophets are come into the World,* &c.

for a Continuance, unless it be such in which he perceives that Doctrine established, which he truly thinks to be the Christian Doctrine; so as that he is put under no Necessity of saying or doing any thing contrary to what he thinks delivered and commanded by Christ.

SECT. II. *We are to join ourselves with those who are most worthy the Name of Christians.*

Amongst Christians that differ from each other, and not only differ, but (to their Shame!) condemn one another, and with cruel Hatred banish them their Society; to agree to any of them without Examination, or, according to their Prescript, to condemn others without Consideration, shows a Man not only to be imprudent, but very rash and unjust. That Congregation which rejects, though but in Part, the true Religion, (a Representation of which he has formed in his Mind,) and condemns him that believes it, cannot be thought by such an one, a truly Christian Congregation in all things; nor can it prevail with him to condemn every Man which that Church shall esteem worthy to be condemned, and cast out of the Society of Christians. Wherefore a wise and honest Man ought above all things to examine, in these Dissentions amongst Christians, who they are which <292> best deserve the holy Name of Disciples of Christ, and to adhere to them. If any one should ask what we are required to do by the Christian Religion, supposing there were no such Christian Society at all, amongst whom the true Doctrine of Christ seems to be taught, and amongst whom there is not a Necessity laid upon us of condemning some Doctrine, which we judge to be true: In this Case, he who apprehends these Errors, ought to endeavour to withdraw others from them; in doing of which, he must use (*a*) the greatest Candour, joined with the highest Prudence and Constancy; lest he offend Men without doing them any Advantage, or lest all Hopes of bringing them to Truth and

---

a. *The greatest Candour,* &c.] Here that Precept of Christ's takes Place, *Matt.* X. 16. where we are commanded, *to be wise as Serpents, and harmless as Doves;* that is, to be so far simple, as not to fall into Imprudence; so wise, as not to be crafty, and offend against Sincerity; in which Matter there are but few who know how to steer their Course in all things, between the Rocks of Imprudence and Craftiness.

Moderation be too suddenly cast off. In the mean time, we are to speak modestly and prudently what we think to be the Truth; nor should any one be condemned by the Judgment of another, as infected with Error, who seems to think right. God has never forsaken, nor never will forsake the Christian Name so far, as that there shall remain no true Christians, or at least none such as cannot be brought back into the true Way; with whom we may maintain a stricter Society, if others will not return to a more sound Opinion; and openly withdraw ourselves from the obstinate, (which yet we ought not to do without having tried all other Means to no Purpose;) (*a*) if it be not allowed you to speak your Opinion <293> fairly and modestly amongst them, and to forbear condemning those whom you think are not to be condemned. The Christian Religion forbids us speaking contrary to our Mind, and falsifying and condemning the Innocent; nor can he be unacceptable to God, who out of Respect and Admiration of those Divine Precepts, can endure any thing rather than that they should be broke. Such a Disposition of Mind arising from a Sense of our Duty, and a most ardent Love of God, cannot but be highly well-pleasing to him.

Wherefore amongst Christians who differ from each other, we are to examine which of them all think the most right; nor are we ever to condemn any but such as seem to us worthy to be condemned, after a full Examination of the Matter; and we are to adhere to those who do not require any Doctrines to be believed which are esteemed by us to be false, nor any to be condemned which we think to be true. If we cannot obtain this of any Christian Society, we, together with those who are of the same Opinion with ourselves, ought to separate from them all, that we betray not the Truth, and utter a Falsity. <294>

a. *If it be not allowed,* &c.] Whilst it is allowed to have a different Opinion, and to profess our Disagreement, there is no Reason to depart from a publick Society, unless the Fundamentals of Christianity be perverted by it; but where this is not allowed, and we cannot without dissembling or denying the Truth live in it, then we ought to forsake that Society; for it is not lawful to tell a Lie, or to dissemble the Truth, whilst a Lie possesses the Place of it, and claims to itself the Honour due to Truth only. If this be not done, *the Candle is put under a Bushel.* Thus Christ did not depart from the Assemblies of the *Jews,* neither did the Apostles forsake them, so long as they were allowed to profess and teach the Doctrine of their Master in them. See *Acts* XIII. 46.

SECT. III. *They are most worthy the Name of Christians, who in the purest Manner of all, profess the Doctrine, the Truth of which hath been proved by* Grotius.

But it is a Question of no small Importance, and not easily to be resolved, who of all the Societies of the present Christians have the truest Opinions, and are most worthy of that Name by which they are called. All the Christian Churches, as well those who have long since separated from the *Romish* Church, as the *Romish* Church itself, do every one of them claim this to themselves; and if we lay aside all the Reasons, we ought no more to give Credit to the one than to the other; for it were a very foolish thing to suffer such a Choice (*a*) to be determined by Chance, and to decide all Controversies as it were by the Cast of a Die.

Now since *Grotius* has not proved the Truth of the particular Opinions of any present Sect of Christians, but only of that Religion which was taught Mankind by Christ and his Apostles; it follows, that that Sect of Christians is to be preferred before all others, which does most of all defend those things which Christ and his Apostles taught. In a Word, That is in every particular truly the Christian Religion, which without any Mixture of human Invention, may be wholly ascribed to Christ as the Author. To this agree all those Arguments of Truth, which are laid down in the IId Book *Of the Truth of the Christian Religion;* nor do they agree to any other, any further than it agrees with that. <295>

If any one adds to, or diminishes from the Doctrine delivered by Christ; the more he adds or diminishes, so much the farther he goes from the Truth. Now when I speak of the *Doctrine of Christ,* I mean by it, the Doctrine which all Christians are clearly agreed upon to be the Doctrine of Christ; that is, which according to the Judgment of all Christians, is either expressly to be found in the Books of the New Testament, or is by necessary Consequence to be deduced from them only. As to those Opinions, which, as some Christians think, were delivered by Word of Mouth

---

a. *To be determined by Chance,* &c.] See Note the 9th, on Sect. the IId.[1]

1. Actually Section I, above, note c, p. 253 of the present volume.

by Christ and his Apostles, and derived to Posterity in a different Method, namely either by Tradition; which was done by speaking only, or which were preserved by some Rite, as they imagine, and not set down in Writing till a great while after; I shall pass no other Judgment upon them here, but only this, that all Christians are not agreed upon Them as they are upon the Books of the New Testament. I will not say they are false, unless they are repugnant to right Reason and Revelation; but only that they are not agreed about the Original of them, and therefore they are controverted amongst Christians, who in other Respects agree in those Opinions, the Truth of which *Grotius* has demonstrated; for no wise Man will allow us (*a*) to depend upon a thing as certain, <296> so long as it appears uncertain to us, especially if it be a Matter of great Moment.

Sect. IV. *Concerning the Agreement and Disagreement of Christians.*

Though the Controversies amongst Christians be very sharp, and managed with great Heat and Animosity, so that we may hear Complaints made on all Sides, of very obvious things being denied by some of the contending Parties; yet notwithstanding there are some things so evident, that they are all agreed in them. And it is no mean Argument of the Truth of such, that they are allowed of by the common Consent of those who are most set upon Contention, and most blinded by Passion. I do not mean by this, that all other things about which there is any Contention, are doubtful or obscure; because all Christians are not agreed in them. It may easily happen that that may be obscure to some, which would be very plain, if they were not hindred by Passion; but it is hardly possible that the fiercest Adversaries, who are most eager in disputing, should agree about an obscure Point.

a. *To depend upon a thing as certain,* &c.] This is the very thing St. *Paul* means, *Rom.* XIV. 23. where he teaches us that *whatsoever is not of Faith is Sin.* On which Place we have quoted the Words of *Philo,* out of his Book concerning Fugitives. *Ed. Paris.* p. 469. *The best Sacrifice is being quiet, and not meddling in those things which we are not persuaded of.* And a little after, *To be quiet in the Dark is most safe;* that is, where we are not agreed what is to be done.

First then, all Christians now alive are agreed concerning the Number and Truth of the Books of the New Testament; and though there be some small Controversies amongst learned Men about (*a*) some Epistles of the Apostles, this is no great Matter; and they all acknowledge that there is nothing but Truth contained in them, and that the Christian Doctrine is not at all altered, either by keeping or rejecting them. And this Consent is <297> of no small Moment in a Discourse about the undoubted Original of a Divine Revelation under the new Covenant. For all other Records or Footsteps of ancient Revelation, that have been preserved according to the Opinions of some, are called in question by others.

Further, Christians are agreed in many Articles of Faith, which they embrace, as things to be believed, practised, and hoped for. For instance; all who have any Understanding, believe (I shall mention only the principal Heads here,) I. That there is one God, eternal, all-powerful, infinitely good and holy; in a Word, endued with all the most excellent Attributes, without the least Mixture of Imperfection; that the World and all things contained in it, and consequently Mankind, were created by this same God; and that by him all things are governed and directed with the highest Wisdom. II. That Jesus Christ is the only Son of the same God; that he was born at *Bethlehem* of the Virgin *Mary,* without the Knowledge of a Man, in the latter Part of the Life of *Herod* the Great, in the Reign of *Augustus Caesar;* that he was afterwards crucified and died, in the Reign of *Tiberius,* when *Pontius Pilate* was Governor of *Judaea;* that his Life is truly related in the History of the Gospel; that he was therefore sent from the Father, that he might teach Men the Way to Salvation, redeem them from their Sins, and reconcile them to God by his Death; and that this his Mission was confirmed by innumerable Miracles; that he died, as I before said, and rose again, and, after he had been very often seen by many, who had discoursed with him, and handled him; he was taken up into Heaven, where he now reigns, and from whence he will one Day return, to pass a final Judgment according to the Laws of <298> the

---

a. *Some Epistles of the Apostles,* &c.] The Epistle to the *Hebrews,* the Second Epistle of *Peter,* the two last Epistles of *John,* the Authors of which are disputed by learned Men.

Gospel, upon those who were then alive, and upon all them that are dead, when they shall be raised out of their Graves; that all the things that he taught, are to be believed, and all that he commanded are to be obeyed, whether they relate to the Worship of God, or to Temperance in restraining our Passions, or to Charity to be exercised towards others; that nothing could be appointed more holy, more excellent, more advantageous, and more agreeable to human Nature than these Precepts; however that all Men (Jesus only excepted) violate them, and cannot arrive at Salvation, but through the Mercy of God. III. That there is a Holy Ghost who inspired the Apostles of Jesus Christ, worked Miracles to recommend them, and inclines the Minds of pious Men constantly to obey God, and supports them in the Afflictions of Life; that we are to give the same Credit, and in all things to obey this Spirit speaking by the Apostles, as we do the Father and the Son. IV. That the Christian Church owes its Original and Preservation from the Days of Christ to this time, to the Father, Son, and Holy Ghost; that all they who believe these things, and observe the Precepts of the Gospel, shall obtain Mercy of God, whereby they shall be made Partakers of the Resurrection, (if they be dead when Christ shall come,) and of a happy Life to Eternity; on the contrary, all they who have diminished from the Faith of the Gospel, and have not observed its Precepts, shall rise, (if they be dead,) to be punished, and their Punishment shall be eternal Death. V. Lastly, That Christians ought to profess all these things, both at their Baptism, in which we declare that we will lead a Life free from the Filthiness of Iniquity, according to the Direction of the Gospel; and also at the Lord's Supper, <299> in which we celebrate the Death of Christ, according to his Command, till he comes; and show that we are willing to be esteemed his Disciples, and the Brethren of those who celebrate it in like Manner; moreover, that those Rites, if they are observed by us as is reasonable, and are celebrated with a religious Mind, convey heavenly Grace and the Divine Spirit to us.

(*a*) *These* things, and others that are necessarily connected with them (for it is not to our present Purpose to mention them all particularly,) all

a. *These things, and others,* &c.] In the foregoing Explication of the Christian Doctrine we have followed the Method of that which they call the Apostles Creed, and have avoided all Expressions which have caused any Controversies amongst Christians,

Christians believe; nor is there any other Difference but only this, that some add many other things to these, whereby they think the foregoing Doctrines ought to be explained or enlarged with Additions; and those such as they imagine were <300> delivered to Posterity, not by the Writings of the Apostles, but by the Tradition and Custom of the Church, or by the Writings of latter Ages. Concerning these Additions I shall say nothing more than what I before advised; that Christians are not agreed upon them, as they are upon the Doctrines now explained, which are put beyond all manner of Doubt by their own Plainness, if we allow but the Authority of the Holy Scripture, which no Christian in his Senses can refuse.

If any one weighs the Arguments by which the Truth of the Christian Religion is proved, with these Doctrines in his View; he will observe, (and if it be well observed, it will be of great use) that all the Force of the Argument is employed about these things, and not about those Points which divide the Christian World, as was before hinted.

SECT. V. *Whence every one ought to learn the Knowledge of the Christian Religion.*

In this Agreement and Disagreement amongst Christians, prudent Men will judge it most safe to take their Knowledge of the Christian Religion from the Fountain, which is not in the least suspected, and whose Streams all confess to be pure and undefiled. And this Fountain is not

---

because we are treating of those things in which they are agreed: And we do not for this Reason condemn as false, any thing that may be added by way of Explication or Confirmation; on the contrary, we highly approve of their Endeavours, who explain and confirm Divine Truths; and we doubt not but that many things have been already found, and may yet be found, to illustrate it. *Tertullian* judges rightly of this Matter, in the first Chap. of his Book concerning veiling Virgins. "The Rule of Faith is altogether one and the same, entirely firm and unalterable; namely, that we believe in one all-powerful God, the Creator of the World, and in his Son Jesus Christ, who was born of the Virgin *Mary,* was crucified under *Pontius Pilate,* was raised from the Dead the third Day, was taken up into Heaven, sits now at the Right-hand of the Father, and will come to judge the Quick and Dead by the Resurrection of the Flesh. Keeping to this Rule of Faith, other Matters of Discipline (*or Doctrine*) and Behaviour, admit of Correction, *viz.* the Grace of God operating and perfecting to the End, etc."

the Creed or the Confession of Faith of any particular Church, but only the Books of the New Testament, which all acknowledge to be genuine. I confess some Christians do sometimes say, that those Books cannot be understood but by the Doctrine of their Church; but others again deny it; and (to mention but this one thing,) that Opinion is very suspicious which depends only on the Testimony of those that affirm it, and they such, whose chief Interest it is that it should seem true. Others say, that there is need of the extraordinary Assistance <301> of the Holy Spirit, not only in order to the Belief of the Scripture, (which may without any great Difficulty be allowed,) but also in order to understand the Meaning of the Words contained in it; which I do not see how it can be proved; but we will grant this also, provided they will acknowledge that all Men, who read the Books of the New Testament with a religious Mind, intent upon the Truth, are afforded this Spirit by the Goodness of God; there is no need of contending for any thing more than this. Every one therefore may wisely and safely gather his Knowledge of the Christian Religion from these Books; yet making use of those Helps that are necessary or profitable for the understanding of such Books; which we will not now enquire after.

Whoever therefore believes that the Revelation of the Will of God made by Christ, is faithfully related in the Books of the New Testament; such an one must of necessity embrace all things which he there meets with, according as he understands them, as Matters of Faith, Practice and Hope; for whoever believes in Christ, ought to receive with a religious Mind, every thing which he thinks comes from him; he cannot defend himself with any Excuse, whereby to admit some, and reject others of those things which he acknowledges to come from Christ. And such are those Doctrines I before explained, and concerning which all Christians, as I said, are agreed.

As to the rest, about which they contest, since they are not so very plain, a religious and pious Man may and ought to deliberate concerning them, and with-hold his Judgment till they appear more evident to him. For it is very imprudent to admit or reject any thing, before it sufficiently appears to be either true or false. Nor is eternal <302> Salvation, in the Books of the New Testament, promised to any one who embraces this or that controverted Opinion; but to him who heartily receives in his Mind, and expresses in his Actions, the Sum of the Christian Religion, as we have described it.

SECT. VI. *Nothing else ought to be imposed upon Christians, but what they can gather from the New Testament.*

(*a*) This therefore is the only thing that can justly be imposed upon all Christians, *viz.* that they embrace whatever they think is contained in the Books of the New Testament, and obey those things which they find there commanded, and abstain from those things which are there forbidden; if any thing further be required of them as necessary, it is without any Authority. For would any fair Judge require a Christian to believe a Doctrine came from Christ, which he does not find in the only faithful and undoubted Records, in which all are agreed the Revelation of Christ is derived down to us? Let other Doctrines be true; let us <303> take this for granted a little while; they cannot however be esteemed as true by him, who, amongst the different Sorts of Christians, follows the middle way, and allows of no certain Record of the Revelation of Christ, but the Books of the New Testament. Whilst he believes this, nothing else can justly be required of him; and he will believe this, till it shall be made appear to him by plain Arguments, that the Knowledge of Christianity is safely to be had somewhere else, which I believe will never be done.

(*b*) *If* any one therefore attempts to take away from Christians the Books of the New Testament, or to add to them such things as do not

a. *This therefore is the only thing,* &c.] To this belongs what Christ saith, *Matt.* XXIII. *ver.* 8. and following. "Be ye not called *Rabbi,* for one is your Master, even Christ, and all ye are Brethren. And call *no Man* your Father upon the Earth, for one is your Father which is in Heaven: Neither be ye called Masters, for one is your Master even Christ." See also *James* III. 1. To the same Purpose, *Rev.* III. 7. where Christ is said to have the *Key of David,* which is thus described, *which opens* (namely heaven) *and no one shuts, and which shutteth and no one openeth.* If we are to believe Christ only, and there remains no other certain Record of the Revelation made by Christ, but the New Testament; it is manifest from hence, that in Matters of Faith, we ought to give Credit only to these Books.

b. *If any one therefore attempts,* &c.] To this relates that Saying of *Paul, Gal.* I. 8. "If we, or an Angel from Heaven preach any other thing for the Gospel, than that

appear to be true; we are by no means to hearken to such an one; because
he requires that of us, which no prudent Man will allow, *viz.* that we
should believe that which we are not certain of, or neglect that which all
own to be the sure Record of the Revelation of the Gospel. There is no
need of examining all Controversies singly, and one by one: which would
be an endless thing, and cannot be done but by very learned Men, who
have abundance of Leisure. Whoever imposes any thing upon us, as necessary to be believed, which we cannot believe; he drives us from himself;
because Belief cannot be extorted by Force; nor will any one who fears
God, and is a Lover of Truth, suffer himself to profess what he does not
believe, for the sake of another. <304>

But they who differ from this, object; that if every one be left to their
own Liberty in judging of the Meaning of the Books of the New Testament; there will be as many Religions as there are Men; and Truth, which
is but one, will immediately be oppressed by a Multitude of Errors. But I
think, that before an Opinion which is established upon solid Arguments
be opposed by Objections, the Foundation upon which it is built ought
to be overthrown; because so long as that remains firm, the whole Super-
structure raised upon it cannot be shaken; as we see here. For if any Inconvenience should follow from what has been said, it is nevertheless true,
till it be made appear not to be fixed on a firm Bottom. But to pass by this
now; it is false that the Revelation of the New Testament is so obscure,
that the Sum of the Christian Religion cannot be truly learned from it,
by any one of a sound Mind, who is desirous of Truth. It is evident from
Experience, that it may be truly learned from thence; for all Christians,
as has been already shewn, agree in the principal Parts of it; which was
observed by *Grotius,* Book II. Sect. XVII. We have no Regard here to a
few simple or wicked Men; since whole Societies of Christians, who in
other Respects, out of their too great Eagerness of Contention, are ready
to differ from one another, and to run into the contrary Extremes, are
here agreed.

Gospel we have preached to you, let him be accursed." And indeed it is no Man's Business to add any thing to the Gospel, as necessary; nor to diminish any thing from it,
as unprofitable.

SECT. VII. *The Providence of God in preserving the Christian Doctrine, is very wonderful.*

In this Particular, as in numberless others which relate to the Government of human Affairs, the Divine Providence is very wonderful; which, notwithstanding so many Differences as were of old, and are at this Day amongst Christians, yet hath <305> preserved the Books of the New Testament untouched, even to our times; that the Christian Doctrine may be recovered out of them, as often as it happens to be corrupted. Nor has it only delivered down to us this Treasure entire; but also in the midst of the hottest Differences, has so secured the Christian Doctrine itself, that the Sum of Religion has never been forgot amongst Christians.

No inconsiderable Number of Christians at this Day contend, that many Errors in former Ages crept by Degrees in amongst the Sects of Christians; which when others denied, in the XVIth Century after the Birth of Christ, that famous Separation in the *West* was made upon that Account, by which Christianity was divided into two Parts, not very unequal. Yet in those Ages, whose Errors are reproved by that Part of the Christians which made the Separation I now mentioned, and whose Faults were highly aggravated by both Sides, and that not without Grounds; the Sum of the Christian Religion before drawn up by us, was all along maintained. (*a*) There is no Age so thick <306> clouded with Ignorance and Vice, but the forementioned Articles of Faith may easily be collected from their Writings that remain. It must not indeed be dissembled, that many things foreign and unknown to the Books of the New Testament, have been added and thrust into the Christian Theology; whence it is,

---

a. *There is no Age so thick clouded,* &c.] None have a worse Report, than the Xth and XIth Centuries, as is granted by those who stick to the See of *Rome,* as much as by those who have made a Separation from it. Yet if any one, for his own Satisfaction, will read *amongst the Books of the Fathers,* the Writings of those Centuries, he may easily collect all the Doctrines mentioned in the IVth Sect. At the Beginning of the XIIth Century, lived *Bernard,* Abbot of the Monastery of *Claravallis,* whose Learning, Piety and Constancy, are commended by very many, and whose Writings were often read in the following Ages, and never condemned. Now from thence an entire Body of the Christian Doctrine may easily be collected; and it is no less certain of the following Centuries down to the XVIth. Nor is there any Doubt of those that follow.

that the true Wheat of the Sower in the Gospel, hath not brought forth so much Fruit as it would otherwise have done, had the Ground been cleared of Thorns and hurtful and unprofitable Weeds. Many Vices and Faults were not only admitted or born with, but applauded also. Yet was not found Doctrine ever the less safe, whilst the Books of the New Testament remained, and whilst Christians were endued with common Sense; for by this means, very eminent Men were often raised up, who corrected the Errors and Vices of their Age, and ventured to oppose the Torrent. Thus according to the Promise of Christ, God hindred (*a*) *the Gates of Death from prevailing against the Church;* that is, did not suffer every Society wherein the Christian Doctrine was preserved entire, to be extinguished; though sometimes they were blended and obscured with foreign and contrary Opinions, and sometimes were more sincere and pure. Wherefore (to observe this by the Way) unless this Doctrine was really sent to us from God, it could never have escaped <307> out of such a Deluge of Vices and Errors, but would at length have been overwhelmed by the Changeableness and Folly of Human Nature, and have entirely perished.

Sect. VIII. *An Answer to that Question, Why God permits Differences and Errors to arise amongst Christians.*

Perhaps some may here object against what has been said, that the Divine Providence would have better consulted the Preservation of the Christian Doctrine, if it had prevented the Errors that are and have been amongst Christians, and maintained Truth and constant Agreement, which is the Companion of it, amongst them, by its Omnipotence. But it is not for

---

a. *The Gates of Death from prevailing,* &c.] So we explain ᾅδης, because neither that Word, nor the *Hebrew* שׁאול *Scheol,* which answers to it, ever signifies in the Sacred Writings, an evil Spirit, but only the Grave, or the State of the Dead, as *Grotius* and others have observed. Therefore this one thing may be gathered from this Place, that it will never happen, that the Christian Church should entirely perish, or that there should be no Society left, amongst whom the Sum of the Doctrine of the Gospel should not remain.

us to instruct God how he ought to direct himself, in the Government of human Affairs, that they might be better. On the contrary, it is our Duty to think that God had very wise Reasons for suffering what he did suffer, tho' we cannot so much as guess at what they are. But if any probable Reasons can be given for the Things that are done; we ought to believe, that God permits those Things which daily come to pass, to be done for these, or more weighty Reasons.

To make a Conjecture from the Reason of Things; we are above all Things sure, that the Design of God was (*a*) to create Men free, and to <308> suffer them to continue so to the End; that is, not so good that they should necessary continue good always, nor so Bad as that they must of Necessity always submit to Vice; but mutable, so as that they might pass from Vice to Virtue, and again from Virtue to Vice; and this with more or less Ease, according as they had longer or shorter Time given up themselves to Virtue or Vice. Such we see the *Hebrew* People of old were, and such were the Christians afterwards. Neither of them were drawn by an irresistible Force either to Virtue or Vice; but only restrained by Laws, which proposed Reward to the Good, and Punishment to the Bad; to which were added by the Divine Providence, various Incitements to Virtue, and Discouragements from Vice; but yet neither of them deprived Man of his native Liberty, whereby he had a Power of obeying or disobeying God, as is evident from Experience; for there were always Good and Bad, though the Divine Laws prescribed Virtue, and prohibited Vice equally to all. That this would be so amongst Christians, Christ has plainly signify'd in two Parables, (*b*) the one of the Tares which the Enemy sowed after the Wheat was sown; (*c*) the other of the Net which took good and bad Fish alike; by which he signified, that there would

a. *To create Men free,* &c.] This is taught with the highest Consent by all Christian Antiquity. See *Justin* the Martyr's Apology I. ch. LIV. and LV. *Irenaeus* Book IV. ch. 9. ch. 29. towards the end, ch. 71, and 72. *Origen's Philocalia,* ch. 21. *Eusebius's* Gospel Preparation, Book VI. ch. 6. and others, whose Sayings are quoted by *Dionysius Petavius,* in his Theological Doctrines, Tom. I. Book VI. ch. 6. There are also many Things to this Purpose, Tom. III. Book III, IV. and V.

b. *The one of the Tares,* &c.] *Mat.* XIII. 24. and following.

c. *The other of the Net,* &c.] *Mat.* XIII. 47. and following.

always be in the Church a Mixture of good and bad Christians; whence it follows, that he very well saw the Evils that would always be in the Christian Church. Moreover *Paul* admonisheth the Christians, (*a*) *that there must be Sects* amongst Christians, <309> *that they who are approved may be made manifest.* (*b*) And indeed unless there had been Differences among Christians concerning Doctrine, there had been no room left for Choice, and for that sort of Virtue, by which Truth is preferred to all Things. Therefore even in this Particular also, the Divine Wisdom shines bright; which caused an excellent Virtue to flourish out of the midst of the Vices of Men.

If any one should object here, (*c*) as some do; that it were better there were no such kind of Virtue, than that there should be Vices contrary to it, from whence so many horrid Crimes, so many Calamities, and so great Miseries should befal Mankind, and such heavy Punishment attend them after this Life; To this we will answer, that these Evils were not of such a Consideration with God, that upon their Account he should not give an Instance of his Power in creating free Agents. Unless this had been done, no Creature would have believed, that it could have been done. Nay, God himself would not have been thought to be free, unless he himself had planted this Opinion of himself by his Omnipotence in the Minds of Men, which otherwise they never could have conceived from his <310> Works. Nor could he have been worshipped, if he had been thought to do, or to have done all Things, not out of his free Goodness, but by a certain fatal Necessity; unless by a fatal Worship also, and such an one as is not at all free. The Vices and Calamities of this or

a. *That there must be Sects,* &c.] 1 *Cor.* XI. 19. *For there must be also Heresies among you, that they which are approved, may be made manifest among you;* that is, as they are Men, there is a Necessity, unless they were changed for the better, that there should arise Sects amongst you, by which the Good may be distinguished from the Bad; whilst the Good stick to Truth and Charity, and the rest run into all other Things. See *Mat.* XVIII. 7.

b. *And indeed unless,* &c.] See this handled more at large in my *Ecclesiastical History* Century I *Anno* LXXXIII. 8. *Le Clerc.*

c. *As some do,* &c.] This Objection is largely proposed, and set off with Rhetorical Flourishes by *Peter Bayle;* whom we have confuted in some of the Volumes of the *Choice Library,* and especially in the Xth, XIth, XIIth, in *French.*

the other Life, are not comparable to so great an Evil, as the supposing God to be ignorant of any Thing; For if we find any Difficulty about them, we ought to consider that God is most good, just, powerful, and wise, and will not act otherwise than agreeable to his Perfections; and will easily find a Way and go in it, whereby to clear those Things which seem to us to be intangled; and to show to all intelligent Creatures, that nothing was done by him, which ought not to have been done. In the mean Time, till that Day spring, in which all the Clouds of our Ignorance shall be dispersed; he has given us such Experience of himself, and such Instances of his Perfections, on the Account of which we may and ought entirely to confide in him, and patiently to wait for what he will have come to pass. More might be said on this Matter, but that it would divert us from that End we are tending to, and carry us to what does not belong to this Place.

SECT. IX. *They profess and teach the Christian Doctrine in the purest Manner of all, who propose those Things only as necessary to be believed, practised, or hoped for, which Christians are agreed in.*

To pass by these Things therefore, and return to the Choice of our Opinion amongst the different Sects of Christians; nothing seems possible to be done more safe and wise, in this State of Affairs, than for us to join ourselves with that Sect of Christians, which acknowledges the New Testament only for the Rule of their Faith, without any Mix-<311>ture of human Decrees; and who think it sufficient that every one should learn their Form of Faith from thence, conform their Lives to its Precepts, and expect the Promises which are there made. Which if it be done sincerely, and without any Dissimulation; the End of such a Search will be that very Form of sound Words, which we have made appear to have remained the same, amidst so many and so great Storms of Errors and Dissentions, during the passing away of so many Ages, and the Changes of Kingdoms and Cities. In it are contained all Things that are necessary to Faith and Practice; to which if any one would have any other Things added, it may lawfully be done, according to the Circumstances of Time and Place; provided they be not imposed as necessary (*a*) (which belongs only to the supreme Lawgiver,) nor contrary Doctrines to these obtruded.

  Christians disposed in the Manner we have been speaking of, ought not to submit their Neck to the Yoke of human Opinions, nor to profess they believe what they do not believe; nor to do that, which they cannot approve in their own Minds, because they think it contrary to the Precepts of Christ. Therefore, where-ever that Christian Liberty, which I have now mentioned, is not allowed, they must of Necessity depart thence; not as if they condemned all that are of a different Opinion from themselves, but because every one is absolutely obliged to follow the Light of his own Mind, <312> and not that of another's; and to do that which he judges best to be done, and to avoid that which he thinks to be Evil.

SECT. X. *All prudent Persons ought to partake of the Sacrament, with those who require nothing else of Christians, but what every one finds in the Books of the New Testament.*

Since Christ has appointed two Signs or Symbols of Christianity, Baptism and the Lord's Supper; it was not indeed in our Power to receive Baptism where we judged the Christian Religion to be most pure, because we were baptized very young; but since we do not come to the other Sacrament till we are of riper Age, we may distinguish that Society of Christians in which we are willing to be Partakers of it; which if we have not already done, we ought to do it now.

  There are some who make the Sacrament, (which according to Christ's Institution, (*b*) is a Token of that Peace and Love which is between

---

a. *Which belongs only to the Supreme Lawgiver,* &c.] See what *Paul* says upon this Matter, *Rom.* XIV. 1. *and so on.* Where he speaks of those who impose Rites on others; or who condemn those that observe them; which Right he declares to belong to Christ only. And to this may be referred what St. *James* says. ch. IV. 12. *There is but one Lawgiver, who is able to save and to destroy.*

  b. *Is a Token of that Peace and Love,* &c.] See 1 *Cor.* X. 16, 17. where mentioning the Sacramental Cup and Bread, of which many are Partakers, the Apostle adds; *For we being many, are one Bread and one Body, for we are all Partakers of that one Bread.* Which Words show, that by the Sacrament is signified the mutual Agreement of Christians; and so the best Interpreters understand it.

Christians,) a Mark of Distinction; and exclude from it all those, who do not think it safe to submit to any Yoke, but what Christ has laid upon them; or to receive any Things as necessary to be believed, practised or hoped for, but those which they are verily perswaded are contained in the Books of the New Testament; and who are therefore very cautious of admitting any other Forms of Faith, be-<313>sides that which we have mentioned. It is but just and reasonable indeed, that we should maintain Peace with such Men as these; (*a*) But for receiving the Sacrament upon this Condition, that we should embrace any other Rule of Faith and Practice, beside the Books of the New Testament, and think all those excluded the Church who will not admit them; this a religious and prudent Man will think very wicked. But all they who are true Lovers of the Gospel, safely may and ought to approach the Sacramental Table of them who know no other Laws of obtaining eternal Salvation, but those laid down by Christ and his Apostles in the Books of the Gospel Covenant, as every one can understand them. For whoever acknowledges the Books of the New Testament for the only Rule of Faith and Practice; who sincerely conform their Lives to that Rule; in a Word, who allow of no Idolatry, nor treat others ill, that they may profess they believe certain Doctrines which they do not believe; all such are received by these, and also invited to this Table. It is manifest indeed, that Communion cannot be maintained with him, who makes use of Force to impose his Opinions upon others; who worships other Gods, besides the true God the Father, Son, and Holy Ghost; or who by his Conversation, shows that he makes light of the Precepts of the Gospel; or who owns any other Laws of Salvation, than those wrote in the Books of the eternal Covenant: But he who behaves himself the direct contrary, is worthy to have all Christians <314> maintain Communion with him, and to be preferred

---

a. *But for receiving the Sacrament,* &c.] And this was the Opinion of *Grotius,* as appears from that little Book of his, *Whether we ought always to join in receiving the Sacrament;* where he speaks of the Reasons of forbearing the Communion. Tom IV. of his Theological Works, page 511.[2]

2. Actually Tome III (Tome II is in two volumes).

to all the rest who are of a different Opinion. (*a*) No mortal Man, nay no Angel can impose any new Gospel upon Christians, to be believed by them; Now according to this Gospel, he is a true Disciple of Christ, who from his Heart believes his Doctrine, and his only, so as to obey it the best he is able, according to the Infirmity of this Life; who worships one God, loves his Neighbour as himself, and lives temperately in respect to all other Things. If any Thing be diminished from this, the Laws of the Covenant, which none but God can abate any Thing of, are maimed: and if any Thing be added, it is an useless Yoke, which none ought to impose on Christians. Such Laws can be received from God only, who alone is the Determiner of eternal Salvation.

Perhaps some may here ask me by what Name these Christian Socie-ties, which I have now described, may be distinguished? But it signifies nothing what Denomination they go under; The Reader may conceive all Churches to be meant, in which, what I have said, is to be found. Where-soever that only Rule of Faith, and that Liberty which I have described, is; there they may be assured true Christianity is, and they need not en-quire for a Name, which makes nothing to the Purpose. I believe there are many such Societies; and I pray the good and great God, that there may be more and more every Day; that at length *his Kingdom may come* into all the Earth, and that Mankind may obey it only. <315>

Sect. XI. *Concerning Church-Government.*

A small Difficulty may here be objected to us, which arises from the Form of Church-Government and Discipline, commonly called Ecclesiastical: For no Society, such as a Church is, can subsist without Order, and there-fore there must be some Form of Government appointed. Now it is de-bated amongst Christians, what Form of Government was appointed by the Apostles; for that seems preferable to all others, which was appointed from the Beginning; and therefore of two Churches, in which the Gospel is taught with equal Purity and Sincerity in all other Respects, that is to

a. *Mortal Man,* &c.] See the Notes on *Sect.* I.

be preferred, in which the Form of Government is Apostolical; though Government without the Thing itself, that is, the Gospel, is only the faint Shadow of a Church.

There are now two Forms of Government, one of which is that wherein the Church acts under one Bishop, who alone has the Right of ordaining Presbyters, or the inferior Order of the Gospel Ministers; the other is that, where the Church is governed by an Equality of Presbyters, joined with some Lay-Persons of Prudence and Honesty. They who without Prejudice have read over the most antient Christian Writers that now remain, (*a*) very well know, that the former Manner of Discipline, which is called Episcopal, such as that in the South Part of *Great Britain,* prevailed every where in the Age immediately after the Apostles; whence we may collect, that it is of Apostolical Institution. The other, which they call *Presbyterian,* was insti-<316>tuted in many Places of *France, Switzerland, Germany,* and *Holland,* by those who in the XVIth Century made a Separation from the Church of *Rome.*

They who read with Attention the Histories of that Century, are fully satisfied that this latter Form of Government was introduced for this Reason only, because the Bishops would not allow to them who contended that the Doctrine and Manners of Christians stood in need of necessary Amendment; that those Things were to be reformed, which they complained were corrupted. Otherwise, if the Bishops every where at that Time, had been willing to do of their own accord, what was not long after done in *England;* that Government had prevailed even to this Day, amongst all those who separated from the *Romish* Church; and the numberless Calamities which happened when all Things were disturbed and confounded, had then been prevented. For if we would judge of the Matter truly, there was no other Reason for changing the Government but this, that whilst the ancient Government remained, nothing could be procured, however just in itself. Therefore the Presbyterian Form is appointed in many Places; which after it was once done, was so much for the Interest of all them who presided in the State-Affairs in those

---

a. *Very well know,* &c.] See my *Ecclesiastical History,* Century I. to the Year LII. 6. and LXVIII. 8. *and the following ones. Le Clerc.*

Places, and is so at this Time not to have it changed, that it must of neces-
sity continue; unless any one had rather upon that Account, that all the
Dominions in which it prevails, should be put into the most dangerous
Disorders; which prudent Men will never allow, nor is to be wished. The
Form of Government was appointed of old, to preserve the Christian
Doctrine, and not to disturb the Commonwealth, which can scarce hap-
pen without endangering the Religion itself. <317>

Wherefore prudent Men, though they above all Things wish for the
Apostolical Form of Church-Government, and that it might be every
where alike; yet they think Things had better be left in the State in which
they now are, than venture the Hazards which always attend the Attempt
of new Things. In the mean Time, they that are wise, will by no means
hate, reproach, nor condemn one another upon that Account, as the most
violent Men are apt to do; as if eternal Salvation depended upon either
Form, which do not seem to be taught any where in the apostolick Writings, nor can it be gathered from the Nature of the Christian Religion.

Sect XII. *The antient Church-Government was highly esteemed by* Grotius, *without condemning others.*

Whoever reads over the Works of that great Man *Hugo Grotius,* and examines into his Doctrine and Practice; will find that he had entertained
in his Mind (*a*) that Form of sound Words, the Truth of which he has
proved; nor did he esteem any thing else as true Religion; but after he had
diligently read the Writings of Christian Antiquity, and understood that
the Original Form was that of <318> Episcopacy, he highly approved of it

a. *That Form of sound Words,* &c.] See amongst other Things, *The Institution
of Children that are baptized,* which the Author himself translated out of *Dutch* Verse
into *Latin.* In his theological Works, Tom. IV. pag. 629.[3] And in his latter Works, he
often affirms that whatever is necessary to Salvation, is plainly enough contained in
the *New Testament.* See his Annotations on *Cassander's* Consultation towards the End,
where he speaks *of the Sufficiency and Plainness of the Scripture.* Which being granted,
it is manifest from thence, that the Sum of the Christian Religion, as it was before
produced by us, may be collected thence by any one.

3. Actually Tome III.

in the Manner it is maintained in *England,* as appears (*a*) from his own express Words, which we have wrote down at the Bottom of the Page.

Therefore it is not to be doubted, but if it had been in his Power, and he had not been so vehemently tossed to and fro by Adversity, and exasperated and vexed by the Baseness and Reproachfulness of his Enemies, at whose Hands he did not deserve it; he would have joined himself with those who maintained the antient Form of Discipline, and required nothing further than what has been already said, the Truth of which he has proved excellently well; the Arguments for which Practice appear to us to be so weighty, that we have thought good to add them to this little Treatise.

Sect. XIII. *An Exhortation to all Christians who differ from each other, not to require of one another any Points of Doctrine, but such as every one finds in the* New Testament, *and have always been believed.*

Seeing these Things are so, we cannot but earnestly exhort all Christians who differ in Opinions, to remember that That only is the true Sum and Substance of the Christian Religion, the Truth of which can be proved by the Arguments *Grotius* has <319> alleged; and not those controverted Points which each Side deny, and which have been the Cause of so many Evils; Further, no one that reads over the *New Testament* with a religious Mind, and meditates upon it, can be perswaded that there is (*b*) any other Lawgiver but Christ, upon whose Law eternal Life depends; nor that any

---

a. *From his own express Words,* &c.] In his Annotations on the Consultation of *Cassander,* Acts XIV. *Bishops are the Heads of the Presbyters, and that Preheminence was foreshewn in* Peter, *and was appointed by the Apostles whereever it could be done, and approved by the Holy Ghost, in the Revelations. Wherefore as it was to be wished that that Superiority were appointed every where,* &c.] See also what follows, concerning *the Ecclesiastical Power, and the Discussion of* Rivetus's *Apology,* p. 714. col. 2. Other Things are also alleged, in the Epistles added to this little Treatise.

b. *Any other Lawgiver but Christ,* &c.] The Words of *James,* ch. IV. 12. quoted in Sect. I. are very express in this Matter; where more is said relating hereto. Besides, the Thing itself speaks here; because amongst the different Sects of Christians, none of them believe their Adversaries Authority.

one who is so disposed, can or ought to persuade himself to admit of any Thing as necessary to Salvation, beside what is the Doctrine of Christ and his Apostles; or to believe that to be true, which he thinks is contrary to it: Wherefore there is none more certain and present Remedy of their Differences, than this, that nothing be imposed upon Christians, but those Things which every one is fully satisfied in his own Mind are revealed; nor need we fear any Inconvenience from hence, since it is evident from the Experience of all Ages past from Christ to this Time, that the Sum of the Christian Religion before laid down, was never rejected by any. (*a*) If this one Thing only <320> were at this Time required of all Christians as necessary, all their Differences would immediately cease; and whatever Disagreement remained in Opinions, it would not belong to the Body of the Church, but to private Persons; every one of which must render an Account of their Conscience to God. If they did but once understand that they were agreed in the principal Matters, as they really are agreed, and would bear with one another in other Things; and would not endeavour to bring over others to their Opinion or Rites, by Force or other wicked Arts; this would be the only Agreement that can be expected on Earth. (*b*) In this Ignorance and Want of Knowledge in Mankind, hindered by so many Passions; no prudent Person can expect that all can be brought, either by Force or Reason, to think and do the same Thing. The more generous and understanding Minds, can never approve

a. *If this one Thing only,* &c.] This was the Opinion of *James* I. King of *Great-Britain,* if we may give Credit to *Isaac Casaubon,* who has these Words, *in his Answer to* Cardinal Perron's *Epistle,* on the third Observation, p. 30. Edit. Lond. 1612. "It is most truly written, in the Explication of those Things which are absolutely necessary, that it is the King's Opinion, that the Number of those Things which are absolutely necessary to Salvation, is not great. Wherefore his Majesty thinks, that there is no shorter Way to enter in an Agreement, than by carefully separating those Things that are necessary, from those that are not; and that their whole Care be employed in agreeing about the necessary Things; and that in those Things that are not necessary, there be an Allowance made for Christian Liberty, &c."

b. *In this Ignorance and Want of Knowledge,* &c.] It was very well said by *Hilary* concerning the Trinity, Book X. c. 70. "That God does not invite us to *Happiness,* through difficult Questions, nor confound us with various Sorts of Eloquence. Eternity is plain and easy to us, to believe that God raised up Jesus from the Dead, and to confess him to be Lord."

of Force; which is the Attendant of Lies, and not of Truth: Nor do they who are less learned, or who are blinded by Passion, or the Prejudices of Education, or any other Thing, as the far greatest Part will always be; fully understand the Force of Reason; nor in the mean Time are they to be compelled to do or speak contrary to what they think. Let them who preside in the Government of the Church think it sufficient, that Men through the Help of the immortal God, believe the Gospel; that that Faith <321> alone is to be preached as necessary; that the Precepts of it are alone to be obeyed, and Salvation to be expected from the Observation of its Laws; and all Things will go well. Whilst human Things are made equal with Divine; and doubtful Things, to say no worse of them, equalled with those that are certain, there can be no End of Contention, no Hopes of Peace; which all pious Men ought, with their most earnest Wishes, to desire of the great God, and to endeavour to promote as far as is in their Power. <322>

Against Indifference in the Choice of our Religion.

Sect. I. *That we ought to have a Love for Truth in all things, but more especially in such as are of great Moment.*

I think that Person judged very rightly, (*a*) whoever he was, that said, there is an eternal Alliance betwixt Truth and the Mind of Man; the Effects of which, though they may sometimes be, as it were suspended or discontinued for a while, by reason of the Inconstancy and Affections of Human Nature; yet the Alliance itself can never be entirely broke. For no body is desirous of being deceived; nay, there is no body <323> but had rather know the Truth, in any Matter whatsoever, but especially in any Matter of Moment, than be mistaken, though it be only in things of mere Speculation. We are naturally delighted with Truth, and have as natural an Aversion to Error; and if we knew any way in which we could certainly arrive at Truth, we should most readily enter into it. Hence it is, that there always have been found very eminent Men, whom all the World have most highly applauded, because they spent their whole Lives in the Pursuit of Truth. There have been, and are at this Day, innumerable

---

a. *Whoever he was that said, &c.*] *John Smith*, in his select Discourses published at *London*, 1660. Hence St. *Austin*, in his CXLth Sermon, concerning the Words of the Evangelist St. *John*, Tom. V. Col. 682. *Every Man searches after Truth and Life; but every Man does not find the Way to them.* And again, Sermon CL. Col. 716. *The Mind cannot endure to be deceived. And how much the Mind naturally hates to be deceived, we may learn from this single thing, that every Man of Sense pities a Changeling. If it were proposed to any one, whether he would choose to be deceived, or to persist in the Truth; there is no body but would answer, that he had rather persist in the Truth.*

natural Philosophers and Geometricians, who have taken incredible Pains to come at Truth; and who affirm, that they never feel (*a*) so great Pleasure as when they find out a Truth which they have long been in search after. So that the Love and the Knowledge of Truth, may very justly be reckoned amongst the many other things that Men excel Brutes in.

But all Truths are not of the same Moment, and many theoretick Notions, though they be true, may be laid aside, because little or no Advantage can be had from them, and therefore it is not worth while to be at much Pains about them; yet, on the other Hand, there are some Truths of so great Moment, that we justly think them worth purchasing at any Rate. Of this sort are all those that relate to our Well-being and Happiness; the Knowledge of which, is most valued by every body, and most diligently pursued by them. To which, if we add, that the Consequence of a well-spent and happy life, (and we must always allow, that what is good, that is, agreeable to Truth, is also an In-<324>gredient of Happiness) during our short Stay here, will be an eternal Happiness hereafter, as all Christians of every Sect whatsoever profess to believe, we cannot but own, that the Knowledge of the Way by which we may arrive at such Happiness, cannot be purchased at too dear a Rate.

SECT. II. *Nothing can be of greater Moment than Religion; and therefore we ought to use our utmost Endeavours to come at the true Knowledge of it.*

Our Business is not now with such Persons as despise all Religion; these have been sufficiently confuted by that great Man *Hugo Grotius,* in the foregoing Books; which whosoever has read, with a Mind really desirous of coming at the Truth, can have no doubt but that there is a God who would be worshipped by Men; and as things now are, with that very Worship which is commanded by Christ; and that he has promised everlasting Happiness, after this mortal Life, to all who thus worship him.

---

a. *So great Pleasure,* &c.] See the Life of *Pythagoras* in *Diogenes Laertius,* Book VIII. 12.

Thus much being allowed, no body can doubt but that Religion is a Matter of the highest Concern; and therefore, as we see that Christians do not consist of one entire Body, we ought to endeavour to find out, which Sect of them is most agreeable in its Doctrines and Precepts, to those which are left us by Jesus Christ; for we cannot have an equal Regard for them all, because some of them are so very different from others, both in Doctrine and Worship, that they accuse one another of the greatest Errors, and of having corrupted the Divine Worship; nay, some of them speak of the rest, as absolutely excluded eternal Life. Now if this could be made plainly appear, without doubt we ought to withdraw ourselves from <325> all other Sects as soon as we can, and join with that alone which with Truth makes such Objections against all others. For not only this present short Life lies at stake, which is subject to innumerable Evils and Misfortunes, let us live how we will; but we render ourselves liable to the Punishments which God has threatned to those who do not believe the Gospel, and hazard that Happiness which has no Defect and will have no End. Yet there are some Men, not indeed very learned, nor very much addicted to reading the Scriptures seriously, in order to judge of the Divisions amongst Christians, and to find out on which Side the Truth lies; for they have no Concern at all for that; but their Notion of these Divisions is, that they think it all one, let their Opinions be what they will, and that it is the same thing whatever Worship they follow, They imagine it to be quite indifferent, what Party of Christians we really join ourselves with, or indeed only profess to join ourselves with. I do not now speak of the common People only; there are Kingdoms, in which not only the common People, but the Magistrates and Nobility have separated from the See of *Rome,* and yet in a very short time, upon having a new King, have returned to it again; and then after this, have been assisting to the supreme Power in opposing the same See. In the Reign of *Henry* VIII. of *England,* there were many Acts made not only by the King, but agreed to by the Parliament, against the See of *Rome,* which King *Henry* was angry with, for a Reason that few People approved of. After his Death, when his Son, *Edward* VI. joined in with that Party, who had not only renounced all the Authority of the See of *Rome,* as his Father had done; but also had embraced other Opinions, which were condemned by that See;

<326> *they* likewise openly declared that they approved of them. A little after King *Edward* died, when Queen *Mary,* a great Bigot to the Pope of *Rome,* succeeded her Brother, this very Nobility assisted this Queen to oppress that Party who had despised the Authority of the Pope, and were in so flourishing a Condition, when *Edward* was King. Some time after, upon the Death of *Mary,* Queen *Elizabeth* succeeded, who was of the same Sect with her Brother *Edward,* and so strongly established it by a long Reign, that it remains to this Day upon the same Foundation on which it was then built. Whoever peruses the History of those times, will see how fluctuating the Nobility of that Nation were, and he will hardly be able to persuade himself, but that they were of the same Mind with those that believe it to be all one with respect to their eternal Salvation, what Sect of Christians they join themselves with. I agree with those who ascribe these Changes in a good Measure to Fear; but when I consider the Constancy, Courage, and Contempt of Death, which we so frequently see in the *English* Nation, I can hardly persuade myself, but that the Love of this present Life, and an Indifference about Religion, were the principal Causes of these several Changes.

SECT. III. *That an Indifference in Religion, is in its own Nature unlawful, forbidden by the Laws of God, and condemned by all Sects of Christians.*

For any one to think that Religion is one of those things that are of an indifferent Nature; so that we may change it as we do our Clothes; or at least, that we may profess or deny it just as the times change; is a most heinous Crime, as will appear by many Reasons, the principal of which we will produce, from the Nature of the thing, <327> the Laws of God, and the Consent of all Christian Nations.

First, to tell a Lie, is a very dishonest thing, especially in an Affair of any great Moment, when it is not so much as allowed in trifling Matters, unless perhaps in such Particulars where a Lie is upon the Whole more advantageous than the Truth. But in the Affair of Religion, it must be a very grievous Fault for Men to lie, or even to dissemble; because thereby they do all in their Power to confirm a Lie, in a thing of the greatest Importance; to stifle Truth which is contrary to it, and to condemn it to perpetual Obscurity. It is the worst Example that can be set, especially in Persons advanced to any Dignity, which the People of a lower Rank are but too apt to imitate; whence it comes to pass, that they are not only Offenders themselves, but they cause others to offend also by their Example; which has the greatest Influence over the common People, because they give a much greater Attention to the Actions of those they have a great Respect for, than to their Words.

It is also a very dishonourable thing, and altogether unworthy a Man of Courage, to tell a Lie for the sake of this short Life, and to choose to displease God rather than Men. For this Reason the most eminent Philosophers chose rather to expose themselves to certain Death, than to do a thing which they thought was displeasing to the Deity; as we see (*a*) in the Instance of *Socrates,* who chose rather to drink a Dose of Poison, than to leave off the Study of Philosophy, which he had so much <328> accustomed himself to, and live. Other Philosophers also chose rather (*b*) to go to the Plough, than give up those Notions which they believed to be true, and had undertaken to defend. And there have been such valiant Men amongst the Heathens, who by their good Lives severely reproached the Age they lived in; and thought it much more preferable to die, than to flatter Tyrants, and thereby forsake the true way of Life; of which were (*c*) *Thraseas Paetus* and (*d*) *Helvidius Priscus,* who chose to die rather than to dissemble or approve of the Vices and wicked Actions of the *Roman*

a. *In the Instance of* Socrates, &c.] See what I have collected about him in my *Silvae Philologicae,* Book I, Chap 3.

b. *To go to the Plough,* &c.] See *Galen,* in that Book where he says, *That the Passions and Affections of the Mind, depend upon the Constitution of the Body.* In the last Chapter towards the End, where speaking of the Stoicks, *They were fully persuaded, that they ought to forsake their Country rather than their Opinions.*

c. *Thraseas Paetus,* &c.] Who was put to Death by *Nero* because he would not flatter him. See *Tacitus*'s Annals, Book XVI. 24. and following Sections.

d. *Helvidius Priscus,* &c.] The Son-in-Law of *Thraseas,* who, as *Tacitus* there tells us, was commanded to depart out of *Italy* at the same time. He was afterwards slain by *Vespasian,* because he would not pay sufficient Reverence to his new Master, as *Suetonius* informs us in the XVth Chap. of the Life of that Emperor. His Son was slain by *Domitian.* See *Suetonius*'s Life of him, and *Tacitus* in the Life of *Agricola,* Chap. XLV.

Emperors. Now if this was done by Men, who had but faint Hopes of another and more happy Life hereafter; how much more are they obliged to do it, who have so much plainer and more certain Hope of an eternal Happiness afforded them.

All Ages have seen and commended such, as have with an intrepid Mind submitted to Death for the sake of their earthly Country. Now after this, who is it but must applaud all those who pre-<329>fer a heavenly Country to an earthly one; and that eternal Life which the Scriptures have revealed to us, to a temporal one? Who can forbear despising those mean Creatures as choose to preserve such a Life as they have in common with brute Beasts, and which they must lose in a short time; rather than to take the first Opportunity of obtaining a Life that can never be lost? We see Soldiers, with great Bravery, face the most imminent Dangers, in order to obtain the Favour of Kings or Princes to themselves, or their Families after them, and rejoice within themselves that they got such Wounds as they must in a very short time die of. Nay, even hired Troops themselves, will fight very valiantly, and venture their Lives for those who employ them, though it be but for very small Wages; and yet there are some, who will not expose themselves to any Hazard, I do not say of their Lives, but of the Loss of their Goods or of their uncertain Dignities, for the Defence of Truth, which will last to Eternity, is most acceptable to God, and has the highest Reward annexed to it.

Therefore what Christ has commanded us in this Respect, is in the following Words; (*a*) *Whosoever shall confess me before Men, him will I confess also before my Father which is in Heaven; but whosoever shall deny me before Men, him will I also deny before my Father which is in Heaven.* In which Words he tells us, that he will own all those for his Disciples, and will give them eternal Life at the Day of Judgment, who have not dissembled his Doctrine, either in their Deeds or Words. He does indeed in another Place declare, that this <330> ought to be done with Prudence; when he says, (*b*) *That we should not cast Pearl before Swine.* But this Prudence does not extend so far, as to allow us to play the Hypocrite, all our Lives

---

a. *Whosoever shall confess,* &c.] *Matt.* X. 32.
b. *That we should not cast,* &c.] *Matt.* VIII. 6.

long, if need be, or so much as to tell a direct Lie; but only not to try at an improper time and place, to convince such Persons as obstinately persist in their Errors, when we see it will have no Effect upon them. For he expressly declares, a little after, the forementioned Words concerning confessing our Religion; that sometimes it ought to be done, though it brings upon us the Hatred of all those about us, and the imminent Danger of certain Death. (*a*) *He that loveth Father or Mother more than me, is not worthy of me: and he that loveth Son or Daughter more than me, is not worthy of me.* And such are all they who dissemble the Doctrines and Precepts which they have received from Christ, for their Families sake. Nor has Christ omitted to tell us, that Death must be expected for such Constancy; and yet notwithstanding, they ought to persist in their Design; and that he who does lose his Life upon this Account, shall obtain a blessed Immortality in the World to come. (*b*) *And he that taketh not his Cross and followeth after me, is not worthy of me. He that findeth his Life* (in this World) *shall lose it* (in another) *and he that loseth his Life* (on Earth) *for my sake, shall find it,* in Heaven, and that an infinitely more happy and eternal one.

This Doctrine is so plain and evident, that there are no Sects of Christians at this time, that differ at <331> all about it; they who own the Pope's Authority, and they of all sorts who disown such Authority, do every one of them, with one Consent affirm it to be a very wicked thing, to dissemble our Sentiments concerning Religion; when Opinions of the greatest Moment are debated, and where the thing may be done without Sedition and Tumult. For in those things in which Faith towards God and Uncorruptness of Manners may be preserved, it may be right to conceal our Notions, rather than raise perpetual Contentions amongst Christians, when there are so few learned Men who think alike in every thing. I say *conceal,* not *dissemble;* for to conceal your Opinion is not *to lie;* but to affirm you believe that which you really do not believe, this is to lie. To which may be added, that if any Opinion be established by the common Law, which you think to be false; you ought modestly and without Contention or

---

a. *He that loveth Father,* &c.] *Matt.* X. 37.
b. *And he that taketh,* &c.] *Matt.* X. 38, 39.

Tumult to declare your Dissent from it; otherwise instead of that mild and gentle Government of Christian Churches, which does not exclude any Dissent, provided it be done with Charity; we shall run into absolute Tyranny, which will allow of no Dissent at all upon any Account. There are innumerable obscure speculative Questions, especially to those who never took any great Pains in such sort of Studies, in which Christian Liberty ought to be allowed, as is confessed by all Christians; for there are a Multitude of Places in Scripture, and a vast Number of theological Opinions, in which learned Men always have and still do differ from each other with Impunity, even amongst those, who in other things require Consent more strictly than they ought to do. <332>

SECT. IV. *We ought not hastily to condemn those who differ from us, as if they were guilty of such a Crime or such unlawful Worship as is inconsistent with eternal Life; so that none who admit such Persons should be capable of the Mercy of God; nor yet on the other Hand is it lawful for us to profess that we believe what we do not really believe, or to do what at the same time we condemn.*

They who have separated from the Church of *Rome,* do no more agree with each other in all Points than they who continue in it: but according to the Judgment of some of the most learned Men, they do not differ in any thing that is consistent with that Faith which is owing to God, and that Obedience which ought to be paid to him. But they object many things to the Church of *Rome,* both in Doctrine and Worship, which they think are plainly false and unlawful. Whether they judge right in this or no, I shall not now enquire: However thus much is evident, that according to the Opinion even of that Church, it is not lawful for them to profess that they approve of what they do not approve of, nor do they admit any Person to Communion with them, who profess to dissent from it in such things. However, amongst those that dissent from the Church

of *Rome,* there are (*a*) some famous and learned Men, who though they
think it utterly unlawful to join with that Church themselves, on the
Account of those Doctrines, and that Worship in which they differ from
it; yet notwithstanding they do not think it right, to ex-<333>clude from
eternal Happiness, all those both learned and unlearned, who live and
die in it. They indeed who think that there is any thing in them, which
is contrary to the fundamental Principles of Christianity, judge it to be
by no means lawful for themselves to give their Assent to them, and that
it would be the highest Crime in them, to pretend to consent to what
they really condemn, and for which Crime, if they should fall into it,
and continue in it to their Death, they believe they should be excluded
eternal Happiness. But as to such as do sincerely embrace those Doctrines, because they believe them to be agreeable to Divine Revelation, or
at least not so repugnant to it, as to subvert the Faith or Holiness of the
Gospel; whether it be owing to that sort of Study which they have employed themselves in from their Youth, or whether it ariseth from a Defect of Knowledge or Judgment; such Persons as these, I say, they do not
presume to exclude from Salvation, because they cannot tell how far the
Mercy of God may extend, with respect to such Men as these. There are
innumerable Circumstances both of time and place, and various Dispositions of Mind, which are quite unknown to us, which may very much diminish the Crimes of wretched Men in the Sight of God; so as to procure
Pardon for such; which would be condemned in Men of more Learning.
Wherefore they look upon it as a Part of Christian Equity and Prudence,
at the same time that they condemn the Doctrine and the Worship, to
leave the Men to the wise and merciful Judgment of God; though they
themselves are determined neither to assent to their Doctrines, nor to be
present at their Worship, because they think it absolutely unlawful. <334>

Surely no Man can think, that from what has been said it will follow, that any Person, who is brought up in a different Opinion, and
has employed himself in reading the Scriptures in the manner that the

a. *Some famous and learned Men,* &c.] Amongst others, is Mr. *William Chilling-
worth,* in his *English* Book, intitled *The Religion of Protestants, the safe way to Salvation,*
where he mentions others, who also think them as safe.

Reformers do; if he should, contrary to his own Conscience, say or do any thing which he thinks unlawful or false, for any present Advantage; that any such Person, I say, can hope for Pardon from God; if he should die with a Habit of saying and doing what he himself disapproves of; and would have said and done so, if he had lived longer. There is not at present, and I hope there never will be, any Sect which shall go under the Name of Christians, who will allow that such a Man can arrive at Salvation.

Let Hypocrites therefore look to themselves whilst they behave so, as shamefully to despise the Light of Reason and Revelation, to resist the Conviction of them, and to look upon the Judgment of all Christians whatsoever as nothing. Such Persons cannot be thought learned Men, or such as have thoroughly and maturely considered the thing. There are them that so far despise all theological Learning, that they will not so much as attempt it; but without this, there can be no Judgment at all passed upon the Matter. These equally despise that noble Philosophy, which the great Men amongst the *Romans* of old, set such a Value upon, as being deduced from the Light of Nature; in order to indulge those Passions which the heathen Philosophy would not allow of. Having thus secured themselves from the Judgment of past Ages, despising every thing in the present, and having little Concern for what is to come; they are more like Beasts than Men indued with Reason, which they never make use of. They who dissemble and lie in such a manner as this, ought not <335> to be looked upon as Men of any Value or Account, they ought not to be trusted even in temporal and worldly Affairs, because they endeavour to impose upon God and Man in a Matter of the greatest Importance. There are some amongst these, who dare to affirm, that we ought always to be of the Religion that the State is of, and when that changes we ought to change also; but it is not at all to be wondered at, that these Persons should have so ill an Opinion of the Christian Faith, when they have not so much as the common Principles of natural Religion in them, nor do they shew any Regard to right Reason or Virtue. What a wretched Condition are those Kings and States in, who put their Confidence in such Men as believe neither natural nor revealed Religion! Indeed, Men, who are themselves void of Learning, who give no Credit to the Judgment of any learned Men whatsoever; who have no sort of Concern for Truth, but live in perpetual Hypocrisy; are by no means fit to be trusted in any Matters whatsoever, not even to such as relate to the Publick.

Yet these very Men, as much Despisers as they are of Truth and Virtue, look upon themselves as better Subjects and more ingenious Persons than others; though they be neither, and though it be impossible they should be either, whilst they make no Distinction betwixt Truth and Falshood, Virtue and Vice, and whilst they are ready to say or do any thing that may be of Advantage to themselves. All such Men have renounced a right Temper of Mind, and every good Action, and therefore ought to be despised and avoided by every Body. <336>

SECT. V. *A Man that commits a Sin by Mistake, may be accepted of God, but a Hypocrite cannot.*

The Condition of human Nature is such, that a great many Men, who in other Respects are not the worst of Men; and yet, either by bad Education, or for want of Teachers or Books, which might bring them off from their Errors; or because they have not Capacity enough to understand the Controversies amongst Christians, and to form a Judgment of them; lead their Lives as it were, in utter Darkness. Such Persons, as they sincerely believe and obey what they are taught concerning the Christian Religion, so far as their Capacity reaches, are more the Objects of Compassion than of Anger, considering the natural State of Mankind. Their Religion indeed is very lame and defective, and abounds with Mistakes, but yet they themselves are very sincere. Wherefore it is highly probable, that he *who does not reap where he has not sown*, will, out of his abundant Equity, pardon those who are in such Circumstances; or certainly will inflict a much lighter Punishment upon them.

But if we consider that there are Men to be found who have not wanted either Education or Teachers, either Books or Capacity, to understand who have the best and who the worst Side of the Question in Controversies of Religion; and yet have followed the wrong Side only for the Sake of the Wealth, or Pleasure, or Honours that attend them in this present Life; we cannot but have great Indignation against such Men, nor can any one presume to excuse them, much less to defend such a Purpose of Life, without the most consummate Impudence. Whence it is easy to apprehend, that if we ourselves, whose Virtue is very imperfect, <337> could not pardon such Persons, how much more severe the infinite Justice of God will be against those, who have knowingly and designedly preferred a Lie to the Truth, for the sake of the frail and uncertain good things of this present Life.

God, out of his abundant Mercy, is ready to pardon such Ignorance as does not proceed from Vice; to pity our imperfect Virtues; and to allow for the Errors of such as are deceived; especially if there was no previous Iniquity nor no Contempt of Religion; but as our Saviour assures us, he will never pardon those, who when they knew the Truth, chose rather to profess a Lie. We see that such a Hypocrite as this is by no means acceptable to men; for no body would choose a Person for a Friend, who to gain any small Advantage to himself, would trample under Foot all the Rights of ancient Friendship. Whence it follows from what has been said, that there is not a baser nor more dangerous piece of Iniquity, than the Crime of those, who in Matters of the highest Moment and Concern, dissemble that which they really think is the best, and openly favour them who are in the wrong. This is what Reason itself teaches us, and what is confirmed by the Christian Religion, and has the Consent of all Sects of Christians whatsoever. <338><339>

TESTIMONIES

CONCERNING

HUGO GROTIUS's
Affection for the Church of ENGLAND

To the Reader

Having the following Letters from that most excellent and learned Person *Henry Newton*,[1] Ambassador Extraordinary from the most Serene Queen of *Great Britain*,[2] to his Royal Highness the most Serene Grand Duke of *Tuscany*,[3] to whose singular Goodness I am very much indebted; I thought I should do a very acceptable Thing to all who love the Name of *Grotius*, and no small Honour to the Church of *England*, if I published them here. It appears plainly from them, that this very great Man had the highest <340> Opinion of the Church of *England*, and would most willingly have lived in it, if he could. Make the best use of them you can therefore, *Courteous Reader*, and continue to have a good Opinion of a Man that deserved so well of the whole Body of Christians. <341>

1. Sir Henry Newton (1650–1715), English diplomat and judge. In November 1704 he was appointed as envoy-extraordinary to Genoa and Tuscany.
2. Anne, Queen of Great Britain and Ireland (1665–1714; reigned 1702–14).
3. Cosimo III (1642–1723), Grand Duke of Tuscany.

I

Henry Newton to Peter Hieronymus Barcellinus, Abbot of St. Eusebius de Urbe.[4]

Being at length returned safe and well to *Florence,* from *Leghorn* and *Pisa,* where through the Intemperateness of the Air I was very near contracting a Fever; the first thing I had to do, most excellent *Barcellinus,* being furnished with the most noble Library of the illustrious *Magliabechius,*[5] was to discharge my Promise concerning that great Man *Hugo Grotius,* and to show from his Writings, particularly his Letters, in which Truth, Candour, Integrity of Heart, and the inward Thoughts of his Mind are discovered; how highly he thought and wrote concerning us all his Lifetime, and a little before his Departure, and when Death and Immortality were in his View. I know what was said of him by that Chief of his Rank *Petavius, Brietius* and *Valesius,*[6] and many other celebrated Men of your Communion, who wished well and favourably to a Man born for the publick Good of Christianity. It is known to all how greatly he suffered in Goods, Honour and Report, <342> from the Calvinists, both in his own Country and in his Banishment, even after he was advanced to a higher Rank by Foreigners; and how much the Heats of Controversy (whilst he

4. Abbot of the monastery of St. Eusebius in Rome. Until the early nineteenth century, the church of St. Eusebius and adjacent monastery belonged to the Celestines, a branch of the Benedictine Order named after Pope Celestine V (b. 1215).

5. Antonio Magliabechi (1633–1714), librarian to Cosimo III, Grand Duke of Tuscany.

6. Denis Pétau or Dionysius Petavius (1583–1652), French Jesuit and eminent Catholic theologian; Philippe Briet or Philippus Brietius (1601–68), French Jesuit; Henri Valois or Henricus Valesius (1603–76), French philologist who studied under the Jesuits.

set his Mind upon this one thing, to establish Peace in the Commonwealth and between the Churches, which highly displeased many; a strange and grievous thing!) fretted that Disposition, which was otherwise peaceable and modest, after he saw himself treated in such an unworthy manner by his own Friends; and sometimes prevailed over that meek Wisdom which was in him both by Nature and Judgment. Yet these did not hinder his Son,[7] who was also a great Man, from saying those things which I shall presently add, concerning his Father, *to that great Prince,* Charles *the* IId *of* Great Britain,[8] *to whom he dedicated his Father's Works,* and in him to all others; and this when he had no Reason to flatter or fear him, because in the Commonwealth, he was of the contrary Part to *Charles's* Sister's Son;[9] and because he was a private Man, wedded to a country and learned Life, and an old Man, not far from Death, nor consequently from Liberty: For he published his Father's Works, but saw them not after they were published; and his own Life is to be seen and read with the Life of his Father in the same Volume. *For thou,* says *Peter Grotius, art he alone, whom if not the greater, yet the wiser Part of the Christian World, have for a long time acknowledged for their Protector. Thou art he to whose* Protection *or* Defence *the Christian Faith willingly commits itself; in whose Kingdoms principally, that Knowledge of the Sacred Writings, that Worship of the Deity, that Moderation of the too free Exercise of Liberty in disputing concerning the secret Doctrines* <343> *of Faith, is established; whose Agreement with which the Author, my Father, has long since declared, and publickly professed in his Writings.*

Hear now *Hugo Grotius's* own Words, how he expresses his own Sense, in his Epistle to *Johannis Corvinis,*[10] dated in the Year MDCXXXVIII, who was not an *English,* but a *Dutch* Divine, of another Church, and also a Lawyer, and consequently skilled in Matters both Divine and Humane; concerning the Reformation of Religion made amongst us in the last

---

7. Peter Grotius or Pieter de Groot (1615–78).

8. Charles II (1630–85), king of England, Scotland, and Ireland (r. 1660–85).

9. William III (1650–1702), king of England, Scotland, and Ireland (r. 1689–1702), and prince of Orange. He was the son of the sister of Charles II, Mary, princess royal (1631–60), princess of Orange.

10. Hugo Grotius to Johannes Arnoldi Corvinus, 28 May 1638 (*BW* vol. 9, No. 3595, p. 319).

Age. *You see how great a Progress they have made in* England, *in purging out pernicious Doctrines; chiefly for this Reason, because they who undertook that holy Work, admitted of nothing new, nothing of their own, but had their Eyes wholly fixed upon another World.* Then was it in a flourishing Condition, before a Civil War broke out, before the King was vanquished, taken Captive, condemned and beheaded;[11] and it afterwards sprung up and flourished again, contrary to all humane Hopes, when his Son[12] returned to the Throne of his Ancestors, to the Surprize of all *Europe,* and, after various Turns, Threats, and Fears, continues still to flourish secure and unhurt.

Nor had he only a good Opinion of the Church of *England* himself, but also advised his Friends in *Holland,* who were of his Party, and, which was no small Thing, who joined with him in partaking of the same Danger and Losses; to take holy Orders from our Bishops; whom it is certain he did not believe, nor would have others believe, to be Schismatical, or Heretical, upon that Account. He addresses his Brother in these Words.[13] *I would perswade them* (that is, the Remonstrants,) *to appoint some amongst them in a more eminent Station, such as <344> Bishops; and that they receive the laying on of Hands from the* Irish *Archbishop*[14] *who is there, and that when they are so ordained they afterwards ordain other Pastors;* and this in the Beginning of the Year MDCXLV.[15] which was fatal to him, and unfortunate to Learning itself. The Bishop he here speaks of is, if I be not mistaken, *John Bramhall,*[16] who was at that Time Bishop of *Londonderry*

---

11. Charles I (1600–1649; r. 1625–49), king of England, Scotland, and Ireland. During the last years of his reign, a civil war broke out, leading to his arrest, condemnation, and execution in 1649.

12. Charles II (1630–85), son of Charles I. He returned from exile in 1660 and under him the monarchy was restored.

13. Hugo Grotius to Willem de Groot, 31 December 1644 (*BW* vol. 16, No. 7222, p. 288).

14. James Ussher (1581–1656), Church of Ireland archbishop of Armagh and primate of Ireland. Henry Newton thought mistakenly that Grotius was referring to John Bramhall (see note 16, below).

15. Actually 31 December 1644 (see note 13 above).

16. John Bramhall (baptized 1594, died 1663). He became bishop of Londonderry in 1634 but was forced to leave Ireland in 1642. In 1660 he was nominated as Church of Ireland archbishop of Armagh and primate of Ireland. His predecessor as archbishop of Armagh was James Ussher.

in *Ireland,* and, at the Restoration of King *Charles* II. Archbishop of *Armagh,* and next to the most learned *Usher* Primate of *Ireland,* and who afterwards in that Country published a Vindication of our Church against *Mileterius.*[17] See also what he said to the same Person, *April* 8. in the Year MDCXLV.[18] concerning the publick Worship of God amongst us. *The English Liturgy was always accounted the best by all learned Men.*

It seems very probable that this Man, who calls the Reformation of the Church of *England a most Holy Work;* who believed that the Holy Orders given and received from the Bishops of that Church, and the Rites appointed about Holy Things, and the prescribed Form of worshipping the supreme Deity, exceeded all other Churches in the Christian World; would have joined himself to that Church, as well in outward Worship, as in the Judgment of his Mind; and so have become now really what he before was in Wish, a Member of the Catholick Church. But he was never able to effect the Thing, because Death immediately after, overtook him; for in the same Year he went from *France* to *Stockholm* to resign his Ambassadorship, and returning from thence home, and having suffered Shipwreck, he departed this Life at *Rostock* on the 28th of *August,* a Man never enough to be lamented, <345> because Study and Learning decayed with him; and never enough to be praised, upon the Account of what he began and finished in all Parts of Learning. He was a great Lover of Peace, if Truth was not injured, (always having Regard to Times and Differences,) and of the antient Church Government, (freed from Abuses,) as it was settled from the Beginning in *England,* and as it was from the very Apostles Time, if we may believe Ecclesiastical Annals. He always studied and consulted the Peace of Empires and Churches, both in his Discourses, and by his Example, and in his Writings; may he be rewarded with God and our common Lord! and may the Memory of him be ever grateful to Posterity! *Farewel.*

Florence XII. *of the Kalends of* May,
MDCCVI.[19] <346>

---

17. Théophile Brachet de La Milletière (1588–1665).
18. Hugo Grotius to Willem de Groot, 8 April 1645 (*BW* vol. 16, No. 7407, p. 625).
19. 12th of the Calends of May, 1706 (that is, 20 April 1706).

Henry Newton to John Clerc.[1]

Most Learned Sir, I send you a new and ample Testimony concerning *Hugo Grotius,* more weighty than the former, if we consider the Author's Dignity in the Commonwealth, or his Knowledge of Things, or that it was writ while *Grotius* was alive. It is taken from Letters to that great Prelate *William Laud,*[2] then Archbishop of *Canterbury,* with whom he often had Correspondence by Letters; they were written from *Paris, October* 24. *Gregorian* Style, in the Year MDCXXXVIII.[3] and were procured me lately out of *England,* by the Kindness of that most illustrious Person *John* Lord *Sommers,*[4] formerly High Chancellor of that flourishing Kingdom, then President of the Law, now* of the Council. In those Letters that most illustrious Viscount *Scudamore,*[5] at the Time Ambassador for our Nation in *France,* has the following Words concerning *Grotius.*

"The next Time I see Ambassador *Grotius,* I will not fail to perform your Commands con-\<347\>cerning him. Certainly, my Lord, I am

---

1. Jean Le Clerc (1657–1736).
2. William Laud (1573–1645), archbishop of Canterbury from 1633.
3. 24 October 1638, Gregorian style (that is, according to the new calendar introduced in 1582 in Catholic countries following a papal bull issued by Pope Gregory XVIII).
4. John Somers, Baron Somers (1651–1716), lawyer and politician. In 1692 he was made attorney general, in 1697 lord chancellor, and in 1708 lord president of the privy council.
* *In this Year* 1709, *he was President of the Privy Council, to her most Serene Majesty.*
5. John Scudamore, first Viscount Scudamore (1601–71), English diplomat and politician. In 1635 Scudamore was appointed ambassador to France.

perswaded that he doth unfeignedly and highly Love and Reverence your Person and Proceedings. Body and Soul he professeth himself to be for the Church of *England,* and gives this Judgment of it, that it is the likeliest to last of any Church this Day in being."

Genoa XVII. *of the Kalends*
of February, MDCCVII.[6] <348>

6. 17th (actually 18th; see Jean Le Clerc, *Epistolario,* ed. Maria Grazia and Mario Sina [Florence, 1994], 3:56) of the Calends of February (that is, 15 January 1707).

Francis Cholmondly[1] to Alexander Forrester.[2]

That which you desire to know of me concerning *Hugo Grotius,* who was one of the greatest Men that ever any Age produced, is this. It happened that I came to *Paris* a little after the Transaction of that Matter. Being very well acquainted with Dr. *Crowder,*[3] he often told me with Assurance, that it was the last Advice this great Man gave to his Wife,[4] as he thought it was his Duty, that he declared he died in the Communion of the Church of *England,* in which Church he wished her to live. This she discovered when she came on purpose to our Church (which was in the House of *Richard Brown,*[5] who was then in *France* upon the King of *England*'s Account) where she received the Sacrament of the Lord's Supper at the Hands of Dr. *Crowder,* then Chaplain to the Duke of *York.* This was done as soon as Matters would permit, after the Death of that Man. Archbishop *Bramhall,* Primate of *Ireland,* in De- <349>fence of himself and the Episcopal Clergy, against *Richard Baxter* the Presbyterian's Accusation of Popery, speaks thus concerning the Religion of *Grotius,* p. 21.[6] *He was a Friend in his Affection to the Church*

---

1. Probably a member of the Cholmondeley family based in Cheshire (England).

2. Alexander Forrester was possibly a relative of another Alexander Forrester (ca. 1711–87), known especially for his Chancery Court reports of 1732–39.

3. Chaplain at the chapel of the English embassy in Paris.

4. Maria van Reigersberch (d. 1653).

5. Sir Richard Browne (1605–83), diplomat and royalist resident in Paris until 1660; his chapel was the main Anglican place of worship in Paris.

6. *Bishop Bramhall's vindication of himself and the episcopal clergy, from the Presbyterian charge of popery, as it is managed by Mr. Baxter* [Richard Baxter, (1615–91)] *in*

of England, *and a true Son in his Love for it; he commended it to his Wife and other Friends, and was the Cause of their firmly adhering to it as far as they had Opportunity. I myself, and many others, have seen his Wife obeying the Commands of her Husband, as she openly testify'd, in coming to our Prayers, and the Celebration of the Sacrament.* When *Matthew Turner,*[7] a great Friend of *Grotius's*, desired to know why he did not go over to the Communion of the Church of *England,* he answered, that he would very willingly have done it, if the Office of Ambassador to *Swedeland*[8] had not hindered it. Otherwise he very highly approved of our Doctrine and Discipline, and wished to live and die in our Communion. If any one thinks that he can know *Grotius's* Mind better from Conjectures and Inferences, or that he dissembled it before his Wife and Children, let him enjoy his own Opinion, he will not have many agree with him. *Farewel.*

June 23. MDCCVII.[9] <350>

From another Letter, *dated Octob. 6. MDCCVIII.*[10]

I lately told you very fully what I knew of the Widow of that great Man *Hugo Grotius.* Afterwards I called to mind that that pious and singular good Man, Sir *Spencer Compton,*[11] Knt. Son of the Earl of *Northampton,* told me he was present when *Grotius's* Widow profess'd this, and received the Sacrament.

FINIS.

---

his treatise of the Grotian religion together with a preface shewing what grounds there are of fears and jealousies of popery, London, 1672.

7. Matthias Turner had been chaplain to the English ambassador to France, John Scudamore. Only one letter of 9 November 1639 by him to Grotius is published in *BW* (*BW* vol. 10, No. 4375, pp. 725–26).

8. Grotius served in France as Swedish ambassador.

9. 23 June 1707.

10. 6 October 1708.

11. Sir Spencer Compton (d. 1659). He accompanied Charles II into exile.

AUTHORS AND WORKS CITED
BY GROTIUS AND LE CLERC

Grotius and Le Clerc do not specify which edition of a work they are referring to. However, in the cases in which they cite authors with a reference to a specific work, I have, where possible, listed editions that might have been available to them. In a few cases I have listed a later edition for the reader's benefit. Finally, when Grotius and Le Clerc cite authors without any direct or indirect reference to specific works, I have simply identified the author. In a few instances John Clarke added new references (indicated by "Reference added by John Clarke").

The order of authors' entries is as follows: name as cited by Grotius or Le Clerc in the text; name as commonly known; birth and death dates; brief biographical information, if available, identifying the author; work or works referred to in the text (for ancient authors this may be fragments preserved in someone else's work).

Ancient, Early Christian, Patristic, Early Postbiblical Jewish Authors and Works

Aboda Zara/Abuda Zara: Avoda Zara. Talmudic tractate on idololatry. See also entry for "Talmud."

Abydenus: Abydenus (ca. 200 BCE). Greek historian who wrote a history of the Chaldeans and Assyrians; fragments of his work are preserved in Eusebius, *Praeparatio Evangelica,* and in Cyril of Alexandria, *Contra impium Iulianum Libri decem.*

Acusilaus: Acusilaus of Argos (6th century BCE). Greek historian.

Adrian: Adrian (Hadrian, Caesar Traianus Hadrianus Augustus) (76–138 CE). Roman emperor. See also entries for "*Digesta*" and "Justinian."

Aelian: Aelian (or Claudius Aelianus) (ca. 170–ca. 235 CE). Roman author; *Aeliani Variae historiae libri XIIII*, Geneva, 1625.

Aeschylus: Aeschylus (525/524–456/455 BCE). Greek dramatist. *Hepta epi Thēbais* (or *Septem Contra Thebas*). *Persai* (or *Persae*).

African Council. Collections of ancient African councils; *Concilia Africae 345–525*, in *Corpus Christianorum, Series Latina* (Turnhout: Brepols Publishers, 1953–).

Africanus: Sextus Julius Africanus (ca. 160–ca. 240 CE). Regarded as the father of Christian chronography; fragments of his work are preserved by Eusebius.

Akiba, R[abbi]: Akiba ben Joseph (40–ca. 132 CE). A founder of rabbinic Judaism associated with the development of the Mishna. See also entry for "Mishna."

Alexander Aphrodisaeus: Alexander of Aphrodisias (ca. 200 CE). Greek philosopher; *Liber de Fato* in Themistius (4th century CE); *Omnia . . . opera: hoc est paraphrases, et orationes. Alexandri Aphrodisiensis libri duo de anima, et de fato unus*, Venice, 1534.

Alexander Polyhistor/Alexander the Historian: Lucius Cornelius Alexander Polyhistor (ca. 105–ca. 35 BCE). Roman historian, philosopher, and geographer.

Alexandrian Chronicon. *Chronicon Alexandrinum*, translated and edited by Matthaeus Raderus, Munich, 1615.

Alfenus: Alfenus Varus (1st century BCE). Roman jurist; excerpts from his work are included in *Digestorum seu Pandectarum libri quinquaginta [Digesta]*, Paris, 1562.

Amelius: Amelius (3rd century CE). Neoplatonist philosopher. Fragments of his work are preserved in Eusebius, *Praeparatio Evangelica*, and in Cyril of Alexandria, *Contra impium Iulianum Libri decem*.

Ammianus: Ammianus Marcellinus (ca. 330–95 CE). Roman historian and author of a history of the Roman Empire in thirty-one books, of which only the last eighteen survive; *Rerum Gestarum Libri XVIII*, Paris, 1544.

Ammonius: Ammonius of Alexandria (fl. ca. 389 CE). Author of a Greek dictionary of synonyms; *Peri omoiōn*, in B. Vulcanius, *Thesaurus utriusque linguae*, 1600.

Ampelius: Lucius Ampelius (possibly early 3rd century CE). *Liber memorialis*.

Anaxagoras: Anaxagoras (ca. 612–545 BCE). Pre-Socratic Greek philosopher; mentioned in Diogenes Laërtius, *De vitis dogmatibus et apophthegmatibus clarorum philosophorum libri X.* Fragments of his work are quoted by later authors. See number 59 in the standard collection of Pre-Socratic texts, H. Diels and W. Kranz, eds., *Die Fragmente der Vorsokratiker,* 6th ed., 3 vols. (Berlin: Weidmann, 1951–52).

Anaxandrides: Anaxandrides (4th century BCE). Comic poet; quoted in Stobaeus. See also entry for "Stobaeus."

Anaximander: Anaximander (ca. 612–545 BCE). Pre-Socratic Greek philosopher.

Antiphon: Antiphon (fl. ca. 480–411 BCE). Greek writer, orator, and statesman.

Antisthenes: Antisthenes (ca. 445–ca. 360 BCE). Greek philosopher and follower of Socrates.

Apollodorus: Apollodorus of Athens (ca. 180–ca. 120 BCE). Greek scholar and grammarian. Grotius, however, seems to refer to Pseudo-Apollodorus (2nd century CE), the author of the *Bibliotheke,* a work on Greek mythology containing the story of Deucalion.

Apollonius: Apollonius of Rhodes (or Apollonius Rhodius) (born ca. 295 BCE). Greek poet; *Argonautica.*

Appion: Apion (ca. 20/30–ca. 45/48 BCE). Greek-Egyptian grammarian and sophist.

Appion: Appian of Alexandria (fl. 2nd century CE). Greek historian, author of a history of Rome in twenty-four books; *Romanarum historiarum . . . fragmenta quaedam. Item, de bellis ciuilibus libri V,* [Geneva], 1592.

Apuleius: Lucius Apuleius (ca. 124–ca. 170 CE). Roman philosopher and scholar. *Opera omnia quae exstant, e quibus . . . philosophici libri expurgati per B. Vulcanium* [Bonaventura Vulcanius] Leiden, 1594. *Apuleius Madaurensis Platonicus,* Amsterdam, 1624.

Aquila: Aquila (Akilas) (fl. 2nd century CE). Biblical scholar who translated the Old Testament into Greek.

Aratus: Aratus (fl. ca. 315–ca. 245 BCE). Greek poet; *Phaenomena.*

Archedemus: Archedemus of Tarsus (fl. ca. 140 BCE). Stoic philosopher.

Aristaeus: Aristaeus or Aristeas (2nd century BCE). The alleged author of the so-called Letter of Aristeas to Philocrates containing a pseudohistory of the Septuagint translation of the Hebrew Bible; Aristaeus or Aristeas, *Ad Philocratem de lxx interpretibus,* Rome, 1471; Naples, 1474; Erfurt, 1483.

Aristides: Aelius Aristides (ca. 117–ca. 187 CE). Greek rhetorician; *Orationum tomi tres,* ed. Willem Canter [1542–75], Geneva, 1604.

Aristippus: Aristippus (ca. 435–366 BCE). Greek philosopher, founder of the Cyrenaic school of hedonism.

Aristobulus: Aristobulus of Paneas (ca. 160 BCE). Hellenistic Jewish philosopher; quoted by Eusebius, *Praeparatio Evangelica.*

Aristophanes: Aristophanes (ca. 446–ca. 386 BCE). Greek dramatist. *Ornithes* (or *Aves*). *Acharneis* (or *Acharnenses*). *Aristophanis comoediae undecim, graece et latine, ex codd. mss. emendatae: cum scholiis antiquis,* ed. Ludolph Kuster, Amsterdam, 1710.

Aristotle: Aristotle (384–322 BCE). Ancient Greek philosopher. *Topica. De Caelo. De Anima. De Generatione Animalium. Metaphysica. Ethica Nicomachea. Politica.*

Arnobius: Arnobius of Sicca (or Afer, Arnobius the Elder) (4th century CE). Christian apologist; *Disputationum adversus gentes libri septem* [*Adversus nationes libri VII*], Douai, 1634.

Arrius: Arrian (or Lucius Flavius Arrianus) (ca. 86–ca. 160 CE). *Commentariorum de Epicteti disputationibus, libri IV.*

Artapanus: Artapanus (ca. 100 BCE). Jewish historian whose work was quoted by Alexander Polyhistor and, in turn, by Eusebius.

Athanasius: Athanasius (ca. 293–373 CE). Greek church father.

Athenaeus: Athenaeus of Naucratis (fl. 200 CE). Greek grammarian and author born in Egypt; *Deipnosophistai; Athēnaiou Deipnosophistōn biblia pentekaideka.* [*Athenaei Deipnosophistarum libri quindecim*], Lyon, 1612.

Athenagoras: Athenagoras (2nd century CE). Greek philosopher and Christian apologist. *Legatio pro Christianis. De resurrectione mortuorum.*

Augustine: Augustine of Hippo (354–430 CE). Christian bishop and theologian. *Epistulae ad Romanos expositio inchoata. Confessiones. De Doctrina Christiana. De Civitate Dei. Epistulae. Sermones. Opera,* 10 vols., Paris, 1586.

Baba Bathra: Bava Batra (The Last Gate). Talmudic tractate. See also entry for "Talmud."

Baba Kama: Bava Qama (The First Gate). Talmudic tractate. See also entry for "Talmud."

Barnabas: St. Barnabas. Believed to be the author of the so-called Epistle of Barnabas. See *Sancti Barnabae apostoli . . . epistola catholica,* ed. Nicolas Hugues Ménard [1585–1644], Paris, 1645.

Basil/Basilius: Saint Basil the Great (329–379 CE). Greek church father and bishop of Caesarea. *Homiliae. Opera Omnia,* Paris, 1638.

Babylonish Gemara. See entry for "Talmud."

Berachoth: Berakhot. Talmudic tractate on blessings. See also entry for "Talmud."

Berosus: Berosus (or Berossus, Berossos, Berosos) (fl. ca. 290 BCE). Chaldean priest of Bel, author of a work on the history and culture of Babylon cited by Flavius Josephus.

Caesar/Cesar: Gaius Julius Caesar (ca. 100–44 BCE). Roman general and statesman. *De Bello Gallico. De Bello Alexandrino*—not by Caesar; probably by Aulus Hirtius (ca. 90–43 BCE).

Calimachus: Callimachus (ca. 305–ca. 240 BCE). Greek poet and scholar. *Iambi.* Poem on Berenice's hair translated by Catullus.

Calisthenes: Callisthenes of Olynthus (ca. 360–328 BCE). Greek historian.

Capitolinus: Julius Capitolinus (ca. 3rd–4th century CE). In *Scriptores Historiae Augustae,* ed. Isaac Casaubon [1559–1614], Paris, 1603.

Castor: Agrippa Castor (2nd century CE). Christian apologist known to Eusebius and mentioned in Pseudo-Justinus, *Cohortatio ad Graecos.*

Cato Major: Marcus Porcius Cato (Cato the Censor, Cato the Elder) (234–149 BCE). Roman statesman, orator, and writer.

Catullus: Gaius Valerius Catullus (ca. 84–ca. 54 BCE). Roman poet. *Carmina. De nuptiis Pelei et Thetidis epithalamium.*

Cedrenus: Georgius Cedrenus (or Georgios Kedrenos) (fl. 11th century CE). Byzantine historian; *Annales, siue, Historiae ab exordio mundi ad Isacium Comnenum usque compendium,* Basel, [1566].

Celsus: Aulus Cornelius Celsus (1st century CE). Roman medical writer; *De re medica libri octo,* Lyon, 1566.

Celsus: Celsus (2nd century CE). Greek philosopher; *Alēthēs logos* ("The True Doctrine" or "Discourse") (lost; refuted by Origen, *Contra Celsum*).

Censorinus: Censorinus (fl. 3rd century CE). Roman grammarian; *De Die natali.*

Chaeremon: Chaeremon (1st century CE). Egyptian priest and Stoic philosopher.

Chagiga: Ḥagiga (The Festival Sacrifice). Talmudic tractate. See entry for "Talmud."

Chalcidius: Chalcidius (or Calcidius) (4th century CE). Christian exegete and commentator; *Chalcidii V. C. Timaeus de Platonis translatus. Item ejusdem in eundem commentarius,* Leiden, 1617.

Chaldee/Chaldee Paraphrast/*Chaldee* Interpreters: Cf. *Biblia sacra polyglotta,* including texts in Chaldean or Aramaic. See also entry for "Walton," p. 332.

Choerilus: Choerilus of Samo (second half of 5th century BCE). Epic poet; quoted by Flavius Josephus in *Contra Apionem*.

Chrysippus (ca. 280–207 BCE). Stoic philosopher.

Chrysostom: John Chrysostom (ca. 347–407 CE). Greek church father; *Opera Graece*, ed. Henry Savile, 8 vols., Eton, 1612.

Cicero: Marcus Tullius Cicero (106–43 BCE). Roman statesman, orator, and philosopher. *De Inventione. Pro M. Fonteio* [Fonteius, praetor in Gaul 75–73 BCE] *M. Tulli Ciceronis Oratio. Epistularum ad Atticum M. Tulli Ciceronis Libri Sedecim. Post Reditum ad Quirites. De Legibus. De Re Publica. Academica I–II. Tusculanae disputationes. De Divinatione. De Natura Deorum. De Officiis. Opera omnia quae exstant*, Hamburg, 1618.

Claudian: Claudian (Claudius Claudianus) (ca. 370–ca. 404 CE). Roman poet. *De Bello Gildonico. Omnia quae quidem extant opera*, Basel, 1534.

Cleanthes: Cleanthes (ca. 331–232 BCE). Stoic philosopher.

Clearchus: Clearchus of Soli (4th–3rd century BCE). Peripatetic Greek philosopher; fragments of his work (mentioning Aristotle) are preserved by Flavius Josephus in *Contra Apionem*.

Clemens: Clement of Rome (Clemens Romanus, St. Clement I). First Apostolic father, pope from 88 to 97 CE; *Epistula I ad Corinthios*.

Clemens Alexandrinus/Clemens: Clement of Alexandria (ca. 150–ca. 215 CE). Greek church father. *Protreptikos pros Ellenas. Stromata* (or *Strōmateis*). *Hypotyposeis*, quoted by Eusebius, *Historia. Ecclesiastica. Omnia quae quidem extant opera*, 1572.

Cleodemus. See entry for "Malchus."

Clinius the Pythagorean: Clinias the Pythagorean. Philosopher, contemporary of Plato; Saint Basil the Great reports that Clinias preferred to pay a fine rather than to swear.

Ctesias: Ctesias (b. late 5th century BCE). Greek physician and historian of Persia and India; *Persica*.

Cyprian: St. Cyprian (Caecilius Cyprianus) (200–258 CE). Theologian and bishop of Carthage. *Testimonia. Epistola ad Demetrianum. Sententiae episcoporum numero LXXXVII De haereticis baptizandis. Epistolae*, Venice, 1471. *Opera*, Cologne, 1617.

Cyril: Cyril of Alexandria (ca. 375–444 CE). Doctor of the church; *Contra impium Iulianum Libri decem*.

Damascenus. See entry for "Nicholaus Damascenus."

Demetrius: Demetrius the Chronographer (3rd century BCE). Jewish writer; fragments of his works are preserved in Eusebius, *Praeparatio Evangelica*.

Demetrius Phalereus: Demetrius Phalereus (Demetrius of Phaleron) (ca. 345–283 BCE). Greek statesman, orator, and philosopher.

Democritus: Democritus of Abdera (ca. 460–ca. 370 BCE). Greek philosopher, cofounder of classical atomism.

Dicearchus: Dicaearchus (fl. ca. 320 BCE). Greek Peripatetic philosopher.

Digesta: Digesta or *Pandecta* of Justinian. Collection of laws compiled by order of Emperor Justinian. See also entry for "Justinian."

Diocles: Diocles. Author of a Persian history mentioned by Flavius Josephus.

Diodorus Siculus: Diodorus Siculus (1st century BCE). Greek historian; *Bibliothēkē* (or *Bibliotheca Historica*).

Diogenes Laertius/Diogenes: Diogenes Laërtius (fl. 3rd century CE). Greek author especially famous for his history of Greek philosophy; *De vitis dogmatibus et apophthegmatibus clarorum philosophorum, libri X*.

Dion Cassius: Dion (Dio) Cassius (ca. 150–235 CE). Roman historian; *Romaika* (or *Historiae Romanae*).

Dion Prusaeensis: Dion (Dio) Chrysostom (Dion of Prusa, Dio Chrysostomus, Dio Prusaeus, Dio Cocceianus) (ca. 40–ca. 120 CE). Greek rhetorician and philosopher; *Orationes LXXX*, Paris, 1604.

Dionysius Halicarnassensis: Dionysius (Dionysios) of Halicarnassus (fl. ca. 20 BCE). Greek historian; *Antiquitatum Romanarum libri X*, Paris, 1546.

Dius: Dius. Hellenistic historian cited by Flavius Josephus.

Dorotheus Sidonius: Dorotheus of Sidon (1st century CE). Astrological poet.

Empedocles: Empedocles (ca. 490–430 BCE). Pre-Socratic philosopher; cited in Plutarch, *De Placitis Philosophorum*.

Ephonus: Ephorus (or Ephoros) of Cyme (ca. 400–330 BCE). Ancient Greek historian.

Epicharmus: Epicharmus (ca. 530–ca. 440 BCE). Greek poet and philosopher; fragments of his works are preserved in Diogenes Laërtius's life of Plato (see *De vitis dogmatibus et apophthegmatibus clarorum philosophorum, libri X*), in Clemens Alexandrinus, *Stromata*, and in Eusebius, *Praeparatio Evangelica*.

Epicurus: Epicurus (341–270 BCE). Ancient Greek philosopher.

Epiphanius: Epiphanius (ca. 310–403 CE). Bishop of Constantia in Cyprus; *Opera Omnia*, Paris, 1622.

Eupolemus: Eupolemus and Pseudo-Eupolemus. Jewish author; cited by Eusebius in *Praeparatio Evangelica*.

Euripides: Euripides (ca. 480–406 BCE). Ancient Greek dramatist. *Andromache. Hiketides. Ione. Hypsipyle. Aeolus.*

Eurysus: Eurysus or Eurytus (3rd century BCE). Ancient Greek philosopher; fragment preserved in Clemens Alexandrinus, *Stromata.*

Eusebius: Eusebius of Caesarea (ca. 269–d. before 341 CE). Bishop of Caesarea in Palestine. [*Chronicon*]: *Eusebii utriusque partis chronicorum canonum reliquiae Graecae, quae colligi potuerunt, antehac non editae,* in *Thesaurus temporum,* ed. Joseph Scaliger [1540-1609], Leiden, 1606. *Historia Ecclesiastica* (or *Historia Ecclesiae*). *Praeparatio Evangelica. Demonstratio Evangelica.*

Ezechiel, Tragicus Judaeus: Ezekiel the Poet or Tragedian (ca. 100 BCE). Hellenistic Jewish dramatist; fragments of his work are preserved by Eusebius.

Firmicus: Julius Firmicus Maternus (4th century CE). Christian author and astrologer; *Iulii Firmici Materni iunioris Siculi . . . ad Mavortium Lollianum Astronomicon libri VIII, per Nicolaum Prucknerum . . . ab innumeris mendis vindicati,* Basel, 1551.

Florentinus the Lawyer. Excerpts from his work are included in the *Digesta* or *Pandecta* of Justinianus. See also entry for "*Digesta.*"

Florus: Publius Annius Florus (or Lucius Annaeus Florus) (fl. 2nd century CE). Roman historian; *Rerum a Romanis gestarum libri IV* [*Epitome rerum Romanarum*], Cologne, 1605.

Gabinius: Gabinius. Roman author who wrote about Mauritania; cited by Strabo.

Galen: Galen (129–ca. 215 CE). Physician and philosopher from Greek Asia Minor. *De Sectis. De Optima Secta. De usu partium corporis humani lib. xvii. De locis adfectis libri vi. Opera quae ad nos extant omnia,* Basel, 1549. *Hippocrates Coi* [Hippocrates], *et Claudii Galeni . . . opera,* ed. René Chartier, Paris, 1679.

Gellius: Aulus Gellius (fl. 2nd century CE). Latin rhetorician; *Noctes Atticae.*

Gemara. See entry for "Talmud."

Germanicus: Germanicus Julius Caesar (15 BCE–19 CE). *Germanicus Caesar cum commentariis incerti auct. Lat.,* in *Astronomica veterum scripta isagogica, Graeca & Latina,* 1589.

Haestiaeus/Hestiaeus: Hestiaios (fl. before 90 CE). Historian mentioned by Flavius Josephus.

Hagiography: Hagiographa. One of the three groups of books in the Hebrew bible, the other two being the Law and the Prophets. Grotius is referring to targums (see entry for "Targum") on individual books of the Hagiographa.

Halicarnassensis. See entry for "Dionysius Halicarnassensis."

"He [Aelius Lampridius] that wrote the life of this Emperor." Grotius used this epithet to refer to Aelius Lampridius, who probably lived under Emperor Constantine, 409–411 CE. The "Emperor" alluded to by Grotius in the same phrase is Severus Alexander, Roman emperor, 222–35 CE. Lampridius's work was included in *Scriptores Historiae Augustae,* edited by Isaac Casaubon [1559–1614], Paris, 1603.

Hecataeus: Hecataeus of Miletus (6th century BCE). Greek geographer and historian.

Hecataeus Abderita: Hecataeus of Abdera (fl. ca. 290 BCE). Greek writer, living in Egypt, who wrote about the Jews.

Hellanicus: Hellanicus of Lesbos (ca. 480–ca. 395 BCE). Greek historian.

Heraclides Ponticus: Heraclides (Heracleides) Ponticus (ca. 390–died after 322 BCE). Greek philosopher and astronomer, pupil of Plato; lost work concerning the dead mentioned by Diogenes Laërtius.

Heraclitus: Heraclitus of Ephesus (or Heracleitus) (ca. 540–ca. 480 BCE). Pre-Socratic Greek philosopher.

Hermippus: Hermippus of Smyrna (or Hermippus the Callimachian) (ca. 200 BCE). Peripatetic Greek philosopher; cited by Flavius Josephus, *Contra Apionem.*

Herodotus: Herodotus (ca. 484–ca. 430–420 BCE). Greek historian. *Euterpe. Thalia. Melpomene. Terpsichore. Herodoti Halicarnassei Historiarum libri IX,* ed. Gottfried Jungermann, Frankfurt, 1608.

Hesiod: Hesiod (or Hesiodos, Hesiodus) (fl. ca. 700 BCE). *Erga kaí Hemérai* (or *Opera et Dies). Theogonia.*

Hesychius: Hesychius of Alexandria (5th century CE). Greek lexicographer. *Lexicon.*

Hierocles: Hierocles of Alexandria (fl. ca. 430 CE). Egyptian Neoplatonist philosopher; *Avrea Pythagoreorvm carmina: Latinè conuersa, multisqve in locis emendata, illustratáque adnotationibus; quibus etiam Hieroclis interpretationi non parum lucis adfertur,* edited by Théodore Marcile [1548–1617], Paris, 1585.

Hieronym: Hieronymus. An Egyptian who wrote an account of the Phoenician foundations, based on the annals of the city of Tyre; mentioned by Flavius Josephus.

Hieronymus: St. Jerome (or Eusebius Sophronius Hieronymus) (ca. 340–420 CE). Latin church father of vast erudition, translator of the Bible. *Contra Vigilantium Liber Unus. Apologia Adversus Libros Rufini. Quaestiones Hebrai-*

cae in libro Geneseos. Commentariorum In Danielem Prophetam Liber Unus. Adversus Oceanum. Chronicon. Epistola ad Pammachium. Opera omnia, Paris, 1624. *Eusebii Pamphili* [Eusebius] . . . *chronicorum canonum omnimodae historiae libri duo, interprete Hieronymo,* ed. Joseph Scaliger, Leiden, 1606.

Hilary: St. Hilary (Hilarius Pictaviensis) (ca. 315–ca. 367 CE). Bishop of Poitiers and theologian. *De Trinitate Libri Duodecim. Opera,* Paris, 1693.

Hillanicus: Hellanicus of Lesbos (ca. 480–ca. 395 BCE). Greek historian.

Hirom: Hiram (r. 969–936 BCE). King of Tyre, Phoenicia.

Homer: Homer (fl. 9th or 8th century BCE). Greek poet. *Ilias. Odyssea.*

Horace: Quintus Horatius Flaccus (65–8 BCE). Roman poet; *Satirae.*

Hostanes (or Ostanes). Ancient *mage* (magician and sage) mentioned by Minucius Felix in his *Octavius.*

Hypsicrates: Hypsicrates (fl. under Julius Caesar). Historian mentioned by Strabo, *Geōgraphiká.*

Hystaspes: Hystaspes (or Vishtāspa) (fl. 7th and 6th centuries BCE). Local ruler and patron of the ancient Persian prophet Zoroaster.

Ilmedenu. See entry for "Tanchuma/Ilmedenu."

Irenaeus: St. Irenaeus (ca. 120–ca. 200 CE). Church father and bishop of Lyon. *Aduersus Valentini, & similium gnosticorum haereses, libri quinque,* Cologne, 1596. *Epistola ad Victorem.*

Jakumnus on the Pentateuch. Possibly a reference to the Targum of Onkelos. See entry "Onkelos."

Jamblicus: Jamblichus of Chalcis (3rd–4th century CE). Neoplatonic philosopher. *De mysteriis Aegyptiorum, Chaldaeorum, Assyriorum,* Venice, 1497. *De vita Pythagorae et Protrepticae orationes ad Philosophiam,* Franeker, 1598.

Jerusalem Gemara/Jerusalem Talmud. See entry for "Talmud."

Jerusalem Targum. More correctly, a group of targums in Palestinian Aramaic. See also entry for "Targum."

John. Talmudic Rabbi Johanan in whose name there are discussions about Bar Kokhba, leader of a Jewish revolt against Rome (132–135 CE). See also entry for "Talmud."

Joma/Jomach: Yoma. Talmudic tractate on the observance of Yom Kippur. See also entry for "Talmud."

Jonathan/Jonathan R[abbi]: Jonathan ben Uzziel. A pupil of Hillel, the leading 1st century BCE–1st century CE rabbinic sage associated with the development of the Mishna and the Talmud; Jonathan ben Uzziel is credited as the author of a targum to the prophets. See also entry for "Targum."

Josephus: Flavius Josephus (37/38–100 CE). Jewish scholar and historian. *Bellum Judaicum. Antiquitates Judaicae. Contra Apionem. Flauij Iosephi Antiquitatum Iudaicorum libri xx: De bello Iudaico libri vij; Contra Apionem libri ij; De imperio rationis siue De Machabaeis liber unus à D. Erasmo* [Desiderius Erasmus, 1469–1536, Dutch humanist and scholar] *recognitus,* Basel, 1540. *Flavii Josephi Opera,* Basel, 1544.

Josephus Caecus: Josephus the Blind (Josephus the One-Eyed or Josephus Luscus), credited as the author of targums on books of the Hagiographa. See entries for *"Hagiography"* and "Targum."

Josue Rabbi: Joshua ben Hananiah (1st–2nd century CE). Mishnaic Rabbi.

Juba: Juba II (ca. 50 BCE–24 CE). King of Numidia and Mauretania who wrote in Greek on various subjects, including history, geography, and grammar.

Julian: Flavius Claudius Julianus (known as Julian the Apostate) (331/332–362 CE). Roman emperor; *Opera, quae reperiri potuerunt, omnia,* Paris, 1630.

Justin: Justin (or Marcus Junianus Justinus) (3rd century CE). Latin historian; *Epitoma Historiarum Philippicarum Pompei Trogi* [Pompeius Trogus].

Justin Martyr/Justin: Justin Martyr (ca. 100–ca. 165 CE). Greek church father. *Opera quae vndequaque inueniri potuerunt; Gr. textus correctus,* Paris, 1615. *Apologia prima pro Christianis. Apologia secunda. Dialogus cum Tryphone Judaeo. Cohortatio ad Graecos* (Pseudo-Justinus). *De monarchia liber* (Pseudo-Justinus). *Quaestiones et Responsiones ad Orthodoxos* (Pseudo-Justinus).

Justinian: Justinian (or Flavius Justinianus) (483–565 CE). Byzantine emperor noted especially for his work as a codifier and legislator. *Digesta* or *Pandecta. Codex Justinianus.*

Juvenal: Decimus Junius Juvenalis (ca. 55–ca. 127 CE). Roman satiric poet; *Satirae.*

Kelmboth: Ketubot (Marriage Entitlements). Talmudic tractate. See also entry for "Talmud."

L. Falsi Nominis: Papinian (Aemilius Papinianus) (140–212 CE). Roman jurist; book 15 of the *Responsa* (19 books).

Labeus: Cornelius Labeo (fl. 3rd century CE). Cited in Macrobius and Augustine.

Lactantius: Lucius Caecilius Firmianus Lactantius (ca. 240–ca. 325 CE). Christian apologist. *Divinarum Institutionum, Libri VII. Epitome Divinarum Institutionum.*

Laetus: Laetus (2nd century BCE). Historian of Phoenicia mentioned by Tatian, *Oratio ad Graecos*.

Linus: Linus (or Linos). Ancient Greek mythological figure, the personification of lamentation.

Livy: Titus Livius (59/64 BCE–17 CE). Roman historian. Author of a massive history of Rome, *Ab Urbe Condita*, from its founding to Livy's own time; *Titi Liuij Patauani Romanae historiae principis, libri omnes: quotquot ad nostram aetatem peruenerunt*, London, 1589.

Longinus: Longinus (or Dionysius Longinus, Pseudo-Longinus) (fl. 1st century CE). Greek literary critic; *Peri Hypsous*.

Lucan: Marcus Annaeus Lucanus (39–65 CE). Roman poet; *Pharsalia* (or *Bellum civile*).

Lucian: Lucianus of Samosata (ca. 125–ca. 180 CE). Greek writer. *Alexander. De Amoribus. De Dea Syria. Pseudologistes. Philopatris* (spurious work formerly attributed to Lucian).

Lucretius: Titus Lucretius Carus (fl. 1st century BCE). Roman poet and philosopher; *De rerum natura*.

Lycophron: Lycophron of Chalcis (fl. 3rd century BCE). Greek poet; *Alexandra, poema obscurum Cum Isacii Tzetzis* [Isaac Tzetzes, d. 1138] *commentariis*, Geneva, 1601.

Lysimachus: Lysumachus (ca. 2nd century BCE–1st century CE). Author of *Aegyptiaca*, a lost work mentioned by Flavius Josephus in *Contra Apionem*.

Lysis the Pythagorean: Lysis of Tarentum (fl. ca. 400 BCE). Pythagorean ancient Greek philosopher.

Macrobius: Ambrosius Theodosius Macrobius (fl. 400 CE). Roman scholar and Neoplatonist philosopher. *Saturnalia. Opera*, Leiden, 1628.

Malchus: Malchus or Cleodemus the Prophet (2nd century BCE). Hellenistic author of a lost Greek history of the Jews mentioned by Flavius Josephus in *Antiquitates Judaicae*.

Manethos/Manetho/Manethon: Manethos (or Manetho, Manethon) (fl. ca. 300 BCE). Egyptian priest and historian, author of a history of Egypt in Greek.

Marcian: Marcian (Marcianus) (396–457 CE). Eastern Roman emperor.

Marcus Antoninus: Marcus Aurelius Antoninus (Caesar Marcus Aurelius Antoninus Augustus) (121–180 CE). Roman emperor; *De rebus suis . . . libri XII* (Meditations).

Martial: Marcus Valerius Martialis (ca. 38–ca. 103 CE). Latin poet; *Epigrammata.*

Masoreth: Masorah. System of critical notes fixing the orthography, pronunciation, cantillation, and, in general, the correct textual tradition of the biblical texts.

Maximus Tyrius: Cassius Maximus Tyrius (or Maximus of Tyre) (2nd century CE). Greek rhetorician and philosopher; *Dissertationes.*

Megasthenes: Megasthenes (ca. 350–ca. 290 BCE). Greek historian and diplomat, author of a work on ancient India; *Indica.*

Mela: Pomponius Mela (fl. ca. 43 CE). Roman geographer; *Pomponii Melae de orbis situ, libri III. et C. Iulii Solini* [Gaius Julius Solinus], *Polyhistor. Quorum ille descriptionem singularum Orbis terreni partium atque regionum,* Basel, 1576.

Menander: Menander (ca. 342–ca. 292 BCE). Greek dramatist; quoted by Stobaeus.

Menander, Pergamenus: Menander of Pergamus. Historian of Phoenicia mentioned by Tatian, *Oratio ad Graecos,* and Clement of Alexandria, *Stromata.*

Menander, the Ephesian: Menander of Ephesus. Historian mentioned by Flavius Josephus.

Mendesus, Ptolomaeus. See entry for "Ptolemy Mendesius."

Methodius: Methodius of Olympus (d. 311 CE). Christian apologist; quoted by Epiphanius.

Metrodorus: Metrodorus of Chios (4th century BCE). Pre-Socratic philosopher, follower of Democritus.

Mimus. See entry for "Syrus the Mimick."

Minutius: Minucius Felix (fl. between 160 and 300 CE). Church father; *Octavius.*

Mishna (Mishnah). Postbiblical collection and codification of originally oral Jewish laws.

Mnaseas: Mnaseas of Patrae (3rd century BCE). Greek historian; mentioned by Flavius Josephus in *Antiquitates Judaicae.*

Modestinus: Herennius Modestinus (fl. ca. 250 BCE). Roman jurist; excerpts from his work are included in *Digesta* or *Pandecta* of Justinian. See also entries for *"Digesta"* and "Justinian."

Mochus: Mochus. Historian of Phoenicia mentioned by Athenaeus.

Molo: Molo of Rhodes. Believed to be the same person as Apollonius. See entry for "Apollonius."

Nazianzen: Gregory of Nazianzus (ca. 330–ca. 389 CE). Byzantine theologian. *Contra Julianum imperatorem. Opera,* Paris, 1630.

Nicholaus Damascenus: Nicholas of Damascus (or Nicolaus of Damascus) (1st century BCE). Greek historian and philosopher. *Historia Universalis* (cited by Flavius Josephus). Works in *Polybii, Diodori Siculi, Nicolai Damasceni, Dionysii Halicar. Appiani Alexand. Dionis et Ioannis Antiocheni excerpta ex collectaneis Constantini Augusti Porphyrogenetae* [Constantine VII Porphyrogenitus, 905–59], *Henricus Valesius* [Henri de Valois, 1603–76] *nunc primum Graecè edidit, Latinè vertit, notisque ilustrauit,* Paris, 1634.

Nida: Nidda (Menstruant). Talmudic tractate on the laws of family purity. See also entry for "Talmud."

Numenius: Numenius of Apamea (fl. late 2nd century CE). Greek philosopher.

Onkelos: Onkelos. Author of the so-called Targum of Onkelos on the Pentateuch, possibly the earliest targum. See also entry for "Targum."

Oppianus: Oppian of Corycus (or Anabarzus) (fl. ca. 161–180 CE). Poet; *Halieutica* (or *De Piscatu Libri V*).

Origen: Origen (ca. 185–ca. 254 CE). Greek church father. *Contra Celsum. Commentarii in Genesim. Homiliae in Ezechielem. Commentaria in Evangelium secundum Matthaeum. Philocalia* (anthology compiled by Basil the Great and Gregory of Nazianzus).

Orosius: Paulus Orosius (fl. 414–417 CE). Historian and theologian, author of the first world history written by a Christian; *Aduersus paganos historiarum libri septem,* Mainz, 1615.

Orpheus: Orpheus. Ancient Greek mythological hero, mythic founder of a religious sect or school first attested in the 6th century BCE; the so-called Orphic Poems or Orphic Hymns are named after him. *Argonautica.* "Hymn to Night."

Orphick verses. See entry for "Orpheus."

Ovid: Publius Ovidius Naso (43 BCE–17 CE). Roman poet. *Amores. Fasti. Metamorphoses. Phaenomena* (lost work).

Parmenides: Parmenides (early 5th century BCE). Pre-Socratic Greek philosopher; cited in *Divini Platonis opera omnia quae exstant,* Frankfurt, 1602. See also the standard collection of pre-Socratic texts, H. Diels and W. Kranz, eds., *Die Fragmente der Vorsokratiker,* 6th ed., 3 vols. (Berlin: Weidmann, 1951–52).

Paul: Julius Paulus (fl. 200 CE). Roman jurist; *Libri quinque sententiarum.*

Pausanias/Pausanius: Pausanias (2nd century CE). Greek traveler and geographer; *Ellados periēgēsis* (or *Graeciae descriptio accurata*).

Pereck Cheleck/c. Helech: Pereck (chapter) "Chelek." Chapter 11 in the Talmudic tractate *Sanhedrin*.

Persius: Persius (Aulus Persius Flaccus) (34–62 CE). Roman Stoic poet; *Satirae*.

Petronius: Gaius Petronius Arbiter (Titus Petronius Niger) (d. 66 CE). *Satyricon* (*T. Petronii Arbitri satyricum notae, castigationes, emendationes, et variae lectiones clarissimorum . . . virorum*, Frankfurt, 1629).

Pherecydes: Pherecydes of Syros (fl. ca. 550 BCE). Greek pre-Socratic philosopher and cosmogonist.

Philiasius. See entry for "Timon of Phlius."

Philo/Philo the Jew: Philo Judaeus (or Philo of Alexandria) (ca. 10 BCE–ca. 50 CE). Jewish philosopher. *De aeternitate mundi. De agricultura. De Cherubim. De confusione linguarum. De vita contemplativa. Quod deterius potiori insidiari soleat. In Flaccum. De fuga et inventione. Quis rerum divinarum heres sit. Legatio ad Gaium. Legum allegoriae. De vita Mosis. De opificio mundi. De sacrificiis Abelis et Caini. De somniis.* "De Circumcisione" in *De Specialibus Legibus. De Monarchia. Philonis Iudaei opera exegetica in libros Mosis, de mundo opificio, historicos & legales . . . Accessere Philonis sex opuscula; Gr. & Lat. in lucem emissa*, Geneva, 1613. *Omnia quae extant opera*, Paris, 1640.

Philo Biblius: Philo of Byblos (fl. ca. 100 CE). Author of a Phoenician history extensively cited by Eusebius in his *Praeparatio Evangelica*.

Philochorus: Philochorus (3rd century BCE). Greek historian.

Philolaus: Philolaus (fl. ca. 475 BCE). Pythagorean philosopher.

Philostorgius: Philostorgius (368–ca. 433 CE). Byzantine historian.

Philostratus: Philostratus the Athenian (or Flavius Philostratus) (170–ca. 245 CE). Greek biographer and neo-Pythagorean philosopher. *Opera quae extant*, Paris, 1608. *Vita Apollonii*.

Phlegon Trallianus: Phlegon of Tralles (2nd century CE). Greek writer. *De Rebus mirabilibus liber* and *De longaeuis libellus*, in *Historiarum mirabilium auctores Graeci/Iohannes Meursius* [Johannes van Meurs, 1579–1639] *recensuit*, Leiden, 1622. *Olympiades* (fragments quoted by Eusebius and St. Jerome).

Plato (428/427–348/347 BCE). Ancient Greek philosopher. *Crito. Phaedo. Politicus. Symposium. Alcibiades. Gorgias. Respublica. Timaeus. Critias. Leges. Epistulae.*

Plautus: Titus Maccius Plautus (ca. 254–ca. 184 BCE). Roman dramatist; *Poenulus*.

Pliny: Pliny the Elder (or Gaius Plinius Secundus) (23–79 CE). Roman scholar; *Naturalis Historia* (*Historia mundi*, Basel, 1530).

Pliny the Younger: Pliny the Younger (Gaius Plinius Caecilius Secundus) (61/62–ca. 113 CE). Roman author; *Epistolarum libri X. Eiusdem Panegyricus Traiano* [Trajan, emperor of Rome, 53–117] *dictus*, Geneva, 1625.

Plotinus: Plotinus (205–70 CE). Ancient philosopher, founder of Neoplatonism; *Enneades*.

Plutarch: Plutarch of Chaeronea (46–d. after 119 CE). Greek-born philosopher and biographer. *Theseus et Romulus. Solon et Publicola. Themistocles et Camillus. Phocion et Cato minor. Dion et Brutus. Alexander. Demetrius et Antonius. Pyrrhus et Marius. Lycurgus et Numa. Septem sapientium convivium* (*Symposion hepta sophōn*). *De superstitione. Apophthegmata Laconica. De Iside et Osiride. De sera numinis vindicta. De Placitis Philosophorum. De Sollertia Animalium. De animae procreatione in Timaeo. Epitome libri de animae procreatione in Timaeo. Omnia quae exstant opera*, Paris, 1624.

Polemon: Polemon (2nd century BCE). Ancient Greek philosopher.

Polybius: Polybius (ca. 200–ca. 118 BCE). Greek historian and statesman; *Historiae*.

Polychronius: Polychronius (fl. first half of the 5th century CE). Bishop of Apamea.

Porphyry: Porphyry (ca. 232–ca. 304 CE). Neoplatonist philosopher. *De Nympharum Antro. Vita Pythagorae. De abstinentia ab esu animalium. De philosophia ex Oraculis haurienda* (fragments). *Ad Anebon* (fragments).

Procopius: Procopius (ca. 490–507 CE). Byzantine historian; *Historiarum sui temporis libri VIII*.

Ptolemaeus/Ptolomaeus/Ptolemy: Ptolemy (or Claudius Ptolemaeus) (ca. 100–ca. 170 CE). Egyptian mathematician, astronomer, and geographer. *Geographiae libri octo Graeco-Latini*, Frankfurt, 1605. [*Almagest*]: *Kl. Ptolemaiou Megalēs syntaxeōs Bibl. 13. . . . Claudii Ptolemaei Magnae constructionis, id est Perfectae coelestium motuum pertractationis, Lib. XIII*, Basel, 1538. [*Quadripartitum*]: *De praedictionibus Astronomicis cui titulum fecerunt Quadripartitum, Graece et Latine libri IIII*, Basel, 1553.

Ptolemy V Epiphanes (ca. 210–180 BCE). Macedonian king of Egypt.

Ptolemy Mendesius/Mendesus: Ptolomaeus (Ptolemy of Mendes in Egypt). Egyptian priest.

Pythagoras: Pythagoras (ca. 580–ca. 500 BCE). Ancient Greek philosopher and mathematician.

Quintilian: Quintilian (Marcus Fabius Quintilianus) (35–d. after 96 CE). Roman rhetorician; *De institutione oratoria.*

Roch Hasschana: Rosh Hashana. Talmudic tractate on the observance of Rosh Hashana. See also entry for "Talmud."

Ruffinus: Tyrannius Rufinus (ca. 345–410/411 CE). Roman priest, theologian, and translator of Greek works into Latin; *Autores historiae ecclesiasticae. Eusebij . . . libri ix. Ruffino interprete. Ruffini presbyteri Aquileiensis, libri duo,* Basel, 1528.

Rutilius: Claudius Rutilius Namatianus (5th century CE). Roman poet; *Itinerarium.*

Sabbathoth: Shabbat. Talmudic tractate on Sabbath observance. See also entry for "Talmud."

Sallust: Sallustius Neoplatonist (4th century CE). Philosopher; *De diis et mundo, Leo Allatius* [Leone Allacci, 1586–1669] *nunc primus e tenebris eruit et Latine vertit,* ed. Gabriel Naudé [1600–1653], Leiden, 1639.

Salust: Sallust (or Gaius Sallustius Crispus) (ca. 86–35/34 BCE). Roman historian. *Bellum Catilinae. Bellum Iugurthinum.*

Salvian: Salvian (Salvianus) (ca. 400–ca. 480 CE). Christian writer; *De gubernatione dei: & de iusto praesentique eius iudicio libri VIII,* 2d ed., Paris, 1608.

Sanchuniathon: Sanchuniathon (or Sanchoniathon, Sanchoniatho). Pre-Hellenistic Phoenician priest and historian; some fragments of Sanchuniathon's writings were preserved and translated into Greek by Philo of Byblos, ca. 100 BCE, whose work was in turn excerpted by Eusebius in his *Praeparatio Evangelica.*

Sardanapalus' Epitaph. According to Diodorus Siculus (who cited Sardanapalus's Epitaph in the *Bibliotheca Historica*), Sardanapalus (or Sardanapallus) was the last king of Assyria.

Saxo Grammaticus: Saxo Grammaticus (fl. 12th century–early 13th century CE). Danish historian; *Danorum historiae libri XVI.* [*Gesta Danorum*], Basel, 1534.

"Scholiast of Apollonius": Jeremias Hölzlin (d. 1641 CE). Editor and commentator of Apollonius's *Argonauta; Apollonii Rhodii Argonauticorum libri IV ab Jeremia Hoelzlino in Latinem conversi; commentario & notis illustrati,* Leiden, 1641.

Seneca: Seneca (Lucius Annaeus Seneca) (ca. 4 BCE–65 CE). Roman Stoic philosopher and statesman. *De ira. De Consolatione ad Marciam. De Beneficiis. Epistolae. L. Annaei Senecae . . . quae extant opera,* Paris, 1607. *Naturales Quaestiones. Oedipus.*

Seneca the Father: Seneca the Elder (ca. 55 BCE–39 CE). Roman rhetorician; *Controversiae.*

Servius: Maurus Servius Honoratus (fl. end of the 4th century CE). Roman grammarian and commentator on Virgil; *P. Virgilii Maronis Bucolicorum Eclogae X., Georgicorum Libri IV., Aeneidos Libri XII., et in ea Mauri Servii Honorati* [Maurus Servius Honoratus] *Grammatici commentarii,* Geneva, 1610.

Seventy: *Septuagint (LXX)* (3rd–2nd century BCE). Greek translation of the Old Testament from the original Hebrew.

Sextus Rufus: Sextus Rufus (or Rufus Festus, Rufius Festus) (4th century CE). Roman author; *Breviarium rerum gestarum populi Romani.*

Schebnoth/Shebnoth: Shavuot. Talmudic tractate on oaths. See also entry for "Talmud."

Siloh, R[abbi]. Reference to the school of R. Shila in *Sanhedrin.* See entry "Talmud/Gemara."

Simplicius: Simplicius of Cilicia (ca. 490–ca. 560 CE). Neoplatonist philosopher; *Simplicii Commentaria in tres libros Aristotelis de anima Alexandri Aphrodisiei commentaria in librum de sensu et sensibili. Michaelis Ephesii annotationes* [in *Parva naturalia*], Venice, 1527.

Socrates: Socrates (ca. 470–399 BCE). Ancient Greek philosopher.

Solinus: Gaius Julius Solinus (3rd century CE). Latin grammarian and polyhistor. *Collectanea rerum memorabilium. Pomponii Melae* [Pomponius Mela] *de orbis situ, libri III. et C. Iulii Solini, Polyhistor; Quorum ille descriptionem singularum Orbis terreni partium atque regionum,* Basel, 1576. *Plinianae exercitationes in Caii Iulii Solini Polyhistoria: Item Caii Iulii Solini Polyhistor ex veteribus libris emendatus,* ed. Claude de Saumaise [or Claudius Salmasius, 1588–1653], Paris, 1629.

Song of Solomon. The Song of Songs (Bible).

Sopater: Sopater of Apamea (4th century CE). Sophist and Neoplatonist philosopher; *Quaestiones de comp[on]endis declamationibus in causis praecipuae judicialibus,* in *Rhetores,* Venice, 1508.

Sophocles: Sophocles (ca. 496–406 BCE). Greek dramatist. *Ajax. Antigone. Oedipus Coloneus.*

Sota: Sota (The Wayward Wife). Talmudic tractate on wives suspected of adultery. See also entry for "Talmud."

Statius: Publius Papinius Statius (45–96 CE). Roman poet. *Thebais. Opera,* Paris, 1600.

Stobaeus: Joannes Stobaeus (5th century CE). Scholar famous for his compilation of extracts from Greek authors. *Sententiae: ex thesauris Graecorum delectae . . . & in sermones siue locos communes digestae,* Zürich, 1543. *Sententiae: ex thesauris Graecorum delectae . . . Huic editioni accesserunt . . . eclogarum physicarum et ethicarum libri duo,* Geneva, 1609. *Dicta poetarum quae apud Io. Stobaeum exstant, Emendata et Latino carmine reddita ab Hugone Grotio* [Hugo Grotius]; *Accesserunt Plutarchi et Basilii Magni de usu Graecorum poetarum libelli,* Paris, 1623.

Strabo: Strabo (63/64 BCE–ca. 23 CE). Greek geographer and historian; *Geōgraphiká;* Strabo, *Rerum geographicarum libri XVII,* Paris, 1620.

Succha: Sukka (Tabernacles). Talmudic tractate on the observance of Sukkoth (a Jewish autumn festival). See also entry for "Talmud."

Suetonius: Gaius Suetonius Tranquillus (69–d. after 122 CE). Roman historian; *De Vita Caesarum.*

Sulpitius: Sulpicius Severus (ca. 363–ca. 420 CE). Ecclesiastical writer and Christian ascetic; *Sacrae Historiae libri II,* Hanau, 1602.

Symmachus: Symmachus (fl. end of 2nd to beginning of 3rd century CE). Author of a Greek translation of the Hebrew bible.

Synesius: Synesius of Cyrene (d. ca. 414 CE). Bishop and Neoplatonist philosopher.

Syrus the Mimick: Publilius Syrus (1st century BCE). Latin mime writer; *Sententiae* in *Florilegium ethico-politicum nunquam antehac editum,* Frankfurt, 1610.

Taanith/Thaanith: Ta'anit (Public Fasts). Talmudic tractate. See also entry for "Talmud."

Tacitus: Publius Cornelius Tacitus (56–ca. 120 CE). Roman historian and senator. *Historiae. Annales. De moribus et populis Germanorum liber. Agricola.*

Talmud/Talmudists/Gemara. The name "Talmud" refers to two compilations of laws, teachings, and commentaries central to the Jewish religious tradition. These collections were compiled by Jewish scholars between the third and the fifth centuries CE and are known as the Jerusalem (or Palestinian) Talmud (also called Talmud Yerushalmi) and the Babylonian Talmud (or Talmud Bavli).

The Talmud can be regarded as comprising both the Mishna and the Gemara, or as referring only to the Gemara. The Mishna is the first rabbinic compilation of law (ca. 200 CE). Grotius tends to use the term "Gemara" as synonymous with "Talmud."

Talmud/Gemara, "Concerning the Council/s": *Sanhedrin* (The Court). Talmudic tractate. See also main entry for "Talmud."

Talmud, "Concerning Instructions": *Horayot.* Talmudic tractate on decisions. See also main entry for "Talmud."

Talmud, "Concerning the Sabbath": *Shabbat.* Talmudic tractate on Sabbath observance. See also main entry for "Talmud."

Talmud, "Concerning Weights": *Shekalim* (or *Sheqalim*). Talmudic tractate on the annual Temple tax. See also main entry for "Talmud."

Tanchuma/Ilmedenu: Tanḥuma or Yelammedenu. Collection of Pentateuch aggadot, that is, edifying interpretations and illustrations of the nonlegal parts of the Bible.

Targum. Translation or paraphrase of the Hebrew Bible or parts of it into Aramaic.

Tatian: Tatian (2nd century CE). Greek church father; *Oratio ad Graecos.*

Terence: Terence (Publius Terentius Afer) (ca. 195–ca. 159 BCE). Roman dramatist. *Hecyra. Heauton timoroumenos. Eunuchus. Phormio.*

Tertullian: Tertullian (ca. 155–ca. 240 CE). Latin church father. *Apologeticus adversus gentes pro Christianis. De Spectaculis. De Praescriptionibus Adversus Haereticos. Adversus Marcionem. Adversus Judaeos. De Anima. De Virginibus Velandis. De Exhortatione Castitatis. De Monogamia. De Baptismo et de Poenitentia.*

Thales: Thales of Miletus (fl. ca. 585 BCE). Pre-Socratic philosopher.

Thallus: Thallus (possibly early 2nd century CE). Historian who wrote in Greek; mentioned in *Cohortatio ad Graecos* (Pseudo-Justinus).

Theocritus: Theocritus (ca. 300–d. after 260 BCE). Greek poet; *Eidyllia.*

Theodoret: Theodoret of Cyrrhus (ca. 393–ca. 458/466 CE). Syrian theologian and bishop. *Therapeutica . . . Graecarum affectionum curatio,* Heidelberg, 1592. *Quaestiones in Octateuchum. Historia ecclesiastica. Sermones.*

Theodorus: Theodotus (fl. before 190 BCE). Hellenistic Jew; fragments of his poem on the Jews are preserved by Eusebius, *Praeparatio Evangelica.*

Theodotion: Theodotion (fl. 2nd century CE). Author of a Greek translation of the Old Testament.

Theognis: Theognis of Megara (fl. 6th century BCE). Ancient Greek poet.

Theophilus Antiochenus: Theophilus of Antioch (d. 180 CE). Greek church father; *Libri tres ad Autolycum.*

Theophrastus: Theophrastus (ca. 372–ca. 287 BCE). Greek philosopher and pupil of Aristotle.

Theopompus: Theopompus of Chios (378/377–ca. 320 BCE). Greek historian; *Philippica.*

Thucydides: Thucydides (ca. 460–ca. 404 BCE). Greek historian; *De Bello Peloponnesiaco libri VIII,* Frankfurt, 1594.

Tiberius: Tiberius (Tiberius Caesar Augustus) (42 BCE–37 CE). Roman emperor; epistle cited by Tacitus, *Annales.*

Tibullus: Albius Tibullus (ca. 54–19 BCE). Latin poet.

Timon: Timon of Phlius (ca. 320–ca. 230 BCE). Greek philosopher, disciple of Pyrrho of Elis; cited by Diogenes Laërtius, Clement of Alexandria, Eusebius, and Theodoret.

Trogus: Gnaeus Pompeius Trogus (1st century BCE). Roman historian; *Historiae Philippicae;* lost; excerpts preserved in Marcus Junianus Justinus (Roman historian, 3rd century CE), *Epitome.*

Tully. See entry for "Cicero."

Ulpianus: Ulpian (Domitius Ulpianus) (d. 228 CE). Roman jurist and imperial official.

Valerius Maximus: Valerius Maximus (fl. ca. 30 CE). Roman historian; *Factorum et dictorum memorabilium libri ix.*

Varro: Marcus Terentius Varro (116–27 BCE). Roman author. *De re rustica. De lingua latina.*

Vegetius: Flavius Vegetius Renatus (fl. 4th century CE). Roman author of a very influential military treatise; *De Re Militari,* Leiden, 1607.

Verrius Flaccus: Marcus Verrius Flaccus (fl. 1st century BCE). Roman scholar and grammarian.

Victor Uticensis: Victor of Vita (Victor Vitensis) (5th century CE). African Bishop; *Historia persecutionis Vandalorum,* in Bildius (B.) Rhenanus, *Auctores Historiae Ecclesiasticae,* 1535.

Virgil: Publius Vergilius (Virgilius) Maro (70–19 BCE). Roman poet. *Eclogae. Georgicae. Aeneis.*

Vitruvius: Vitruvius (fl. 1st century BCE). Roman architect and engineer; *De architectura.*

"Writers of the Life of Atticus": Cornelius Nepos (ca. 110–ca. 24 BCE). *De viris illustribus.*

Xenocrates: Xenocrates (d. 314 BCE). Greek philosopher, pupil of Plato.

Xenophon: Xenophon (ca. 430–ca. 350 BCE). Greek historian. *Memorabilia. Xenophontis . . . quae exstant opera,* Paris, 1625.

Zeno: Zeno of Citium (ca. 335–263 BCE). Stoic philosopher; only fragments of his works have survived.

Zoroaster: Zoroaster (Zarathushtra, or Zarathustra) (ca. 628–ca. 551 BCE). Persian prophet and religious reformer; *Zoroastri oracula CCCXX,* in *Hermetis Trismegisti* [Hermes Trismegistos] *libelli, & fragmenta,* Venice, 1593.

Medieval and Early Modern Authors and Works

Abarbanel: Isaac Abarbanel (Abrabanel, Abravanel), (1437–1508). Jewish biblical commentator and theologian born in Lisbon. *Leonis Hebraei* [Leo Hebraeus; see entry for "Gerson"] . . . *de amore dialogi tres,* Venice, 1564. *D. Isaaci Abrabanielis & r. Mosis Alschechi comment. in Esaiae prophetiam 30. cum additamento eorum quae r. Simeon è veteris dictis collegit,* Basel, 1631.

Abba: Rabbi Abba, cited in *Ecka Rabbathi.* See entry for *"Echad Rabbathi."*

Abdias: Abdias of Babylon (possibly 6th century). Apocryphal writer; *De historia certaminis Apostolici: libri X,* Paris, 1571.

Abenesdra: Abraham ben Meir ibn Ezra (ca. 1092–1167). Spanish Jewish biblical exegete, man of letters, and astronomer; *Biblia Sacra Hebraica & Chaldaica: cum Masora, quae critica Hebraeorum sacra est, magna & parva, ac selectisissimis Hebraeorum interpretum co[m]mentariis, Rabbi Salomonis Jarchi, R. Abrahami Aben Esrae . . . fido & labore indefesso Johannis Buxtorfi* [Johann Buxtorf (1564–1629)], Basel, 1618–19.

Abraham Salmanticensis: Abraham ben Samuel Zacuto (ca. 1450–ca. 1510). Born in Salamanca; Jewish astronomer, mathematician, and historian. *Almanach Perpetuum. Sefer Hayuhasin* (a compendium of Jewish history from the Creation to 1500).

Acosta: Joseph (José) de Acosta (1540–1600). Spanish Jesuit; *De natura novi orbis libri duo: et de promulgatione evangelii apud barbaros; siue, de procuranda indorum salute, libri sex,* Cologne, 1596.

Adam Bremensis: Adamus Bremensis (Adam of Bremen) (1068–1081). German historian and geographer; *Historia Ecclesiastica,* Leiden, 1595.

Aeneas Gazaeus/Aeneas Gaza: Aeneas of Gaza (5th–6th century CE). Christian Neoplatonist philosopher; *Theophrastus, sive de animarum immortalitate, et corporum resurrectione dialogus, è Graeco in sermonem Latinum conuersus,* Zürich, 1559.

Alcoran: Qur'ān (Koran); cf. *Machumetis . . . eiusque successorum uitae, ac doctrina, ipseque Alcoran . . . Haec omnia in unum uolumen redacta sunt, opera et studio Theodori Bibliandri* [Theodorus Bibliander (Theodor Buchmann), 1506–1564, Swiss theologian] *. . . qui . . . Alcorani textum emendauit, & marginibus apposuit annotationes*, Basle, 1543; 2nd ed., Zürich, 1550.

Alseck: Moses Al-Sheikh (Moses Alshaikh) (fl. second half of the 16th century in Safed, northern Israel). *D. Isaaci Abrabanielis & r. Mosis Alschechi comment. in Esaiae prophetiam 30. cum additamento eorum quae r. Simeon è veteris dictis collegit*, Basel, 1631.

Alvaresius: Francisco Alvarez (ca. 1465–ca. 1541). Portuguese missionary and explorer; *Historia de las cosas de Etiopia*, Antwerp, 1557.

Arabian Geographer: Muhammad Al-Idrisi (1100–1166). Arab geographer and cartographer; *Geographia Nubiensis: id est accuratissima totius orbis . . . descriptio, continens praesertim exactam vniuersae Asiae, & Africae . . . explicationem*, trans. from Arabic by Gabriel Sionita and Joannes Hesronita, Paris, 1619.

Aramas: Isaac ben Moses Arama (ca. 1420–94). Spanish rabbi; *'Aḳedat Yitsḥaḳ: . . . Pe[erush] ha-'Aramah le-ḥamesh megilot*, Venice, 1573.

Azoara/Azoarae. Sura/suras (i.e., chapter/chapters) of the Qur'ān (Koran).

Balance of Truth: Bilibra veritatis et rationis (Amsterdam, 1700), by Jonas Slichting (1592–1661, Socinian theologian).

Baldus: Baldo degli Ubaldi (Baldus Ubaldus) (1327–1400). Italian jurist; *Commentaria in Digestum vetus*, Paris, 1558.

Bechai: Rabbi Baḥya (or Bachya, Baḥia) ben Asher (ca. 1255–1340). Spanish Biblical exegete; author of a commentary on the Torah and of a famous "Book of Discourses" called *Kad ha-Ḳemaḥ*.

Benjamin Benjaminis Tudelensis: Benjamin Ben Jonah of Tudela (1165–73). Famous Jewish traveler; *Itinerarium* [Hebrew and Latin], Leiden, 1633.

Bereschith Rabbah/Beresith Rabba. Bereshit Rabbah (Bereshith Rabba), mainly sixth-century expository Midrash (that is, rabbinical exposition of Scripture) on the Book of Genesis, including passages by a number of commentators (e.g., R. Judah ben Simon).

Bernard: Saint Bernard of Clairvaux (1090–1153). French monk and mystic, founder and abbot of the abbey of Clairvaux.

Bochart: Samuel Bochart (1599–1667). French biblical scholar; *Geographia sacra, seu Phaleg et Canaan*, 3rd improved ed., Leiden, 1692 (1st ed. Caen, 1646).

"Book of Mahomet's Generation." *Machumetis . . . eiusque successorum uitae, ac doctrina, ipseque Alcoran . . . Haec omnia in unum uolumen redacta sunt, opera et studio Theodori Bibliandri* [Theodorus Bibliander (Theodor Buchmann), 1506–64, Swiss theologian] . . . *qui . . . Alcorani textum emendauit, & marginibus apposuit annotationes,* Basle, 1543; 2nd ed., Zürich, 1550.

"Book of the Doctrine of Mahomet." *Machumetis . . . eiusque successorum uitae, ac doctrina, ipseque Alcoran . . . Haec omnia in unum uolumen redacta sunt, opera et studio Theodori Bibliandri* [Theodorus Bibliander (Theodor Buchmann), 1506–64, Swiss theologian] . . . *qui . . . Alcorani textum emendauit, & marginibus apposuit annotationes,* Basle, 1543; 2nd ed., Zürich, 1550.

Buxtorf: Johann Buxtorf (1564–1629). Christian Hebraist born in Germany; *Lexicon chaldaicum, talmudicum et rabbinicum,* Basel, 1639.

Cantacuzenus: John VI Cantacuzenus (1292–1383). Byzantine emperor; *Ioannis Cantacuzeni Constantinopolitani Regis Contra Mahometicam Christiana & orthodoxa assertio, Graece conscripta ante annos ferè ducentos, nunc uero Latinitate donata,* Basel, 1543.

Capel/Capell: Louis Cappel (or Ludovicus Cappellus) (1585–1658). French theologian and Hebrew scholar; *Commentarii et Notae Criticae in Vetus Testamentum,* Amsterdam, 1689.

Carpenter: Nathaniel (Nathanael) Carpenter (1589–ca. 1628). *Philosophia libera . . . in qua adversus hujus temporis philosophos dogmata quaedam nova discutiuntur,* Oxford, 1636.

Cartes: René Descartes (1596–1650). French philosopher, mathematician, and scientist; *Opera Philosophica,* Editio secunda, ab auctore recognita, Amsterdam, 1650.

Casaubon: Isaac Casaubon (1559–1614). Classical scholar and theologian; *The ansvvere of Master Isaac Casaubon to the epistle of the most reuerend Cardinall Peron* [Jacques Davy Du Perron, 1556–1618]. *Translated out of Latin into English,* London, 1612.

Cassander: George Cassander (1513–66). German theologian; *De articulis religionis: inter Catholicos et Protestantes controuersis consultatio,* Cologne, 1557.

Chalcocondilas: Laonicus Chalcocondylas (Laonicus Chalcocondyles, Chalcondyles, Laonikos Chalkokondyles) (ca. 1423–ca. 1490). Byzantine historian; *Chalcocondylae . . . historiarum de origine ac rebus gestis Turcorum, liber primus(–decimus),* in *Historiae Byzantinae Scriptores tres,* Geneva, 1615.

Cieza: Pedro de Cieza de Leon (1519–54). Spanish conquistador and historian; *Crónica del Perú,* Seville, 1553.

Clarke: Samuel Clarke (1675–1729). Anglican clergyman regarded as the best exponent of Newtonian natural philosophy. *A letter to Mr. Dodwell* [Henry Dodwell, 1641–1711]: *wherein all the arguments in his Epistolary discourse against the immortality of the soul are particularly answered, and the judgment of the fathers . . . represented,* London, 1706 (Reference added by John Clarke). *A defense of an argument made use of in a letter to Mr. Dodwel[l], to prove the immateriality and natural immortality of the soul,* London, 1707 (Reference added by John Clarke). *A discourse concerning the being and attributes of God, the obligations of natural religion, and the truth and certainty of the Christian revelation* [Boyle lectures, 1704, 1705], 3rd ed., corrected, London, 1711 (Reference added by John Clarke).

Cocceius: Johannes Cocceius (Johannes Koch, or Coch) (1603–69). Reformed theologian and biblical scholar born in Germany; *Duo tituli thalmudici Sanhedrin et Maccoth: quorum ille agit de synedriis, judiciis, suppliciis capitalibus ebraeorum; . . . cum excerptis utriusque Gemara,* ed. Johannes Cocceius, Amsterdam, 1629.

Copernicus: Nicolaus Copernicus (1473–1543). Polish astronomer; *De revolutionibus orbium coelestium, Libri VI,* Nuremberg, 1543.

Cortius: Sebastianus Curtius (d. 1684). Reformed theologian; *Radices linguae sanctae Hebraeae,* Hofgeismar, 1649.

Cudworth: Ralph Cudworth (1617–89). Cambridge Platonist; *The True Intellectual System of the Universe,* London, 1678.

Curtius: Quintus Curtius Rufus (fl. ca. 41–54 CE). Noted for his biography of Alexander the Great, king of Macedonia, 356–323 BCE; *De rebus gestis Alexandri Magni,* Leiden, 1633.

Cusan: Nicholas of Cusa (Nikolaus von Cusa, Nicolaus Cusanus) (1401–64). Cardinal, philosopher, mathematician, scholar, and experimental scientist; *Cribratio Alchorani,* in *Machumetis . . . eiusque successorum uitae, ac doctrina, ipseque Alcoran . . . Haec omnia in unum uolumen redacta sunt, opera et studio Theodori Bibliandri* [Theodorus Bibliander (Theodor Buchmann), 1506–64, Swiss theologian] *. . . qui . . . Alcorani textum emendauit, & marginibus apposuit annotationes,* Basle, 1543; 2nd ed., Zürich, 1550.

Dale: Anthony (Anton) van Dale (1638–1708). Dutch physician and man of letters; *De oraculis ethnicorum dissertationes duae,* Amsterdam, 1683.

Debarim Rabba: Debarim Rabba. Tenth-century Midrash (that is, rabbinical exposition of Scripture) on Deuteronomy. See also entry for "*Rabboth.*"

"Dispute betwixt a Saracen and a Christian." In *Machumetis Saracenorum principis, eiusque successorum uitae, ac doctrina, ipseque Alcoran . . . quae ante annos CCCC . . . Petrus Abbas Cluniacensis per uiros eruditos, ad fidei Christiana[e] ac sanctae matris Ecclesiae propugnationem, ex Arabica lingua in*

Latinam transferri curauit. His adiunctae sunt confutationes multorum, & qui-dem probatissimorum authorum, Arabum, Graecorum, & Latinorum . . . *Haec omnia in unum uolumen redacta sunt, opera et studio Theodori Bibliandri* [Theodorus Bibliander (Theodor Buchmann), 1506–64, Swiss theologian] . . . *qui* . . . *Alcorani textum emendauit, & marginibus apposuit annotationes,* Basle, 1543; 2nd ed., Zürich, 1550.

Dodwell: Henry Dodwell, the Elder (1641–1711). Scholar and professor of an-cient history; *A discourse concerning Sanchoniathon's Phoenician history,* London, 1681.

Echad Rabbathi/Ecka Rabbathi/Ecka Rabthi: Ekah Rabbathi or *Echa Rabba.* Seventh-century Midrash (that is, rabbinical exposition of Scripture) on Lamentations. See also entry for "*Rabboth.*"

Elias Cretensis: Elias of Crete (9th century). Archbishop of Crete and author of commentaries on St. Gregory of Nazianzus; *D. Gregorii Nazianzeni* . . . *Opera* . . . *quae extant; nunc primum propter novam plurimorum librorum accessionem in duos tomos distincta; cum* . . . *Nonni* [Pseudo-Nonnus, 6th century], *et Eliae Cretensis commentariis,* Paris, 1583.

Enthymius/Euthymius. See entry for "Zigabenus."

Fontenelle: Bernard Le Bovier de Fontenelle (1657–1757). French man of let-ters and scientist; *Histoire des Oracles,* Paris, 1687.

Freita: Frei Serafim de Freitas (ca. 1570–d. 1633). Portuguese jurist and profes-sor in Valladolid; *De iusto imperio Lusitanorum asiatico,* Valladolid, 1625.

Gabriel: Antonius Gabrielius (d. 1555). Italian canonist; *Communes conclusio-nes* . . . *in septem libros distributae,* Frankfurt, 1597.

Gailus: Andreas Gaill (1525–87). German jurist; *Practicarum observationum: tam ad processum iudiciarium* . . . *quam causarum decisiones pertinentium* . . . *libri duo,* Cologne, 1595.

Gemma Frisius: Rainer Gemma Frisius (1508–55). Flemish mathematician, physician, and astronomer; *Cosmographia, siue Descriptio vniuersi orbis, Petri Apiani* [Peter Apian, 1495–1552] *& Gemmae Frisij, mathematicorum insignium, iam demum integritati suae restituta. Adjecti sunt alij, tum Gem-mae Frisij, tum aliorum auctorum eius argumenti tractatus ac libelli varij,* Antwerp, 1584.

Georgivitius: Bartholomew Georgivitius (Bartholomaeus Georgievits, Gyor-gievits). *De Turcarum Ritu,* in *Machumetis* . . . *eiusque successorum uitae, ac doctrina, ipseque Alcoran* . . . *Haec omnia in unum uolumen redacta sunt, opera et studio Theodori Bibliandri* [Theodorus Bibliander (Theodor Buchmann), 1506–64, Swiss theologian] . . . *qui . . . Alcorani textum emendauit, & marginibus apposuit annotationes,* Basle, 1543; 2nd ed., Zürich, 1550.

Gerson: Levi ben Gershom (Gerson, Gersonides, Leo De Bagnols, Leo Hebraeus) (1288–1344). French Jewish Talmudic scholar, philosopher, mathematician, and astronomer; in *Biblia Sacra Hebraica & Chaldaica: Cum Masora, quae Critica Hebraeorum sacra est, Magna & Parva, ac selectisissimis Hebraeorum interpretum commentariis . . . R. Levi Gerson,* Basel, 1618–19.

Gerson the Christian: Christian Gerson (1569–1627). *Der Jüden Thalmud Fürnembster inhalt und Widerlegung,* Helmstedt, 1609.

Gregoras: Nicephorus (or Nikephoros) Gregoras (ca. 1292–ca. 1360). Byzantine scholar, author of a Byzantine history in 37 volumes; *Byzantinae Historiae libri XI. Gr. & Lat.* in *Historiae Byzantinae Scriptores tres,* Geneva, 1615.

Gregory the Great: St. Gregory the Great (Gregorius I Magnus) (ca. 540–604). Pope from 590 to 604; *Epistolae* in *Omnia quae extant opera,* Antwerp, 1572.

Grotius: Hugo Grotius (or Hugo de Groot, Huigh de Groot) (1583–1645). Dutch jurist, political theorist, humanist scholar, and statesman. *De Jure Belli ac Pacis,* Paris, 1625. *De Veritate Religionis Christianae,* Leiden, 1627; Paris, 1640. *An semper communicandum per symbola,* Amsterdam, 1638; also in *Opera omnia theologica,* Amsterdam, 1679, T. III. *Annotata ad Consultationem Cassandri* [see entry for "Cassander"]. *Disquisitio de dogmatibus Pelagianis. Baptizatorum puerorum institutio alternis interrogationibus et responsionibus. Ex Belgicis rythmis . . . ab auctore Latine reddita,* in *Via ad pacem ecclesiasticam,* ed. Hugo Grotius, Paris, 1642; also in *Opera omnia theologica,* Amsterdam, 1679, T. III. *Rivetiani Apologetici, pro schismate contra Votum pacis facti, discussio,* Irenopoli [Amsterdam], 1645; also in *Opera omnia theologica,* Amsterdam, 1679, T. III. *Annotationes in epistolam quae Petri altera dicitur,* in *Opera omnia theologica,* Amsterdam, 1679, T. II, ii. "De Potestate ecclesiastica," in *Opera omnia theologica,* Amsterdam, 1679, T. III, p. 627.

Haiton: Haythonus Armenius (or Hayton of Corycus, Hetoum of Korykos, Haitho, Antonius Curchinus) (d. ca. 1308). Armenian monk and historian; *Historia Orientalis Haythoni Armenii, et huic subiectum Marci Pauli Veneti itinerarium,* Helmstedt, 1585.

Helmoldus: Helmold of Lübeck (12th century). Historian; *Helmoldi . . . historiarum liber . . . ab autore inscriptus Chronica Slauorum,* ed. Siegmund Schorkel, Frankfurt, 1556.

Herera/Herrera: Antonio de Herrera y Tordesillas (1559–1625). Spanish historian; *Historia general de los hechos de los Castellanos en las Islas i tierra firme del mar oceano,* Madrid, 1601–15.

Hesychius: Hesychius of Miletus (fl. 6th century). Byzantine historian; *Opuscula, partim hactenus non edita,* Leiden, 1613.

Isaac's *Bereschith Rabba: Bereshit Rabbah.* Midrash (that is, rabbinical exposition of Scripture) on the Book of Genesis, including the explanations of Rabbi Isaac. See also entries for *"Bereschith Rabbah"* and *"Rabboth."*

Isidore: Isidore of Seville (or Isidorus Hispalensis) (ca. 560–636). Archbishop of Seville and scholar; *Opera omnia,* Paris, 1601.

Israel: *Nezah Israel* (Prague, 1598). Work by Judah Loew ben Bezalel (d. 1609), the maharal of Prague.

Ivon: St. Ivo (ca. 1040–1116). Bishop of Chartres; *Epistolae . . . In illas observationum liber non antea editus. Eiusdem . . . Chronicon de regibus Francorum,* ed. François Juret, Paris, 1610.

Jachiades/Jaccides: Joseph ben David Ibn Yahya (Jacchiades) (1494–1539). *Paraphrasis Dn. Iosephi Iachiadae in Danielem,* Amsterdam, 1633.

Jacob, R[abbi], in *Caphthor:* Jacob ben Isaac Luzzatto (16th century), author of *Caphtor va-pherah* (or *Kaftor va-feraḥ*), Basle, 1580.

Jehuda Levita: Yehudah Halevi (or Judah Ha-Levi, Judah ben Samuel Halevi) (ca. 1075–1141). Spanish Jewish poet and philosopher.

Joachim Raeticus: Georgius Joachimus Rhaeticus (1514–76). *De Libris Revolutionum . . . Nic. Copernici* [Nicolaus Copernicus, 1473–1543, Polish astronomer] . . . *: narratio prima,* Basel, 1541.

Jochnaan [Rabbi Jochanan]. His teaching is included in *Schemoth Rabba.* See entry for *"Schemoth Rabba."*

Joseph Albo/Josephus Albo: Joseph Albo (1380–1444). Spanish-Jewish philosopher and theologian who wrote a work of Jewish dogmatics; *Sefer ha-'ikkarim* (Book of Principles), 1485.

Judas, R[abbi]: Judah ben Samuel (Yehuda the Ḥasiol) (ca. 1150–1217). German Jewish mystic and founder of the movement of German Ḥasidism); *Sefer Ḥasidim* (or *Sefer Chasidim;* Book of the Pious), Bologna, 1538.

Junius: Franciscus Junius (or Franz Junius, François du Jon) (1545–1602). Huguenot scholar; *Testamenti Veteris Biblia sacra: siue libri canonici priscae Iudaeorum ecclesiae à Deo traditi; latini recéns ex hebraeo facti, breuibúsque scholiis illustrati ab Immanuele Tremellio* [Immanuel Tremellius, 1510–80], *& Francisco Junio,* Hanau, 1596.

Juret: François Juret (1553–1626). Canon of Langres, France; *Ivonis Episcopi Carnotensis* [St. Ivo, Bishop of Chartres, ca. 1040–1116] *Epistolae . . . In illas observationum liber non antea editus. Eiusdem . . . Chronicon de regibus Francorum,* ed. François Juret, Paris, 1610.

Kaimchi/Kimchi: David Kimhi (Kimchi, Kimḥi, or Qimḥi) also known as Radak (acronym of Rabbi David Kimhi) (ca. 1160–ca. 1235). Jewish scholar, biblical commentator, grammarian, and lexicographer; cf. *Biblia Sacra Hebraica & Chaldaica: cum Masora, quae critica Hebraeorum sacra est, magna & parva, ac selectisissimis Hebraeorum interpretum co[m]mentariis, Rabbi Salomonis Jarchi, R. Abrahami Aben Esrae, R. Davidis Kimchi,* Basel, 1618–19.

Le Clerc: Jean Le Clerc (1657–1736). Central figure of the European republic of letters. *Aeschinis Socratici* [Aeschines Socraticus] *dialogi tres Graece et Latine, ad quos accessit quarti Latinum fragmentum, vertit et notis illustr. I. Clericus: cujus additae sunt Silvae philologicae,* Amsterdam, 1711. *Ars critica, in qua ad studia linguarum Latinae, Graecae et Hebraicae via munitur,* Amsterdam, 1697; 2nd ed., 1699–1700. *Bibliothèque choisie* (1703–13, 1718). *De l'Incredulité,* Amsterdam, 1696. *Entretiens de Maxime et de Thémiste; ou, Réponse à ce que M. le Clerc a écrit dans son X. tome de la Bibliothèque choisie contre Mr Bayle* [Pierre Bayle, 1647–1706], Rotterdam, 1707. *Genesis, sive Mosis prophetae liber primus,* Amsterdam, 1693. *Harmonia Evangelica, cui subjecta est historia Christi ex quatuor Evangeliis concinnata. Accesserunt tres dissertationes de annis Christi, deque concordia & auctoritate Evangeliorum,* Amsterdam, 1699. *Historia Ecclesiastica,* Amsterdam, 1716. *Novum Testamentum Domini nostri Jesu Christi ex Versione Vulgata, cum paraphrasi et adnotationibus Henrici Hammondi* [Henry Hammond, 1605–60]. *Ex Anglica lingua in Latinam transtulit, suisque animadversionibus illustravit, castigavit, auxit Joannes Clericus,* 2nd ed., Frankfurt, 1714 (Vol. II: *Epistolae Sanctorum Apostolorum*). *Opera philosophica,* 4 vols., Amsterdam, 1710. [*Pentateuchus, sive,*] *Mosis prophetae libri quatuor,* Amsterdam, 1696. *Veteris Testamenti Libri Historici,* Amsterdam, 1708. *XVIII. prima commata capitis primi evangelii S. Joannis paraphrasi et animadversionibus illustrata a Joanne Clerico; ubi demonstratur, contra alogos, evangelium hoc esse foetum Joannis Apostoli; & evertitur sententia Fausti Socini* [Faustus Socinus, 1539–1604], *de sensu primorum ejus commatum,* Amsterdam, 1695.

Leunclavius: Johannes Leunclavius (Löwenklau) (ca. 1533–93). Translator of a history of the Ottoman sultans; *Annales Sultanorum Othmanidarum,* 2nd ed., Frankfurt, 1596.

"Life [of Genghiz-Can] written in French": François Pétis (1622–95). French orientalist; *Histoire du grand Genghizcan* [Genghis Khan, 1162–1227] *premier empereur des anciens Mogols et Tartares*, Paris, 1710.

Lindebrogius: Friedrich Lindenbrog (1573–1648). *Codex legum antiquarum*, Frankfurt, 1613.

Linschotius: Jan Huyghen van Linschoten (1563–1611). Dutch explorer; *Histoire de la navigation de Iean Hugues de Linschot Hollandois: aux Indes Orientales*, 3rd ed., Amsterdam, 1638.

Lipsius: Justus Lipsius (1547–1606). Belgian scholar. *Monita et exempla politica libri duo*, Antwerp, 1605. *Physiologiae Stoicorum libri tres*, Antwerp, 1604.

"Mahomet's Chronicon": *Machumetis . . . eiusque successorum uitae, ac doctrina, ipseque Alcoran . . . Haec omnia in unum uolumen redacta sunt, opera et studio Theodori Bibliandri* [Theodorus Bibliander (Theodor Buchmann), 1506–64, Swiss theologian] *. . . qui . . . Alcorani textum emendauit, & marginibus apposuit annotationes*, Basle, 1543; 2nd ed., Zürich, 1550.

Maimonides: Maimonides (or Moses ben Maimon) (1135–1204). Spanish-Jewish philosopher, jurist, and physician. *Constitutiones de fundamentis legis*, Amsterdam, 1638. *De idololatria liber, cum interpretatione Latina & notis Dionysii Vossii* [Dionysius Vossius, 1612–42], Amsterdam, 1641. *Doctor Perplexorum*, trans. into Latin by Johann Buxtorf, Basel, 1629. *Mishneh Torah*, Venice, 1550–51. *Tredecim articuli fidei Iudaeorum*, Worms, 1529 (Maimonides's commentary on the Mishna, tractate *Sanhedrin*, including the Thirteen Articles of Faith [*Shloshah-Asar Ikkarim*]).

Manasses: Manasseh (Menasseh) ben Joseph ben Israel (Manoel Dias Soeiro) (1604–57). Dutch-Jewish scholar of Portuguese origins. *Conciliator, sive De convenientia locorum S. Scripturae, quae pugnare inter se videntur*, Amsterdam, 1633. *De Creatione problemata XXX*, Amsterdam, 1635. *De resurrectione mortuorum: libri III*, Amsterdam, 1636.

Margarita: Antonius Margarita (Anton Margaritha) (born ca. 1490). Jewish-German convert to Christianity; *Der gantz jüdisch Glaub: mit sampt ainer gründtlichen und warhafften Anzaygunge, aller Satzungen, Ceremonien, Gebetten, haymliche und offentliche Gebreüch*, Augsburg, 1530.

Marsham: John Marsham (1602–85). *Chronicus canon Aegyptiacus Ebraicus Graecus & disquisitiones*, London, 1672.

Masius: Andreas Masius (1514–73). Humanist and biblical scholar, editor of and commentator on the text of the Book of Joshua in Hebrew, with translations in Latin and Greek; *Iosuae imperatoris historia illustrata atq. explicata ab A. Masio,* Antwerp, 1574.

Mendesius de Pinto: Fernão Mendes Pinto (ca. 1510–83). Portuguese traveler; *Peregrinaçam de Fernam Mendez Pinto,* Lisbon, 1614 (French trans.: *Les voyages advantureux de Fernand Mendez Pinto,* Paris, 1628).

Mills: John Mill (1645–1707). English scholar and theologian; *Novum Testamentum cum lectionibus variantibus,* ed. John Mill, Oxford, 1707.

Mornaeus: Philippe de Mornay (or Philippe Duplessis-mornay) (1549–1623). Protestant French diplomat and publicist; *De la verité de la religion chrestienne,* Antwerp, Paris, 1581.

Moses Gerundensis/Moses son of Nehemannus/Moses son of Nachman: Moses ben Nahman (Moshe ben Nahman Gerondi, Naḥmanides, or, by acronym, Ramban) (ca. 1194–1270). Catalan Talmudist and exegete born in Gerona, Spain; commentary on the Pentateuch in *Ḥamishah Ḥumshe Torah,* Venice, 1548.

Nonnus: Pseudo-Nonnus (6th century). Author of commentaries on St. Gregory of Nazianzus; *D. Gregorii Nazianzeni . . . Opera . . . quae extant; nunc primum propter novam plurimorum librorum accessionem in duos tomos distincta; cum . . . Nonni, et Eliae Cretensis* [Elias of Crete, 9th century] *commentariis,* Paris, 1583.

Nubian Geographer: Muhammad Al-Idrisi. See entry for "Arabian Geographer."

Osorius: Hieronymus Osorius (Jeronimo Osorio) (1506–80). Bishop of Silves; *Opera Omnia,* Rome, 1592.

Peiresius: Nicolas-Claude Fabri de Peiresc (1580–1637). French humanist, antiquary, and astronomer.

Petavius: Denis Petau. *Theologicorum dogmatum tomus primus* [*–quartus*], Paris, 1644[–1650].

Peter Abbot of Cluny: Peter the Venerable (Blessed Peter of Montboissier) (ca. 1092–1156). French Abbot of Cluny Abbey who ordered the first Latin translation of the Qur'ān. See also entry for "Dispute betwixt a Saracen and a Christian."

Pocock: Edward Pocock, the Elder (1604–91). Editor of a Latin version of Bar Hebraeus's history of the Arabs; *Specimen Historiae Arabum sive Gregorii Abul Faragii* [Gregorius, Abū al-Faraj, or Ibn Al-'Ibrī, or Bar Hebraeus, 1226–86, Syrian philosopher, historian, and scholar] *de Origine et Moribus*

Arabum succincta narratio, in linguam Latinam conversa, notisque illustrata: opera et studio E. Pocockii. Arab. and Lat., Oxford, 1650.

Prideaux: Humphrey Prideaux (1648–1724). Biblical and literary scholar, dean of Norwich; *The true nature of imposture fully display'd in the life of Mahomet*, 2nd ed., London, 1697.

Rabboth: Rabboth (great commentaries). Collection of ten Midrashim (that is, rabbinical expositions of Scripture), including *Bereshith Rabba* (see entry for *"Bereschith Rabbah"*), *Shemoth Rabba* (see entry for *"Schemoth Rabba"*), *Debarim Rabba* (see entry for *"Debarim Rabba"*), and *Echa Rabba* (see entry for *"Echad Rabbathi"*).

Richardus. *Richardi* [Ricoldus de Montecrucis, Riccoldo da Monte Croce, 1243–1320] *ex ordine fratrum, qui apud Latinos Praedicatores appellantur, Confutatio legis latae Saracenis à maledicto Mahumeto*, in *Machumetis . . . eiusque successorum uitae, ac doctrina, ipseque Alcoran . . . Haec omnia in unum uolumen redacta sunt, opera et studio Theodori Bibliandri* [Theodorus Bibliander (Theodor Buchmann), 1506–64, Swiss theologian] *. . . qui . . . Alcorani textum emendauit, & marginibus apposuit annotationes*, Basle, 1543; 2nd ed., Zürich, 1550.

Rivetus: André Rivet (1572–1651). Reformed minister and professor of theology at the University of Leiden; *Apologeticus, pro suo de verae et sincerae pacis ecclesiae proposito: contra Hugonis Grotii* [Hugo Grotius] *votum*, Leiden, 1643.

Roman Martyrology. *Martyrologium romanum*, Rome, 1583.

Ryckius: Theodorus Ryckius (1640–90). "Oratio de Gigantibus," in *Lucae Holstenii* [Lucas Holstenius, 1596–1661] *Notae et castigationes postumae in Stephani Byzantii* [Stephanus Byzantinus, 6th century] *Ethnika . . . editae a Theodoro Ryckio*, Leiden, 1684.

Saadia, Rabbi/Saaidias/Saaida: Sa'adia ben Joseph (882–942). Jewish Talmudic scholar, exegete, and philosopher; *Biblia Sacra Hebraica & Chaldaica: cum Masora, quae critica Hebraeorum sacra est, magna & parva, ac selectisissimis Hebraeorum interpretum co[m]mentariis . . . R. Saadie . . . fido & labore indefesso Johannis Buxtorfi* [Johann Buxtorf (1564–1629)], Basel, 1618–19.

Salmasius/Salmanus: Claudius Salmasius (or Claude de Saumaise) (1588–1653). French classical scholar; *Plinianae exercitationes in Caii Iulii Solini* [Gaius Julius Solinus] *Polyhistoria*, Paris, 1629.

Samuel, R[abbi]: Samuel Ibn Seneh Zarza (second half of the 14th century). Jewish-Spanish philosopher, author of a philosophical commentary on the Pentateuch; *Mekor Hayim*, Mantua, 1559.

Scaliger: Joseph Scaliger (1540–1609). Classical scholar. *Animaduersiones in Chronologica Eusebii*, in Eusebius (see entry for "Eusebius"), *Thesaurus temporum*, Leiden, 1606. *De emendatione temporum: Addita veterum Graecorum fragmenta selecta*, Geneva, 1629.

Schemoth Rabba: *Shemoth Rabba*. 11th- and 12th-century Midrash (that is, rabbinical exposition of Scripture) on Exodus. See also entry for *"Rabboth."*

Schep-tal: *Sefer Shefa Tal* (Hanau, 1612), by Shabbetai ben Akiba Horwitz (fl. in Prague between the 16th and the 17th centuries). Cabalistic author.

Schindler: Valentin Schindler (d. 1604). German Hebraist; *Lexicon pentaglotton: Hebraicum, Chaldaicum, Syriacum, Talmudico-Rabbinicum, et Arabicum*, Frankfurt a. M., 1612.

Sebundus: Raymundus de Sabunde (or Raymond, Raimundus, Raemundus Sabundus, Sabundius, Sebond, Sibiuda) (d. 1436). Catalan professor of philosophy and medicine at the University of Toulose, Spain; *Theologia naturalis, sive liber creaturarum*, Deventer, ca. 1484–85.

Selden: John Selden (1584–1654). English jurist; *De iure naturali & gentium, iuxta disciplinam Ebraeorum, libri septem*, London, 1640.

Simeon, R[abbi]. See entry for *"Bereschith Rabbah."*

Smith: John Smith (1618–52). Cambridge Platonist; *Select discourses . . . As also a sermon preached by Simon Patrick at the author's funeral: with a brief account of his life and death*, London, 1660.

Solomon, Rabbi/Solomon Jarchi/Solomon Jarchis: Rashi (or Rabbi Shlomo Yitzhaki, Rabbi Solomon Bar Isaac of Troyes) (1040–1105). Medieval Jewish scholar; *Biblia Sacra Hebraica & Chaldaica: cum Masora, quae critica Hebraeorum sacra est, magna & parva, ac selectisissimis Hebraeorum interpretum co[m]mentariis, Rabbi Salomonis Jarchi . . . fido & labore indefesso Johannis Buxtorfi* [Johann Buxtorf (1564–1629)], Basel, 1618–19.

Speculator: Guilielmus Durandus (ca. 1237–96). French canonist; *Speculum iuris*, Frankfurt, 1592.

Speculum Saxonicum: *Sachsenspiegel auffs newe iibersehen*, Leipzig, 1582. Compendium of the customary laws of Saxony compiled by Eike von Repgow in the 13th century.

Spencer: John Spencer (1630–93). English theologian and Hebrew scholar; *De legibus Hebraeorum ritualibus et earum rationibus, libri tres*, Cambridge, 1685.

Stanley: Thomas Stanley (1625–78). First English historian of philosophy, also poet and translator; *The history of philosophy* (including *The history of the*

Chaldaick philosophy), London, 1687; Latin translation by Jean Le Clerc, *Thomae Stanleii Philosophia orientalis*, vol. 2 of Le Clerc, *Opera philosophica*, 4 vols., Amsterdam, 1710.

Stephanus/Stephens: Stephanus Byzantinus (Stephen of Byzantium) (6th century). Author of a geographical dictionary; *Peri Poleōn: De Urbibus*, Basel, 1568.

Suidas: Suidas (or *Suda, Souidas, Souda*). Tenth-century monumental Byzantine Greek lexicon-encyclopedia.

Tzetzes: Isaac Tzetzes (d. 1138). See entry for "Lycophron."

Vega: Garcilaso de la Vega (1539–1616). Peruvian historian; *Le commentaire royal, ou l'histoire des Yncas, roys de Peru*, translated from Spanish by Jean Baudoin, Paris, 1633.

Vives: Joannes Ludovicus (Juan Luis) Vives (1492–1540). Humanist of Spanish origin; *De veritate fidei Christianae*, Basel, 1543.

Vossius: Gerardus Johannes Vossius (1577–1649). Dutch humanist. *De arte grammatica libri septem*, Amsterdam, 1635. *De historicis graecis libri IV*, Leiden, 1624.

Vossius: Isaac Vossius (1618–89). Dutch scholar; *De Sibyllinis aliisque quae Christi natalem praecessere oraculis*, Oxford, 1679.

Walton: Brian Walton (1600–1661). British scholar who, with the help of others, compiled one of the most comprehensive polyglot bibles, comprising six volumes in nine languages; *Biblia sacra polyglotta: complectentia textus originales, Hebraicum, cum Pentateucho Samaritano, Chaldaichum, Graecum. Versionumque antiquarum, Samaritanae, Graecae LXXII interp., Chaldaicae, Syriacae, Arabicae, Aethiopicae, Persicae, Vulg. Lat., quicquid comparari poterat ... Opus totum in sex tomos tributum*, London, 1657.

Zemach David: Zemah David ("offspring of David"), Prague, 1592. Annals of Jewish and general history by David ben Salomon Gans (1541–1613), chronicler, astronomer, and mathematician born in Germany.

Zigabenus: Euthymius Zigabenus (Zigadenus, Zygadenus) (fl. 12th century). Byzantine theologian; *Saracenica, siue Moamethica: in quibus Ismaeliticae seu Moamethicae sectae praecipuorum dogmatum elenchus: ex Euthymii Zigabeni Panoplia dogmatica*, Heidelberg, 1595.

Zonaras: Joannes Zonaras (fl. 12th century). Byzantine historian, author of a world history; *Annales* in *Corpus historiae Byzantinae*, Frankfurt a. M., 1568.

Zuinger: Theodor Zwinger (1533–88). Swiss physician and scholar; *Theatrum humanae vitae*, Basel, 1586–87.

INDEX

This book is set in Adobe Garamond, a modern adaptation by Robert Slimbach of the typeface originally cut around 1540 by the French typographer and printer Claude Garamond. The Garamond face, with its small lowercase height and restrained contrast between thin and thick strokes, is a classic "old-style" face and has long been one of the most influential and widely used typefaces.

This book is printed on paper that is acid-free and meets the requirements of the American National Standard for Permanence of Paper for Printed Library Materials, z39.48-1992. ∞

Book design by Louise OFarrell
Gainesville, Florida
Typography by Apex CoVantage
Madison, Wisconsin
Printed and bound by Victor Graphics, Inc.
Baltimore, Maryland